FORTRAN 77 for Humans
3rd EDITION

REX PAGE
Colorado State University

RICH DIDDAY
Information Tools

ELIZABETH ALPERT
Hartnell College

D1416215

WEST PUBLISHING CO. *St. Paul • New York • Los Angeles • San Francisco*

Library of Congress Cataloging in Publication Data

Page, Rex L.
  FORTRAN 77 for humans.

  Includes index.
  1. FORTRAN (Computer program language)   I. Didday,
Richard L.   II. Alpert, Elizabeth.   III. Title.
IV. Title: FORTRAN seventy-seven for humans.
QA76.73.F25P3   1986   005.13'3   85-20318
ISBN 0-314-93404-9

Cover Designer: Arnold Design
Cover Art: Luis Vega/Image Bank
Production Coordination: Editing, Design & Production, Inc.

1st Reprint—1986

This book is dedicated to all
Rana pipiens *everywhere.*

CONTENTS

PREFACE

We have written this book because we feel that most books specifically about Fortran teach programming as an application of Fortran rather than the reverse. There are, of course, many books designed for use in an introductory computer science course that dwell primarily on programming and skip the details of a particular language. These books are appropriate in a course for computer science majors, but they are not particularly appropriate for a general studies course on Fortran programming.

Because most students learn to program in general studies Fortran courses, we feel that there is a need for a book that provides coordinated introduction to both the rules of Fortran and the creative process of designing algorithms and expressing them in a programming language. The particular notation used in this text to specify algorithm details in a form that can be carried out by a computer is Fortran 77. Access to a computer system that supports Fortran 77, or any Fortran compiler that provides CHARACTER data type and list-directed I/O (the WATFIV compiler, for example), is necessary for practice with the programming concepts covered in this text.

Modern programming practices (the concepts of *structured programming*) are emphasized throughout the book so the student learns to program in a sound, well-organized style. Students also learn modern terminology (while-loop, repeat-loop, etc.), but they are not constantly bombarded with the term "structured programming" because we suspect that repeatedly telling students that they are to use "structured programming only" requires that bad practices be demonstrated for comparison. Instead, we prefer to introduce program design techniques in contexts where they are obviously useful and appropriate.

Of all the improvements made to produce ANSI Fortran 77 from the skeleton of Fortran IV, three have had the most effect on the organization of this book. First is list-directed (FORMAT-free) I/O. In the past, FORMATs have been stumbling block number one for many beginners. Just as students began to understand the idea of a program, a new language was thrown at them—the arcane language of FORMATs. Fortunately, this level of complexity can be avoided now. FORMATs are covered in an independent chapter (Chapter 8) and need not be broached at all in an elementary course.

Stumbling block number two has been in gaining a clear, working understanding of the difference between **looping** and **selection.** This barrier is made lower by the new blocks IF THEN ELSE construct, which allows selection structures to be expressed without GOTOs. To emphasize the distinction between looping and selection, we use the logical IF statement in the form

IF (logical relation) GOTO statement label

only as a loop exit. We implement all selections with the IF THEN ELSE structure. Thus, in all our examples there is a syntactic as well as a semantic distinction between looping and selection. It is unfortunate that standard Fortran provides no direct notation for looping other than that for the counting DO-loop, but we feel that it is important to adhere to the standard language to emphasize the notion of program portability. Our pseudocode for program planning employs a loop notation patterned after the one currently proposed for the next standard version of Fortran. (This notation, incidentally, is functionally identical to the iteration control structure added to Modula 2, the successor to Pascal; it consists of a loop bracketing notation plus an exit command that can appear anywhere inside the loop.) By this means, we emphasize modern loop design, even though the final translation to Fortran 77 code incurs some loss.

A third stumbling block has been dealing with nonnumeric data. The introduction of the CHARACTER data type is a major improvement in this area. It allows the expression of nonnumeric data in a natural way, and it avoids the confusing and obscure use of numeric type arrays for dealing with nonnumeric data that was necessary in Fortran IV.

All of these changes in Fortran find direct expression in the organization of this book. The material can now be presented in a more logical, understandable manner. Now, even more than before, ideas about program design can drive the development, without frequent detours made necessary by defects in the language, to cover abstruse details.

One of our most important goals has been to present each feature of the language in a *useful* context, as opposed to a context in which it *can be used.* Using this approach, we explain how it would be possible to write equivalent programs without using a new feature and, at the same time, why we wouldn't want to do without it. This is necessary because most of the facilities in any programming language are conveniences, not necessities. We could get by with simple variables and restricted forms of assignment and IF statements in Fortran, but our programs would be unwieldy and impractical. Therefore, in order to be motivated to learn new features, students need to understand how the extra notational power makes certain types of programs both easier to create and clearer expressions of the underlying algorithm .

We have arranged the material in the order which we feel is the most pedagogically sound. In many cases this means introducing restricted versions of certain statements a chapter or two ahead of the more general versions. In this way, concepts are reinforced and covered at a deeper level in each new context. There is one unfortunate side effect of this teaching method: it can make the material difficult to use as a reference. To alleviate this difficulty, we have prepared an extensive alphabetical index with multiple references to each discussion in the text. Important definitions and general versions of statements have page references in boldface type. This makes it easier for readers to find what they need. Often, chapters contain optional sections on more advanced topics in order to keep similar material together for easy reference. Finally, we have prepared a Quick Reference Index (just inside the back cover) which, on one page, gives an example of each major type of statement, keyed to relevant pages in the text.

Boxes throughout the text summarize important points and provide additional information.

We have found that we can cover Chapters 1 through 11 in a ten-week, three-hour, beginning course in programming. If students are having trouble understanding arrays, Section 14.2, Multidimensional Arrays, may be helpful. Chapters 1 through 15 provide enough material for a serious sixteen-week programming course. The first nine chapters present a good basic introduction to programming and provide enough material for an elementary course. Since each of these chapters depends strongly on previous material, there is little choice in the order of presentation, except that Chapter 8 (on FORMATs) may be omitted. Chapters 12 through 15 are almost independent of one another and can be rearranged to suit student interest or the goals of the course.

In this, the third edition of **FORTRAN 77 for Humans**, we have made several organizational changes. We have moved the discussion of DO-loops to the chapter that introduces looping. Since the Fortran 77 DO-loop is a pretest loop, it now seems more appropriate to include it in the discussion of loop types. Whenever appropriate, IF . . . GOTO . . . terminator loops have been replaced by DO-loops. The explanation and discussion of arrays now include examples of DO-loops.

We have consolidated the material on arithmetic expressions, including intrinsic functions and statement functions, into one chapter early in the text. The structure of the introductory chapters has been designed so that students can begin running programs on the computer as soon as possible.

A chapter on top-down design has been included as early as practical in the text (Chapter 5, just following the introduction of loops). The design principles presented here are adhered to throughout the text, and expanded upon in Chapter 12. Debugging hints are included throughout the text at crucial points, and an early chapter presents the science of debugging in a highlighted context (Chapter 6). FORMATs are covered early, but remain optional until Chapter 13.

There are three types of programming exercises in the text: (1) review exercises at the end of each section, with answers in an appendix, to help students confirm their understanding of the material, (2) practice problems at the ends of the chapters, which provide relatively straight-forward applications of chapter concepts, and (3) programming design problems at the ends of the chapters, which present an opportunity for creative problem solving, applying the design principles of the chapter and earlier chapters.

Since the trend of computing is away from cards and batch process-ing, we have eliminated references to data cards. The data line is the unit record and may be a line of data entered at the terminal, a line of data from a file, or a card.

In the first edition, we used high-level flowcharts as a design tool. We have replaced them with what we call "plans." These are pseudocode descriptions which use boxes to group related operations and distin-guish options. Whether or not we agree with using the "writing" meta-phor for programming to the exclusion of other metaphors like "drawing," "sculpting," or "managing," we have found that flowcharts are becoming past history.

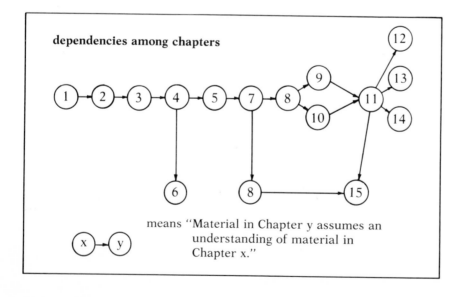

dependencies among chapters

means "Material in Chapter y assumes an understanding of material in Chapter x."

We hope that students will find learning to program an enjoyable experience and that this text will ease some of the difficulties and frustrations everyone encounters in that process. Good luck!

Acknowledgments

We would like to thank our students, who taught us how to teach Fortran, Ed Noyce for giving us the idea and getting us started, Walter Orvedahl for his encouragement and philosophical influence, Rebecca Daniels, George Porter, and Jessica Porter for their tremendous effort on the program listings, and Beverly Page for not giving up.

We would also like to thank Adolpho Guzman, Terrence Pratt, Michael Tindall, Peter Neeley, Nell Dale, Jennifer Scrivner, Carolee Drotos, Gary Sager, Janice Kurasz, Jerome A. Smith, Walt Brainerd, John Backus, R. J. Beeber, S. Best, R. Goldberg, H. L. Herrick, R. A. Hughes, L. B. Mitchell, R. A. Nelson, R. Nutt, D. Sayre, P. B. Sheridan, H. Stern, I. Ziller, Walt Kelley, Merl Miller, Tonio K., and Halliday and Resnick, Mort Drucker, Rector Page, Maj. C. S. Brown, Ryo Arai, E. K. "Mo" Moyer, Nora Huff, Harwood Kolsky, R. A. Didday, Mamie K. Moyer, Warren Page, Mildred Hill, Althea G. Hoerner, Bertrand Russell, William Hill, Herman C. Didday, Ruby G. Latham, Adolph Coors, E. W. Dijkstra, David Ossman, Phillip Proctor, Phillip Austin, Peter Bergman, Ken Friedenbach, David Carter, Steve Naslund, and Tim Priddy for the parts they played.

R. L. Page
R. L. Didday
L. Alpert

1 BASIC IDEAS

1.1 ADVICE TO YOU WHO ARE ABOUT TO LEARN FORTRAN

You will probably find learning to program a new kind of experience. Insofar as programming is like planning a task, it is a familiar process. What makes it difficult is that the planning must be much more complete than most people are used to.

For example, suppose a carpenter decides to write a set of directions for hanging a door. The difficulty of the task would depend to a large extent on the audience. It would be much easier to write a set of directions addressed to another carpenter than it would be to write directions addressed to the general public. For the public, the directions would have to be much more complete because most people don't know much about carpentry. In fact, a layman who happened to know how to hang a door would probably write better instructions for the general public than would the expert carpenter. While the carpenter might be tempted to say "rout strike box in jamb," the layman would realize that he would have to explain what a door jamb is, what the strike of a lock is, and what "routing" is before he could make any such statement.

It is usually the case that the programmer, like the carpenter, knows much more than his audience, the computer, about the process he is trying to describe. The computer does know some things in the sense that it can perform certain operations, but it is up to the programmer to describe the process in terms the computer understands. If a computer system runs Fortran, then it already can perform all the operations specified in Fortran. It is up to the programmer to describe the process in terms of those operations.

Learning to describe processes in terms of Fortran operations is not easy. The operations are very limited in scope—almost simpleminded, in fact. You will be as frustrated as the carpenter trying to explain a simple job like routing a strike box. Probably more frustrated! Because the computer will not tolerate even the most minor deviations in the form of the instructions you give it. One comma out of place and it blows you out of the water. You have probably never been in a situation that requires as much attention to detail as writing Fortran programs for a computer. That's the first hurdle you will have to cross—getting accustomed to the required level of detail.

Fortunately, once you get by this hurdle the whole process of writing programs seems a lot easier. It's fun too. That's what leads to your second hurdle: "friends." Since programming is easy and fun for those who know how to do it, you will probably have lots of friends who want to help you do your Fortran problems. Unfortunately, helping another person learn to write programs takes patience, thought, and planning. It takes time.

It might be interesting for you to keep track of the number of times someone says to you: "Oh, that's no good. Why don't you do it *this* way?" Your helper won't take the time to look at what you did, discover your reasons for doing it that way, and help you see the flaws in your approach. Instead, you get the answer on a platter, usually in terms of Fortran statements you've never seen before. These new statements will fall into one of four categories:

1. (OK) They are described in the text and you will learn them soon.
2. (POOR) They are advanced constructions and shouldn't be used until you know more about the basics.
3. (BAD) They are outmoded ways of doing things which are holdovers from more primitive languages.
4. (FREQUENT) They don't exist at all.

We offer this advice: Listen politely to friends who want to help, but always try to write the program yourself using techniques you know from the part of the text you have read. You can't learn to ride a bicycle by watching someone else ride one, and you can't learn programming that way either.

1.2   ORGANIZATION OF THE TEXT

Fortran 77 for Humans is arranged as a sequence of chapters, each subdivided into sections. Each section introduces a specific new concept within the general area covered by its chapter. Each chapter begins with a short summary of the general area to be covered (a "chapter plan"). This is intended to elaborate the chapter title and give you a few hints about what you will be studying. It may also help you locate topics for review or further study.

Each section ends with a short list of review exercises designed to help you confirm your understanding of the material in the section. We recommend that you work out these exercises for yourself faithfully, and read the answers to them, which are provided near the end of the book.

Important concepts within sections are summarized in boxed displays. This serves to emphasize important ideas during initial study and to provide focal points during review.

The programming problems at the ends of the chapters suggest ways to practice what you have learned. You will need to do some of these problems (one or two per chapter) to learn what this text aims to teach: programming, from design through coding. The programming problems are of two types: practice problems and program design problems. The practice problems require straightforward application of techniques described in the chapter; the design problems require more creative problem-solving skills. In most cases, these problems are mere sketches of ideas. You will have to provide your own data and interpret your results. Or perhaps an instructor will elaborate some of the problems for you or provide even better problems to help you learn to design and code programs.

The first few chapters contain many new concepts, you will probably be able to grasp them quickly. Later chapters contain more and more complex combinations of these basic concepts and will probably require more thought. You can't learn to program in a day. It will take lots of thought and practice, but we think you will find it an enjoyable experience.

1.3   THE BIG PICTURE

This book is intended to help you learn to program computers using the programming language Fortran. In practice, the only way to learn to program is to do it, so this book is really only an aid to reduce the number of errors in your trial-and-error learning process.

> **computer:** a machine that can perform symbol manipulation tasks, such as arithmetic operations, and make choices based on given data by following, automatically, the instructions in a computer program

Fortan is a **computer language,** a language that can be used to give commands to a computer. A **computer** is a machine that manipulates symbols by following the instructions in a computer program (written in a computer language, of course). Humans may interpret these symbols as they please. For example, a person might want to interpret a certain set of symbols as the results of a questionnaire, write a program (a sequence of commands) in Fortran that would cause some of the symbols to be matched up in pairs, call the process "computer dating," and make a lot of money.

> **program:** a sequence of instructions

Motivation for development of computers has come from efforts to mechanize symbol manipulation tasks. An adding machine is a familiar device that manipulates symbols and, in so doing, winds up with symbols that we call the "sum" of the symbols we put in. Early computers were little more than assemblages of devices that added, multiplied, divided, and so on, and could do these operations in sequence. Thus, a person who wanted to add a large list of numbers, then divide the sum by another number, then subtract this from yet another number, could write down a series of commands which would be *stored in the machine* and carried out in order automatically. The key word here is *stored.* The instructions that the computer is to follow are stored in the machine, and they can be changed by the user of the computer, which makes the computer a very flexible machine that can be used to solve many different types of problems.

Computers are typically designed to perform about two hundred different types of simple operations, ranging in complexity from moving a small piece of information from one place in a computer to another to finding the location of a given sequence of digits in a table of numbers. The set of operations that a computer can perform directly is called its **machine language.** Every different type of computer has a different machine language, and in the early days of computing all programs were composed entirely of machine language commands. It was tedious, time-consuming work because the operations were so elementary that even the simplest tasks required long sequences of commands.

> **machine language:** a set of operations that a computer is built to perform. Different computers have different machine languages. Machine language programs run on their computer directly, without being translated.

In the early fifties, a group of computer scientists under the leadership of John Backus formulated a bold new plan. They designed a program that translated sequences of mathematical formulas into machine language commands. Programmers could then write their programs in an algebraic notation (albeit a restricted form) with English-like constructions to control things such as repetition, selection of alternative sequences, getting data, and printing results. Their translator program was the first **compiler** and their algebraic language, Fortran, was the first **higher-level** language.

---

compiler: a program that translates a higher-level language into machine language

---

higher-level language: a computer language that appears more like a human language than a machine language and is designed to be used on many different types of computers

---

Fortran was designed around the needs of scientists and engineers who needed to use computers primarily to perform large numeric calculations. They wanted to be able to drive the computer to the limits of its performance, and the developers of Fortran realized that their language would never be used if it could not translate mathematical formulas into very efficient machine language programs. They did such a good job that Fortran captivated the scientific community. No subsequent development in computing has reduced the level of effort required to develop efficient programs as dramatically as did Fortran when it began to replace machine language, and Fortran remains today the foremost language for scientific and engineering calculations.

Higher-level languages like Fortran have two big advantages over machine languages. One is ease of use. Many application programs can be written ten times faster in Fortran than in machine language, and this makes the computer directly accessible by people who would never have the time to fiddle with machine language programs. The other is portability. Programs written in Fortran will run on many different types of computers; machine language programs will run only on one type. Better yet, programmers who know Fortran don't have to learn a whole new language every time they switch computers. The amount of effort saved by the use of higher-level languages has been phenomenal.

Through the years, as people have become more familiar with programming techniques, they have found certain types of statements more useful than others. *Higher-level languages have evolved.* New ones have been designed, hundreds of them. Most of these have fallen by the wayside, but a few have found niches. Many of the important ones are described and classified in Chapter 15.

Fortran itself has evolved. The first version was never widely available, but Fortran II (introduced in 1958) became the first popular, commercially available higher-level language. Its successor, Fortran IV, was introduced in 1962. It was formally standardized by the American National Standards Institute in the document ANSI X3.9-1966, and is sometimes referred to as Fortran 66 for this reason. Fortran 66 is no longer supported by the American National Standards Institute because it has adopted a new standard, ANSI X3.9-1978. This latest version of Fortran, usually called Fortran 77, is a substantial improvement over Fortran 66.

> **Fortran:** the first commercially available higher-level language. Throughout this text, the word Fortran refers to the language described in the document ANSI X3.9-1978, which is commonly referred to as Fortran 77.

This text focuses on Fortran 77 as a vehicle to help you learn about programming. Deficiencies are inevitable in every programming language. You can't expect the notation supported by a language to match the notation you would design to specify problem solutions if you were unrestricted. Through careful use of names and hierarchical design, you can break the problem into a few subproblems, depending on specialized operations and make a program written in any higher-level language look very much like a custom-designed notation for the problem at hand.

Your plans and notes for the solution of a problem will be in a notation that you devise, which can have infinite variety. When you encode your solution for a computer, you will have to stay within the restrictions of a programming language. Your computer system's version of Fortran will support some notations that are not included in standard Fortran 77. Since this text stays strictly within Fortran 77, you will not find coverage of other notations here. We are inclined not to use them because they restrict the portability of our programs, and we find that we frequently want to use our programs on several different computer systems.

Fortran is continuing to evolve. We expect that sometime within this decade a new version of Fortran will be standardized that will extend the notations of Fortran 77, making Fortran a truly modern language of an even "higher" level (in the sense that its notations will be closer, in many cases, to those you would employ for the solution of a problem if you were not limited by programming language restrictions). A committee working under the auspices of the American National Standards Institute is at work on such an extension of Fortran 77. We have taken their deliberations into consideration, and we use the sense of some of their projected extensions in our program plans, which precede all of the Fortran 77 programs in this text. In this way, the text looks forward to the next version of Fortran.

It is important to understand what it is that you are to learn about programming. We are not going to try to teach you to "think in Fortran"—in fact, this is undesirable. We want you to learn first, how to analyze a problem from the real world and divide it into subproblems each of which you know how to solve, and second, how to communicate the results of your analysis to a computer in terms of a Fortran program. Figure 1.3.1 illustrates the process.

Figure 1.3.1   The Big Picture

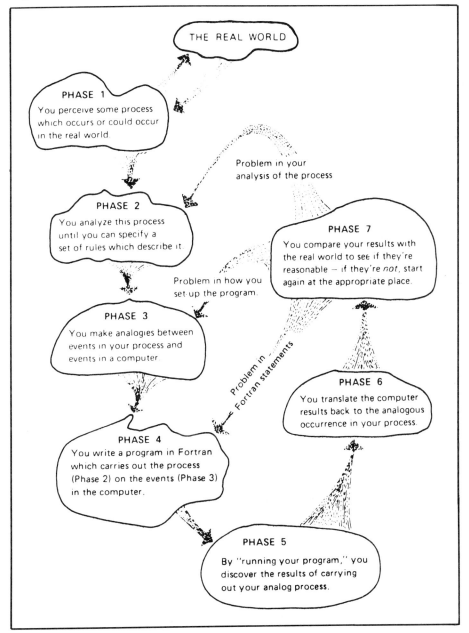

Phases 2 and 3 of Figure 1.3.1 are the most important to learn—and if you do learn them, you will be in a much better position to understand what can be done with computers. Unfortunately, they are virtually impossible to learn out of context. You will have to learn about reasonable analogies between real-world processes and computer processes by learning about computers through programming.

Let's apply the scheme shown in Figure 1.3.1 to a specific problem. Figure 1.3.2 suggests a concrete example of a case in which it is easy to make appropriate analogies. We don't expect you to understand all the details, just the general idea.

Figure 1.3.2   Financing a New Car

Phase 1. You decide you want to know the monthly payment on a new car, given the purchase price, the money you have for a down payment, the best interest rate you can get on a personal loan (which you know is better than the rate the dealer will give you), and the number of months you will have to make payments.

Phase 2. You dust off your old annuity tables, and you find the formula

$$\text{pmt} = P/[(1 - (1 + i)^{-n})/i]$$

where P stands for the amount you will have to borrow, i the monthly interest rate, and n the number of monthly payments. You figure that if you know the annual percentage rate *(APR)* for your loan, then i will be *APR*/1200 (12 months in a year and 1 percent means 1/100).

Phase 3. You decide to put the price of the car, the amount of your down payment, the number of payments you will have to make, and your bank's APR into data storage cells in the computer. Then you will use the formulas to get the monthly interest rate and the monthly payment. At the end, you will have the computer print the monthly payment it computed.

Phase 3

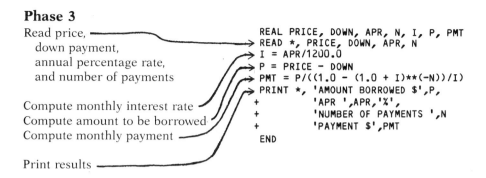

Read price,
  down payment,
  annual percentage rate,
  and number of payments

Compute monthly interest rate
Compute amount to be borrowed
Compute monthly payment

Print results

```
REAL PRICE, DOWN, APR, N, I, P, PMT
READ *, PRICE, DOWN, APR, N
I = APR/1200.0
P = PRICE - DOWN
PMT = P/((1.0 - (1.0 + I)**(-N))/I)
PRINT *, 'AMOUNT BORROWED $',P,
     +        'APR ',APR,'%',
     +        'NUMBER OF PAYMENTS ',N
     +        'PAYMENT $',PMT
END
```

Phase 4. You write a Fortran program to carry out the steps you planned in Phase 3. You can probably guess what each of the Fortran statements shown here as the product of Phase 4 means, although you will not understand all the details at this point. Basically, the program retrieves the given data from an external source (this is the READ statement); then it uses the formulas to compute the monthly payment (I = . . . , P = . . . , and PMT = . . .); finally, it prints the result (PRINT). The other statement in the program tells the computer what type of data to expect (REAL).

Phase 5. You run your program on some test data where you know what the results should be. For example, you know that if the amount you borrow is zero, your monthly payment should also be zero. You also know that if the APR is zero, the monthly payment should be the amount borrowed divided by the number of payments. You may also have borrowed money in the past, and you can test your program with that data too. Finally, you will run the program on the data for the loan you are considering.

Phase 6. You examine the printed results and interpret them as dollar amounts for monthly payments.

Phase 7. If the results of the test cases are what you expected, and if the monthly payment for the loan you are considering seems reasonable, compared, for example, to the monthly payment the car dealer is offering, then you accept the results as correct. If some results are out of line, you check your analysis (Phase 2), your computation plan (Phase 3), and your Fortran program (Phase 4), and repeat the process from the point where you believe there is an error.

Writing programs and using the results of computations is (or should be) a very logical process. The stories about credit card foul-ups, statements like "we have student numbers because that's easier for the computer," and the assumption that computers are like people, only dumber and faster, show that, unfortunately, many people don't understand the BIG PICTURE. As you go through this book, recalling the ideas in Figure 1.3.1 may help you to keep your perspective.

While the process of using the computer is basically logical, Phase 4, in which your ideas are translated into Fortran commands, may not seem to be. Don't worry if certain requirements in Fortran don't seem rational to you—they're probably not. Don't forget that Fortran was designed before anyone had used higher-level languages. Since then, committees and special-interest groups have added parts, usually trying to keep the new version enough like the old so that old programs will run on new compilers. Such an evolution is bound to produce some clumsy appendages. In this book we are trying to protect you from as many idiosyncrasies as possible; in fact, we will occasionally lie to you. That is, initially we will leave certain details out of the language we describe. But these will be only little white lies, and we think they're for your own good (the details often add little but confusion at first). We fill in details when it becomes necessary so that by the end of the text you'll have the whole picture.

By the way, you might consider that English, which was developed by a *huge* committee, isn't exactly logical either.

1.3   EXERCISES

1. Write down some of your current opinions about computers and how they work, what they do, what they will be able to do, how they affect the life of the average person, and so on. Attach what you've written to the last page of this book so that when you've finished the book you can see in what ways your ideas about computers have changed.
2. Read more about the history of Fortran in the chapter on Fortran in *Programming Languages: History and Fundamentals* by Jean E. Sammet (New York: Prentice-Hall, 1969), pp. 143–172.

1.4   THE IDEA OF ALGORITHMS

Algorithm is a word used by the computing community to mean a rule, procedure, or sequence of instructions. An algorithm is a description of how to do some task, and each step of the description, while incompletely specified, is understood by the person or machine that is to perform the task. Each step will always be incompletely specified simply because it's impossible to describe anything *completely.* You just hope to be understood most of the time. Our first example of an algorithm is so incompletely specified that one important instruction is totally left out. Look at Figure 1.4.1 and see if you can discover what is missing.

Since the ZAPPO instructions fail to tell you when to stop, you would wash your hair forever if you followed them unswervingly. There is little doubt that sometime, someone you know, maybe even (perish the thought) *you*, will write a computer program that acts like the ZAPPO directions in Figure 1.4.1. Saying, "but that isn't what I *meant*" will get you sympathy but not results.

---

infinite loop: a list of instructions that cannot be performed in a finite amount of time

---

Figure 1.4.1   The ZAPPO Algorithm

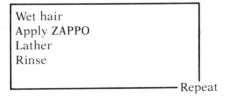

The most important things to notice in the **ZAPPO** algorithm are:

1. When performed in order, the instructions lead you through the process of "washing your hair with **ZAPPO**"—presumably this is a difficult task which must be explained.
2. Each instruction is incompletely specified—if you don't know how to "lather," this algorithm is of no use to you.
3. Each step within the algorithm seems reasonable, but the overall effect is not reasonable (namely, it never stops).

Programmers need a special method of describing algorithms. Saying what a program does in English is useful in dealing with your customers or boss, but is only the first step in writing a program. Writing down a sequence of computer commands in Fortran takes time, effort, and patience, and can only be done once the programmer really understands the problem. Most of the real work is done using **plans**, which are expressed in a form somewhere between English and actual computer code. Here's a plan for the **ZAPPO** algorithm.

Plan

```
Wet hair
Apply ZAPPO
Lather
Rinse
                              Repeat
```

Notice that the fifth instruction on the **ZAPPO** bottle ("repeat") is written differently from the other four in the plan. If you think about it a bit, you'll realize that it is a markedly different sort of instruction from the other four. Instructions 1 through 4 tell you to perform specific acts, whereas number 5 tells you where to get your next instruction. That is, it refers to the list of instructions itself rather than to something you're to do with ZAPPO. In the plan, we draw a box around the instructions that we're to repeat.

So that you will be more comfortable thinking in terms of algorithms, we'll show you a few more examples. In each case we'll present the algorithm using an accepted terminology, then convert it to our "plan" notation. Try to see how the one relates to the other.

The knitting book description in the algorithm may look strange to you, especially if you don't know that *sts.* means "stitches" and that *K2, P2* means "knit 2, purl 2," but this is a characteristic of special languages (including programming languages)—they contain symbols that mean precise things to the person or computer being instructed.

Knitter's terminology:

Starting at lower edge, cast on 116 sts. 1st row: *K2, P2. Repeat from * across. Repeat 1st row until total length is 60 inches.

Plan   Cast on 116 stitches

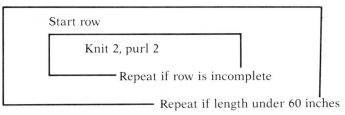

Notice that in the knitting book description a symbol (*) is used to identify a place to repeat from and that the "repeat from * across" instruction refers to that place. Compare with the plan. Also, you will notice that, unlike the ZAPPO algorithm, the commands to "repeat" are conditional. You don't repeat forever; you repeat to the end of the row ("across"), or until the total length is 60 inches.

The plan for the knitting algorithm is relatively complicated, yet it is easy to understand. The main part of the process consists of repeating a repetition. We keep repeating rows until the scarf is long enough. To make a row, we keep repeating K2, P2. You probably won't write a program as complicated as this until you have read Chapter 3.

Computing Compound Interest. Suppose you want to put some money in a savings account, and you want to decide whether it would be better to get 5 percent interest compounded quarterly or 4.85 percent interest compounded weekly. One way to find out which is better is to compute your interest for one year at each rate and then compare the results.

financial formula: $FV = P \times (1 + i)^n$

Plan   Let N = number of compounding periods in year
        P = amount of intial deposit
        A = P (A will be your account's running balance)
        R = annual interest rate (in percent)
        i = R/(100 × N) (i is the monthly interest rate)

Do N times
            Increase A: multiply it by 1 + i
                                        Repeat

Your profit: A − P

This algorithm has a characteristic that is common to many algorithms—it repeats one of its statements several times. Computers are often used to perform difficult tasks by repeating many simple tasks, as in this example. Possibly this is where the characterization of computers as "high-speed idiots" comes from.

1.4 EXERCISE

1.   Write a verbal description of and a plan for one or two of the following:
    a. Making a dessert (following a recipe)
    b. Making a desert (altering an ecosystem)
    c. Fixing a flat rear tire on a bicycle
    d. Buying a pair of shoes
    e. Figuring your grade point average

1.5 MACHINE IDEAS

You will recall from Section 1.3 that Fortran was designed for use on many different computers. Fortran assumes that every computer has certain characteristics. These assumed characteristics can be described in simple terms and are helpful to know. The Fortran statements you will soon be learning will make sense if you visualize them as affecting the various parts of the **conceptual computer** shown in Figure 1.5.1.

The conceptual computer has three parts, a **processor** which carries out the commands that make up your program, a **memory** which stores your program and any values it may use or produce, and **input** and **output devices** through which values are fed in and printed out. We'll describe each part in concrete terms.

The memory consists of some number of words or **cells. A memory cell** is a collection of two-state elements. At any point in time each element is in one or the other state. These two states are commonly named "1" and "0" by machine designers, and although we'll rarely think of memory cells in these terms, the size of a memory cell is usually measured in **bits** (**binary digits**), the number of two-state elements making up the cell.

Figure 1.5.1   The Conceptual Computer

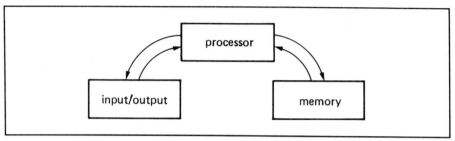

---

memory: the part of a computer that stores programs and data

The size of a memory cell may also be given in **bytes,** which are eight-bit chunks of memory. A computer's array of memory cells is often called its *random access memory*—RAM, for short. (People over 40 occasionally refer to RAM as "core memory," after an obsolete technology for RAM fabrication.) The size of a computer's RAM is usually given in bytes, and it may run from 16,000 bytes on a very small microcomputer up to a few million bytes on a large micro- or minicomputer on up to tens of millions of bytes on a large mainframe computer. For example, a VAX 11/780 computer has 32-bit words. Each word is a sequence of four bytes, and the RAM on a VAX typically has a total of two to four million bytes, or, in other terms, one-half million to a million words.

---

byte: an eight-bit sequence of bits

Each cell in memory has an **address** (denoting where it is) and a **value** (the particular pattern of 1's and 0's that it contains). In Fortran programs we give a **name** to each memory cell we wish to store a value in; the name can be thought of as the address of the memory cell. We can issue commands which will copy the value from a particular memory cell into another part of the machine by using the name of that memory cell. As the term *copy* implies, doing this does not disturb the value in the memory cell. We will also be able to store values in memory cells, and since there is only a fixed storage capacity (a fixed number of bits) in a cell, the value that previously occupied that cell is destroyed when a new value is stored in it.

We use the terms word, cell, memory word, memory location, and memory cell interchangeably.

The **processor** is the central coordinator of the conceptual computer. Your program, when stored in the memory, is really just a bunch of values (patterns of 1's and 0's) in a bunch of memory cells. The values that make up your program are examined by the processor, and the 1's and 0's work like electrical switches turning on the various subunits required to carry out the command. We're not trying to say that a computer is just a lot of 1's and 0's. That would be a vast oversimplification. But we want to emphasize that the processor simply carries out the instructions or commands specified by bit patterns in memory cells. The processor can get values from memory cells, can manipulate them, can put new values back in memory, and can supervise the input and output devices.

> **processor:** the part of a computer that carries out commands from a program

Input and output devices (**I/O devices**) provide the means of communication between people and the machine. Every Fortran system will have a standard input device and a standard output device for people/machine communication. The most common standard I/O device is the keyboard and screen of a CRT (cathode ray tube) computer terminal (sometimes referred to as a VDT for *v*ideo *d*isplay *t*erminal). However, your system may have a card reader for an input device and a line printer for an output device.

Not all I/O devices are designed for communication between people and computers. Some types of I/O devices serve to expand the computer's memory and to act as a permanent storage facility. (RAM normally functions as a temporary storage facility to record intermediate results while a program is running.) Disks, magnetic tapes, and bubble memories fall into this category. Magnetic tape drives are especially favored by makers of grade B science fiction movies as symbols of how computers look and behave, probably because the tape reels spin quickly, stop on a dime, reverse their direction, and generally display a lot of action. Computers themselves are boring to watch. Nothing moves at all in the processor or the memory (except electrons, and they're hard to see).

The computer you'll be using is almost surely much more complex than the simple picture we have described in the processor-memory-I/O device model, but this "conceptual computer" will serve very well as a context for thinking about how Fortran statements work. If you think we're being elusive, look at the manual describing your computer. It will probably be as murky as Weird Al's musical history.

> **input/output:** the parts of a computer that allow communication between users and the computer

1.5 EXERCISES

1. Look at the computer you will be using. Locate the various I/O devices, the processor, the various types of memory, and so on.
2. Find out something about the machine you will be using—the number of bits per word, the number of words in the memory, the brand and model number, the price, what it smells like, and so on.
3. List the parts of the conceptual computer and their functions.
4. What is the difference between the name of a memory cell and its value?

1.6 A PROGRAM FOR THE CONCEPTUAL COMPUTER

To get an idea of how computers operate, it will be helpful for you to simulate a computer running a program. The idea is to play the roles of the various parts of the conceptual computer as it goes through the steps of a program. This is a realistic simulation. Every command is directly analogous to a Fortran statement, and all of the parts of the conceptual computer are used.

The program you'll be simulating computes a new bank balance, given the old balance and the recent deposits and withdrawals (checks). (Fig. 1.6.1 describes the general process. To carry out the simulation, you will need some 3-by-5 cards to write on, some patience, and a little common sense.

Some of the cards will be identified by "name." To get started, write the names BAL, AMT, and TYPE at the tops of three of the cards, and the names CMD1, CMD2, up through CMD8 on eight other cards. Each of these "named" cards represents a "memory cell" in the computer. Finally, put aside a special card to use for "output," and a stack of cards for input, which we'll call the "data stack."

On the bottom card on the data stack, write the number zero and the words NO MORE DATA. On the top card of the data stack, write the balance in your checking account when you received your last bank statement followed by the words LAST BALANCE. On the rest of the cards in the middle of the data stack, write the amounts of recent transactions on your account. Write the word CHECK after each amount that represents a withdrawal from your account; write the word DEPOSIT after each amount that reflects a deposit. (At this point, each card in the data stack should have a number and one of the following phrases written on it: LAST BALANCE (top card only), NO MORE DATA (bottom card only), CHECK, or DEPOSIT.)

The eight cards called CMD1, CMD2, . . . CMD8 will contain the instructions your "computer" is to follow (i.e., the "program" for the computer). On these cards write the following instructions.

CMD1	Write a zero on the card named BAL.
CMD2	Remove the top card remaining on the data stack and copy the number on it onto the card named AMT.

Figure 1.6.1   Balancing a Checkbook

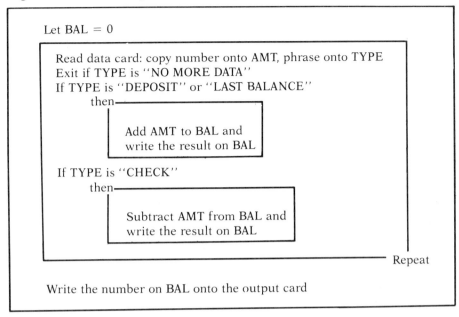
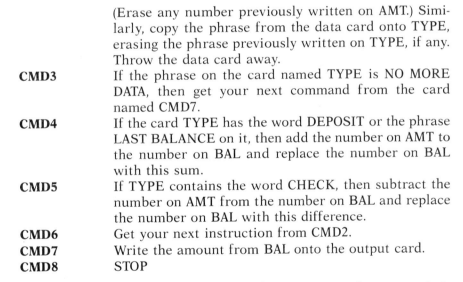

Let BAL = 0

Read data card: copy number onto AMT, phrase onto TYPE
Exit if TYPE is "NO MORE DATA"
If TYPE is "DEPOSIT" or "LAST BALANCE"
    then——

    Add AMT to BAL and
    write the result on BAL

If TYPE is "CHECK"
    then——

    Subtract AMT from BAL and
    write the result on BAL

Repeat

Write the number on BAL onto the output card

(Erase any number previously written on AMT.) Similarly, copy the phrase from the data card onto TYPE, erasing the phrase previously written on TYPE, if any. Throw the data card away.

CMD3   If the phrase on the card named TYPE is NO MORE DATA, then get your next command from the card named CMD7.

CMD4   If the card TYPE has the word DEPOSIT or the phrase LAST BALANCE on it, then add the number on AMT to the number on BAL and replace the number on BAL with this sum.

CMD5   If TYPE contains the word CHECK, then subtract the number on AMT from the number on BAL and replace the number on BAL with this difference.

CMD6   Get your next instruction from CMD2.

CMD7   Write the amount from BAL onto the output card.

CMD8   STOP

This program is a list of instructions for computing the current balance in a checking account. It uses data from the data stack, "variables" (BAL, AMT, and TYPE) to record intermediate (temporary) values, and the output card to deliver the final answer.

To carry out the program, simply start with CMD1 and proceed through the commands in sequence, 1, 2, 3, and so on. Some commands say to break the sequence. In this case, you again proceed sequentially after starting from the new command.

There are a great many things to be learned from going through a simulation like this one. The commands that you (simulating the processor) carry out are very similar to commands that can be written as Fortran statements. This should give you a feeling for the degree of explicitness required to write programs.

The following exercises will give you a little more practice in choosing and expressing commands.

1.6 EXERCISES

1. Write a program for the conceptual computer that computes the average of a group of numbers.
2. Write a program that finds the longest name in a list of names. Write a bunch of your friends' names on cards, and simulate a computer executing the program to find the longest name.

1.7 COMPUTING ENVIRONMENTS

Before you start writing Fortran programs you will need to learn more about your computing environment and how you will enter and run your programs. If your computer system is card oriented, you will be punching your program and data on cards. The card reader will transmit the information to the computer and after your program has been run you will receive a listing of the output. This is a **batch processing** type of environment.

Figure 1.7.1   Fortran Coding Sheet

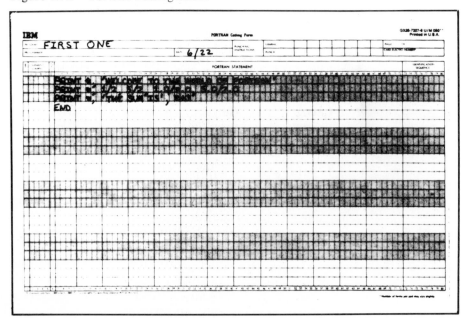

Conventions concerning the physical appearance of Fortran statements are based on the assumption that the statements are punched on 80-column cards. If you are using a terminal or microcomputer, follow the same conventions on an 80-column line. Certain columns are used for certain purposes. There are four fields on a Fortran statement card:

1. the label field (columns 1-5)
2. the continuation field (column 6)
3. the statement field (columns 7-72)
4. the identification field (columns 73-80)

The identification field is completely ignored by the compiler, but it is printed on your program listing and is often used for card numbering. In all fields, blanks are ignored; you should use blanks freely to make your program readable.

You write one statement on each card. However, if your statement is too long to fit in the statement field of one card, you may continue it into the statement field of the next card by placing any mark (other than zero) in the continuation field (colum 6) of the second card. (This doesn't work for comment statements.)

There is one additional convention: a C in column 1 will cause the compiler to ignore the entire card. Since the card will be printed on the program listing, you may use this convention to intersperse your program with comments.

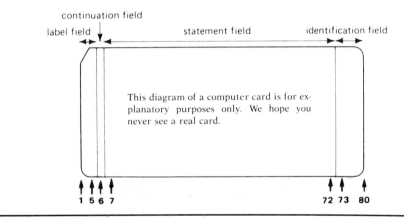

This diagram of a computer card is for explanatory purposes only. We hope you never see a real card.

In a **time-sharing** environment you will use a terminal connected to a computer whose processor is being shared by other users. You will enter your programs and data at the terminal keyboard. You may have to learn how to use a text editor. A text editor helps you enter information into the computer system. Each system has its own text editor so you will have to learn the one for your particular system. You can have your program listing and output displayed at the terminal or you can have it printed on the line printer.

If you have a microcomputer, you will be working in an environment very similar to time-sharing. The main difference is that you are the only one using your computer's processor.

In all of these environments, you will have to use special control commands to run your programs. Your local experts will help you get started.

It's probably a good idea to try running a program in your computing environment. Figure 1.7.1 is a complete program written on a Fortran coding sheet. A coding sheet indicates the columns where information belongs. (You don't need to use a coding sheet, but some people find them helpful.) Enter the program using your computing system, making sure you key the information in the right columns. Then run the program and see what happens.

1.7   EXERCISE

1.   Enter and run the program in Figure 1.7.1.

2 WRITING PROGRAMS

CHAPTER PLAN
- *Describe the declaration and use of REAL memory cells and constants*
- *Define and describe the use in programs of these statement types:*
  - *assignment*
  - *PRINT*
  - *READ*
  - *END*
- *Introduce expressions and functions*
- *Introduce CHARACTER constants*

2.1 MEMORY CELLS

Of the three parts of the computer, the memory is probably the most confusing. The I/O apparatus's purpose is straightforward; the processor carries out commands, some of which you can imagine from your class simulation; and the memory is used to store values. This seems simple enough, but confusion seems to arise from the fact that each memory cell has a **name.** Because of the way computer programs are written, many people tend to confuse the name of a memory cell with the **value** stored in it, a mistake similar to confusing a box with its contents. Try to keep in mind that *a memory cell is a container for a value.*

We've said a number of things about memory already (that it's made up of cells, each of which has an address or name, and a value, and that both your program and data are stored there). In this chapter we'll make these ideas more concrete and begin to get some notion of how to use the computer's memory.

To use the memory in the Fortran language, you need a name for each memory cell you intend to use. You can use any names you like, as long as you follow a few rules.

The rules are these: start each name with a letter, use only letters and digits in the name, and don't use more than six characters (letters and digits) in all. Some Fortran systems relax these rules a little. Many systems allow seven-character names, or even eight-character names, but standard Fortran specifies the six-character limit. If you stay within this limit, your names will work on *any* Fortran system, not just the one you happen to be using now.

Rules for Naming Memory Cells

- start with a letter
- use *only* letters and numerals
- use no more than six characters

Within these rules, you have *complete freedom!* For example, you may name a memory cell DRAT, if you like, or any other four-letter word, or POPE or CELL12 or COFFEE. But you may not name a memory cell EVANGELIST or ASPIRINS because these names have too many characters, nor can you name one D––N because two of the characters in that name are neither letters nor numerals.

You can do virtually nothing in Fortran without memory cells. They are used for storing information. Any information your Fortran program deals with in any way must be stored in memory cells. "What kind of information?" you might be asking. "Any kind" is the answer, as long as you can devise a way to represent your information in Fortran's terms.

Devising generally useful ways to represent information can be a complex and difficult problem. In fact, it is one of the primary areas of study in the field of computer science. The problem is this: given a class of data to deal with, devise a way to denote each distinct item using the notational symbols available. A questionnaire is a familiar example of this process. Suppose you want to find out about the musical tastes of your friends. You might put together a list of multiple-choice questions to ask them:

1. Who do you like best? (a) Frank Zappa, (b) Beethoven, or (c) Cyndi Lauper.
2. What is better for a party? (a) Pat Benatar, (b) Charlie Daniels, or (c) Glenn Miller.

And so on.

You might represent the results of the questionnaire as tallies of answers: 1(a:3, b:1, c:2); 2(a:2, b:4, c:0); and so on. You have chosen to represent your data in terms of familiar symbols: letters, numbers, and punctuation marks, and these symbols have a specific meaning to you in terms of the questionnaire results they represent.

You will have to go through a similar process every time you write a Fortran program, except that you will have to choose symbols that Fortran can process. Fortran can handle six different kinds of data: four kinds of numbers (all processed and interpreted by Fortran in different ways, most of which will match your intuition about how numbers behave); raw "characters" (letters, digits, and a limited collection of special characters like punctuation marks, asterisks, and the like); and two-valued logic data (with true/false-type interpretations). These are known as the **data types** of Fortran.

As you progress in your study of programming, you will think of more and more clever ways to interpret the data types that Fortran provides in the context of the problems you are solving. However, in the beginning we will try to stick with problems where this interpretation is very straightforward. In fact, to keep things as simple as possible in the early going, we will use only one data type, known as REAL numbers. These are the familiar decimal numbers that your pocket calculator uses: 293.44, 8.5, 0.01, and so on. Fortran places a limit on the size of these numbers, and, just as with pocket calculators, this limit varies, depending on the brand and type. IBM Fortran, for example, allows 7 digits; many microcomputers allow 17 digits. We'll go into more detail on this topic in Chapter 3. For now, just try to stay within reason and you probably won't run into trouble.

Of the three other kinds of Fortran numbers, only one is frequently used by novice programmers. This is the INTEGER data type (numbers without decimal fractions, like 101, 12, and 29). You will learn about INTEGERs and the other kinds of Fortran numbers in Chapter 3, and you will use INTEGERs extensively in subsequent chapters, but for now you have enough details to worry about without having to concern yourself with things like different kinds of numbers. One kind will do nicely for now.

---

data type: a particular class of information
Fortran programmers must place each item of data into one of six classes. There are four different types of *numbers,* all used in different ways. There is a type for characters. In addition, there is a *logical* data type for decision making. In this section, to keep things as simple as possible, we'll learn about just one of the numeric classes: REAL.

When you want to use a memory cell in a Fortran program, you must decide what kind of information it will contain; that is, you must choose its **type.** Within a program you may use many memory cells containing many different types of information, but any *one* memory cell is allowed to contain only *one* kind of information. That is, you will associate *one* name and *one* data type with each memory cell you use.

FORTRAN is not a legal memory cell name in standard Fortran.

The data type we'll start with is the REAL data type. REALs are ordinary numbers and are always written with a decimal point, as in 137.9, 4932.1, 32.00, and −17.472.

In Fortran programs, numbers containing decimal points are known as **REAL** numbers. Thus a *REAL* number is a sequence of digits with a decimal point located somewhere in the sequence. In addition, the sequence may be preceded by a plus or a minus sign.

REALs	unREALs
1497.3	1,497.3
+83.0	+83
−983.25	−983¼
1.0	1
0.5	½

At the beginning of each Fortran program we use declaration statements to name the memory cells we intend to use and we say what type of information we intend to store in them. For example, the declaration statement

```
REAL X, Y, Z
```

gives names to three memory cells, X, Y, and Z, and decrees that each will be used to store REAL numbers.

Declaration Statement

form
type list
type is the name of a Fortran data type (REAL, for example)
list is a list of memory cell names, separated by commas.

meaning
instructs the compiler to attach the names in *list* to memory cells, which will be used to store information of the *type* declared at the beginning of the statement

examples

```
REAL W, ALPHA, Z27, STUDNT
REAL R, SP, TRACK
```

If you forget to declare a memory cell that your program uses, you may get by with it. Fortran doesn't require declarations, but it does make certain assumptions when you omit declarations. Our policy is to *declare all memory cells*, whether they need it or not, and we recommend that you follow this procedure too, at least until you have gotten through Chapter 3. (We follow our policy throughout the text, and in our own programming, too.)

2.1 EXERCISES

1. Which of the following are legal names for memory locations? If not, why not?

    ```
    23SKIDOO
    SKIDOO23
    SALE3
    TORQUE
    OILWELL
    LIMIT
    TONY THE TIGER
    FORTRAN
    ```

2. Which of the following are legal declaration statements?

    ```
    REAL J, Z, BETA
    REAL HIGH, LOW
    REAL A, 149.2
    ```

3. Write a Fortran statement that declares that we want to use two memory cells, AJAX and FOAM, to store REALs.

4. Circle the REALs and place a check mark by the ones that aren't REALs.

    41.7
    349
    692.0
    81
    −49
    −896.721
    0

2.2 THE ASSIGNMENT STATEMENT

There are two ways of getting information into memory cells. You can specify a cell's value directly by writing down the cell's name and a number to be assigned to it, or you can tell the processor to get a cell's value from an input device such as the keyboard of a video terminal or from a card reader or a disk. Programmers use the direct method more frequently because it permits values to be specified in terms of computations (addition, multiplication, etc.). In fact, it is the primary means of computation in Fortran. The input method, on the other hand, makes it possible to write generalized programs that can handle varied batches of data. This chapter discusses both methods—the direct method (known as the assignment statement) now, and the input method later.

An **assignment statement** is a memory cell name followed by the assignment operator (the equal sign, =), followed by the value that you wish to place into the memory cell. The assignment operation transfers the value on the right into the memory cell named on the left.

The assignment statement confuses many people, perhaps because the assignment operator (=) is a familiar sign, but the operation it designates is *not* familiar. The action in an assignment statement proceeds from *right* to *left*: the value on the right is placed into the memory cell named on the left. This is an important thing to remember, so important that you should probably read this paragraph again.

= Remember! In Fortran the equal sign does not mean equals in the mathematical sense. A statement like $A = B$ places the value in the memory cell B into the memory cell A. It is true that immediately after the statement is executed the values in A and B are the same, but at some later time the values in the two memory cells may be different. For example, the next statement in the program may assign a different value to B. This won't affect the value of A, so at that point $A's$ value will be different from $B's$.

Examples

```
TWO = 2.0
```

The value 2.0 is placed into the memory cell named TWO.

```
M1 = -1.0
```

The value −1.0 is placed into the memory cell named M1.

```
STUDNT = 3.982
```

The number 3.982 is placed into the memory cell named STUDNT.

```
TRACK = -1.95
```

The number −1.95 is placed into the memory cell named TRACK.

```
FOUR = 2.0
```

The value 2.0 is placed into the memory cell named FOUR. FOUR is a lousy name for a memory cell containing the value two. The reason it's lousy has nothing to do with the rules of Fortran. The computer doesn't care what names you associate with which values. But there are enough complications in writing programs without increasing the problems by choosing misleading names. Choose names that at least hint at the ways in which the values stored will be used.

Of course, for these assignment statements to work properly, the declaration statement

```
REAL TWO, M1, STUDNT, TRACK, FOUR
```

must appear at the beginning of the program.

It would soon get boring just writing programs that assigned values to a bunch of memory locations. Fortunately, the right-hand side of an assignment statement can be more complex than just a single number. It

Assignment Statement

form
v = *e*
v is a memory cell name
e is an expression

meaning
computes the value of *e* and places it in *v*

examples
```
A1 = 3.0
TAX = PRICE*0.06
TOTAL = 11.99 + 2*4.95
```

may be an **expression** involving some arithmetic computations. In Fortran, the familiar operations of addition, subtraction, multiplication, division, and exponentiation may be used in the usual ways (see Table 2.2.1).

The Fortran symbols denoting addition (+), subtraction (−), and division (/) are widely used and are probably familiar to you, but the symbols for multiplication (∗) and exponentiation (∗∗) are "Fortranisms." The problem is that the usual multiplication sign looks like an "x" and the usual notation for exponentiation is superscripting. Neither is available on standard computer input devices, so the asterisk and double asterisk are used instead.

Parentheses can be used for grouping subexpressions into single quantities. Operations inside parentheses are done first, and the result is reduced to a single value before being combined with other values outside the parentheses. Again, this method of grouping quantities is widely used and probably familiar to you.

Example
```
REAL TOTAL
TOTAL = 12.00*(1.0+0.05)
```

The value of the arithmetic expression above (namely 12.60) is placed into the memory cell named TOTAL.

Expressions can be considerably more general than the ones you have seen so far, which have involved only constants. It is also permissible to use memory cell names in an expression. Thus, names of memory cells may appear on both sides of an assignment statement, but the names are used in very different ways. As you already know, the name on the *left* side tells where to *store* the value which results from the computation on the right side. Memory cell names on the *right* side mean "go to this place in memory, and use whatever value is stored there in the computation." It is important to realize that the values of memory cells on the right remain unchanged by the process of evaluating the expression.

Example
```
REAL TAX
TAX = TOTAL*0.06
```

The value of the arithmetic expression on the right is placed into the memory cell named TAX. To compute the value of the expression, the processor must first determine the contents of the memory cell TOTAL, then do the indicated multiplication. If we assume the value of the memory cell TOTAL hasn't changed since the last time we used it in this chapter, then TOTAL has the value 12.60, so TAX will be assigned the value 12.60*0.06, that is, 0.756.

Example
```
REAL COST
COST = TOTAL + TAX
```

The value of the expression on the right (TOTAL + TAX) is placed into the memory cell on the left (COST). If TOTAL has the value 12.20 and TAX has the value 0.756, then COST gets the value 12.956.

Example
```
TOTAL = TOTAL + 4.25
```

The value of the expression on the right is placed into the memory cell named TOTAL. This example may appear odd at first because the memory cell to be given a value is involved in the expression on the right. This is one time when it is especially important to remember that the action goes from right to left. First the computer looks up the current value of TOTAL; our last assignment made that value 12.60. Adding 4.25 to 12.60, the value of the expression is 16.85, and this value is put into the memory cell TOTAL. The assignment destroys the old value of TOTAL.

In most cases, writing arithmetic expressions to make computations is quite natural and the results fit in pretty well with your past experience. However, there is one big difference to keep in mind. Remember that each memory cell is made up of a fixed number of "bits," 1's and 0's. That means that some numbers will be too long to fit.

For example, REAL-valued memory cells in IBM 370 Fortran cannot handle numbers with more than seven **significant digits.** (The significant digits in a number are those between the first and last nonzero digits, inclusive. The number 2.007 has four significant digits; the number 0.00000059 has two significant digits.) There is also a restriction on the range of the numbers: there cannot be more than 38 digits to the left of the decimal point; nor more than 38 digits to the right of the decimal point in IBM 370 Fortran.

This may not seem especially restrictive, and it usually isn't, but it is important to realize that REAL numbers in Fortran are not the same as numbers in mathematics. There is an infinite collection of different mathematical numbers, but the number of different Fortran REALs is finite. You can lose digits in a Fortran computation just as you can lose digits on a pocket calculator. The difference is that you normally see on your calculator all the numbers you are computing. They appear on the

Table 2.2.1   Fortran Operations

Operation	Standard Symbols	Example	Fortran Symbol	Examples
addition	+	a + b	+	A + B 1 + 1
subtraction	−	a − b	−	A − B 3 − 2
multiplication	×	a × b	*	A*B 4*4
division	÷ or /	a ÷ b a/b	/	A/B 10/2
exponentiation	superscript	a^b	**	A**B 2**10

display. A Fortran program runs on its own, and you don't see all of the numbers. You can lose digits without knowing it, and these **rounding errors,** as they are known, can cause lots of difficulty in certain types of computations.

We will discuss arithmetic expressions in more depth in Chapter 3. For now, rely on your past experience to guide you. Use parentheses to denote subexpressions that are to be treated as single quantities. For example, 1.25 + (2.50*2.0) is 6.25, but (1.25 + 2.50)*2.0 is 7.50. The usual algebraic rules of precedence apply, so you don't always have to use parentheses. This means that multiplication and divisions are performed before additions and subtractions, so that 1.25 + 2.50*2.0 is the same as 1.25 + (2.50*2.0) and 5.0/2.0 − 12.3*9.1 is the same as (5.0/2.0) − (12.3*9.1). Exponentiations are performed before multiplications and divisions, so that 32.0/4.0**2.0 is 32.0/(4.0**2.0). Whenever you are uncertain about how an expression will be evaluated, use parentheses to make your intentions clear. It's much better to put parentheses into an expression, even when they are unnecessary, than it is to leave them out and get the wrong answer.

Variables

Memory cells are often called **variables.** The use of variables is the essence of programming. It is important to remember that *variables vary.* They change values. This is a new concept for novice programmers. It differs from the concept of variables in mathematics. In mathematics, variables *don't* vary! $x + 10 = 15$ means that x must stand for 5, but that's all x stands for. The single value 5 is the only one associated with x in this mathematical problem. In programming, the name "X" stands for a memory cell whose value will be changed and rechanged as the computation proceeds.

2.2   EXERCISES

1.   At the end of the following program fragment, what are the values of A and B?

```
REAL A, B
B = 10.0
A = B
B = 2.0
```

2.   What values would be stored in memory cell B by these assignment statements?

```
B = 2.0*3.0*4.0
B = (5.0/2.5) + 1.0
B = -9.5*4.0
```

3.   Which of these are legal assignment statements? It not, why not?

```
A = A*A + A
BO = 2.0
-AT = 2.0
CAT + DOG = FIGHT
CAT + DOG -3.0
FIGHT = CAT + DOG
```

4.   What value will be stored in memory cell SOUP by these assignment statements?

```
SOUP = 1.0  + (7.0*4.0)/2.0
SOUP = 7.0/2.0 + 4.5
SOUP = (2.0 + 3.5)*(1.0 + 9.0)
SOUP = (8.0/16.0)*1024.0
```

5.   Write statements which will
   a.   declare a REAL memory cell named FIRST and assign FIRST the value 2
   b.   assign FIRST its old value times 4
   c.   assign FIRST its old value plus 1

2.3   THE PRINT STATEMENT

So far you have learned how to attach names to memory cells and to place values in them. You can also make the computer perform computations. Unfortunately, however, you have no way at this point of finding out the results of the computations. The PRINT statement will solve this problem, as the following example demonstrates.

Suppose you are buying a car, and you want to compute the total price, including an optional FM radio and supersport airfoil spoiler. The computation might proceed like this:

1. Note the base price.
2. Note the price of the FM radio option.
3. Note the price of the airfoil spoiler option.
4. Add the above three figures to get a total.

What we have written here is a step-by-step plan for our computation. Conscientious programmers always write a computation plan before writing a program. They study the plan until they are sure it is correct. When they are confident that the plan describes the essential features of the computation, then they look at each step in the plan and find a way to say the same thing within the restricted conventions of Fortran. Writing the plan in English allows you to solve the problem without worrying about the finer points of Fortran.

In our plan for computing the total price of a car, we think we have included everything except directions for writing out the results. These directions wouldn't be important if the plan were to be used by another person. Anyone using such a list of instructions would know what to write down. However, a computer doesn't automatically know the goal of the computation. It has to be told exactly what values to print and exactly when to print them. Otherwise the results of the computation will be lost.

Let's decide what needs to be printed. Obviously the total cost must be printed, but it would be nice to have other costs printed too (the base price and the price of each option). This means we'll have output associated with each step of the computation. Our plan now is:

1. Note base price and print.
2. Note the price of the FM radio option and print.
3. Note the price of the airfoil spoiler and print.
4. Add the above three figures to get the total and print.

We've simply added a print command along with each step in the plan.

Now that our plan is complete, we need to translate it into Fortran. Looking at step 1, it's easy to see that we can enter the base price in the computer's memory by assigning a number to a memory cell:

BASEPR = 4127.00.

The second part of step 1, printing the base price, is another matter. For that we need a new kind of Fortran statement—a **PRINT statement.** The purpose of the PRINT statement is to write out values from memory cells. For example, the statement

```
PRINT *, BASEPR
```

tells the computer to copy the number of BASEPR onto a printed line as shown below.

```
4127
```

PRINT Statement

form
PRINT*, *list*
list, an **output list** contains one or more values (i.e., constants, memory cell names, or expressions) separated by commas.

meaning
prints each of the values in the list on a line. If the values won't all fit on one line, as many lines are used as are needed to complete the printing of the entire *list*.

examples

```
PRINT *, X
PRINT *, C
PRINT *, X, X+Y, 'STRING'
PRINT *, (X*Y-X)
```

We can use a PRINT statement like this with every step in our plan. Then the program becomes a sequence of assignment statements and PRINT statements as shown below.

```
REAL BASEPR, RADIO, SPOILR, TOTAL
BASEPR = 4127.00
PRINT *, BASEPR
RADIO = 232.00
PRINT *, RADIO
SPOILR = 248.00
PRINT *, SPOILR
TOTAL = BASEPR + RADIO + SPOILR
PRINT *, TOTAL
END ◀─────────────────────
```
─an END statement is required at the end of all programs

Output

```
4127.000
232.0000
248.0000
4607.000
```

The output from this program, as you can see, consists of four numbers, one from each PRINT statement. It may be suitable for our immediate purposes, but it could be improved. Some explanatory information along with the numbers would help.

Desired Output

```
BASE PRICE     $4127.00
     RADIO       232.00
   SPOILER       248.00
     TOTAL     $4607.00
```

To get this information printed along with the numbers we want, we put CHARACTER constants in the PRINT statements. CHARACTER constants are strings (sequences) of symbols enclosed by apostrophes.

(When apostrophes are used in this way, they're often called "single quotes," or "quote marks" in programming circles.)

CHARACTER Constants

> strings of symbols enclosed in quote marks (single quotes, like apostrophes, rather than double quotes)
>
> ```
> 'HOUSE'
> 'FARM'
> 'K7 SPOT REMOVER'
> '$43.27***TOTAL'
> ```
>
> The quote marks aren't part of the CHARACTER string. They serve only to delimit the ends of the string which may contain any characters, including blanks.

The statement

```
PRINT *, 'BASE PRICE  $', BASEPR
```

tells the computer to write the characters between the quote marks on the first part of a line, and then to print the value of BASEPR. When we enclose something in quote marks, that means we want it treated *verbatim*. We don't have BASEPR in quotes because we don't want to print BASEPR, we want to print the **value** of BASEPR.

In this case the line above would cause the computer to print

```
BASE PRICE  $        4127
```

You're probably surprised to see all those spaces between the dollar sign and the number of decimal places printed. When we use this form of PRINT statement (the word PRINT followed by a *, followed by a list of the things we want PRINTed), we are leaving it up to the computer to decide on the spacing between items and on the format of individual items. If we don't like the spacing it chooses, we will have to replace the * with detailed information about the spacing we want used. For now, we'll let the computer handle the format decisions.

END Statement

> **form**
>
> ```
> END
> ```
>
> **meaning**
> tells computer to stop doing statements in your program; must be the last statement

Using the new PRINT statements, our program looks like this.

```
COMMENT:                  FIND TOTAL PRICE OF CAR WITH OPTIONS
        REAL BASEPR, RADIO, SPOILR
        REAL TAX, TOTAL
        BASEPR = 4127.00
        PRINT *, ' BASE PRICE      $', BASEPR
        RADIO = 232.00
        PRINT *, '       RADIO      $', RADIO
        SPOILR = 248.00
        PRINT *, '     SPOILER      $', SPOILR
        TOTAL = BASEPR + RADIO + SPOILR
        PRINT *, '        '
        PRINT *, 'TOTAL PRICE       $', TOTAL
        END
```

don't forget the END; it tells the computer to stop

this statement says to PRINT a line of nothing,
and here is the result

Output

```
BASE PRICE    $      4127.000
    RADIO     $      232.0000
  SPOILER     $      248.0000

TOTAL PRICE   $      4607.000
```

2.3 EXERCISES

1. What is the first step in writing a program?
2. What is the second step?
3. What is the last step in writing a program?
4. Write a PRINT statement which would write out the value of a memory cell POP containing the population of Omaha.
5. Write a sequence of PRINT statements which would write out the lines below with the x's replaced by values from memory cells HOME and VISIT.

   ```
         SCORE
       ROCKETS        xxx
       BULLDOGS       xxx
   ```
6. What would the following program print?

   ```
   COMMENT: DOUBLE A VALUE AND SHOW THE RESULT
           REAL M,N
           N = 37.0
           M = N*2.0
           N = M*2.0
           PRINT*, 'SINGLE=' ,M, '      DOUBLE=' ,N
           END
   ```
7. What would be printed if we changed the PRINT statement in Exercise 6 to the following?

   ```
   PRINT *, 'SINGLE=, M,        DOUBLE=, N'
   ```

2.4   USING FUNCTIONS

Now that you can write complete, working programs, it's time to try out some fancy operations. Fortran is like a calculator with lots of keys. It has all of the standard "keys" (multiplication, division, etc.) of course. And it has exponentiation, which is a key found on some calculators but not others. It also has square root, logarithm, trigonometric functions, absolute value, and a host of others that are listed in Appendix B.

The following program uses the square root function, called SQRT, and the logarithm function, called LOG10. (Don't let it bother you if you don't know what a logarithm is. Just think of it as a mathematical operation that tells you, when you round it up to the next whole number, how many digits a given number has before the decimal point.)

```
REAL X, T, SQRX
X = 144.0
SQRX = SQRT(X)
PRINT *, 'SQUARE ROOT OF 144=', SQRX
T = LOG10(X/12)
PRINT *, 'LOGARITHM OF 144/12=', T
END
```

Output

```
SQUARE ROOT OF 144= 12.00000
LOGARITHM OF 144/12= 1.079181
```

Square Root

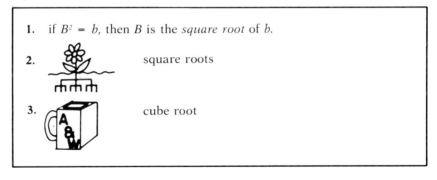

1.   if $B^2 = b$, then B is the *square root* of b.

2.   square roots

3.   cube root

A function is something like an ordinary arithmetic operator (plus, minus, etc.) in the sense that it transforms numbers into other numbers, but the notation is different. The number to be transformed by the function, which is known as the **argument,** is enclosed in parentheses, and the name of the function is put in front of this argument, as in SQRT(2.0). This is known as "prefix notation" for an operation, as opposed to "infix notation," which is what we use for addition, subtraction, and the like, as in 12.95 + 3.47.

The argument for a function can be an arbitrarily complex expression. It can use both ordinary operations, as in SQRT(X + Y), or it can use functions, as in LOG10(3.9 + SQRT(9.1*X)/4.0).

So functions make Fortran like a calculator with lots of keys. But the nice thing about Fortran is that you can make up your own functions. This is a little like being able to program new keys for a calculator. It works like this. Suppose you decide you'd like to have a function that computes the price of an item, given a 30 percent discount. All you have to do is to think up a name for the function (following the six-letter rule for names), and write the formula for the function in your program.

```
DIS30(PRICE) = PRICE - 0.30*PRICE
```

In the formula you use a name for the argument, and you put this name in parentheses after the function name, then an equals sign (=), and finally the formula. There are two conventions you must observe: the names you choose must be declared, just as if they were memory cells (which they are not), and the formula for the function must come after all of the declarations in your program and before all of the other statements. Thus, the declaration

```
REAL DIS30, PRICE
```

should precede the formula for the above function.

Statement Function

form
f(plist) = *e*
where
f, the function name, is a name,
plist, the parameter list, is a list of names separated by commas,
and
e is an expression, which may use other functions and operations.

meaning
Defines a function that you can use to form expressions in your program. When you use the function, you supply arguments to take the place of the *plist* parameters wherever they occur in the formula *e*.

note
The data types of the name *f* and all the names in *plist* should be specified in a declaration statement prior to the statement function

examples
```
ROUND(X)  = INT(X+0.5)
PLACES(X,D) = NINT(X*(10.0**D))/(10.0**D)
COT(X)  = COS(X)/SIN(X)
```

Functions that you define in this way are called "statement functions," and functions that Fortran provides automatically are called "built-in functions." Together, the standard arithmetic operations plus the built-in functions provide a great many "automatic" operations that you can use to get your computational job done. You can use them directly in expres-

Table 2.4.1 Built-in FUNCTIONS

Function	Value Computed
SQRT(r)	$\sqrt{r}$
LOG10(r)	log to the base 10 of r
LOG(r)	natural logarithm of r
EXP(r)	e^r, where e is the base of natural logarithms
SIN(r)	trigonometric sine of r radians
COS(r)	cosine of r radians
TAN(r)	The angle $\left(-\dfrac{\pi}{2} \text{ to } \dfrac{\pi}{2}\right)$ whose tangent is r
ABS(r)	the absolute value of r, $\lvert r \rvert$
NINT(r)	nearest INTEGER to r (rounding): NINT(-3.7) is -4
INT(r)	integer version of r (truncation): INT(-3.7) is -3
MAX($r_1, r_2, \ldots, r_n$)	largest value of $r_1, r_2, \ldots, r_n$; $n \geq 2$
MIN($r_1, r_2, \ldots, r_n$)	smallest value of $r_1, r_2, \ldots, r_n$; $n \geq 2$

sions, or you can combine them to form statement functions, then use the statement functions as a shorthand notation for a complex expression in your program.

Some of the commonly used built-in expressions are listed in Table 2.4.1. The rest of them appear in Appendix B.

---

infix operator: an operator which is written between its arguments

examples

$$+, -, *, /, **$$

as in

$$A + 375$$

---

prefix operator: an operator which appears before its arguments

examples

SQRT
LOG10
ABS

as in

$$ABS(-1.75432)$$

Here are a few statement functions to show you how they can be used. Compute discount price, given regular price and discount percentage:

```
DISCPR(PR,DISC) = PR - PR*(DISC/100.0)
```

Compute discount percentage, given regular price and discount price:

```
DISC(PR,DISCPR) = 100.0*(PR - DISCR)/PR
```

Round a given number to two decimal places:

```
TWODEC(X) = NINT(X*100.0)/100.0
```

Compute the average of two numbers:

```
AVG(X,Y) = (X + Y)/2.0
```

Compute fraction of distance traveled, given current position, starting point, and destination:

```
P(X,S,D) = (X - S)/(D - S)
```

Compute fraction of distance remaining, given current position, starting point, and destination:

```
Q(X,S,D) = 1.0 - P(X,S,D)
```

Interpolate for missing table entry at X, given surrounding table entries:

```
TRPLAT(X,X1,Y1,X2,Y2)=Y1*Q(X,X1,X2)+Y2*P(X,X1,X2)
```

The following program features the use of a statement function. It computes the length of the hypotenuse of a right triangle given the lengths of the legs. If you know a little geometry, you will be familiar with the formula given in the statement function.

```
REAL A, B, C
REAL HYP
HYP(A,B) = SQRT(A**2 + B**2)
A = 3.0
B = 4.0
C = HYP(A,B)
PRINT *, ' LEGS:', A, B,' HYPOTENUSE:', C
END
```

Output

```
LEGS:   3.000000  4.000000    HYPOTENUSE:  5.000000
```

The exercises for this section suggest a few ways for you to experiment with expressions and functions. It will help you immeasurably if you practice using these concepts in some short programs that compute a few values according to formulas and print them out. You may do these exercises using expressions only, no functions; but using functions in these short programs will help you even more because, in a sense, functions embody the whole idea of programming, but in a simplified form. The idea is that you can combine few basic operations to form more complex computations. You can program new computations, given a few to start with, then use the new ones you put together to form still more complex ones, and so on.

2.4 EXERCISES

1. Write an assignment statement that changes the number in a memory cell X into the square root of double its current value.
2. What is the value of the expression SQRT(4.0*(3.4 + 0.6))?
3. What is the value of the expression SQRT(6.0-SQRT(4.0))?
4. Write a statement function that doubles a given number and adds ten to that.
5. Write a statement function that computes the average of three numbers.
6. Use the functions INT and LOG10 to write an expression that computes the number of digits in front of the decimal point in the number stored in the memory cell X. The trick is to use the logarithm function LOG10 to get close to the answer, drop the fraction from the approximation using the function INT, and finally to add 1 to get the exact answer.
7. If you know a little about trigonometry, use the functions SIN and COS to write a statement function that computes the tangent of a given number.

2.5 THE READ STATEMENT

In most cases the most convenient and efficient way to place values into memory cells is to use the assignment statement we have just discussed. There is, however, a second way to give values to memory cells that, in certain cases, makes a program easier to use: the READ statement. Its main advantage is that it allows you to change the data the program uses in its computations without changing the program itself. The following example illustrates the point.

Suppose you are in charge of computing the weekly averages for your bowling team. Every week your team plays in a league match, and each team member rolls three lines (a "line" is what real bowlers call their games—it consists of ten or eleven "frames," depending on the result in the tenth frame). To compute a team member's average for the week, you have to compute the average of the three scores bowled in the match.

To write a simple program to figure such an average, all you need to do is to write an expression that totals up the three scores, divides by three, and writes out the result, which is the average of the three scores. The program would look something like this (depending on what the actual scores were):

```
REAL AVG
AVG = (167.0 + 142.0 + 159.0)/3.0
PRINT *, 'AVERAGE:', AVG
END
```

Output

```
AVERAGE:   156.0000
```

There are two disadvantages of using such a simple approach. One is that it doesn't write out a permanent record of the actual scores. It only prints the average. To make it provide a permanent record, you could declare a memory cell for each score and assign each score to one of the memory cells. Then your formula for the average would be the sum of the values in these cells divided by three, and you could have the computer write out the scores as well as the average. That would alleviate the first disadvantage.

The second disadvantage is that the program has to be changed every time you run it because you need to put in different scores. That's not so bad, but if it's a special tournament week and you have four matches instead of two, then you'll have to add more statements and change the number you divide by. On the other hand, if a match is canceled for some reason, you have to delete some statements and change the division factor.

In other words, the program isn't very adaptable. It's probably a lot easier to use your pocket calculator instead of Fortran. With the READ statement, however, we can make the program much easier to use. The idea is to bring the scores in as data from outside the program. As each score comes in, it is printed for a permanent record and added to a running total. In addition, the program counts the number of scores involved by adding 1.0 to a running count of the number of scores every time a new score is brought in. At the end, when all of the scores have been accounted for, the total score is divided by the number of scores involved and the resulting average score is written out.

In this procedure there are only three memory cells involved: SCORE, which handles one score at a time; TOTAL, which keeps track of the running total (TOTAL = TOTAL + SCORE); and G, which keeps track of the number of games scored (G = G + 1.0). The idea is to get a score, print it for a permanent record, add it to the total, and increment the number of games. These four operations are repeated three times, once for each score. If there are more or fewer scores, the four-step procedure is simply repeated more or fewer times.

Plan

```
get score
print score
add score to total
increment number of games
```
———————————————————— Repeat as needed

compute average
print average

There is a flaw in the plan, but it is easily remedied. The flaw is that before starting, the memory cells that are being used to keep track of the running sums (that is, TOTAL and G) must be initialized to zero. Otherwise, the first time the computer comes to the statement TOTAL = TO-TAL + SCORE, it will look up the value of TOTAL and use it to compute

TOTAL + SCORE. If we haven't assigned any value to TOTAL, the computer will use whatever "garbage" was in there before our program started running, and the final average will be based on that "garbage value." The remedy is to assign 0.0 to TOTAL and to G before we start the repetitions of the four-step totaling procedure.

If we write our program according to this plan, we can use the same program every time we want to compute a weekly average. So we have avoided having to change the program every week. However, it is clear that *something* must be changed every time we run the program because the individual scores will be different every time.

This is where the READ statement comes in. To get a score, we use a READ statement that tells the computer to retrieve a number for the score from some data written outside the program. This data may be written on a data file, or it may come from the keyboard of a video computer terminal, or it may come from punched data cards. It all depends on what type of computer system you are using, and you will have to consult a local expert to find out how to provide data for your program. Regardless of the source of the data, however, it will be brought into the memory cell SCORE in your program by a READ command.

A READ command directs the processor to get values from a data source outside the program and to put them into memory cells. The data source will be a collection of **data lines.** (Whenever we mention a data line, we will mean either a data card, a line of data entered at the terminal during execution, or a line of data from a data file.)

A READ statement consists of the word READ followed by an asterisk, then a comma, and finally a list of memory cell names. The READ statement places a value into each memory cell in the **input list,** getting these values from a data line. The first value on the line goes into the first memory cell in the input list, the second value, into the second memory cell, and so on. The values must be separated by spaces or commas, and each value must be a constant of the same data type as the corresponding memory cell in the READ list. If the first data line does not contain

READ Statement

---

form
READ*, *list*
list, an **input list,** is a list of memory cell names separated by commas

meaning
Places values into the memory cells in *list*, taking the values from a data line or lines. If there is more than one memory cell in *list*, the values on the data line(s) must be separated by commas or spaces. The first value on the line(s) will be stored in the first cell in the list, the second value in the second cell, etc.

examples

```
READ *, TCELL
READ *, A, B, C
```

enough values to fill all the memory cells in the list, then the next line will be used, and so on until all the memory cells in the input list have values. If there are leftover values on a line used by a READ statement, they will be totally ignored by the program. The next READ statement will start at the beginning of the next line.

You may recall that in Chapter 1, when you were simulating a computer, the processor executed some statements similar to READ. It was a two-step process: first the processor told the card reader to read a card, and then it told certain memory cells to remember the values on that card. The Fortran READ statement is executed in the same way.

No data line can be read twice. Each time a READ statement is performed, it starts at the beginning of a new data line.

---

data lines: lines with data values on them. They are not statements in your program, but they contain values to be stored in memory cells used by your program.

Since data lines are not inside your program, they are not bound by the rules for Fortran statements. You may use any or all of the 80 or more character positions available.

The data source used by READ statements is not part of your program. If you are using a "file-oriented" system, the data source will probably be a file that you will prepare separately from the program. If you are using an "interactive" system, the data source may be the keyboard of your video terminal. If you are using a "punched card" system, the data source will probably be a separate part of your "card check"; typically, the data source portion of a card deck follows the program part and is separated from it by a special card. In any case, you will have to consult a local expert on how to prepare the data source for your program.

Now let's see how we can use the READ statement to solve the bowling-average problem. Recall that we wanted to write the program in such a way that we could use it every month without change. Thus, the program itself can depend neither on the actual scores nor on the number of scores. This calls for careful planning, and we will take several stabs at the problem before coming up with a complete solution.

Our first approach is to READ the scores one by one and keep a running total. Our program will assume that there are exactly six scores. You can easily change the program so that it will handle more or fewer scores, but this dependence on six scores is an objectionable feature which we will remove later in an improved version of the program. Read the program carefully, and try to understand what it does. We'll describe it in detail after you've read through it.

```
COMMENT:                  CALCULATE AVERAGE BOWLING SCORE
C                         DATA:  THREE LINES, ONE SCORE PER
C                                LINE
       REAL SCORE, TOTAL, G, AVG
C                         INITIALIZE RUNNING SUMS
       TOTAL = 0.0
       G = 0.0
C                         GET SCORE, PRINT, AND TALLY
       READ *, SCORE
       PRINT *, 'SCORE:', SCORE
       TOTAL = TOTAL + SCORE
       G = G + 1.0
C                         ...AGAIN...
       READ *, SCORE
       PRINT *, 'SCORE:', SCORE
       TOTAL = TOTAL + SCORE
       G = G + 1.0
C                         ...AND AGAIN...
       READ *, SCORE
       PRINT *, 'SCORE:' SCORE
       TOTAL = TOTAL + SCORE
       G = G + 1.0
C                         COMPUTE AVERAGE AND PRINT

       AVG = TOTAL/G
       PRINT *, '   AVERAGE:', AVG
       END
```

Data

```
167.0
142.0
159.0
```

Output

```
SCORE:    167.0000
SCORE:    142.0000
SCORE:    159.0000
   AVERAGE:  156.0000
```

An important thing to notice about the program is the high degree of redundancy. The statements READ, PRINT, assign, assign, are repeated over and over. There are always ways to avoid rewriting the same statements over and over, and you will learn one in the next chapter, but for now this will have to suffice.

Another important feature is the technique of computing the sum of the scores using a single memory cell in which the running sum builds up. In this case, that memory cell is called TOTAL. First we put zero into TOTAL. This step is called **initialization.** Each time the computer gets a new score from a data line, it changes TOTAL by that amount. This technique, called **accumulating a sum,** is very common in computer programming. You will see it again and again. In this case the sum accumulates one term at a time in the memory cell TOTAL. The same technique is used to keep track of the number of games, G, but the number added each time (1.0) is the same. This is called adding an **increment** to G.

2.5 EXERCISES

1. Prepare some data for the preceding program, assuming that you bowled the scores 182, 176, and 165. What results would be printed if the program were executed with this data?
2. Which of the following are legal Fortran I/O statements? If a statement is not legal, explain why.

```
READ* A, B, D
PRINT*, A, B, D
READ*, A, A+B, 2
PRINT, A
PRINT*
READ*, X
```

3. Write a program that READs four numbers from a data line and WRITEs their sum.

*

2 PROBLEMS

Practice Problems

1. Construct a program that prints your name and address (as they would appear on a mailing label), using one PRINT statement for each printed line. Sample output:

```
CHESTER P. FARNSWORTHY
1704 MONDO VERDE LN.
FERNLY, NEVADA 89408
```

2. Write a program to (a) print your name, (b) assign the result of a computation to a memory cell, and (c) print the result of this computation below your name.
3. Write a program that computes and prints the sum of the squares of the first 10 numbers, $1^2 + 2^2 + 3^2 + \ldots + 10^2$.
4. Design a program that computes your car's gasoline mileage. READ three REAL values from one data line. The three values are previous mileage reading, current mileage reading, and gallons of gas used. Be sure to print out the three input values as well as the computed mileage.
5. Write a program that READs the lengths of the sides of a rectangle and prints out those lengths followed by the area of the rectangle.

6. Write a program that PRINTs your name in a box of asterisks, like this:

7. Write a program that takes a value in inches and PRINTs the equivalent length in centimeters (1 inch = 2.54 cm.).

Program Design Problems

8. You are about to paint your house. Why not write a program to compute the amount of paint you need? The front-to-back measurement of the house is 62 feet, side-to-side is 85 feet. The house is 12 feet high, and all sides are rectangular. There are 240 square feet of windows on the front and back of the house and 188 square feet of window space on the sides. Assume that you can cover 200 square feet with a gallon of paint. In addition to computing the amount of paint you need, compute the time it'll take you to paint the house, assuming that you can apply a gallon of paint in two hours.

9. Design a program that helps you visualize the effects of inflation. READ in the inflation rate (say, 0.06 if the rate is 6 percent per year), and print out
   a. The amount of money you will need in four years to buy what $1.00 will buy today (if the rate is 15 percent, then this is given by $1.00*1.15*1.15*1.15*1.15)
   b. The amount of money you would have needed four years ago to buy what $1.00 will buy today ($1.00/(1.15*1.15*1.15*1.15))

10. Do problem 9 again, but change the program so that it accepts not only the rate of inflation, but also the number of years the comparison is to be made for. (*Hint:* Use exponentiation.)

11. Write a program that figures out how long it will take to mow a rectangular lawn with a rectangular house on it. READ in the dimensions of the lawn and house. Assume you can mow at a rate of 100 square feet per minute.

12. Do problem 11 again, but include more accurate information about your personal mowing habits. In addition to the input data that allows you to compute the area to be mown, use these three input values:
   a. The width of your mower's cut (e.g., 18 inches)
   b. Your walking speed (e.g., 1.5 miles per hour)
   c. The fraction of the time you spend resting or drinking lemonade (e.g., 0.25 if you rest a quarter of the time)

3 DATA TYPES

CHAPTER PLAN
- *Discuss the representation of numbers*
- *Discuss operator precedence*
- *Emphasize useful differences between INTEGER and REAL*
- *Mention DOUBLE PRECISION and COMPLEX*
- *Introduce CHARACTER variables*
- *Show how to name constants (PARAMETER statement)*

3.1 NUMBERS

There are four kinds of numbers in Fortran: INTEGER, REAL, DOUBLE PRECISION, and COMPLEX. We use them for different purposes.

You are already familiar with **REAL** numbers. They are ordinary numbers with decimal points that people use to represent measurements of all kinds: length, diameter, elapsed time, weight, temperature, and so on. REAL constants are written as signed or unsigned strings of decimal digits containing a decimal point. Sometimes, for writing super-big numbers like the national debt or super-small numbers like the diameter of a chlorine atom, people use scientific notation. For convenience, Fortran

REAL Constants

---

form

$$x$$
$$x\mathrm{E}s$$

x is a signed or unsigned string of decimal digits containing a decimal point.

s is a signed or unsigned string of decimal digits with no decimal point.

meaning
specifies a number indicated by x with its decimal point shifted s places (positive s indicates right shift; negative s, left shift)

---

provides a version of scientific notation. This consists of writing a REAL constant in the usual form followed by a decimal point shift factor (which is an E followed by a whole number with no decimal point). The decimal point shift factor in a REAL constant indicates how far to move the decimal point in the number that precedes the E. Positive shifts indicate shifts to the right, negative shifts to the left.

Examples of REAL Constants

form	meaning
1.00	
−7.7254	
+.000137	
.472E5	47200.
+7.21E − 2	.0721
−1.22E − 12	−.00000000000122
+6.023E + 23	Avogadro's number
.002E3	Avis's number
1,482.5	invalid, no comma allowed
723	invalid, needs decimal point
−4.18732E − .5	invalid, shift factor must be INTEGER

DOUBLE PRECISION numbers in Fortran are simply another kind of REAL number, but they make it possible to express more precise measurements than Fortran REALs allow. We will have more to say about this later when we discuss how Fortran represents REAL numbers.

If you measure a pizza, you get a REAL number.

COMPLEX numbers occur in certain types of mathematical formulas that describe electromagnetic wave forms, fluid flow, and other complex phenomena. Fortran is one of the few programming languages that has built-in facilities for handling COMPLEX numbers. We will describe them briefly in this chapter, but not in any great detail because any meaningful example involving the use of COMPLEX numbers would require a heavy mathematical background. All of you engineers and mathematicians out there will be able to see from our brief description, together with the general knowledge of programming that you are beginning to develop, how to apply COMPLEX numbers to problems that interest you.

INTEGERs are used for counting, which is fundamentally different from measuring. Measurements are never exact. A measurement with a 0.01 percent error tolerance is more nearly exact than one with a 10 percent tolerance, but all measurements incorporate some error. A count, on the other hand, can be an exact quantity. A grocery bag may contain *exactly* five apples and two bars of soap. You may want the computer to perform *exactly* five iterations of a loop.

When your program is counting things, use INTEGERs; when it is calculating with measurements, use REALs.

The number of '54 Chevys you've seen in your lifetime is an INTEGER.

3.1   EXERCISES

1. What type of number, INTEGER or REAL, should be used for computing gas mileage? gas purchased? miles traveled? babies born in
   Scripps Hospital in November? glasses broken in Stern Hall in 1963?
   runs scored in a baseball game?
2. Write the number "four and one-half" as a Fortran REAL constant.
3. Circle the pairs in which both numbers denote the same Fortran
   constant.
   a. 49.2   0.492E2
   b. 4.92   4.92E − 1
   c. 492.0   0.004920E + 05
   d. 0.004920   492.0E − 05

3.2   INTEGERs

INTEGERs are counting numbers: 1, 2, 3, and so on. Negative counts
(− 1, − 2, − 3, etc.) and zero (0) are also allowed. A Fortran **INTEGER
constant** is a signed or unsigned string of digits: 4922, − 39, + 200, and
00 are all examples of Fortran INTEGERs; 4,922, − 39., and 0.0 are not
Fortran INTEGERs (no commas or decimal points allowed).

INTEGER Constant

form
string of decimal digits which may be preceded by a plus or a minus sign
 	
+1497
−392
−01124
  33421
 	
+1,497
−392.0   invalid, no comma allowed
  33,492.1   invalid, no decimal point allowed

To use INTEGER values in Fortran, you need INTEGER variables:
memory cells to store INTEGER values. You declare INTEGER variables
just like you declare REAL variables, but you use the word INTEGER
instead of the word REAL.

The statement INTEGER SCORE, TOTAL, G declares three variables
for storing INTEGER values. The following program is like the bowling-
average program of Chapter 2, but uses INTEGER variables instead of
REAL variables for SCORE, TOTAL, and G, which are always whole numbers. The average, AVG, is properly a REAL, however, since it is a fraction.

INTEGER Declaration Statement

form
INTEGER list

list is a list of memory cell names, separated by commas.

meaning
instructs the compiler to attach the names in *list* to memory cells, which will be used to store INTEGERs

examples
```
INTEGER A, B, C, TWO, THREE, Q1
INTEGER M
```

```
COMMENT:               CALCULATE AVERAGE BOWLING SCORE
C                      DATA:  THREE LINES, ONE SCORE PER LINE
          REAL AVG
          INTEGER SCORE, TOTAL, G
C                      INITIALIZE RUNNING SUMS
          TOTAL = 0.0
          G = 0.0
C                      GET SCORE, PRINT, AND TALLY
          READ *, SCORE
          PRINT *, 'SCORE:', SCORE
          TOTAL = TOTAL + SCORE
          G = G + 1.0
C                ...AGAIN...
          READ *, SCORE
          PRINT *, 'SCORE:', SCORE
          TOTAL = TOTAL + SCORE
          G = G + 1.0
C                ...AND AGAIN...
          READ *, SCORE
          PRINT *, 'SCORE:', SCORE
          TOTAL = TOTAL + SCORE
          G = G + 1.0
C                      COMPUTE AVERAGE AND PRINT
          AVG = REAL(TOTAL)/REAL(G)
          PRINT *, '  AVERAGE:', AVG
          END
```

Data

```
167
142
159
```

Output

```
SCORE:  167
SCORE:  142
SCORE:  159
   AVERAGE:   156.000ᴜ
```

In computing the average, we need to perform division using fractional parts, so the program makes use of a new function called "REAL" to convert INTEGER data to REAL data. If we had written AVG = TOTAL/G without converting TOTAL to a REAL value, the division would have been performed in INTEGER mode, and the fraction would have been dropped. You'll learn more about this in the next section.

3.2 EXERCISES

1. Write a program that reads two INTEGERs from a data line and computes their sum (+), difference (−), and product (*).
2. Identify the error in the following statement.

```
POP = 204,397,000
```

3.3 INTEGER DIVISION: QUOTIENTS AND REMAINDERS

Back in the third grade when we all learned to do division, we got answers in two parts—**quotients** and **remainders.** INTEGER division in Fortran is like third-grade division. We get the quotient with the "/" operator; we can compute the remainder with the MOD function: 13/5 is 2; MOD(13,5) is 3.

There are lots of problems in which this kind of division is useful. A typical one is in converting inches to feet and inches. A man who is 70 inches tall is 5 feet, 10 inches tall. The number of feet in 70 inches is the quotient of 70 divided by 12 (the number of inches in a foot). The number of inches left over is the remainder in that division. In general, the number of feet in N inches is the Fortran quotient N/12, and the number of inches left over is the remainder MOD(N,12).

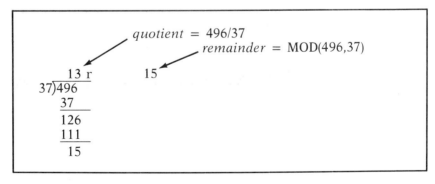

```
INTEGER IN, FEET, INCHES
IN = 70                 [measurement in whole inches]
FEET = IN/12
INCHES = MOD(IN,12)
```

You can use the same principle to compute gallons and quarts from total quarts or to compute hours, minutes, and seconds from total seconds.

```
INTEGER SEC, HOURS, MINUTS, SECNDS
SEC = 23487      [elapsed time in whole seconds]
HOURS = SEC/3600
MINUTS = MOD(SEC,3600)/60
SECNDS = MOD(MOD(SEC,3600), 60)
```

Another use of INTEGER division is in **unpacking** data. Suppose a date is written on a data line in the form *mmddyy*, where *mm* is the month, *dd* is the day, and *yy* is the year. For example, the number 102186 would represent month 10, day 21, and year 86 (October 21, 1986). If we want to print the date separately in its component parts, we need a way to split the number into three pieces. We can do this using quotients and remainders. The last two digits of the number *yy* are the remainder in the division by 100. Thus, YY = MOD(DATE,100) splits off the year digits. To get the month digits, notice that in dividing by 100, the quotient throws away the last two digits in the date, leaving a four-digit number. The last two digits in this four-digit number give the day *dd*. Thus, DD = MOD(DATE/100, 100). Finally, the month can be computed by chopping off the last four digits (i.e., dividing by 10,000). MM = DATE/10000.

```
INTEGER DATE, MM, DD, YY
READ *, DATE
MM = DATE/10000
DD = MOD(DATE/100,100)
YY = MOD(DATE,100)
PRINT *, 'MONTH:', MM,',  DAY:', DD,',  YEAR:', YY
END
```

Data

```
102186
```

Output

```
MONTH:        10,  DAY:        21,  YEAR:        86
```

Even though INTEGER division in Fortran can be confusing because we are surprised when the Fortran quotient 1/3 turns out to be zero, this type of division can also be useful. We can put it into a familiar context by harkening back to the third grade when we first learned to divide. When you see INTEGERs in Fortran, think "third-grade arithmetic." Then it won't seem so tricky.

3.3 EXERCISES

1. Devise a formula for the last digit in an INTEGER (e.g., the last digit of 397 is 7).
2. Devise a formula for the hundreds digit in an INTEGER (e.g., the hundreds digit in 1812 is 8).

3. Write an assignment statement to change the hundreds digit of a nonnegative INTEGER stored in the variable N to a zero.
4. Write an assignment statement to change the hundreds digit of N to the digit stored in the variable D.

3.4 ARITHMETIC EXPRESSIONS

You have already seen many examples of arithmetic expressions. We purposely kept those expressions quite simple in order to defer a detailed explanation of the rules of evaluation until now.

Arithmetic expressions are formed of memory cell names and arithmetic constants separated by arithmetic operators (+, −, *, /, **). In addition, parentheses may be used to force the processor to perform the operations in the desired order, and functions may be used to extend the basic operations.

Consider the following examples of arithmetic expressions:

```
COUNT+1
```

Find value of COUNT and add 1 to it.

```
(1+BRATE-DRATE)*POPUL
```

Find value of BRATE, add it to 1, subtract the value of DRATE, and multiply the result by the value of POPUL.

```
PI*(R**2)
```

Raise the value of R to the power 2 (i.e., square R) and multiply the result by the value of PI.

In each of these examples the meaning of the expression is not hard to see, but consider a more complicated expression like

```
SUMXSQ/(N-1.0)  -  SUMX**2/(N*(N-1.0))
```

In this case the expression appears ambiguous because it is not clear which operations should be performed first. Should we proceed from left to right, from right to left, or by some other set of rules? Surely we should perform the operations grouped by the parentheses first, but after that there is still ambiguity. Are we to raise SUMX to the power 2 or to the power $2/N*((N - 1.0))$? Do we divide SUMXSQ by $(N - 1.0)$ or by $(N - 1.0) - $ SUMX? The expression would be easier to interpret if we didn't have to write it all on one line, but Fortran requires us to do so.

In normal algebraic notation the expression is

$$\frac{sumxsq}{n-1} - \frac{sumx^2}{n(n-1)}$$

In Fortran the order of operations proceeds according to the following rules of precedence, which are the same as those used in ordinary algebra.

( ) First	compute the expressions within parentheses
** Second	perform exponentiations
*,/ Third	perform multiplications and divisions
+, − Fourth	perform additions and subtractions
→ Tiebreaker	perform adjacent additive operations (+, −) from left to right
	perform adjacent multiplicative operations (*,/) from left to right
	perform adjacent exponentiations (**) from right to left

Now no ambiguity remains. The expression is equivalent to

`(SUMXSQ/(N-1.0)) - ((SUMX**2)/(N*(N-1.0)))`

Consider the expression

`A/B*C-D+E`

The rules of precedence tell us to perform multiplications and divisions before additions and subtractions. Therefore, A/B*C must be evaluated first. But does that mean (A/B)*C or A/(B*C)? Using the tiebreaker rule, (A/B)*C would be the interpretation.

Evaluating an Expression Step by Step

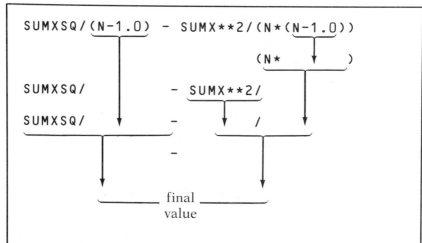

Notice that the subtraction in the middle of this expression is performed dead last.

Arithmetic operators may be used with either REALs or INTEGERs, so that both 2/4 and 2.0/4.0 are legal expressions, which yield the values 0 and 0.5, respectively. But how should something like 2/4.0 be interpreted? The first value is an INTEGER constant, the second a REAL. Such an expression, which combines values (or memory cells) of differing types, is said to be **mixed mode.** In these expressions, INTEGERs are converted to REALs before an arithmetic operation involving both data types.

One exception is in the case of exponentiation. Here is one place where it is desirable to mix REAL and INTEGER in the same expression; it is not considered mixed mode. For example, the expression 4.73**8 means to form a product containing eight factors, 4.73 times itself eight times. The result of this computation is, of course, a REAL.

It is also possible to raise a REAL to a REAL power, but the computation which is performed is very different. For example, 4.73**1.79256 clearly cannot mean to multiply 4.73 times itself 1.79256 times. To make this computation, the processor first computes the logarithm of the base in the exponentiation, multiplies that by the exponent, getting a product *p*, and finally raises the logarithm base-constant to the power *p*.

$$x^y = 10^{y\log(x)}$$

Since logarithms of negative numbers do not generally result in REAL values, *it is illegal to raise a negative number to a REAL power.* No logarithms are involved in raising a number to an INTEGER power, however, so there is nothing wrong with an expression like (-4.73)**8 even though the expression (-4.73)**8.0 would be illegal. Use INTEGERs for exponents whenever you can. There is one other thing that can cause trouble. We said that INTEGER constants could be numbers like -2 or 3 and that you could use an arithmetic operator between two constants; however, $3* -2$ is illegal in Fortran. In addition to the rules for forming arithmetic expressions that you've seen so far, there is the rule that *no two operator symbols (*, /, +, −, **) may come in a row*, no matter what they're used for. The expression $3* - 2$ can be written legally as $3*(-2)$.

Arithmetic Expressions

form
basic arithmetic elements (numeric memory cells, unsigned numeric constants, or parenthesized subexpressions) separated by arithmetic operators (+, −, *, /, or **) with an optional sign (+ or −) at the beginning of the expression

meaning
specifies a numeric value, namely, the value obtained by following the rules of precedence and carrying out the operations denoted by the arithmetic operators

examples

legal	illegal
X**(-2)	X***2
COL*(COL-1)/2 + ROW	DVN-3*
DVN-3*QUO	A*-4
Z**3/3.0	
4*(-3)	
-4*A	

A**3   A**3.0
/   /
use this   *not this*

---

illegal: negative base with REAL exponent
(−4.0)**0.5 *illegal*
(−4.0)**2.0 *illegal*

3.4 EXERCISES

1. Using the precedence rules, compute the value of the expression (−1**4).

2. Use parentheses to make the meaning of the following arithmetic expressions perfectly clear. When the expression is ambiguous, use the tiebreaker rule.

```
MOUSE + CAT**DOG**2
S + D - R*F + A**B**C
DIXIE/MELLOW/DEE
```

3. Suppose A has the value −3.7. Then A**2 is legal, but A**2.0 isn't. Why?

4. In algebraic notation we write the product of two terms like *a* and *b* as *ab*. Why isn't this allowed in Fortran?

3.5 INTEGERS VERSUS REALS

Some computations naturally involve both INTEGER and REAL values. Because of the way Fortran handles these two kinds of data, they can be mixed only with great care and understanding. We will start by studying how they can be mixed in assignments.

Recall that an assignment statement is a memory cell name followed by the assignment operator (=) followed by an expression. The assignment statement tells the processor to evaluate the expression and store the result in the memory cell named to the left of the assignment operator. In this way the processor gives the cell a new value. For example, if we had made the declarations

```
INTEGER PURCH1, PURCH2, TOTAL, CENTS
REAL DOLARS
```

then these assignment statements

```
PURCH1 = 75
PURCH2 = 50
```

```
TOTAL=PURCH1 + PURCH2
CENTS = 125
DOLARS = 125.0/100.0
```

would leave the memory cells with these values:

PURCH1 | 75 |

PURCH2 | 50 |

TOTAL | 125 |

CENTS | 125 |

DOLARS | 1.25 |

Everything was nice and easy—each expression on the right was of the same type as the memory cell named on the left, so it was obvious what to store. But what if a statement like

```
CENTS = DOLARS*100.00
```

had appeared? The memory cell named on the left is an INTEGER: the expression on the right is REAL. A very important rule about assignment statements takes care of this situation. (Notice that this is *not* an example of a mixed mode expression. The expression on the right involves the multiplication of two REAL values.)

The rule is that *the expression to the right* of the replacement operator *is evaluated first* without any concern being given to the memory location named on the left. After the expression has been evaluated, a check is made to see if the type of the result agrees with the type of the memory cell where the result is to be stored. If it does not agree, then *the value stored in the memory cell is the value of the expression after being converted to the data type required by the memory cell.*

So, in the preceding example, first DOLARS*100.0 is evaluated to get the REAL value 125.0, and then, since CENTS is declared to be an INTEGER, the corresponding INTEGER value 125 is stored in CENTS.

This is a very important rule to understand. Let's see it in action again.

Suppose at some point in a program we need to compute a term N/M. Since we've been counting with M and N, they are declared INTEGERs, but the use we make of the term requires it to be REAL. Since we're not certain how our compiler treats mixed mode operations, we will use assignment statements to control the conversions ourselves. Can you see why these two program fragments produce different results?

```
INTEGER M,N                    INTEGER M,N
REAL TERM,FRAC,NUM             REAL TERM,NUM,DENOM
N=2                            N=2
M=3                            M=3
```

```
NUM=N                          NUM=N
FRAC=1/M                       DENOM=M
TERM=NUM*FRAC                   TERM=NUM/DENOM
```

M	3		M	3
N	2		N	2
NUM	2.0		NUM	2.0
FRAC	0.0		DENOM	3.0
TERM	0.0		TERM	0.666666

The key difference is caused by the statement

```
FRAC = 1/M
```

The INTEGER expression 1/M is evaluated first (giving the INTEGER value 0). Then (and only then) the computed value is converted to REAL (0.0), and stored in FRAC.

There are two functions that can be used to convert between INTEGER and REAL values. The REAL function converts an INTEGER value to a REAL value: REAL(3) is 3.0; REAL(−12) is −12.0. Thus, we could get what we get with the fraction 1/M computed as a REAL number by using the expression 1.0/REAL(M). If M is 2, for example, then FRAC = 1.0/REAL(M) assigns 0.5 to FRAC.

The function INT converts a REAL value to an INTEGER value by dropping the fraction: INT(4.9) is 4; INT(−3.23) is −3—in both cases the digits after the decimal point are simply dropped.

Often, you would rather round off REALs to get INTEGERs. You can use the NINT (nearest integer) function to round off instead of dropping the entire fraction.

3.5 EXERCISES

1. Using the REAL function, change the program fragments at the end of this section to make all the implicit data type conversions in the assignment statements explicit.
2. Change the computation of the average in the bowling program of Section 3.2 to figure the average rounded to the nearest whole number.
3. In the following program, SNAFO takes on several different values at different times. What values are they?

```
INTEGER A, B, C
REAL SNAFO, R1,R2
R1 = 1
R2 = 2
A = 1
```

```
B = 4
C = 16
SNAFO = R1*R2
SNAFO = A*R2
SNAFO = B/(A+B)
SNAFO = B
SNAFO = C/B
END
```

3.6 CHARACTER VARIABLES

The CHARACTER data type, one of the two nonnumeric Fortran data types, is extremely useful. People often fall into the trap of believing that computers deal only with numbers. Computers are *symbol* manipulators—there is a whole world of computing outside "number crunching." Of all the written symbols you've seen today, numbers probably are only a small part, so it is natural that computers are equipped to handle nonnumeric data.

CHARACTER*(n) constants are strings (sequences) of one or more characters (any character you can find on your keyboard should be OK) enclosed by single quotes. The quote marks are not considered part of the string, so the *length* of a string is the number of characters inside the quotes (except that two apostrophes in a row count as only one character, an apostrophe).

CHARACTER* (n) Constant

---

form
a string of n ($n \geq 1$) characters enclosed by single quotes (apostrophes). If one of the characters in the string is intended to be an apostrophe, you must indicate it by two successive apostrophes to avoid ambiguity.

examples
```
' '
'12'
'STRING'
'SNOW BALL4'
'BRUCE''S BAR'
```

illegal forms
```
''
'BRUCE'S BAR'
```

In order to use a memory cell to store CHARACTER values, you must not only specify that the cell is to be of type CHARACTER, you must also give the capacity of the cell. For instance, the declaration

```
CHARACTER*(7) A
```

associates the name A with a memory cell with a capacity of seven characters. We could put a value into the cell with an assignment statement like

```
A = 'KUMQUAT'
```

Declaring CHARACTER Memory Cells

---

forms

CHARACTER *list*
CHARACTER*(*n*) *list*

n is an unsigned INTEGER ($n > 0$)
list is a list of memory cell names. The first form is equivalent to the second with $n = 1$

meaning
instructs the compiler to attach the names of *list* to
memory cells which can contain CHARACTER strings of length *n*

Or we could use a READ statement to put a value into A.

```
READ *, A
```

The data line for this READ would have a CHARACTER constant (that is, a string enclosed in quotes) like 'KUMQUAT' on it.

When the computer prints the value of a character variable, it leaves off the quote marks.

```
PRINT *, A
```

Output

```
KUMQUAT
```

The quote marks are used as delimiters. They set the boundaries of the CHARACTER constant and are needed because the constant may contain blanks.

```
A = ' SQUAT '
```

CHARACTER variables are useful in many programs. You will probably use them about as often as numbers. To get started, let's look at a simple example, a program which prints personalized fortunes for Chinese fortune cookies. To keep the program from being too elaborate, let's assume that the fortune cookie factory uses only one fortune: "You are about to receive a gift." For special customers (and a small fee) they will personalize the message: "You are about to receive a gift, Mary Grace."

We want to write a program which will print these personal fortunes after it gets the name from a data line. The program is displayed below. We have shown two sample runs so that you can see how the name varies with the data line.

```
CHARACTER*(10) NAME
READ *, NAME
PRINT *, 'YOU ARE ABOUT TO RECEIVE A GIFT, ',NAME,'.'
END
```

Data

```
'MARY GRACE'
```

Output

```
YOU ARE ABOUT TO RECEIVE A GIFT, MARY GRACE.
```

Data

```
'BIG JOHN'
```

Output

```
YOU ARE ABOUT TO RECEIVE A GIFT, BIG JOHN  .
```

The capacities of CHARACTER variables don't always match the lengths of the strings we want to store in them. ('BIG JOHN' is only eight characters, and we put it in a cell with a ten-character capacity.) A mismatch between capacity and length may happen in either direction. When the length of the string is less than the capacity of the cell (as in the 'BIG JOHN' case), the extra places on the end of the cell are filled with blanks. Thus, if the cell NAME has a ten-character capacity, and we write NAME = 'BIG JOHN', then the string which actually gets stored in NAME has two blanks on the end: 'BIG JOHN*bb*', where *b* stands for "blank."

On the other hand, if the string is too long to fit, it is cut down to size by chopping characters off the end. The assignment statement

```
NAME = 'BIG BAD JOHN'
```

Conversion of CHARACTER Values

given
A value of type CHARACTER*(n) to be stored in a memory cell of type CHARACTER*(m)

rules
If $m = n$, no conversion is necessary.
If $m > n$, add $m - n$ blanks to the right of the value.
If $m < n$, drop the rightmost $m - n$ characters.

would put the string 'BIG BAD JO' into the cell NAME. By the same rule, if we ran our program with a data card containing 'BIG BAD JOHN', the fortune printed would be

```
YOU ARE ABOUT TO RECEIVE A GIFT, BIG BAD JO.
```

3.6 EXERCISES

1. What line of output will this program produce?

```
CHARACTER*(4) WAIT, WALK
WAIT = 'WAIT'
WALK = 'WALK'
PRINT *, WAIT, 'FOR RED, THEN ', WALK
END
```

2. How would you change the program in Exercise 1 to make the output more legible? Can you think of two different ways to do it?
3. One of these two programs

```
CHARACTER*(8) DAY, PLACE
DAY = 'TUESDAY'
PLACE = 'BELGIUM'
PRINT *, 'IF IT''S' ,DAY, 'IT MUST BE ', PLACE
END

CHARACTER*(8) DAY, PLACE
DAY = 'TUESDAY'
PLACE = 'BELGIUM'
PRINT *, 'IF IT''S ', DAY, ', IT MUST BE ', PLACE
END
```

produced this line of output:

```
IF IT'S TUESDAY , IT MUST BE BELGIUM
```

Which one?

3.7 NAMING CONSTANTS

Constants are used in a program when a symbolic name for the constant value would be more descriptive than the literal specification of the value. For example, in a program involving calculations on circles, the name PI would be more descriptive of the constant's purpose than would the literal approximation 3.14159. By using a name rather than a literal denotation to designate a constant, the programmer can associate a meaning with the constant relative to the program context. In a sense, the name associates units with the constant: is it two pounds or two inches?

The PARAMETER statement provides a way to give symbolic names to constant values. These names are like variable names, but when they are given values by PARAMETER statements, they denote constants, not memory cells.

A PARAMETER statement looks like a list of assignment statements enclosed in parentheses and preceded by the keyword PARAMETER. Each parameter assignment in the list names the constant on the left and gives its value on the right of the equal sign. The constant value in the PARAMETER statement must be a *constant expression*. A **constant expression** is any expression which involves no FUNCTION references and no variables. Each value within the expression must be a constant or the name of a constant previously set up by a PARAMETER statement.

If the name of a constant is of a numeric data type, whether it gains its type of explicit declaration or by implicit typing, then the value given for it in a PARAMETER statement can be of any numeric data type and will be assigned to the constant name under the same rules that apply for assignment statements. If the constant name is of CHARACTER type, then the value given must also be of CHARACTER type, and the rules for assignment statements apply. The name for the constant may be of CHARACTER type with an assumed length, CHARACTER*(*). In this case the constant name takes on the length of the constant value on the right of the equals sign.

PARAMETER Statement

---

form

PARAMETER $(p_1 = c_1, p_2 = c_2, \ldots, p_n = c_n)$
p_i is an unsubscripted identifier
c_i is a constant expression of a type which could be assigned to a variable of the data type of the name p_i

meaning
Henceforth within this program unit, the name p_i may be used anywhere that a constant expression of the data type of p_i would be used, and the value p_i stands for the value of the expression c_i converted as necessary to match the data type of p_i.

restriction
All PARAMETER statements in a program unit must precede the executable statements.

examples

```
PARAMETER (PI=3.14159, N=2, TWOPI=2*PI)
PARAMETER (NAME = 'WAXLEY')
```

The PARAMETER statement has two purposes. First, it allows you to make your program more readable by naming things which would have been only numbers before. Second, it allows you to design programs which can be easily modified to meet new requirements simply by changing the values of certain constants listed in PARAMETER statements.

Constant Expression

> An expression in which the operands are constants, names of constants defined previously in PARAMETER statements, or constant expressions in parentheses and in which none of the operators are FUNCTIONs is a **constant expression.** Any exponentiation in a constant expression must be to an INTEGER (constant) power.
>
> The term may be modified by the data type of the resulting value. An INTEGER **constant expression** is a constant expression whose value is an INTEGER. An **arithmetic constant expression** is one whose value is a number. Similar definitions can be made for CHARACTER **constant expressions,** etc.

Throughout the remainder of the text, unnamed constants will be extremely rare. We will use PARAMETER statements to name almost all of the constant values used in programs (e.g., loop termination values, Chapter 4; array bounds, Chapter 9; etc.) and we recommend this practice to you for your programs.

3.8   HOW FORTRAN REPRESENTS INTEGERs AND REALs

The memory of a computer is organized as a collection of **cells.** All the cells are identically composed of a collection of *binary digits* (**bits**) and may be set to an arbitrary pattern of 1's and 0's. The number of bits per cell is known as the **word size** of the computer and will vary from machine to machine. IBM/360-370 computers have 32-bit words: PDP-10's have 36-bit words; CDC CYBER1xx's have 60-bit words; IBM PC's have 16-bit words. There are two times when you need to be aware of the size of your computer's memory: when something goes wrong and when your algorithm is taxing the limits of the machine's accuracy. So that you can understand what's happened when things go wrong and how you can run up against problems with accuracy, we'll explain how INTEGERs and REALs are represented as patterns of 1's and 0's stored in memory cells.

Externally (i.e., in a Fortran program or on a data line), an INTEGER constant is written as a signed or unsigned string of digits. But internally (i.e., inside a memory cell), an INTEGER is represented by a pattern of 1's and 0's. All large modern computers build this bit pattern by converting the INTEGER to its **binary** or **base 2 encoding.** In the **decimal** system each digit is a decimal digit—0, 1, 2, 3, 4, 5, 6, 7, 8, 9—representing a multiple of a power of 10. On the right, we have the units digit, then the tens digit, the hundreds digit, and so on. In the **binary** system, integers are written with binary digits—0, 1—with each digit standing for a multiple of a power of 2. On the right there is the units bit, then (moving left) the twos bit, the fours bit, the eights bit, the sixteens bit, and so on. Because each cell has a finite capacity (32 bits, for example), the size of the integers that may be stored is limited.

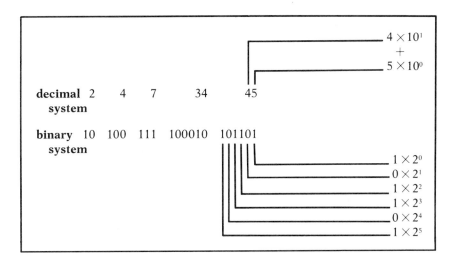

Negative numbers present another problem. Most computers handle them with the **two's-complement** system. To represent a negative number, the binary notation for the positive number is computed first, then all the bits are reversed (1's become 0's; 0's become 1's). Finally, the integer 1 is added to the number obtained after reversing the bits. Thus, small positive numbers start with lots of 0-bits at the beginning of the word, and negative numbers start with 1-bits. The two's-complement form for negative numbers makes it possible to do subtraction with the same algorithm as addition, thus making it unnecessary to build a separate subtraction component for the processor.

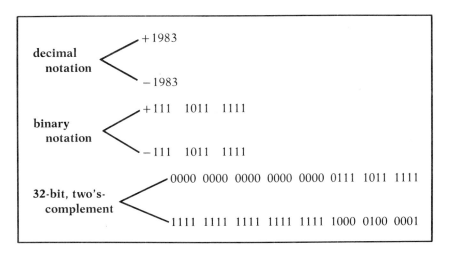

INTEGER Range

The upper and lower bounds of the INTEGERs which may be stored in a memory cell. For example, machines like the IBM/360-370 computers which use 32-bit, two's-complement notation, have a range from −2,147,483,648 up to +2,147,483,647.

At this point, it is important to realize that when a machine with 32-bit words uses a 32-bit, two's-complement representation for INTEGERs, all the possible bit patterns are used up. With 32-bit words there are 2^{32}, or 4,294,967,296, possible patterns, precisely the number of different INTE-GERs in the range of such a machine ($-2,147,483,648$ to $2,147,483,647$). The obvious question is: if all the bit patterns have been used up in representing INTEGERs, how is it possible to put REAL values in memory cells? The answer is that the processor uses an entirely different encoding method. The declaration statements tell the computer which cells will contain REALs and which will contain INTEGERs, so the processor will know how to interpret their contents. It interprets INTEGER cells as two's-complement binary numbers. For REAL cells it follows a different method of interpretation known as **floating point.**

The processor uses the first bit of the memory cell for the sign of the number (0 for positive, 1 for negative). It uses another group of bits for the significant digits in the REAL number, and it uses the rest of the bits for the decimal point shift factor. The bits used for the significant digits are known as the **significand** portion of the word (sometimes called the **mantissa** in older literature), and the bits for the decimal point shift factor are known as the **exponent.** Both the significand and the exponent are represented in binary notation.

Floating-Point Word

sign bit	exponent bits	significand bits

The exponent, in effect, multiplies or divides the significand by a power of 2, just as the decimal point shift factor in a REAL number multiplies or divides the number in front of the E by a power of 10. On most machines the exponent is represented as an unsigned binary integer and is interpreted with a "bias." That is, the processor computes the true exponent from the binary integer in the exponent field of the floating-point word by subtracting a standard bias. The bias is normally half as large as the largest unsigned integer which will fit in the exponent field. For example, if the exponent field is seven bits long, then the bias is 2^6, or 64.

We don't expect you to understand all the details of floating-point notation, and we haven't explained all of them, either. But there is one important fact that you can glean from all this: when all the bits in the exponent field are zeros, the true exponent is as large as possible in the *negative direction.* Thus, the significand is being divided by a large power of two, and the number represented, whether it is positive or negative, is very close to zero, something like ± 0.00000000000001. The reason it is important for you to understand this is that sometimes a bit pattern which is intended to represent an INTEGER gets put into a memory cell of type REAL. You probably haven't seen this happen yet, but when you study FORMATs, arrays, or subprograms, you will encounter this type of error unless you are very careful, phenomenally lucky, or happen to be using a computer system with exceptionally good error-checking facilities.

If an INTEGER bit pattern gets mistakenly put into a REAL memory cell, the exponent field will be all zeros (unless the INTEGER is extremely large). Then what you thought was a number of ordinary size (such as 742693) turns out to be a number very close to zero (such as 0.00000000001). It's something to watch for. That kind of error can hang you up for days if you don't know where to start looking.

The second most important fact about REALs that you can glean from this discussion is that *they're not represented precisely*. In the decimal system there are some fractions that can't be written with a finite number of digits. Take $1/3$, for example. In the decimal system it's 0.33333333333 . . . , and you can keep writing threes forever and still not get the exact representation of $1/3$. This can occasionally cause some embarrassing situations, because in Fortran

```
1.0/3.0 + 1.0/3.0 + 1.0/3.0
```

doesn't necessarily equal 1.0!

In the binary system there are analogous problems. A number like $1/10$, which has a short decimal representation, 0.1, has no exact binary representation. Not in a finite number of bits anyway. As a result, many numbers that you would expect to be exactly the same often turn out to be just a little bit different. The small errors which creep into calculations with REALs are called **roundoff errors.** In certain applications roundoff errors, each one seemingly insignificant, can add up to make a final answer completely wrong. This is a serious problem, and numerical analysts have spent enormous effort trying to understand how to avoid getting such erroneous results, and how to tell when they occur if they can't be avoided.

3.9 IMPLICIT TYPING

Fortran does not require memory cell names to be listed in type statements. If a memory cell name is not explicitly given a type, Fortran makes an assumption. The convention is: if the memory cell name starts with I, J, K, L, M, or N, it is assigned the type INTEGER; otherwise, the type assigned is REAL.

This has one side effect which may have already brought you grief. If you make a typing error and misspell a memory cell name, the compiler won't print an error message. Instead, it asssumes you want to have a memory cell of that name and assigns it a type according to the convention. The result is a program which may look like it works, but produces incorrect results.

The question of whether or not to explicitly type INTEGER and REAL variables can lead to heated debate (believe it or not). Here are some arguments.

pro: It's crucial for the programmer to be aware of the use he or she intends to make of each memory cell. Explicitly naming the type ensures that the programmer is conscious of each memory cell, its name, and its type.

con: If you don't follow the naming rules, you have to look all the way up to the top of the program to see what type a given memory cell is. That takes your mind off what you're doing.

pro: It's important to choose memory cell names which are strongly suggestive of the use made of the cell. Often, six letters are inadequate to the task, and further restricting the choice of the first letter to fit the implicit typing convention becomes unbearable.

con: There's too big a deal made of using fancy memory cell names. People see a memory cell named IDEAS and think that the program does something significant. It's better to use names like A, B, and C—they don't mislead anyone about what the computer is actually doing.

pro: You have to use type statements for all the Fortran data types besides INTEGERs and REALs—why not be consistent and do it for all of them?

con: Consistency is the hemoglobin of small minds. Besides, it's just a waste of time to punch the type statements. Let the compiler figure out what types the memory cells have.

3.10 OTHER NUMERIC DATA TYPES

REALs and INTEGERs are the most commonly used types of Fortran numbers, but there are two other types. One of them, DOUBLE PRECISION, makes it easy to deal with numbers which have more digits than are allowed in REALs. Typically, DOUBLE PRECISION constants have more than twice the accuracy of REALs.

DOUBLE PRECISION Constants

```
examples
129.748239
-49734004.88
1.00000000
-4.72D - 8
.31415926535898D + 01
2.7182818204590D0
5.77215664901D - 01
```

DOUBLE PRECISION variables are declared using the usual form of a declaration statement with the *type* position occupied by the phrase DOUBLE PRECISION, as follows.

```
DOUBLE PRECISION A, D, Z
```

DOUBLE PRECISION constants and variables may be mixed with REAL values in arithmetic expressions, and the result is a DOUBLE PRECISION value. As with REALs, and for the same reason, negative DOUBLE PRECISION values cannot be raised to non-INTEGER powers Thus, $(-4.7D00)**0.5$ is not a legal expression.

COMPLEX is the other type of Fortran number. COMPLEX numbers have two parts, a real part and an imaginary part, and are written in the form (*r part, i part*), where *r part* (the real part) and *i part* (the imaginary part) are REAL constants.

COMPLEX Constants

---

examples
$$(1.0, 0.0)$$
$$(0.0, 1.0)$$
$$(1.0, -1.0)$$
$$(4.93, 7.948)$$
$$(-5.221, 6.14)$$

COMPLEX variables are declared in exactly the way you would expect.

```
COMPLEX ZETA, MU, A
```

As with the other types of Fortran numbers, COMPLEX values can be used in arithmetic expressions, and they can be mixed with REAL values to produce a COMPLEX result, using +, −, /, or *. There are two restrictions to be aware of: (1) the exponent in a ** operation can never be COMPLEX, and (2) if the base in a ** operation is COMPLEX, the exponent must be of type INTEGER.

---

number**COMPLEX is illegal
COMPLEX**INTEGER is legal
COMPLEX**non-INTEGER is illegal

3.10   EXERCISES

1. What are the values of the following expressions?
   a. 2.0*(1.4,3.7)
   b. (0.0,1.0)**2
   c. A*(1.0,0.0) + B*(0.0,1.0), where A and B are REALs
   d. ZETA*(1.0, −1.0), where ZETA is COMPLEX
2. What distinguishes a REAL constant from a DOUBLE PRECISION constant?

---

3 PROBLEMS

Practice Problems

1. Write a program that will compute the weighted average of three test scores. The first midterm is worth 25 percent of the grade, the second midterm is worth 35 percent, and the final is worth 40 percent. Write a program that will READ in a student's name and the three test scores. Then compute and PRINT the weighted average along with the student's name and the three scores.

2. If 1.0/3.0 + 1.0/3.0 + 1.0/3.0 doesn't quite equal 1.0, how far off is it? How about 1.0/4.0 + 1.0/4.0 + 1.0/4.0 + 1.0/4.0? Answer these questions by computing these sums (and others with denominators up to 10.0) and printing the difference between the sums and 1.0.

3. Find the number of half-dollars, quarters, dimes, nickels, and pennies returned as change from one dollar. READ a purchase price (in pennies), and print out how many of each coin go into the change.

4. Write a program a publisher could use to print form letters. The main parts of the letter stay the same, and should be incorporated in PRINT statements in your program. The parts shown in brackets change from letter to letter and should be read in from data lines. Run your program at least twice, once to create an acceptance letter, once to make a rejection letter.

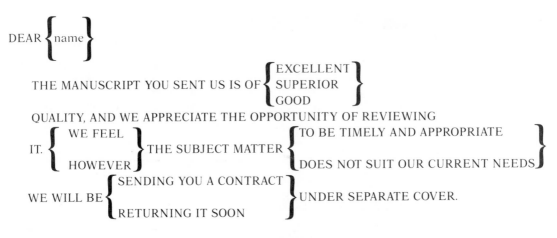

THANK YOU FOR YOUR INTEREST

COLLAPSE OF THE EMPIRE PRESS, INC

5. The truncation that occurs when a REAL value is converted to an INTEGER value is useful for getting rid of unwanted fractional parts. But what if you want to print out a value in dollars and cents? You don't want to get rid of all the fractional part—just everything past two digits to the right of the decimal place. Write a program which accepts a REAL value and prints it out after removing the unwanted fractional digits.

Program Design Problems

6. Do problem 5 again but accept two values per data card, one a REAL value and the other an INTEGER which tells how many digits to the right of the decimal point to retain. (*Hint:* It requires only a minor change to the solution to problem 4.)
   Examples:

input		output
1.2345	1	1.2000
327.1039	3	327.1030
98.7219	0	98.0000
123.3217	−1	120.0000

7. Design a program that READs a pair of INTEGERs from a data line. This pair represents a fraction, with the first value being the numerator, the second the denominator. Print out the fraction as a whole number with a proper fraction.
   Examples:

input		output	
2	3	0	2/3
7	3	2	1/3
22	7	3	1/7
19	10	1	9/10

8. Write a program that reverses the effect of problem 7. Each data card should contain three INTEGER values which represent a number and a proper fraction. Print the equivalent improper fraction.
   Examples:

input			output
2	1	3	7/3
2	5	7	19/7
0	1	3	1/3

9. Write a program which solves this problem when you READ the appropriate numbers:

   Generous Electric's 60-watt, 820-lumen, "long life" light bulbs cost $1.39 for 2 and last 1500 hours (each) on the average. Generous Electric's 60-watt, 855-lumen, "regular" light bulbs cost $2.13 for 4 and last about 1000 hours each. Assuming it costs you nothing to change a light bulb when it goes out, which type of bulb gives the most lumens*hours for the dollar? Which one gives you the most hours per dollar?

10. Write a program to estimate the cost of siding for a house. Assume the siding comes in 4-foot-by-9-foot panels. READ the cost of the siding per panel and the length and width of the house. Assume that the house is a simple, rectangular, one-story ranch style house and that a 9-foot panel is long enough, placed vertically, to go from the foundation to the top of the exterior walls.

11. In a typical house with six inches of fiberglass insulation in the roof and none in the walls, 40 percent of the heating bill is for heat loss through the walls.

    The insulating effectiveness of materials is given by the "R-rating." A normal wall with no insulation in it has an R-rating of R4.

Installing three-and-a-half-inch-thick fiberglass insulation increases the R-rating to R13. The R-rating is inversely proportional to the amount of heat flow through the material, so 4/13 as much heat is lost through an R13 wall as through an R4 wall.

It costs about $400 to buy enough insulation for the walls of a 2000-square-foot house.

Write a program which illustrates the cost effectiveness of installing insulation in the walls. Your program should READ in the size of the house (in square feet) and the average monthly heating bill for a 2000-square-foot house with uninsulated walls in this part of the country. Assume that heating bills and cost of insulation are proportional to the area of the house. Print the monthly saving obtained by installing insulation in the walls.

12. Improve the program from problem 11 in two ways. First, include figures based on both three-and-a-half-inch insulation and on five-and-a-half-inch insulation (in some areas, houses are being built with 2-by-6 framing members instead of 2-by-4's to allow thicker insulation). A wall with five-and-a-half-inch insulation has an R-rating of R21, and costs about $600 for a 2000-square-foot house.

Second, compare the monthly savings to the interest that would be earned on $400 or $600 if it were put in the bank at 10 percent interest instead of being spent on insulation.

13. Mrs. Bigelsby has just purchased a ten-unit apartment building for $320,000. She paid $80,000 down and makes mortgage payments of $1,845 per month. During the first year, taxes are $3,425, insurance is $450, power and gas cost $250, water and garbage cost $660, and repairs to the building cost $950. One of the units is provided free to the manager of the apartment. If Mrs. Bigelsby wants to make a 10 percent profit each year on her investment of $80,000, how much rent should she charge per apartment?

4 LOOPS

4.1 INTRODUCTION

By now you know enough to write programs that perform numerical computations and print the results. You also know that the numbers used in the computations can be either written within the program itself or obtained from a data source outside the program. Thus, you are able to use a computer to do computations similar to those you can do on a calculator. In some cases it might actually be more convenient to use a computer to do these calculations, but most of the time it would be easier to use the calculator. The computer might have a slight advantage if the expression is written with lots of parentheses that make it hard to untangle, and the calculator might have a slight advantage in simply totaling up a list of numbers since the procedure is simple enough to be remembered without being written down in the form of a program. Thus, the computer may not seem particularly useful to you right now, but by the end of this chapter you will begin to see how useful it can be.

Totaling a list of numbers on a calculator is a very repetitious task: enter a number, punch the add key, enter a number, punch the add key, and so forth. The program we wrote in Section 2.5 to compute bowling averages was also very repetitious.

```
        .
        .
        .
READ *, SCORE
PRINT *, 'SCORE:', SCORE
TOTAL = TOTAL + SCORE
G = G + 1.0
        .
        .
        .
```

A repetitious program can always be written in a much more compact way using a program structure known as a **loop.** Instead of writing the same statements over and over, we tell the computer to repeat the statements.

loop:

Looping is probably the most important programming technique you will learn. It's not the most difficult concept in programming, but it has broad applications. The technique of **looping** allows us to put explicit instructions for repetition directly in our program instead of having to type the same statements over and over again.

A loop is a sequence of statements which are to be repeated. Each time the statements are performed, a decision must be made to repeat or not to repeat. You will learn about three different kinds of loops in this chapter, and the distinctions among them are based on how and when the decision to repeat is made. If the decision comes at the beginning of the loop, it is a **pretest loop.** When the decision comes at the end, the loop is called a **posttest loop.** In the third kind of loop, known as a **READ-loop,** the decision for repetition is made on the basis of information fetched from a data line. A READ-loop always begins with a READ statement, which is followed immediately be the repeat decision. Because READ-loops fit nicely into our bowling-average program, we'll discuss them first.

4.2 READ-LOOPS

The plan for our bowling-average program, as it stands in Chapter 2, has some looping in it.

Plan

> Get score
> Print score
> Add score to total
> Increment number of games
> ──────────────────────── Repeat as needed

Compute average
Print average

A four-step sequence (get score, print, add to total, increment) is repeated three times, once for each score. In the program, we simply copied the four statements three times in a row. This approach will always work, but it has some disadvantages. First, it's tedious to copy the statements, and it makes the programs very long. Second, the programs don't generalize easily. If the bowling team plays two matches in a week, the program won't work as it is. The statements need to be repeated three more times to include the three scores from the second match.

It would be better if we had a plan that automatically repeated only "as needed"—no more, no less. One way to do this is to stop repeating after processing the last score. But how will the computer know which is the last score? Will it be the third score? the sixth? or maybe the fourth score (in case a special kind of match is being played)?

This is a common problem in computer programming: telling the computer when it has come to the end of the data. The usual solution is to put a special piece of data, known as the **termination signal,** at the end. This is simply a data value that is easily distinguished from "regular" data. The program tells the computer how to recognize the termination signal, and when it finds the signal, it discontinues the repetitions.

In the bowling-average program, it's easy to choose a termination signal. All of the scores will be numbers between 0 and 300. We could choose any number outside that range as a termination signal. Suppose we choose a negative number. Then the plan would look like this:

Plan

```
 _____
| Get score                              |
| Exit if score < 0                      |
| Print score                            |
| Add score to total                     |
| Increment number of games              |
|                                        |
|_____ Repeat |
```

Compute average
Print average

The "exit" command, which is a new wrinkle, means to get out of the loop, that is, to go on with the commands after the "repeat."

There are now five types of commands in the plan: get value, exit-if, print, compute value (add, increment, etc.), and repeat. You already know that "get value" translates into a Fortran READ statement and that you can use assignment statements to compute values and WRITE statements to print results. You also know a way to "repeat" using multiple copies of the statements that need repeating, but that is not really a satisfactory way to repeat things. Now you'll learn a better way to repeat commands, and you'll learn how to exit from a loop.

First the repeat. It's easier. When we come to a point in a program where we want to repeat previous statements instead of proceeding in the usual sequence to the next statement, we must have some way of telling the processor where to begin that repetition. In Fortran this is done by placing a **label** on the statement to be repeated and referring to that label to initiate the repeat. To tell the processor to repeat from the statement whose label is *s* we write

GO TO *s*

The label *s* is a number between 1 and 99999. The statement to be repeated will have the number *s* in its label field, columns 1 through 5 (see the box in Section 1.6 describing the statement format). Any statement may be labeled, but it is wise to put a label on a statement only if it is necessary to refer to the statement from some other point in the program.

Now we can easily translate everything but the "exit-if" in the plan into Fortran. The following program is the partial translation, leaving space for the exit from the loop, which we'll discuss next.

```
COMMENT:                    CALCULATE AVERAGE BOWLING SCORE
C                           DATA:  THREE LINES, ONE SCORE
C                                  PER LINE, COL. 1-5
        INTEGER SCORE, TOTAL, G, AVG
C                           INITIALIZE RUNNING SUMS
        TOTAL = 0
        G = 0
C                           GETS SCORES, PRINT, AND TALLY
  100   READ *, SCORE
C                           EXIT IF SCORE<0

        PRINT *, 'SCORE: ', SCORE
        TOTAL = TOTAL + SCORE
        G = G + 1
        GO TO 100
C                           COMPUTE AVERAGE AND PRINT
  200   AVG =  NINT( REAL(TOTAL)/REAL(G) )
        PRINT *, '   AVERAGE:', AVG
        END
```

To implement the exit from the loop in Fortran, we need a way to go to the assignment statement when we come to the negative number. What we need is a "conditional GO TO statement," which is a Fortran IF statement. The IF statement has the form

IF (e_1 *rel* e_2) GO TO *s*

where *s* is a statement label, e_1 and e_2 are arithmetic expressions like the right-hand side of an assignment statement, and *rel* expresses a relation

IF-GOTO Statement

---

form
IF (e_1 *rel* e_2) GO TO *s*
e_1 and e_2 are arithmetic expressions
rel is a relational operator
s is a statement label

meaning
decide whether or not the expressed relationship between the expressions is true; if so, proceed from statement *s*; otherwise, continue from the next statement as usual

examples
```
IF (A+B .GT. 0) GO TO 130
IF (3*(A/B) .GT. C*B) GO TO 500
```

between e_1 and e_2. The six possibilities for *rel* are shown in Table 4.2.1.

If e_1 *rel* e_2 is true, then the processor proceeds to statement *s*; otherwise, the processor continues from the statement following the IF statement in the usual sequence. For instance, the IF statement

```
IF (SCORE .LT. 0) GO TO 200
```

means: IF the value of memory cell SCORE is less than zero, then GO TO statement 200; otherwise, just go on to the next statement.

Table 4.2.1 Relational Operators

Relation	Usual Symbol	Fortran Symbol
Less than	$<$	.LT.
Less than or equal to	$\leq$	.LE.
Equal to	$=$	.EQ.
Not equal to	$\neq$	.NE.
Greater than or equal to	$\geq$	.GE.
Greater than	$>$	.GT.

Now (finally!) we can write the complete program. Compare the following program with our latest plan. Do you see how each statement in the program is a direct translation of the plan into Fortran? This is an important principle to follow: *complete your plan before writing your program.*

```
COMMENT:                CALCULATE AVERAGE BOWLING SCORE
C          DATA:  THREE LINES, ONE SCORE PER LINE
           INTEGER SCORE, TOTAL, G, AVG
           INTEGER ENDSCR
           PARAMETER (ENDSCR=0)
C                        INITIALIZE RUNNING SUMS
           TOTAL = 0
           G = 0
C                      GET SCORES, PRINT, AND TALLY
  100      READ *, SCORE
             IF (SCORE .LT. ENDSCR) GO TO 200
             PRINT *, 'SCORE:', SCORE
             TOTAL = TOTAL + SCORE
             G = G + 1
             GO TO 100
C                      COMPUTE AVERAGE AND PRINT
  200      AVG = NINT(REAL(TOTAL)/REAL(G))
           PRINT *, '    AVERAGE:', AVG
           END
```

Data

```
167
142
159
-1         (this is the termination signal)
```

Output

```
SCORE:  167
SCORE:  142
SCORE:  159
   AVERAGE:     156
```

The program initializes the memory cells TOTAL and G, then adds each score into the total until it reaches the negative value that denotes the end of the scores. At that point it hops out of the loop.

Indentation

> Loops are such an important part of Fortran programs that we need some way to emphasize their place in our programs. There are many ways of doing this, and we can have chosen one particularly popular technique: **indentation**. We indent all the statements in the loop except the first one. The indentation serves as a visual bracket for the loop. See Figure 4.2.1.

Figure 4.2.1 The Skeletal Form of the READ-Loop

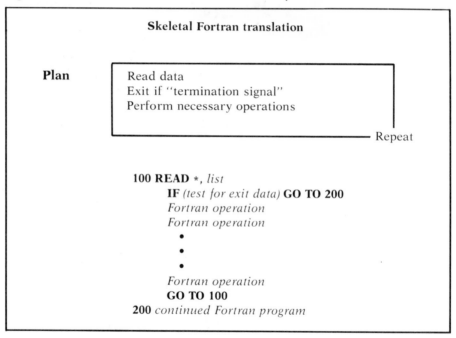

Skeletal Fortran translation

Plan

Read data
Exit if "termination signal"
Perform necessary operations

—— Repeat

100 **READ** *, *list*
    IF *(test for exit data)* **GO TO 200**
    Fortran operation
    Fortran operation
    •
    •
    •
    Fortran operation
    GO TO 100
200 *continued Fortran program*

4.2 EXERCISES

1. Which of the following IF statements are legal?

```
IF (X .GT. Y)  GO TO 35
IF (X*2 + 17 .LE. Y**2)  GO TO 100
IF (14 .EG. 2)  GO TO 10
IF (X .SGT. A)  GO TO 15
IF Y .EQ. 0,  GO TO 20
```

2. Translate the following plan into Fortran.

> Read two numbers
> Exit if first number is zero
> Print the numbers and their sum
> ────────── Repeat

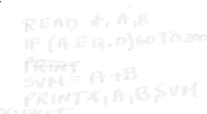

3. What happens if the data for our bowling-average program includes a score of 407.0?

4. What is the goal of the following computation?

Start with P = 1

> Read number
> Exit if the number is zero
> Multiply P by the number
> ────────── Repeat

Print the value of P

5. Translate the plan in exercise 4 into Fortran.

6. Make a plan for computing the sales taxes on a sequence of individual purchases.

4.3 PRETEST LOOPS

The next time you get caught with a calculator that doesn't have a square root key, and you need to compute a square root, try this method: make a guess; if the guess (when you square it) is close enough, then you're done; if not, compute the average of the (1) guess and (2) the number whose square root you're trying to find divided by the guess. This average will be closer to the square root, and you can repeat the process to get still closer if you need to.

Newton's Method

> The procedure for computing square roots that is based on the formula $r = (r + x/r)/2$ is known as Newton's method. (The formula it's based on is known as Heron's formula.) Newton's method can be used with other formulas to compute other types of roots and, more generally, to solve many kinds of equations. If you are interested in this topic, look it up in a book on numerical analysis. (Practically any book on that subject will do; your library should have several.)

This is a very quick and easy way to compute square roots. It is, in fact, the way your Fortran system does it when you use the SQRT function. You'll never need to program this method in Fortran, of course, because you can always use SQRT to get the answer automatically, but we're going to use it as a simple example to get more practice with looping. First, we can describe the procedure using our "plan" notation. We let x stand for the number that we're trying to find the square root of, and we let r be the best approximation we've found as we go through the calculations.

Exit if r^2 is close enough to x
Let $r = 0.5*(r + x/r)$

— Repeat

This type of loop, with the exit positioned at the beginning, is known as a pretest loop because the test to determine whether to continue occurs prior to the commands that need to be repeated. Many programmers believe this to be the safest kind of loop because it forces a decision about whether to proceed before any damage has been done. It's a little like signaling before making a left turn.

The hardest part of translating the Newton's method plan to Fortran is in figuring out what "close enough" means. That probably sounds easy, and you wouldn't have much trouble with it if you were using the procedure yourself on a pocket calculator. But "close enough" turns out to be very difficult to express as a general concept in a computer program. Treatises on numerical procedures devote a great deal of space to the topic.

To keep our example as simple as possible without being too misleading, we will use the concept of "relative error" to decide the "close enough" question. When the square of our approximation (r) is within 1 percent of the number we're trying to get the square root of (x), we'll say that's close enough. Mathematically, this means that $|r^2 - x| <$ $0.01x$. The vertical bars in this formula stand for "absolute value," which means the value enclosed inside the bars, ignoring its sign (plus or minus). We need to use the absolute value because we don't know whether the approximation is going to be too large or too small. If it's too small, the difference $r^2 - x$ will be negative, and that would be algebraically less than $0.01x$, regardless of how far off the approximation is (consider $r = 1$ and $x = 100$, for example). To get the absolute value in Fortran, we use the ABS function.

With the close-enough question out of the way, the plan for Newton's method translates easily into Fortran statements that you already understand.

```
100  IF (ABS(R**2 - X) .LT. 0.01*X) GO TO 200
        R = 0.5*(R + X/R)
        GO TO 100
```

Remembering Heron's Formula

If r is the square root of x, then so is x/r, which means that

$$r = (r + x/r)/2.$$

Furthermore, if r exceeds the square root of x, then x/r is smaller than the root (and vice versa), so it's not surprising that the average of those two quantities, that is, $(r + x/r)/2$, is closer to the root than either r or its counterpart, x/r.

The other question is how to make the first guess. This turns out to be very easy if we're not too concerned about how many iterations through the loop the computer has to make before getting the answer. Namely, you can make any guess you like, as long as it's not a negative number. The simplest thing to do is to start with $r = 1.0$, regardless of the value of x. We'll leave it to you to do the exercises of this section to expand the program fragment into a full program that gets a value for x from a data source, goes ahead with Newton's method, and prints the square root.

Figure. 4.3.1 illustrates the type of plan we draw up for pretest loops, and the layout of the corresponding Fortran implementation. Note the indentation of the statements inside the loop.

Figure 4.3.1   The Skeletal Form of the Pretest Loop

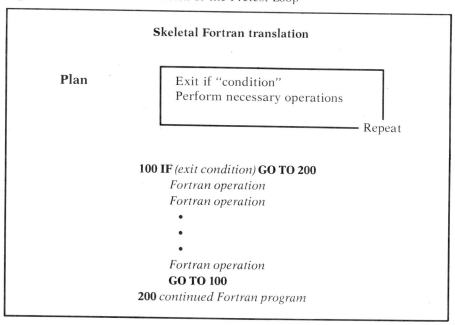

4.3 EXERCISES

1. How would you change the exit test in the loop to compute square roots if you wanted the square of the answer to be within 0.1 percent of the number whose square root is being computed?
2. What if you wanted the square of the answer to match the given number to three decimal places?
3. Use the square root loop of this section as the main part of a program that gets a number from a data source (READ), computes its square root, and prints the given number, the square root computed in the loop, and the square root computed by the SQRT function.
4. What happens if your program gets a negative number to compute the square root of?
5. Any number x has a sequence of **doubles:** $x, x + x, (x + x) + (x + x),$ etc. The sequence can be computed by repeatedly replacing x by $x + x$. Write a plan for computing the largest double of a given number that doesn't exceed 100. (Assume the given number x is between 1 and 100. For example, if x is 20, then the doubles are 20, 40, 80, and 160, and 80 is the largest one that doesn't exceed 100.)
6. Translate your plan for exercise 5 into Fortran.

4.4 POSTTEST LOOPS

Now that you understand the basic idea of a loop, you will probably want to view the rest of this chapter as variations on a theme: how to describe repetitive processes to a computer.

In most algorithms where repetition is needed, the operations to be repeated must be performed at least once. After the first pass through the operations, a decision is made on whether to repeat. Loops of this kind in which the decision to repeat is made *after* each pass through the operations within the loop are known as posttest loops. Figure 4.4.1 displays their general form.

Figure 4.4.1 The Skeletal Form of the Posttest Loop

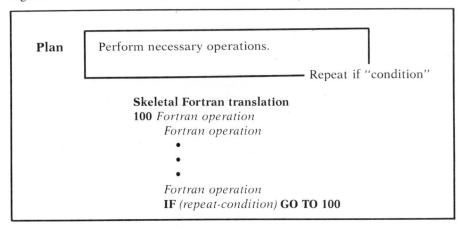

To see this kind of loop in action, let's suppose we're thinking of getting a bank loan to buy a new car. Suppose we can budget $100 a month for car payments, and to buy the car we want we'll have to borrow $5000. The bank will lend us the money at an annual interest rate of 14 percent. The question is, how long will it take to pay off the loan? One way to find out is to call the bank and ask, but let's do it the hard way. We'll write a program and let the computer do the calculations.

The first step is to decide exactly what results we want the computer to print. A loan payment schedule showing the status of the loan after each monthly payment would probably be the most helpful thing. To print a table like this, we need to use one basic formula:

```
BAL = AMT + R*AMT - PAYMNT
```

The formula says that the balance (BAL) remaining to be paid after a monthly payment can be computed by adding the amount (AMT) owed before the payment to the accumulated monthly interest (R*AMT) and subtracting the amount of the monthly payment (PAYMNT). The R in the formula stands for the monthly interest rate. In our problem R is 0.14/12 (one-twelfth the annual interest rate of 14 percent).

Figure 4.4.2   Plan for Computing a Loan Payment Schedule

```
Determine amount of loan.
Determine interest rate.
Determine amount of payment.
Start with MONTH = 1.

    Compute monthly interest.
    Compute new balance.
    Print figures for this month.
    Increment MONTH.
    Update amount of loan to new balance.
                            Repeat if balance exceeds zero
```

The program to print the loan payment schedule must repeat the monthly calculation until the balance goes to zero (indicating that the loan is paid off). The details of our computational plan shown in Figure 4.4.2 illustrate the use of a posttest loop. The idea is to calculate the remaining balance (using the formula) and repeat if it still exceeds zero. On each pass through the loop, we print one line of the schedule.

The following program implements our computational plan in a direct fashion, and embellishes the output with the original loan conditions and with column headings on the schedule so that anyone who looks at the output will be able to understand what the numbers mean.

```
C                          LOAN PAYMENT SCHEDULE

C                          P       ---AMOUNT ORIGINALLY BORROWED
C                          AMT     ---AMOUNT (UPDATED MONTHLY)
C                          PAYMNT  ---MONTHLY PAYMENT
C                          R       ---MONTHLY INTEREST RATE
C                          APR     ---ANNUAL INTEREST RATE (PERCENT)
C                          MONTH   ---MONTH NUMBERS (1, 2, 3, ... ETC.)
C                          INTRST  ---MONTHLY INTEREST ($)
C                          BAL     ---NEW BALANCE EACH MONTH
          REAL P, AMT, PAYMNT, R, INTRST, BAL, APR
          INTEGER MONTH
          PARAMETER (P=5000.00, PAYMNT = 100.00, R = 0.14/12,
     +              APR = R*12*100)
          AMT = P
          PRINT *, 'PRINCIPAL', AMT
          PRINT *, 'ANNUAL INTEREST RATE', APR
          PRINT *, 'MONTHLY PAYMENT', PAYMNT
C                          COMPUTE PAYMENT SCHEDULE
          PRINT *, ''
          PRINT *, '   MONTH OLD BALANCE     INTEREST          ',
     +            'PAYMENT     NEW BALANCE'
          MONTH = 1
  100     INTRST = AMT*R
            BAL = AMT + INTRST - PAYMNT
            PRINT *, MONTH, AMT, INTRST, PAYMNT, BAL
            MONTH = MONTH + 1
            AMT = BAL
            IF (BAL .GT. 0.00) GO TO 100
          END
```

Output

```
PRINCIPAL   5000.000
ANNUAL INTEREST RATE   14.00000
MONTHLY PAYMENT   100.0000
```

MONTH	OLD BALANCE	INTEREST	PAYMENT	NEW BALANCE
1	5000.000	58.33333	100.0000	4958.333
2	4958.333	57.84725	100.0000	4916.181
3	4916.181	57.35544	100.0000	4873.536
4	4873.536	56.85792	100.0000	4830.394
5	4830.394	56.35460	100.0000	4786.749
6	4786.749	55.84540	100.0000	4742.594
7	4742.594	55.33026	100.0000	4697.924
8	4697.924	54.80911	100.0000	4652.733
9	4652.733	54.28188	100.0000	4607.015
10	4607.015	53.74850	100.0000	4560.763
.				
.				
.				
71	527.5999	6.155333	100.0000	433.7552
72	433.7552	5.060478	100.0000	338.8157
73	338.8157	3.952850	100.0000	242.7686
74	242.7686	2.832300	100.0000	145.6009
75	145.6009	1.698677	100.0000	47.29957
76	47.29957	.5518283	100.0000	-52.14861

4.4 EXERCISES

1. Translate the following into Fortran.

   Get values for X and N.
   Let $P = X$.

   > Multiply P by X.
   > Reduce N by 1.

   Repeat if $N > 1$

   Print P.

2. What is the goal of the computation in exercise 1?
3. Write a plan for a program to compute the sum of the first 50 cubes: $1^3 + 2^3 + 3^3 + 4^3 + \ldots + 50^3$.

4.5 DO-LOOPS

So far, we have divided loops into three categories according to the placement of the exit: pretest loops, posttest loops, and READ-loops. This is not the only way to classify loops. Another way is to divide them into two categories: **counting loops** and **noncounting loops.** In a **counting loop** the statements are to be repeated a fixed number of times. The number of iterations, known as the **iteration count,** is computed before the first pass through the loop. By using DO statements, Fortran programmers don't have to write explicit initialization, repetition, and exit statements for counting loops. The DO statement handles all three of these details automatically.

A surprisingly large proportion of program loops are counting loops. This makes the DO-loop very useful. However, many Fortran programmers try to force their loops to fit this category even when they could be more clearly written in some other way. Choose your loops wisely, based on the problem.

Here's an example of a DO-loop in use:

```
COMMENT:                    LIST THE SQUARES AND CUBES OF 1,2, ..., TOP
          INTEGER N, TOP
          TOP = 10
          PRINT *, ' NUMBER        SQUARED        CUBED'
COMMENT:                    HERE'S THE DO-LOOP
          DO 10 N = 1, TOP, 1
            PRINT *, N, N**2, N**3
   10       CONTINUE
          END
```

Output

NUMBER	SQUARED	CUBED
1	1	1
2	4	8
3	9	27
4	16	64
5	25	125
6	36	216
7	49	343
8	64	512
9	81	792
10	100	1000

You can probably tell what's going on just by staring at the program and the output for a while. There are a number of formal rules, however.

Each DO-loop starts with a statement called a **DO statement**, which specifies five things:

1. the **DO variable,**
2. the **starting value** of the DO variable,
3. the **ending value,**
4. the **increment,** and
5. the **range** of the DO-loop (that is, the statements which are part of the DO-loop).

The DO variable must be an unsubscripted variable. The range is specified by a statement label in the DO statement that indicates the last statement in the loop. This last statement conventionally is a CONTINUE statement, which does nothing but mark the end of the range. Thus, the loop includes all the executable statements *following* the DO statement, up to and including the terminal statement. The DO statement itself is *not* part of the loop; it merely sets up the loop.

The DO statement sets the DO variable to the starting value and establishes the iteration count. The iteration count is the number of repetitions of the loop. The DO variable begins with the starting value, and the increment is added after each pass through the loop until the ending value is matched or surpassed. For example, if the starting value is 1, the ending value is 10, and the increment is 1, the iteration count will be 10. The DO variable will take the values 1 = starting value, 1 + 1 = 2, 2 + 1 = 3, 3 + 1 = 4, and so on up to 10. The statements in the range of the DO-loop are automatically repeated once for each value of the DO variable.

Let's dissect the DO-loop in the example above to see how it fits the rules. While we're at it, we'll write out a program that does exactly the same thing but which doesn't use a DO-loop. That way you can always refer to the non-DO-loop form if you have a question about some detail of how DO-loops work.

DO-loop form	non-DO-loop form

```
        DO 10 N=1,TOP,1                N = 1
           PRINT *, N, N**2, N**3  10   IF (N .GT. TOP) GO TO 11
10         CONTINUE                        PRINT *, N, N**2, N**3
                                           N = N + 1
                                           GO TO 10
                                    11   ...
```

The DO statement comes first and specifies the number of times the loop will be repeated and the values the index will take. The statement label specifies the range of the loop. In our example the range is all statements *after* the DO statement up to and including statement 10. The memory cell called N serves as the index, and its value is changed on each pass through the loop. The DO variable N is initialized to the value 1 (the starting value) and is increased by 1 (the increment) on each pass. The statements of the loop are repeated as long as the index is less than or equal to the value of TOP (the ending value). Compare the DO-loop to the equivalent form using the conditional GO TO again. You'll probably agree that the DO statement is easier to read, once you understand the notation.

Let's look at another example. Suppose you want to compute an approximation of the infinite sum $1 + 1/4 + 1/9 + 1/6 + \ldots + 1/n^2 + \ldots$ To see how the sum is progressing, you want to print it after every hundredth term has been added. This is a perfect situation for a DO-loop; while you are adding terms, you want to count to 100 over and over again and print out the sum each time you get to 100. The following program does this computation. It stops adding terms when they get very small.

```
COMMENT:                COMPUTE 1 + 1/4 + 1/9 + ... + 1/N**2 + ...
            REAL N, SUM, SMALL
            INTEGER COUNT
            PARAMETER (SMALL = 1.0E-6)
COMMENT:                INITIALIZE SUM AND N
            SUM = 1.0
            N = 1.0
```

(Continued on following page)

```
COMMENT:                    ADD A HUNDRED TERMS
10         DO 20 COUNT = 1,100,1
               N = N + 1.0
               SUM = SUM + 1.0/N**2
20             CONTINUE
           PRINT *, 'SUM SO FAR', SUM
COMMENT:                    ADD NEXT 100 TERMS UNLESS LAST TERM WAS VERY SMALL
           IF (1.0/N**2 .GT. SMALL) GO TO 10
           END
```

Output

```
SUM SO FAR          1.635082
SUM SO FAR          1.639971
SUM SO FAR          1.641617
SUM SO FAR          1.642444
SUM SO FAR          1.642940
SUM SO FAR          1.643272
SUM SO FAR          1.643509
SUM SO FAR          1.643686
SUM SO FAR          1.643825
SUM SO FAR          1.643935
```

In both of the above examples it was easy to compute the iteration count because the DO variable was essentially counting in an ordinary way from one up to the ending value. This is not always the case, however. It is also possible to increment the DO variable by two or three or any other number. This is like "counting by twos," "counting by threes," or whatever. It is even possible to count backwards with the DO variable by using a negative increment. For example, if the starting value is 10, the ending value is 1, and the increment is -1, then the DO variable begins at 10 and goes to $10 + (-1) = 9$, $9 + (-1) = 8$, $8 + (-1) = 7$, and so on down to 1, the ending value.

Actually, "ending value" is a misnomer. It's the iteration count that matters. The iteration count is computed before the repetitions begin and determines the number of repetitions exactly. The formula is complicated and tricky because it takes into account both the forward and backward cases, as well as "counting by twos" or "threes" and so on. The formula is written here primarily for reference. You will probably understand it better later. You can usually figure out the iteration count more easily by using your common sense.

For example, if the starting value is 3, the ending value is 9, and the increment is 1, then the iteration count is 7. If the starting value is 1, the ending value is 10, and the increment is 2, then the iteration count is 5. The value of the DO variable during the last iteration is 9, which is why the term "ending value" can be misleading.

Iteration Count

```
IC = MAX(INT((EV-SV+INC)/INC),0)
```

where IC = iteration count, EV = ending value,
SV = starting value, and INC = increment.

The DO variable is automatically initialized and incremented so that it takes on successive values from the sequence s, $2 + i$, $s + 2i$, $s + 3i$, and so on up to $s + ni$ where n is the iteration count, s is the starting value, and i is the increment. When the DO-loop is completed, the DO variable has the *first value in the sequence beyond the ending value*. For example, if the starting value is 1, the ending value is N, and the increment is 1, then the DO variable will have the value N + 1 when the loop is completed.

To sum things up: DO-loops provide a flexible way to write counting loops in Fortran. An equivalent loop can always be written as a pretest loop using IF statements and GO TOs, but the DO statement provides the loop control automatically, making the loop easier to write and, once you get used to it, easier to read.

Because counting loops are used in many applications and because we'll use DO-loops to express them in Fortran, we will use a special notation for counting loops in our plans. We'll list the values of the DO variable in a heading at the beginning of the loop. Normally there are too many values to list explicitly, so we'll use an ellipsis (. . .) to span the gap once the pattern has been established. For example, if the DO statement is DO 100 I = 1, 10, then the DO variable takes the values 1,2, . . . , 10 (that is, all the numbers from 1 to 10, incrementing by one at each step). If the DO statement is DO 100 K = 1,N,2 then K takes the values 1,3,5,. . . , N. In this case K takes only odd-numbered values. It may happen that N is an even number, in which case K will never have the value N. Remember: the DO variable takes all the values in the established sequence up to, but not including, the first one that goes *beyond* the ending value. In Figure 4.5.1, we use this technique to outline the DO-loop in the program at the beginning of this section.

There are two fairly common techniques associated with DO-loops that programmers use to improve the readability of their programs. One is to indent the statements in the range of the DO-loops. The other is to place a CONTINUE statement at the end of the range of every DO-loop so that the DO statement and the CONTINUE act as visual "brackets" for the DO-loop. The CONTINUE statement has no effect other than to act as a place to attach a statement label. Figure 4.5.1 illustrates this use of the CONTINUE statement.

Figure 4.5.1   A Typical DO-Loop

Fortran Translation

```
        DO 10 N = 1, TOP
          PRINT *, N,N**2,N**3
  10      CONTINUE
```

For N = 1, 2, . . . , TOP

Print N, N^2, and N^3

CONTINUE

> **CONTINUE** is an executable statement. Its (rather unusual) meaning is to *do nothing*. It is often used as the terminal statement in the range of a DO-loop.

There are a few natural restrictions placed on DO-loops. The first one is that the value of the DO variable may not be altered by any statement in the range of the DO-loop. This is because its value is being automatically incremented each time through the loop.

DO Statement

> **forms**
> *DO r v = s, e, i*
> *DO r v =s, e*   (*i* assumed to be 1 in this form)
>
> *r* is a statement label (on the terminal statement of the DO-loop)
> *v* is an unsubscripted variable (the DO variable)
> *s, e,* and *i* are arithmetic expressions (the starting value, ending value, and increment, respectively)
>
> **restrictions**
> *i* cannot be zero
> *v* cannot be altered by any statement in the range of the DO-loop
> The terminal statement cannot be a GO TO, IF-THEN, ELSE IF, ELSE, ENDIF, END, STOP, RETURN, or DO statement
>
> **meaning**
> the following loops are equivalent:
>
> ```
> DO r v = s, e, i          v = s
>     statement 1           N = MAX(INT((e−s+i)/i, 0))
>     statement 2           K = 1
>       •               r IF   (K.GT.N) GO TO exit
>       •                      statement 1
>       •                      statement 2
> r   CONTINUE                   •
>     statement after loop       •
>                                •
>                             terminal statement
>                             v = v + i
>                             K = K + 1
>                             GO TO r
>                      exit statement after loop
> ```

Making further changes would foul up the sequence of values the DO variable is supposed to take on as the iterations proceed.

The second restriction is that the terminal statement must not be an unconditional transfer of control (like a GO TO statement or a STOP or RETURN statement, which you will learn about later). Nor can it be an

END statement or an IF-THEN, ELSE IF, ELSE, or ENDIF statement (which you will learn about in a subsequent chapter). Finally, it cannot be another DO statement. This last restriction makes especially good sense because placing a DO statement at the end of a DO-loop would imply some kind of **weird** overlapping loop structure. If you use CON-TINUE statements to end all your DO loops, you needn't worry about these restrictions.

DO-loops don't provide you with any capability that you didn't have before. They simply provide a better notation for counting loops. You will see later that they are especially helpful in implementing array processing loops, array search loops, and array READ-loops.

The DO statement is a command to repeat a sequence of Fortran statements n times, where n is the iteration count. Additionally, it initializes the DO variable and automatically increments it after each repetition.

4.5   EXERCISES

1. In the first DO-loop example program, what will be printed if TOP has the value -1?
2. In what way would the output of the second example program be changed if its DO statement was changed to

```
DO 20 COUNT = 1,100
```

3. How many lines will this bizarre and possibly senseless program print?

```
COMMENT:            THIS PROGRAM IS BIZARRE AND POSSIBLY SENSELESS.
C                   READ IT AT YOUR OWN RISK.
          INTEGER OUTER, INNER, MIDDLE
          DO 300 OUTER = 2,8,2
            DO 200 MIDDLE = OUTER,2,1
              DO 100 INNER = 1,4,2
                PRINT *, 'LINE'
100           CONTINUE
200         CONTINUE
300       CONTINUE
          END
```

(handwritten annotations: "DONE 2" next to the DO 100 INNER line; "PRINTS LINE TWICE" beside lines 100–300)

4. What's wrong with this?

```
          DO 110 I = 1,10
100           N = N + 1
              PRINT *, I
110           CONTINUE
          IF (N .LT. 100) GO TO 100
```

5. Write a loop which is equivalent to the one below without using a DO statement.

```
          S = 0.0
          DO 100 X = A,B,DX
            S = S + X
100       CONTINUE
          S = S*DX
```

4.6 SUMMARY

We have studied four kinds of loops:

1. READ-loop

> Read data
> Exit if "final data"
> •
> •
> •
>
> _____ Repeat

2. pretest loop

> Exit if "condition"
> •
> •
> •
>
> _____ Repeat

3. posttest loop

> •
> •
> •
>
> _____ Repeat if "condition"

4. DO-loop

> For v = s, s + i, s + 2i, . . ., e _____
> •
> •
> •

The type of loop to use for a given problem is mostly a matter of your approach to the problem. You can always contort your logic to make your program use either pretest or posttest loops. You should try to pick the one that best suits the requirements of your problem. The common thread among all types is the **Loop** . . . **Repeat** sequence with an exit condition included somewhere therein. It is important to realize that each loop has only *one exit*. It is possible to write loops with more than one place to get out (multi-exit loops), but programmers have found them hard to use without making errors. It seems that loops are a difficult concept to master. To keep them under control, we have to write them as simply as possible.

> ☐ Loops lead to problems.
> ☐ Complicated loops lead to worse problems.
> ☐ Therefore, keep loops simple—**one exit.**

It's unfortunate that loops are so hard to manage because they are essential. Automatic repetition is the capability that makes computers more powerful than calculators. We must be able to use repetition, and in Fortran as well as nearly every other programming language, *repetition means looping*. (See Chapter 15 for a discussion of some programming languages—LISP and APL—where repetition can be accomplished without explicit loops.)

Loop Indentation

```
              REAL P, D, T
              P = 0.0
              D = 1.0
              T = 4.0                    first statement
        100 P = P + T/D                  not indented
              T = -T
              D = D + 2.0                remaining statements
              IF (D .LE. 200.0) GO TO 100    indented

              PRINT *, P
              END                        not indented
```

loop { (bracket spanning `100 P = P + T/D` through `IF (D .LE. 200.0) GO TO 100`)

first statement not indented

remaining statements indented

not indented

nested

```
              INTEGER N
              REAL X, P
        100 READ *, X, N                 not indented
              IF (X .EQ. 0.0) GO TO 200  indented one level
              PRINT *, X, N
              P = X
        110   IF (N .EQ. 0) GO TO 120    indented one level
                P = P*X                  indented two levels
                N = N-1
                GO TO 110
        120   PRINT *, P                 indented one level
              GO TO 100

        200 END                          not indented
```

outside loop { inside loop {

- [ ] Repetition is essential.
- [ ] Repetition means looping.
- [ ] Therefore, loops are essential.

4.6   EXERCISES

---

1. Describe the four basic types of loops.
2. State the rules for loop indentation.

4 PROBLEMS

Practice Problems

1. Write a program to READ two numbers per line and print these two numbers and their difference on one line; the last line will contain zeros.
2. Write a program which will calculate the area of the right triangle given the lengths of the two legs. Each data line will contain two INTEGERs representing the length of the legs. Assume that the last data line will contain two zeros.
3. READ in data, containing the ages, heights, and weights for ten of your friends. PRINT out a list of the ages, heights, and weights. At the end of the list, PRINT the average age, height, and weight for all those on the list.
4. Write a program that computes the average of the first n INTEGERs, where the value n is READ as data.
5. A good friend of yours needs a table of numbers to look up squares, cubes, and quads. You decide to help so that both of you can make it to the TGIF bash. Write the program to do the computation for the numbers 1 through 100. Arrange your output as follows.

NUMBER	SQUARE	CUBE	QUAD
1	1	1	1
2	4	8	16
3	9	27	81
•			
•			
•			

6. Write a program which computes the sum of the first n odd integers where the value of n comes from a data line.

Program Design Problems

7. Write a program which computes the first perfect square larger than 84,123. A perfect square is an integer which is the square of another integer (perfect square = $n*n$). Use a loop in your program. (An easy technique is to square each integer, starting at 1 and going up until you find a square larger than 84,123.)
8. In making fudge candy, a thermometer is handy; unfortunately, accurate candy thermometers are difficult to find. The ones we've used have been off by several degrees. To test thermometers for accuracy, we use them to measure the temperature of boiling water and compare their readings to the (known) temperature of boiling water.

    At sea level water boils at 212°F. At higher altitudes it boils at lower temperatures. Use the computer to print out a table of boiling points at various altitudes: sea level, 500 feet, 1000 feet, 1500 feet, and so on in steps of 500 feet up to 15,000 feet above sea level. The boiling point changes by about 1°F for each 550-foot change in altitude. You can use the formula below to compute the boiling point in Fahrenheit degrees when the altitude is measured in feet above sea level.

$$\text{boiling point} = 212 - \frac{\text{altitude}}{550}$$

If your thermometer reads in Celsius (centigrade) degrees and you know your altitude in meters, the formula is

$$\text{boiling point} = 100 - \frac{\text{altitude}}{170}$$

9. Use the computer to print a table of boiling points as in problem 8, but in steps of 100 meters up to 5000 meters above sea level.

10. You have decided to take a job for the Christmas holidays and have negotiated an unusual pay scale. You will work for 1¢ for the first day (a paltry sum), 2¢ the second day, 4¢ the third, 8¢ the fourth (still not much money), and so on, with your pay doubling each day. This will go on for the entire month of December with only one day off— Christmas Day, of course. Use the computer to figure out how much you'll make. Is the old man a Scrooge or not?

output

$	.01	DEC. 1
$	.02	DEC. 2
$	.04	DEC. 3
$	.08	DEC. 4

11. Many infinite series have sums equal to π. Leibnitz's formula (1674) is one with a nice property.

$$\pi = 4 - 4/3 + 4/5 - 4/7 + 4/9 - 4/11 + \cdots$$

It consists of alternating positive and negative terms. If we stop adding after a positive term, the sum is a little larger than π, and if we stop after a negative term, it's a little smaller. Thus we can get upper and lower bounds on π. Write a program to estimate π using Leibnitz's formula. Print the estimate after 99 terms and after 100 terms. Use the fact that ATAN (1.0) = $\pi/4$ to determine whether the 99-term sum or the 100-term sum is closer to π.

12. Businesses depreciate capital assets for tax purposes on a year-by-year basis. Write a program which READs (1) the name of a capital asset, (2) the cost of the asset, (3) the expected life of the asset, and (4) the estimated salvage value of the asset at the end of its expected life. The program should print out a depreciation table using the **straight-line depreciation** method. Each year the asset is depreciated by an amount equal to the difference between its cost and its salvage value divided by its expected life. Its book value decreases by that amount each year. Your table should cover the years of expected life for the asset.

```
ASSET: TRS 80 - LEVEL II
          COST: $1000
          LIFE: 5 YEARS
       SALVAGE: $500
```

(Continued on following page)

```
DEPRECIATION TABLE

YEAR     DEPRECIATION      VALUE
 1          $ 100         $ 900
 2          $ 100         $ 800
 3          $ 100         $ 700
 4          $ 100         $ 600
 5          $ 100         $ 500
```

13. Print a table of the value of an annuity on a yearly basis. READ in (1) the amount invested, (2) the annual interest rate, and (3) the number of years desired in the table. Print the value at the end of each year, compounding the interest yearly.

```
AMOUNT INVESTED:      $1000
ANNUAL INTEREST RATE: 10%

YEAR     INTEREST         VALUE
 1        $ 100         $ 1100
 2        $ 110         $ 1210
 3        $ 121         $ 1331
 4        $ 133.1       $ 1464.1
 5        $ 146.41      $ 1610.51
```

14. Print a table showing the amount owed on an installment loan with monthly payments. READ in (1) the amount of the loan, (2) the annual interest rate, (3) the amount of each payment, and (4) the number of payments to be made. PRINT, on a monthly basis, the current amount owed, the interest paid this month, and the amount paid on the principal this month. Interest is charged on the unpaid balance (current principal) each month.

```
AMOUNT OF LOAN: $1000
ANNUAL INTEREST RATE: 12%
MONTHLY PAYMENT: $47.08
PAYOFF PERIOD: 24 MONTHS
```

MONTH	INTEREST PAID	PRINCIPAL PAID	CURRENT PRINCIPAL
1	$ 10	$ 37.08	$ 962.92
2	$ 9.63	$ 37.45	$ 925.47
3	$ 9.25	$ 37.83	$ 887.64
4	$ 8.88	$ 38.2	$ 849.44
5	$ 8.49	$ 38.59	$ 810.85
6	$ 8.11	$ 38.97	$ 771.88
7	$ 7.72	$ 39.36	$ 732.52
8	$ 7.33	$ 39.75	$ 692.77
*			
*			
*			
18	$ 3.17	$ 43.91	$ 272.7
19	$ 2.73	$ 44.35	$ 228.35
20	$ 2.28	$ 44.8	$ 183.55
21	$ 1.84	$ 45.24	$ 138.31
22	$ 1.38	$ 45.7	$ 92.61
23	$ .98	$ 46.15	$ 46.46
24	$ .46	$ 46.62	$ -.16

15. If you get 23 people together and ask them all their birthdays, the odds are a little better than fifty-fifty that two of them will have the same birthday.

Hard to believe? Pick a person. That eliminates one birthday, and the odds that the next person you pick will have a different birthday are about 365/366 (this includes February 29 birthdays—the leap year people). That eliminates two birthdays. The third person will have yet another birthday with a likelihood of about 364/366. For the fourth person the odds are 363/366, and so on.

In the end, the odds that at least two people have the same birthday are the inverse of the likelihood that they all have different birthdays.

$$1 - \begin{array}{l} \text{likelihood of} \\ n \text{ people all} \\ \text{having different} \\ \text{birthdays} \end{array} = 1 - \frac{365}{366} * \frac{364}{366} * \frac{363}{366} * \ldots * \frac{367 - n}{366}$$

Write a program which READs the number of people at the party and uses a DO-loop to compute the odds that at least two of the people have the same birthday. Use your program to find out how many people it takes to make the odds 90 percent or better.

16. Supposedly, if you take more and more terms of the series $1 + (1/2) + (1/3) + (1/4) + \ldots + (1/n)$, you can get as large a total as you want. But if you just leave out a term here and there so that you have the series $1 + (1/4) + (1/9) + \ldots + (1/n^2)$, the sum never gets very large.

    Write a program which prints an appropriately formatted table of the values of the two series for $n = 1, 2, 3, \ldots, 180$. Try to fit the entire table on one output page.

17. Write a program to illustrate the difference between REAL and DOUBLE PRECISION values. Add terms to the sum $1 + 1/2^2 + 1/3^2 + \cdots + 1/n^2 + \cdots$ until adding the next term does not affect the sum. Then print the total. Do this first using REAL variables, then with DOUBLE PRECISION variables.

18. Find out how many "bits" your Fortran system puts in floating-point significands by doing the following experiment. Start with NUMBIT = 1 and X = 0.5. Check to see if X + 1.0 equals 1.0. If so, exit and print NUMBIT. If not, halve X, increment NUMBIT, and repeat.

5 TOP-DOWN DESIGN

CHAPTER
PLAN
- *Introduce the concept of hierarchical decomposition*
- *Illustrate top-down design*

5.1 COMPLEXITY AND HIERARCHY

People manage complexity by constructing hierarchical descriptions. For example, a particular computer system might be described as a CPU, a memory, and an I/O system. The CPU itself might consist of a control unit and an arithmetic/logic unit; the memory, a collection of bytes and a refresh system; the I/O system, a printer, terminal, and disks. So far, there are three levels in this description of a computer system hierarchy. The top level, "computer system," is described as a collection of three components; each of the second-level components is described as a collection of subcomponents (e.g., CPU breaks down to arithmetic/logic and control), and this breakdown could continue *ad infinitum*. If the breakdown terminates when the functions of the components on the bottom level are evident or well explained to the intended audience, the system can be understood. If the explanation skips all the middle levels and goes directly to the bottom level, a person trying to understand it would have to group components, and reconstruct the intervening levels, to be able to comprehend the system as a whole.

Programs that describe complex processes should be constructed in this same hierarchical fashion. An overall plan for the program should enumerate and relate its three or four major steps. A second level plan should be constructed for each major step, and so on.

Steps in Program Design

---

1. **Problem statement:** *State the problem you are trying to solve as precisely as you can.*
2. **Input/output description:** Describe in precise terms the input your program will have, how it is to manipulate the input, and the output it will have.
3. **Stepwise refinement:** Describe the process your program is to perform in terminology closer to that which the computer can understand. Continue refining your description until you have something you can code directly into Fortran.
4. **Fortran coding:** Translate the statements in your final refinement from step 3 into Fortran.

The technique of expanding the plan in several levels of detail is known as **top-down design** or the method of **stepwise refinement.** It is an important concept in programming. In fact, it is an important concept in the more general task of problem solving. The idea is to start with an overall description of an algorithm in which the tasks to be performed are described in general terms and laid out in the correct order. Then you look at each task and explain in greater detail how to carry it out. The plans you come up with in this step are subplans that refine the general description in the overall **(top-level)** plan. Sometimes even the subplans are not yet detailed enough for the computer. If they aren't, you refine the complicated steps in the subplans and continue this re-

How to program

finement process until you're satisfied with the level of detail. Using this technique the programmer can handle more and more complex problems by avoiding the consideration of minor details until the overall design is established. The levels of complexity in the solution are sorted out, and the plans at each level are short and comprehensible.

So far your programming experience is limited, but even at this stage you can probably see some advantages in the top-down approach because you realize that details can be overwhelming. They can obscure the solution if you worry about them too soon.

5.2 PROGRAM DESIGN EXAMPLE

To illustrate the use of top-down design, consider the development of a more elaborate version of the bowling-average program of Section 4.2. We would like to make the program handle the scores for the whole team in one run. As it stands, to get the averages for the whole team, we have to make up a data set for an individual team member, run the program on that data set, then make up another data set for another team member, run the program again, and so on. It gets tedious.

It would be more convenient to be able to put all the data sets together and run the program just once. Let's consider what sorts of things we would need to do to convert our old program to handle the one-run mode of operation. First, we would need some way to identify team members so we could tell whose average was whose in the printout. For this data, we'll use a CHARACTER variable to record their names.

Here's how we'll make up the combined data set: on the first line put a team member's name; then on the next three lines put that member's scores for the match; on the next line put a negative number (that's the termination signal). After that, we start the sequence again: name, score, score, score, termination signal, and so on—one group like this for each team member. At the end, we put a special name, say, "*END*".

We plan to have a loop that gets a team member's identifier from a data line, computes that member's average score, and then moves on to the next team member.

Figure 5.2.1 Team Bowling Averages

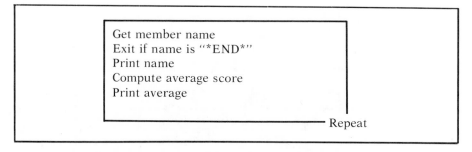

In this way we can use our old program as a component of our new program. The overall strategy (the **top level** in our design) is shown in Figure 5.2.1. The algorithm is simply one big READ loop that exits when the computer encounters the termination signal—the data line that has a negative number instead of a team member's identifier.

Since we have already written the component of our program which adds up an individual's list of transactions, it is easy for us to view that process as a single operation. The top-down design process isn't usually this easy. The components of the algorithm need to be separated out and clearly identified as subtasks even before we know exactly how we'll design the subtask algorithms. Usually, the hardest step is to choose a good way to split up the problem at the top level. The essence of good problem solving is to find a good way to decompose the problem into subproblems.

> **problem decomposition:** slicing a problem into subproblems. Good decomposition leads to good solutions.

Figure 5.2.2, a stepwise refinement of the top-level plan, details the operations summarized by "compute average score." You may want to look at Section 4.2 again to review the process of computing the average. The plan in Figure 5.2.2 is the same as the one in Section 4.2 where we solved the bowling-average problem for a single individual.

Figure 5.2.2   Computing an Individual's Bowling Average

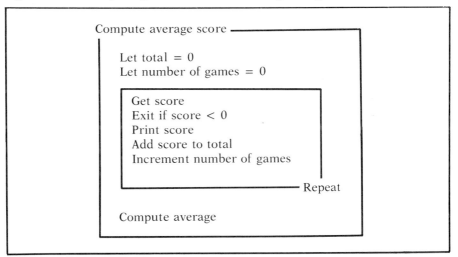

```
COMMENT:            CALCULATE AVERAGE BOWLING SCORES FOR
C                   ALL TEAM MEMBERS
C                   DATA:  ONE GROUP FOR EACH TEAM MEMBER
C                   GROUP:MEMBER NAME
C                         SCORE
C                         SCORE
C                         SCORE
C                          -1   (MEMBER TERMINATION SIGNAL)
C                   NOTE: *END* FOLLOWING THE LAST GROUP
C                         SERVES TO TERMINATE THE GROUPS.
```

(Continued on following page)

```
            INTEGER SCORE, TOTAL, G, AVG, ENDSCR, NAMELEN
            PARAMETER (NAMLEN=20)
            CHARACTER*(NAMLEN) MEMBER, ENDMEM
            PARAMETER (ENDSCR=0, ENDMEM='*END*')
C                       GET MEMBER IDENTIFIER
  100       READ *, MEMBER
             IF (MEMBER .EQ. ENDMEM) GO TO 400
C                       PRINT MEMBER IDENTIFIER
            PRINT *, MEMBER
C                       COMPUTE MEMBER'S AVERAGE

            TOTAL = 0
            G = 0
C                       GET SCORES, PRINT, AND TALLY
  200       READ *, SCORE
             IF (SCORE .LT. ENDSCR) GO TO 300
             PRINT *, '     SCORE:', SCORE
             TOTAL = TOTAL + SCORE
             G = G + 1
             GO TO 200
C                       PRINT AVERAGE
  300       AVG = NINT(REAL(TOTAL)/REAL(G))
            PRINT *, '    AVERAGE:', AVG
            GO TO 100
  400       END
```

Data

```
'BOB'
 167    (SCORE FOR BOB)
 142    (SCORE FOR BOB)
 159    (SCORE FOR BOB)
  -1    (TERMINATION SIGNAL FOR BOB)
'JON'
 139    (SCORE FOR JON)
 186    (SCORE FOR JON)
 152    (SCORE FOR JON)
  -1    (TERMINATION SIGNAL FOR JON)
'*END*'
```

Output

```
BOB
    SCORE:  167
    SCORE:  142
    SCORE:  159
      AVERAGE: 156
JON
    SCORE:  139
    SCORE:  186
    SCORE:  152
      AVERAGE: 159
```

Finally, Figure 5.2.3 displays the whole process as a nested loop, inserting the plan of Figure 5.2.2 at the appropriate place in the plan of Figure 5.2.1. The expanded plan matches the Fortran program.

Figure 5.2.3   Bowling-Average Algorithm as a Nested Loop

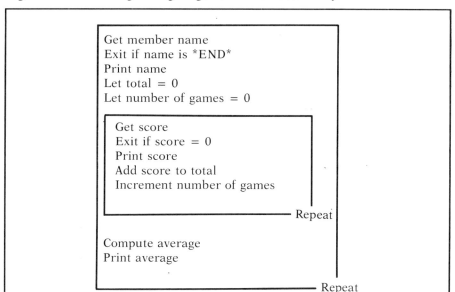

5.2 EXERCISES

1. Describe the similarity between the knitting algorithm of Section 1.4 and the bowling-average program in this section.
2. What happens in our bowling-average program if some players bowl more lines than others?

5 PROBLEMS

Program Design Problems

1. The phone company has asked you to write a program that PRINTs phone bills. Basic service costs $4.00 plus $1.25 for each extension phone; local calls are computed at the rate of 4.5¢ per message unit; local tax is 5 percent; federal tax is 10 percent. Be careful not to tax past-due balances or local calls. Input to your program is the customer's account number, the number of extensions, long distance expense, message units, and the past due balance. The output should include the account number, the past-due amount, the total bill, the service cost, local call cost, long distance expense, and local and federal taxes. PRINT out at least five phone bills.
2. The Good News Ice Cream Company sells 500,000 quarts of ice cream a year. The stores pay 85¢ a quart for each of Good News' 12 "natural" flavors. Raw materials cost 30¢ a quart.

Good News' research department reports that a new process has been developed that will cut the cost of raw materials by one-third, to 20¢ a quart; however, the new process has the side effects of making the ice cream a little foamy and slightly less smooth. The marketing department estimates that sales will be hurt by these changes. When pressed for figures, they say sales could drop by as little as 10 percent or by as much as 50 percent—they can't tell.

Assume that Good News still charges the stores 85¢ a quart and that the conversion of the plant to handle the new process is paid for with a 10-year loan, with payments of $32,000 a year. Write a program which, given the percentage loss of sales, shows the loss or gain that would result each year for the first 10 years if a switch to the new ingredients is made.

3. Write a program that uses the trapezoidal rule to approximate the area under the curve $f(x) = x^3$ from $x = 0$ to $x = 1$. The formula is:

Area $= (h/2)[f(0) + 2f(h) + 2f(2h) + \cdots + 2f(1 - h) + f(1)]$

The step size h should be chosen so that $1/h$ is a whole number (integer). What this formula does is to divide the area into strips of width h and to sum up estimates of the area of each strip.

(*Optional:* Use a loop to compute the area for several values of h, say 0.1, 0.01, and 0.001, and compare the results.)

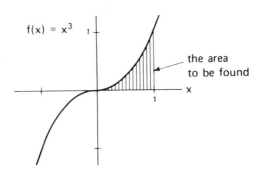

4. Write a program to compute the mean and variance of a set of numbers.

Mean   = sum of numbers/n
Variance = (sum of squares/n) − mean^2

where n is the number of terms in the sum.

5. The thermostat in a heating system generates a command to the furnace on the basis of the difference between the setting on the thermostat dial and the current room temperature.

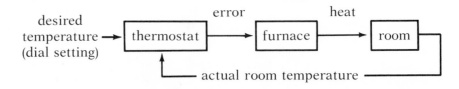

In the particular heating system we're dealing with here, the command to the furnace is proportional to the difference between the desired temperature and the actual temperature. (Most thermostats just send one of two commands to the furnace—"all the way on" or "all the way off.")

Convert the following plan into a program and run it to study the effects of changing the proportionality constant k. Try $k = 0.5$, 0.95, 1.0, and 1.5 (and others if you like). The assumption in the plan is that the room temperature starts at 65°F and that the thermostat is set to 72°F. It also includes a term that corresponds to the time delay while the room heats up. Use the output to draw graphs of the various cases. Choose a value that you would like k to have if the system were controlling the heating of *your* house.

Take care to print appropriate messages if strange things happen— like temperatures below freezing or above 120°F. In such cases the setting of k must be poor. Stop the loop and try another setting.

```
Read k
Exit if k < 0
Let Old Temp = 65
Let Temp = 65
Let Thermo = 72
Let Time = 0

    Print current Temp

    Let Command = k*(Thermo − Temp)
    Let Delay = (Temp + 0.1*Old Temp)/1.1
    Let New Temp = Delay + Command

    Let Old Temp = Temp
    Let Temp = New Temp
    Increase Time by 1
                                    Exit if Time > 30
                                        Repeat
```

6. Write a program that simulates fleas on a dog, using the equations below. Perform the simulation for several different values of the parameters and see what happens. (For some values, the fleas die out, for some they overwhelm the poor dog, for some they reach an uncomfortable compromise with the dog.) For each set of parameter values, print the flea population each minute for a total of 60 simulated minutes.

   Equations:

   SCRACH = (SCRATE*FLEAS) or TIRED, whichever is less (use the MIN function for this)

   FLEAS (next minute) = FLEAS + NEWFLE*FLEAS − DEATHF*FLEAS − SCRACH

Memory Cell	Meaning	Typical Value
FLEAS	The total number of fleas on the dog this minute.	50
SCRACH	The number of scratches the dog makes this minute.	10
SCRATE	The number of scratches the dog makes per minute per flea.	.1
TIRED	The maximum number of scratches the dog can make each minute.	20
NEWFLE	The fraction of fleas born or hopping on the dog each minute.	.2
DEATHF	The fraction of fleas which die or jump off the dog each minute.	.1

6 DEBUGGING YOUR PROGRAMS

CHAPTER PLAN
- *Emphasize program design*
- *Distinguish compile-time errors from execution-time errors*
- *Present an example of the debugging process*

6.1 INTRODUCTION

So far it must seem that we think if you read this book you'll be able to write programs that contain no errors. After all, all our examples have involved programs that work properly. Probably you are spending most of your time rewriting programs that *don't* work. As you know, the often laborious task of getting a program to run the way you want is called **debugging.** This chapter gives hints about how to proceed.

The best course, obviously, would be to avoid errors in the first place. By using plans, and by designing your program carefully before you write down anything in Fortran, you can avoid an amazing number of bugs. By using comment statements in your program, you can make it much easier to follow the logic of the troublesome parts of your program. By taking your time and checking each card carefully after you punch it, you can eliminate a number of typing errors. Even if you do all these things, however, you will, no doubt, still have bugs in your programs. Everybody does, and everybody *will* for a long time. Try to think of designing programs as a four-step process, as described in Chapter 5: (1) problem statement, (2) input/output description, (3) stepwise refinement of the solution, and (4) Fortran coding. It won't always be possible to keep these steps completely separate. Sometimes you'll have to repeat parts of the process (see Section 1.3), but using this general approach can be very helpful.

> **debug:** to remove the errors (bugs) from a program

Let's assume that you've done all you can beforehand, you've run your program, and it doesn't work right. There are three main ways your program can fail. First, it might be that you have written some illegal statements and the compiler couldn't figure out what you meant. We'll call these errors **compile-time errors** because they are detected in the process of translating your Fortran statements into machine language. Another possibility is that, even though you've written a legal Fortran program, it has illegal consequences; for example, it might wind up dividing by a variable which has the value zero. We'll call such errors **execution-time errors** because they are detected while the machine language instructions corresponding to your program are being performed (executed). The third possibility is that, while your program produces results, the results are wrong. For example, if your program was supposed to compute the area of a basketball court and it gave a negative number as the answer, you'd know right away that something was wrong. We'll call these kinds of errors **logic errors** because they are caused by flaws in the way you wrote your program, errors in your logic. Often logic errors cause execution-time errors, and we'll tend to lump the two together for that reason.

6.2   COMPILE-TIME ERRORS

Compile-time errors are easy to find—the compiler itself will carefully mark where they occur and will supply an error message that usually has something to do with the problem. Typographical errors often cause this sort of error. Things like accidentally leaving out the replacement operator (=), forgetting to mark column 6 on continuation lines, leaving out an asterisk (*), using too many letters in a memory cell name, and not balancing parentheses are typical compile-time errors. If you're not absolutely certain of the form of a statement you want to use, look it up.

Sometimes one error can lead to lots of error messages. For example, an error in a type statement which was supposed to declare an INTE-GER variable

```
INTERGER P
```

may result in additional messages each time you try to use the variable, as in N = MAX0(P,N), because the compiler won't know that P is of type INTEGER (it will assume P is REAL). The mistake in your declaration (misspelling INTEGER) causes this cascade of errors. Fortunately, it is likely that some error messages in this cascade caused by the erroneous declaration will suggest the possibility that a memory cell of the wrong type is being used, a good hint toward what went wrong.

> **error cascade:** Each compile-time error leaves the compiler with less information than it needs to compile the program properly. Often this lack of information causes the compiler to flag errors in statements which are actually correct. This is an error cascade.

Another thing to watch for is this: if you have *two* errors in one expression, e.g.,

    A = 2(1+AARDOR))

sometimes only the *first* error is discovered by the compiler. If you don't look closely, you might correct the statement to read

    A = 2 * (1+AARDOR))

only to discover another error message staring at you after your next run. There are too many right parentheses. Look over your statements carefully to find all the errors at once.

> **multiple errors:** Because people tend to make errors in groups, it is quite common for one statement to have several errors. When this happens, the compiler often fails to catch some of them. Check each erroneous statement carefully for multiple errors.

Compile-Time Errors

6.3 EXECUTION-TIME ERRORS

We face a problem in writing this section—many errors that will occur are errors which are detected by the actual machine hardware, when the Fortran compiler isn't around to help you. This means that the details of errors are machine-dependent and vary widely from one model to another (let alone the variations from manufacturer to manufacturer). What we'll do is go through an example and indicate the nature of the errors. Your instructor should be able to tell you exactly what the error messages will look like on your system.

To correct an error you need to know (1) where in your program the error occurred and (2) what caused it. To help locate the error, we'll describe three (increasingly difficult) ways to proceed. First, you may be fortunate and be provided with a message that tells you which line of your program the error occurred in or at least at which memory location in the machine it occurred. Second, by studying which of your PRINT statements were printed before the error occurred, you may be able to deduce in what part of your program the error occurred. This is a reason to put extra PRINT statements in programs you are debugging. (On some systems, with some types of errors, the last few PRINT statements' results may not appear even though they were executed, however.) Third, you may be able to infer where the error occurred from the nature of the error. For example, if your program exceeded its time limit, then it probably was in a loop at the time. If it tried to divide by zero, then obviously it was carrying out some statement which involved a division. If you absolutely cannot locate the error, you will have to insert additional PRINT statements in suspicious spots of your program and run it again.

> The precise nature of an execution-time error, that is, the error mentioned in the resulting error message, is often only the tip of the iceberg. You must deduce the underlying cause.

To fix the error once it's located, you must determine its cause. If the error is for time limit, then the conditions for stopping a loop must not have been met for some reason. If it is an arithmetic sort of error (overflow, underflow, division by zero), then some variable is getting a value you didn't expect. If it is an "address out of range," that means your program attempted to use a memory cell it shouldn't have—this is almost always caused by an array subscript which has an improper value. You will learn about arrays later.

Many errors result from bad logic in the program, which ultimately makes the instructions in your program impossible to perform, thus helping you detect the errors. However, some logic errors simply cause your program to produce incorrect results without asking the computer to perform impossible operations. These errors are often more difficult to fix—you simply may not notice that there is anything wrong. Just because something comes out of a computer doesn't mean it's right! It's a good idea to run a small test case in order to verify that your program really is working properly. If the small test doesn't work as you expect, you may be able to locate the trouble, or you may be forced to get more information by sprinkling your program with PRINT statements to give you partial results. Once the error is located and you know what caused it, alter the program and run it again. It is an *extremely* bad bet ever to assume that the error was a fluke and to run the program again hoping the error will go away by itself!

Test your program on simple data where you know the results before you assume it is producing correct results on more complicated data.

Print partial results to trace the execution of the program and find errors.

Once you get the hang of it, debugging is almost fun. There's a Sherlock Holmes flavor to it. To illustrate, we'll run through an actual case from our programming diary.

Debugging Example. The following program is supposed to compute the average cost of all the laundry detergents we found at the supermarket. Here's what we started with after drawing a plan, converting it to Fortran, and removing the compile-time errors.

```
COMMENT:                   THIS IS A PROGRAM TO FIND THE AVERAGE COST
C                          OF LAUNDRY DETERGENT
          REAL SUM, PRICE, WGT, AVG
          INTEGER N
          N = 0
          SUM = 0.0
C                          READ PRICES AND WEIGHTS.
   10     READ *, PRICE, WGT
C                          ANOTHER BRAND TO AVERAGE IN
          N = N + 1
C                          IF PRICE IS NEGATIVE, WE'RE DONE.
          IF (PRICE .LE. 0.0)  GO TO 20
C                          ADD IN UNIT PRICE OF THIS BRAND
          SUM = SUM + PRICE/WGT
          GO TO 10
COMMENT:                   GOT THEM ALL--COMPUTE AVERAGE
   20     AVG = SUM/N
          PRINT *, 'THE AVERAGE PRICE PER POUND IS', AVG
          END
```

We made up some data with a few easily computed results to test our program before turning it loose on our real data.

```
 2.00   2.0
10.00   5.0
```

Selecting a Laundry Detergent

If our program had worked the way we had wanted, it would have gotten the result (2./2. + 10./5.)/2 = 1.5. We ran it and, not only didn't we get 1.5, we didn't get anything at all except an error message telling us that an "end of file" had been reached.

```
'ERROR 65--EOF ON FILE INPUT'
```

Needless to say, we were a little disappointed. The error message seemed a bit obscure, but since statement 10 is the only READ (i.e., "input") statement, we realized that the error must have occurred in statement 10. This set us to thinking . . . The program must not have stopped READing soon enough and must have gone on past what we intended to be our last data line, looking for another one, and finally READing beyond the end of our data.

When eliminating complicated errors, especially in large programs, it helps to form a hypothesis, keeping notes on the hypotheses you have checked. Eventually, you can deduce the roots of the problems.

We checked our data and, sure enough, we'd forgotten to put a termination line at the end of the data. We added a final data line with −1.0 in the first field and tossed our program in to be run again. This, by the way, is a *mistake*. If we had taken a little more time to go over our program carefully, we could have avoided the next round of errors.

This time we got no error messages, but the result was

```
THE AVERAGE PRICE PER POUND IS $1.000000
```

"What?" we said. "We expected a much higher average!" We stared at the statements for a while but didn't see anything wrong. We looked at the data cards carefully to see if we had mispunched any (wishing all the time that we had placed statements like

```
PRINT*, 'PRICE:', PRICE, ', WEIGHT:', WGT
```

after the READ statement). Since we didn't find anything wrong, we began a time-honored process. We wrote down the names of all the memory cells we used in the program and drew a box beside each. Then we put one finger beside the first statement of the program, keeping one hand free to write values into the 'memory cells' as necessary. We analyzed the effect of the statement our finger was on. If it altered a memory cell value, we crossed out any old value we had for that cell and wrote in the new one. If it was a control statement like

```
GO TO 10
```

we moved our finger appropriately. After a while we found the problem. By the time we got to statement 20, N had the value 3.0. even though there were only two brands of detergent in the data. Our program was counting the end-of-data signal as part of the regular data!

---

mirror printing: It is usually a good idea, especially in the debugging stage of writing a program, to print values obtained by READ statements immediately after READing. This is called mirror printing. It helps discover errors in the program which cause the data to be misinterpreted.

Now that our attention was drawn to it, we were embarrassed to discover that our loop wasn't even one of the recommended forms (pretest, posttest, or READ-loop). We made the loop into a READ loop by moving the statement

```
N = N+1
```

and its associated comment so that they appeared immediately *after* the IF test, not before. This had the twin benefits of making the loop into a standard form and of allowing 1 to be added to N only when the data represented a legitimate detergent price and weight.

We looked our program over carefully, decided to change the PRINT statement to

```
PRINT*,'AVERAGE PRICE:', AVG,
+ ',NUMBER OF BRANDS:',N
```

and ran it again. If we'd been awake enough to use this more informative PRINT statement to begin with, we would have been able to find the problem more quickly.

The computer is a "great humbler." It seems that no matter how careful you are, there will always be bugs in your programs. Learning to

avoid them requires great patience and self-control. Like a master crafts-man, a good programmer produces well-thought-out, finely finished work.

Postmortem

The following is a summary of what we learned from the example:

1. **Plan:** No matter how simple a program may be, always start with a plan.
2. **Use approved structures:** Deviating from the approved methods for writing loops can cause errors, some of which are very subtle and hard to find.
3. **Mirror printing:** Print the values that are read in. It could be the data that causes errors.
4. **Trace:** If there are errors in the results, trace through the program by hand, keeping track of the values of all memory cells.
5. **Keep notes:** Write down everything that occurs during the debugging process. Your notes may help you deduce the problem.

For a number of good ideas about how to improve your programs, make them more readable, more easily debugged, more efficient, and so forth, see the little book *Elements of Programming Style*, 2nd edition, by B. W. Kernighan and P.J. Plauger, McGraw-Hill, 1978.

7 SELECTING ALTERNATIVES

CHAPTER PLAN
- *Introduce the concept of selection*
- *Show how to implement if-then-else*
- *Introduce logical operators (AND, OR, and NOT)*
- *Introduce logical variables*
- *Explain CHARACTER comparisons (collation)*

7.1   TWO ALTERNATIVES (IF-THEN-ELSE)

In addition to the ability to automatically *repeat* complex sequences of commands, computers can also *select* an appropriate list of operations based on the result of previous calculations. The programmer can describe two different calculations and direct the computer to use the one which is relevant under the current conditions of the computation. The choice between them is made in the same way as the decision to repeat in a loop. The programmer sets up a test using relational operators (.EQ., .NE., etc.) and then specifies which calculations are to be performed if the relationship is verified, as well as those to be performed if the relationship doesn't hold.

Suppose, for example, that you wanted to write a program to convert between Fahrenheit and Celsius temperatures. If the program is to be able to handle the conversion in either direction, from Fahrenheit to Celsius or from Celsius to Fahrenheit, then you must specify both formulas in the program and provide a way to select between them. Basically, the algorithm proceeds like this:

Plan   Get temperature and type.
              If type is Fahrenheit
                  then ——————————————
                      | Convert to Celsius.
                      | Print results.

                  else ——————————————
                      | Convert to Fahrenheit.
                      | Print results.

The idea is to select the appropriate conversion formula depending on which type of temperature was provided as input. The key words in selecting the alternative are **if, then,** and **else.** They form a sentence.

A selection like this can be coded in Fortran with an IF statement. Figure 7.1.1 illustrates the form of such a selection.

Fahrenheit and Celsius

$$F = \frac{9}{5} C + 32$$

$$C = \frac{5}{9} (F - 32)$$

where F stands for degrees Fahrenheit and C stands for degrees Celsius

Figure 7.1.1   The Skeletal Form of Selection

```
If "condition"
then ─────────────
    │ Perform first alternative.

else ─────────────
    │ Perform second alternative.

Fortran translation:

IF (test for condition) THEN

    Fortran operation
        •
        •           these statements perform
        •           the first alternative
    Fortran operation
ELSE
    Fortran operation

        •
        •           second alternative
        •
    Fortran operation
ENDIF
```

As you can see in the program, we have assumed that the temperature's type is indicated by putting an "F" (for Fahrenheit) or a "C" (for Celsius) after the temperature. Thus, the data line will have two values on it: a REAL number specifying the temperature measured in degrees and a letter (CHARACTER*1) indicating which type of degree was used in the measurement.

IF-THEN Statement

form

IF (e_1 *rel* e_2) **THEN**
   then-block
ELSE
   else-block
ENDIF
e_1 and e_2 are both arithmetic expressions or both character
   expressions.
rel is a relational operator.
then-block is a sequence of Fortran statements.
else-block is a sequence of Fortran statements.

meaning
Perform the commands in the *then-block* if the expressed relationship
between e_1 and e_2 holds; otherwise (else) perform the commands in
the *else-block*.

example

```
IF (D .NE. 0.0) THEN
   QUO = X/D                            }   the
   PRINT *, X,'/',D, '=',QUO                then-block

ELSE
   QUO = UNDEF                          }    the
   PRINT *, X,'/',D, '= UNDEFINED'          else-block

ENDIF
```

```
COMMENT:              CONVERTING BETWEEN TEMPERATURE SCALES
      REAL TEMP, F, C, FFREEZ, DRATIO
      CHARACTER*(1) TYPE, FAHREN
      PARAMETER (FFREEZ = 32.0, DRATIO = 5.0/9.0, FAHREN = 'F')
      READ *, TEMP, TYPE
      IF (TYPE .EQ. FAHREN) THEN
            C = DRATIO*(TEMP - FFREEZ)
            PRINT *, TEMP, ' DEG F IS', C, ' DEG C'
      ELSE
            F = (1.0/DRATIO)*TEMP + FFREEZ
            PRINT *, TEMP, ' DEG C IS', F, 'DEG F'
      ENDIF
      END
```

Input

98.6   'F'

Output

98.60000 DEG IS   37.00000 DEG C

(Continued on following page)

Input

100.0   'C'

Output

100.0000 DEG C IS   212.0000 DEG F

7.1   EXERCISES

1. Explain the difference between **looping** and **selection.**
2. Which of the following tasks require selection? Which need looping?
   a. Computing the total of a large collection of numbers
   b. Counting the number of data cards
   c. Printing an "L" or an "S" depending on the result of a previous computation
   d. Determining the sex of an insurance applicant
3. Write a plan for an algorithm to print the larger of two given numbers.
4. Translate your plan from exercise 3 into Fortran.
5. What would happen in the temperature conversion program if the person typing the data card accidentally typed

   98.6 'G'

   instead of

   98.6 'F'

7.2   MANY ALTERNATIVES (IF-THEN ELSE-IF)

Sometimes a computation calls for selection among several possible calculations. For example, a program for tabulating data on the populations of various water fowl in Big Thicket Wildlife Preserve might need to compute the number of observations of curlews, egrets, blue herons, and whooping cranes. If the data is entered as one observation per data line, then the central step in the calculation is to increase the observation count for the appropriate bird when the species of the bird is fetched from the data line. In other words, the program is going to contain a READ-loop in which we fetch the type of bird from a data line and then increase one of four observation counts depending on which type of bird was named.

We are obviously selecting among four different actions. Figure 7.2.1 details our strategy. The question is: how can we implement the algorithm in Fortran?

Figure 7.2.1   Bird Counting Algorithm

Start with C, E, H, and W = 0.

> Read bird type
>
> Exit if type is "no bird"
>
> Select type of bird
>
>   curlew: let C = C + 1
>
>   egret: let E = E + 1
>
>   heron: let H = H + 1
>
>   whooper: let W = W + 1
>
> ———————— Repeat

Print C, E, H, and W.

We need a generalized form of selection for multiple alternatives. To do this, we list the alternatives one after another with an **else-if block** for each one. Each else-if block is encoded like a two-way if-then-else.

ELSE IF Statement

form

ELSE IF (e_1 *rel* e_2) **THEN**
  else-if-block

meaning
Perform the commands in *else-if-block* if the relation e_1 *rel* e_2 is true

note
An ELSE IF statement may be used in place of or in addition to the ELSE part of an IF-THEN STATEMENT.

example

```
IF (B .EQ. 'C') THEN
   PRINT *, 'CURLEW'
ELSE IF (B .EQ. 'E') THEN
   PRINT *, 'EGRET'
ELSE IF (B .EQ. 'H') THEN
   PRINT *, 'BLUE HERON'
ELSE
   PRINT *, 'WHOOPING CRANE'
ENDIF
```

```
COMMENT:                    COUNTING BIRD OBSERVATIONS IN THE BIG THICKET
C                           DATA ENCODING
C                           'C' STANDS FOR CURLEW
C                           'E' STANDS FOR EGRET
C                           'H' STANDS FOR BLUE HERON
C                           'W' STANDS FOR WHOOPING CRANE
C                           'N' STAND FOR 'NO MORE BIRDS'
            INTEGER C, E, H, W
            CHARACTER*(1) BIRD, CURLEW, EGRET, HERON, WHOOP, ENDBRD
            PARAMETER (CURLEW = 'C', HERON = 'H', EGRET = 'E',
      +               WHOOP = 'W', ENDBRD = 'N')
            C = 0
            E = 0
            H = 0
            W = 0
100         READ *, BIRD
            IF (BIRD .EQ. ENDBRD) GO TO 200
               IF (BIRD .EQ. CURLEW) THEN
                  C = C + 1
               ELSE IF (BIRD .EQ. EGRET) THEN
                  E = E + 1
               ELSE IF (BIRD .EQ. HERON) THEN
                  H = H + 1
               ELSE
                  W = W + 1
               ENDIF
               GO TO 100
200         PRINT *, 'CURLEW SIGHTINGS:', C
            PRINT *, 'EGRET SIGHTINGS:', E
            PRINT *, 'BLUE HERON SIGHTINGS:', H
            PRINT *, 'WHOOPING CRANE SIGHTINGS:', W
            END
```

Input

```
'H'
'E'
'C'
'C'
'E'
'E'
'C'
'N'
```

Output

```
CURLEW SIGHTINGS:              3
EGRET SIGHTINGS:               3
BLUE HERON SIGHTINGS:             1
WHOOPING CRANE SIGHTINGS:            0
```

Indentation

In a selection (two-way or multi-way) the IF (. . .) THEN, ELSE IF (. . .) THEN, ELSE, and ENDIF statements should all start in the same column. The blocks of Fortran statements for each alternative should be indented.

IF *(condition)* **THEN**
   Fortran statement
     •
     •   ‖ indented
     •
   Fortran statement
ELSE IF *(condition)* **THEN**
   Fortran statement
     •
     •   ‖ indented
     •
   Fortran statement
ELSE
   Fortran statement
     •
     •   ‖ indented
     •
   Fortran statement
ENDIF

IF-THEN Statement with ELSE IF

form

IF *(logical-exp)* **THEN**
   then-block
ELSE IF *(logical-exp)* **THEN**
   then-block
   •
   •
   •
ELSE IF *(logical-exp)* **THEN**
   then-block
ELSE
   else-block
ENDIF

meaning
Perform the then-block associated with the first logical expression that is true; if none of the logical expressions is true, perform the else-block if it's present; if none is true and the else-block is omitted, take no action—just move on.

7.2 EXERCISES

1. What happens in the program for counting birds if some of the data lines have 'M' on them (standing for mallard ducks)?

2. Fix the program so that sightings of all types of birds other than curlews, egrets, blue herons, and whooping cranes get counted in a generalized counter for type "other."

3. What does your program for exercise 2 do if there are three ducks ('D') and seven sandpipers ('S') in the data? (Assume all other sightings are of type 'C', 'E', 'H', or 'W'.)

4. If your program from exercise 2 doesn't get 7 + 3 = 10 sightings of type "other" for the data given in exercise 3, fix it so it does.

5. Write a program which will print "BOX CARS," "CRAPS," or "SNAKE EYES" depending on whether a data card has a 12, 3, or 2 on it (respectively). Have it print "O.K." if the data line has any other number on it.

7.3 LOGICAL OPERATORS

Some algorithms require more complex decisions than can be easily expressed as relationships between one pair of values. For example, it may be necessary to decide whether a given number is between 90 and 100. None of the relational operators (.LE., .GE., etc.) is adequate by itself to express a test like this. What we need is a kind of composite operation: is the number both greater than 90 *and* less than 100? We can write combinations of relationships in Fortran with the .AND. and .OR. conjunctions.

The meaning of .AND. is just what you would expect. When two relations are connected with .AND., the composite has the value **true** when *both* relations are true. If either one is **false,** then the composite is false. This conforms with the common usage of "and" in English. If the weatherman reports, "It is raining and the sun is shining," then we would expect to see *both* sunshine *and* rain if we looked out the window. If either were missing, we'd lose confidence in the weatherman.

> A sunshiny shower
> won't last half an hour

On the other hand, when we use "or" in English, we normally mean that either one or the other is true, but not both. "He is heavy or he's wearing a pillow under his overalls." It's possible that both are true, but it's not what we expect. The .OR. in Fortran allows for *either* or *both*

> .AND. and .OR. need dots (periods) around them in Fortran. Otherwise the compiler would have trouble distinguishing them from memory cells named AND and OR.

parts being true. When two relationships are connected by .OR., then the composite is true if either one is true or if both are true. It is false only when both are false. For this reason the Fortran .OR. is referred to as the **inclusive or.** In English, "or" is normally used in the *exclusive* sense so we have to be a little careful with the Fortran .OR.. Its meaning occasionally fails to conform exactly to our intuition.

A composite relation in Fortran is written by putting one of the conjunctions (.AND. or .OR.) between two ordinary relational expressions. .AND. is used in the IF-THEN statement below.

```
IF (DISP .GT. 442.0 .AND. WEIGHT .LT. 3000.0) THEN
  PRINT *, 'HOT CAR'
ELSE
  PRINT *, 'NOT SO HOT'
ENDIF
```

This would print the first message (HOT CAR) if the contents of memory cell DISP exceeded 442.0 *and* the contents of WEIGHT were less than 3000.0; otherwise it would print NOT SO HOT.

.OR. is used similarly.

```
IF (PRICE .GT. 9000.00 .OR. NUMCYL .GT. 8) THEN
  PRINT *, 'CANNOT PURCHASE'
ELSE
  PRINT *, 'O.K. TO BUY'
ENDIF
```

The computer would print CANNOT PURCHASE for a Ferrari (price exceeds 9000.00 and there are 12 cylinders) or a Porsche (price is too high, even though number of cylinders, 6, is o.k.). On the other hand, a $7000.00 Sunbird with 6 cylinders would be O.K. TO BUY.

A common error is to leave out parts of logical expressions, assuming the computer will get the gist.

```
IF (M .GT. 0 .AND. .LT. 100)  GO TO 200
```
incomplete relation

corrected version
```
IF (M .GT. 0 .AND. M .LT. 100)  GO TO 200
```

A third operation may be applied when algorithms require a complicated decision. The .NOT. operation reverses the value of the test.

For example, suppose we are interested in studying the sum 1/2 + 1/3 + 1/4 + 1/5 + ...Obviously, as we include more and more terms in the sum, the total gets bigger and bigger, but how big and how fast? We decide to begin our investigation by writing a program which keeps adding terms until either a thousand terms are included, or the total exceeds 10.0, whichever happens first. Once we have a rough idea of how the sum grows, we can change our program and refine our investigation.

Our plan is shown in Figure 7.3.1. We can express our loop-exit criteria with this composite relation:

```
D .GT. 1000.0 .OR. SUM .GT. 10.0
```

We must repeat if this composite is *not true,* and we can do it in Fortran by using the .NOT. operation. Putting a .NOT. in front of the whole thing reverses the result.

```
 IF (.NOT. (D .GT. 1000.0 .OR SUM .GT. 10.0))
+  GO TO 100
```

will cause a repetition from statement 100 as long as the sum is not yet completed.

Figure 7.3.1   Adding Successive Fractions

```
Let SUM = 0.0
Let D = 1.0

    ┌─────────────────────────────┐
    │ Let D = D + 1.0             │
    │ Let SUM = SUM + 1.0/D       │
    └──────────┬──────────────────┘
               └── Repeat if not finished

Print SUM and the number of terms included in SUM.

Note: We are "finished" if D > 1000.0 or if SUM > 10.0
```

We need the extra parentheses in the IF statement because the .NOT. operation applies to the shortest possible part of the expression it's used in. If we had written

```
IF (.NOT. (D .GT. 1000.0 .OR. SUM .GT. 10.0)) GO TO 100
```

then .NOT. would apply only to the first relation, D .GT. 1000.0. In this case we could just as well have used the opposite relation D .LE. 1000.0 to avoid the .NOT. altogether (D .LE. 1000.0 and .NOT. D .GT. 1000.0 mean the same thing).

The Fortran version of Figure 7.3.1 is shown below.

```
          REAL SUM, D
          SUM = 0.0
          D = 1.0
100       D = D + 1.0
              SUM = SUM + 1.0/D
              IF (.NOT. (D .GT. 1000.00 .OR.
      +              SUM .GT. 10.0))  GO TO 100
          PRINT *, 'SUM = ', SUM
          PRINT *, D - 1, ' TERMS USED'
          END
```

Output

```
SUM =       6.486470
        1000.000 TERMS USED
```

There are two more logical operators, .EQV. and .NEQV. . They are roughly analogous to equality and inequality. Two logical values are **equivalent** if they have the same value (i.e., both are true or both are false). Thus, this test

```
IF ((A .GT. 10) .EQV. (B .GT. 5)) THEN
```

can succeed in two different ways. The test succeeds if A is greater than 10 and B is greater than 5 (both parts are true); and it succeeds if A is not greater than 10 and B is not greater than 5 (both parts are false). In every other case (for example, if A has the value 9 and B the value 6) the test fails.

The equivalence operator (.EQV.) and its counterpart, **nonequivalence** (.NEQV.) provide easier ways to express tests which can be made using the .AND., .OR., and .NOT. operators alone, if you wanted to go to the trouble.

---

equivalent logical expressions
```
(A .GT. 10) .EQV. (B .GT. 5)

((A .GT. 10) .AND. (B .GT. 5)) .OR.
 (.NOT. (A .GT. 10) .AND. .NOT. (B .GT. 5))
```

equivalent logical expressions
```
(A  .GT. 10) .NEQV. (B .GT. 5)

((A .GT. 10) .AND. .NOT. (B .GT. 5)) .OR.
      ( .NOT. (A .GT. 10) .AND. (B .GT. 5))
```

Composite relations which use .AND., .OR., .EQV., .NEQV., and .NOT. operators are known as **logical expressions.** In general they are built from one or more ordinary relational expressions connected by .AND., .OR., .EQV., or .NEQV. operators. In addition, .NOT. can be used to reverse the meaning of an expression.

---

logical: a term borrowed from a branch of mathematical philosophy known as "logic," which is concerned with the study of symbolic expressions whose values must be either "true" or "false"

---

precedence: In general it's best to avoid using very complicated logical expressions with many operators in one expression, but if you find it unavoidable, you need to know that in the absence of parentheses the computer will do the .NOT.'s first, then the .AND.'s, then the .OR.'s, and finally the .EQV.'s and .NEQV.'s

7.3 EXERCISES

1. Write an IF statement which will cause a repetition if the value of X is less than half as large as that of Y and Y is nonzero.

2. What gets printed?

```
REAL X, Y
X = 2.0
Y = 3.0
IF (X + 2.0 .GE. Y AND Y .LT. 0.0) THEN
  PRINT *, 'ONE'
ELSE
  PRINT *, 'TWO'
ENDIF
END
```

3. What gets printed?

```
        INTEGER N, M
        N = 2
        M = 10
100     IF (N .GT. M .OR.
    +       (N .GT. 100 .AND. M .GT. 100))  GO TO 200
          N = N * N
          M = M + M
          GO TO 100
200     PRINT *, 'M=', M, ' N=', N
        END
```

4. What would get printed in the program of exercise 3 if we changed the third statement to M = 50?

5. What if we changed the third statement to M = 20?

7.4 IF-THEN, NO ELSE

Some algorithms call for a selection between two alternatives where one alternative requires some action to be taken and the other needs *no* action. This is like an IF-THEN-ELSE structure with the else-block empty. To handle this type of problem, we are allowed to leave out the else-block in our Fortran IF-THEN statement.

To see how this can be useful, suppose the chamber of commerce of Socorro, New Mexico, has asked us to compute the average nighttime temperature for the year. They will provide us with data containing temperature readings (°F) and time of day (24-hour clock). A line with the numbers 31.3 and 1830 would represent a temperature reading of 31.3°F at 6:30 P.M. (1830 on the 24-hour clock is 6:30 P.M.).

The data has been obtained from a machine at the weather bureau which automatically records a reading every 4 hours. As a result, some of the data contains daytime temperatures. Our program must ignore them.

This is the type of situation where an IF-THEN is needed without any else-block, as shown in the plan of Figure 7.4.1. We need to add up all the nighttime temperatures, but we take no action on daytime temperatures. Translating to Fortran is no problem; just omit the ELSE and put the ENDIF right after the then-block as shown on the program below.

Figure 7.4.1 Computing the Average Nighttime Temperature

```
Set SUM and N to 0.

    ┌────────────────────────────────────────────────┐
    │ Read TEMP and TIME                               │
    │ EXIT if "end of data"                            │
    │                                                  │
    │ If nighttime                                     │
    │    then ┌──────────────────────────────┐         │
    │         │ Add TEMP to SUM.             │         │
    │         │ Increase N.                  │         │
    │         └──────────────────────────────┘         │
    └──────────────────────────────────────────── Repeat
Print SUM/N.

Note: Nighttime is before 0600 or after 2100.
```

```
          REAL AVNITE, TEMP
          INTEGER NITES, TIME, SIXAM, NINEPM
          PARAMETER (SIXAM = 0600, NINEPM = 2100)
          NITES = 0
          AVNITE = 0.0
    100   READ *, TEMP, TIME
          IF (TIME .LT. 0) GO TO 200
             IF (TIME .LT. SIXAM .OR. TIME .GT. NINEPM) THEN
               AVNITE = AVNITE + TEMP
               NITES = NITES + 1
             ENDIF
             GO TO 100
    200   PRINT *, 'AVERAGE NIGHTTIME TEMPERATURE', AVNITE/NITES
          END
```

Data

```
78.0    2200
66.0    0500
68.2    0600
44.1    1600
73.5    0200
66.0    1000
56.3    1800
91.7    0900
77.0    1200
88.0    1500
0.00     -1
```

Output

```
AVERAGE NIGHTTIME TEMPERATURE          72.50000
```

Even multi-alternative selections may omit the else-block. If the chamber of commerce had wanted us to compute the average temperature during the midday hours (9:00 A.M. to 3:00 P.M.) in addition to the average nighttime temperature, we would have to put a second alternative in our algorithm, but we still would have to ignore some of the data. As a result, we would have an IF-THEN-ELSEIF statement with no ELSE at the end. The following program illustrates this case.

```
            REAL AVNITE, TEMP, AVDAY
            INTEGER NITES, TIME, DAYS, SIXAM, NINEPM, NINEAM, THREEPM
            PARAMETER (SIXAM = 0600, NINEPM = 2100, NINEAM = 0900,
       +              THREEPM = 1500)
            DAYS = 0
            NITES = 0
            AVDAY = 0.0
            AVNITE = 0.0
  100       READ *, TEMP, TIME
              IF (TIME .LT. 0) GO TO 200
              IF (TIME .LT. SIXAM .OR. TIME .GT. NINEPM) THEN
                AVNITE = AVNITE + TEMP
                NITES = NITES + 1
              ELSE IF (TIME .GT. NINEAM .AND. TIME .LT. THREEPM) THEN
                AVDAY = AVDAY + TEMP
                DAYS = DAYS + 1
              ENDIF
              GO TO 100
  200       PRINT *, 'AVERAGE NIGHTTIME TEMPERATURE', AVNITE/NITES
            PRINT *, 'AVERAGE DAYTIME TEMPERATURE', AVDAY/DAY
            END
```

Data

```
78.0    2200
66.0    0500
68.2    0600
44.1    1600
73.5    0200
66.0    1000
56.3    1800
91.7    0900
77.0    1200
88.0    1500
0.00     -1
```

Output

```
AVERAGE NIGHTTIME TEMPERATURE     72.50000
AVERAGE DAYTIME TEMPERATURE       77.00000
```

7.5   LOGICAL VARIABLES

As LOGICAL expressions get more complex, they become hard to understand and look bulky and forbidding. We can avoid long expressions by breaking them into pieces and evaluating the pieces one at a time. To save the result from each piece, we use memory cells of LOGICAL type. These cells are named in LOGICAL declarations and may be used only to store LOGICAL values—true or false.

LOGICAL Declaration

> **form**
> *LOGICAL list*
> *list* is a list of memory cell names separated by commas
>
> **meaning**
> Attach the names in *list* to memory cells for storing LOGICAL values
>
> **examples**
>
> ```
> LOGICAL P, Q, FINISH
> LOGICAL ADULT
> ```

Suppose you have two friends, Mary and Jane, who have established minimum criteria for men they will date.

Mary's criteria—6 feet tall and decent looking
                or has $1 million and a Porsche
                or is in college and very good looking

Jane's criteria—decent looking and owns a car
                or isn't broke and is very good looking
                or is a medical student

The relevant data are height, looks, money, car, and type of student. If this data is keyed on one line, as in Figure 7.5.1, we can write a program to decide whether a man with the given characteristics can date Mary or Jane. We could write it using ordinary LOGICAL expressions with lots of .AND.'s and .OR.'s but they would be very long and ominous looking. Better to shorten them with LOGICAL variables as illustrated in the program below.

```
      INTEGER HEIGHT, LOOKS, MONEY, CAR, STYPE
      LOGICAL TALL, VGL, DL, RICH, BROKE
      LOGICAL ANYCAR, PORSCHE, COLL, MED
      READ *, HEIGHT, LOOKS, MONEY, CAR, STYPE
C               SET LOGICAL VALUES
      TALL = HEIGHT .GE. 6*12
      VGL = LOOKS .GE. 9
      DL = LOOKS .GE.5
      RICH = MONEY .GE. 1000000
      BROKE = MONEY .LE. 0
      ANYCAR = CAR .GT. 0
      PORSCHE = CAR .EQ. 3
      COLL = STYPE .GE. 2
      MED = STYPE .EQ. 3
C               USE LOGICAL VARIABLES TO DECIDE
      IF (TALL .AND. DL
     +    .OR. RICH .AND. PORSCHE
     +    .OR. COLL .AND. VGL) THEN
         PRINT *, 'MAY DATE MARY'
      ELSE
         PRINT *, 'MAY NOT DATE MARY'
      ENDIF
```

(Continued on following page)

```
      IF (DL .AND. ANYCAR
   +      .OR. .NOT. BROKE .AND. VGL
   +      .OR. MED) THEN
          PRINT *, 'MAY DATE JANE'
      ELSE
          PRINT *, 'MAY NOT DATE JANE'
      ENDIF
      END
```

Data

```
70      50      9000    1       2
```

Output

```
MAY NOT DATE MARY
MAY DATE JANE
```

Figure 7.5.1   Data Format for Dating Criteria

height (inches)	looks (on a scale of 0–10)	money ($)	car (0 = none 1 = ordinary 2 = new 3 = Porsche)	type of student (0 = high school dropout 1 = high school diploma 2 = college student 3 = medical student −1 = graduate student)

As you can see in the program, LOGICAL variables are given values in assignment statements where the right-hand side is a LOGICAL expression. These were all simple relational expressions, but they could have been more complex. They may even involve other LOGICAL variables, just as values specified in arithmetic assignment statements may involve several variables.

> **LOGICAL constants**
> **.TRUE.** is Fortran notation for the logical value "true."
> **.FALSE.** stands for the logical value "false."

LOGICAL values may be PRINTed and READ. If a LOGICAL variable is included in a PRINT statement, either a T or an F will appear in the output, depending, of course, on the value stored in that variable. Any sequence of characters which has T as the first letter will be READ as the LOGICAL value. TRUE.; any sequence of characters on a data line which has F as the first letter will be READ as the LOGICAL value .FALSE.. That means you can put T, .T., TRUE, or .TRUE. on a data line, and it will be READ as a .TRUE. LOGICAL value by the appropriate READ statement.

There is one common error made in using LOGICAL variables. If DONE is a LOGICAL variable, then the test

```
IF (DONE) THEN
```

succeeds if DONE has the value .TRUE. and fails if DONE is .FALSE.. For some reason, people often try to perform the test in this incorrect way:

```
IF (DONE. .EQ. .TRUE.) THEN
```

People who do this are probably making an (incorrect) analogy between arithmetic relations and LOGICAL tests. If you absolutely insist on making the decision explicit, you may use this form:

```
IF (DONE .EQV. .TRUE.) THEN
```
                    EQUIVALENT

Test on a LOGICAL variable

```
IF ( DONE) THEN
IF ( .NOT. DONE) THEN
```

equivalent form

```
IF ( DONE .EQV. .TRUE.) THEN
IF ( DONE .NEQV. .TRUE.) THEN
```

incorrect form

```
IF ( DONE .EQ. .TRUE.) THEN
IF ( DONE .NE. .TRUE.) THEN
```

7.5 EXERCISES

1. What gets printed if the data line contains a 7?

```
INTEGER N
LOGICAL BIG
READ *, N
BIG = N .GT. 10
IF (BIG) THEN
  PRINT *, 'BIG', N
ELSE
  PRINT *, 'SMALL', N
ENDIF
END
```

2. What value would SPREAD get if the data line contained a 10 and a 100?

```
INTEGER M, N
LOGICAL SPREAD
READ *, M, N
SPREAD = M .GT. N+50 .OR. N .GT. M+50
```

3. Alter the Mary/Jane program so that Mary's second criterion requires only $1 million and no Porsche.

4. If

```
LOGICAL A, B, C
A = .TRUE.
B = .TRUE.
C = .FALSE.
```

then what values do the following expressions have?

```
A .OR. B
.NOT. C
(A .OR. B) .AND. C
.TRUE. .OR. C
.TRUE. .AND. C
(.NOT. C) .OR. B
```

7.6 CHARACTER COMPARISONS

In Section 4.2 we introduced the relational operators (.EQ., .LT., .GE., etc.). Besides using these operators to compare numbers, they can be used to compare CHARACTER values. If one CHARACTER value comes after another in normal alphabetical order, Fortran treats it as if it were greater than the one that comes earlier. In most cases, this is all you need to know.

There are a few cases in which the story isn't quite so simple. For instance, how will this test turn out?

```
IF ('$100.00' .GT. '+100') THEN
```

Another time you need to know the details is when you're developing a program to be sent to someone who will run it on a different computer system. Unfortunately, comparisons between string values are not guaranteed to work exactly the same on all versions of Fortran 77, unless you go to a little extra effort.

If SONG is a CHARACTER*(14) memory cell, then the statement

```
IF (SONG .EQ. 'BORN IN THE USA') THEN
```

performs a test which succeeds only if the value in SONG is 'BORN IN THE USA'. Two CHARACTER*(n) values which start out the same are still considered equal even if they have a different number of blanks at the end. For example, the test in

```
IF ('BEST' .EQ. 'BEST        ') THEN
```

succeeds.

Comparisons for alphabetical order are also possible. The test

```
IF ('JONES' .LT. 'SMITH') THEN
```

succeeds because the string 'JONES' comes before 'SMITH' in normal alphabetical order.

Here are the details of how the tests are performed. First the leading (leftmost) characters of the two strings are compared. If they are not the same, then one must come before the other alphabetically, and the test is decided. If the leading characters *are* the same, then the characters in the next position are compared. This process continues until some difference is found, or (if the strings are actually the same) the ends of the strings are reached. If the two strings are not of the same length, the shorter one is treated as if blanks had been added to its right end—enough blanks to make the strings the same length.

As long as the two strings being compared contain just letters (and, possibly, blanks), there are no surprises. 'A' comes before (is Less Than) 'B' or any other letter. And 'A' comes before 'AARDVARK'. As long as the two strings contain nothing but digits and blanks, there are no surprises. '1' comes before '2', and '12' comes before '9'. (Remember: when you compare CHARACTER values, you're making an *alphabetical* comparison, not a *numerical* comparison.) If, however, the two strings contain characters like '$', '+', and '=', or contain some combination of letters and digits, there can be trouble. Is '2' before or after 'A'? While the result will be consistent on your specific computer system, it can vary from computer system to computer system.

Each computer system has some built-in ordering of the characters it makes available. The ordering of the characters is called a **collating sequence.** (Collating is derived from the Latin *collatus*, meaning "compared.") This collating sequence determines whether '2' is Greater Than or Less Than 'A' on your system. All you are *guaranteed* is that

1. ' '(blank) precedes all letters and all digits;
2. letters go in alphabetical order;
3. individual digits go in numerical order;
4. letters and digits are not intermingled (i.e., either all the digits precede all the letters, or vice versa).

The collating sequences for the two most common character sets are shown in Table 7.6.1—but there are others. Consult a local expert.

If you are still with us at this point, you must be wondering one of two things. Either you are wondering what difference it makes that the collating sequence can be different from computer to computer, or else you are wondering why the Fortran standards don't specify one specific sequence.

The answer to the first question is that one of the main advantages to using Fortran is that it *is* a standardized language, and a good one to choose if you intend to use, sell, or promote computer programs on a wide range of computers. People who make a living by selling programs use Fortran because, if they take care to write their programs in accord with the standards, no changes will be necessary to run the same program on many different computers. To these people, the fact that '2' may

Table 7.6.1   Collating Sequences

ASCII	EBCDIC	
blank	blank	
! (boxed)	.	characters not included in standard Fortran are boxed
" (boxed)	(	
$	+	
% (boxed)	! (boxed)	
'	$	
(	*	
)	)	
*	; (boxed)	
+	-	
,	/	
-	,	
.	% (boxed)	
/	?	
0–9	:	
:	'	
; (boxed)	=	
=	"	
? (boxed)	a–z	
A–Z	A–Z	
a–z (boxed)	0–9	

come before 'A' on one system and after 'A' on another is *totally unacceptable.* It would cost them money and time to make the changes in their programs to make them run properly on different systems. The most obvious solution to the problem would be for the standards to specify one specific collating sequence. Which brings us to the second question: Why don't the standards specify one specific sequence?

A complete answer to the second question would require a politico-socioeconomic analysis of the computer field. Suffice it to say that since many computer manufacturers use different collating sequences, no agreement could be reached on a specific sequence.

As a compromise, Fortran 77 provides a number of **lexical operators** (see Table 7.6.2), which provide for comparisons of CHARACTER values in accordance with the ASCII collating sequence.

The lexical operators shown in Table 7.6.2 produce LOGICAL (.TRUE., .FALSE.) values by comparing the two (CHARACTER) arguments in accord with the ASCII collating sequence (see Table 7.6.1). For example, the statement

```
IF ( LLE( 'JONES' , 'SMITH') ) THEN
```

uses the LLE lexical operator (Lexically Less than or Equal to) to see if 'JONES' is less than or equal to 'SMITH' according to the ASCII collating sequence.

The four lexical operators (LLT, LLE, LGE, and LGT) have the meanings you would expect. Like the corresponding relational operators, .LT., .LE.,

Table 7.6.2 The ASCII Lexical Operators (assumes that A and B have been declared to be CHARACTER memory cells)

Lexical Operator	Example	Meaning
LLT (arg_1, arg_2)	`IF ( LLT('$', 'A') ) THEN`	The first argument comes before the second, according to the ASCII collating sequence
LLE (arg_1, arg_2)	`IF (LLE(A, 'A  ') ) THEN`	The first argument comes before or is the same as the second
LGE (arg_1, arg_2)	`IF ( LGE(A, B) ) THEN`	The first argument comes after or is the same as the second
LGT (arg_1, arg_2)	`IF ( LGT('O', B) ) THEN`	The first argument comes after the second in (ASCII) lexical order

.GE., and .GT., they compare the two strings character by character and pad the shorter string with blanks. The only difference is that, with the lexical operators, you are *guaranteed* that the ASCII collating sequence is used.

7 PROBLEMS

Practice Problems

1. Write a program which will help a person figure how much cloth to buy to make a tablecloth for a rectangular table. READ values giving the dimensions of the table, the length of overhang desired, and the width of cloth to be used. If the cloth is too narrow for a single width to cover the table, your program should assume that 5/8 inch will be taken from the material on each side of each seam.

2. Write a program that READs INTEGERs, one from each data line, and that prints the word TRUE only if the latest number is larger than the one immediately before. When a data line with a value greater than 1000000 is READ, print a message value telling whether all the numbers were in increasing order.

3. You are given eight sets of three values each.

23.37	19.51	8.37
57.46	40.06	27.57
42.09	35.78	61.65
8.63	15.74	12.38
61.94	78.07	10.87
19.56	23.54	33.28
84.37	61.98	15.93
37.80	49.24	23.51

Write a program to determine whether or not the three values of a set could represent the lengths of the sides of a triangle. If the three sides could make a triangle, calculate its area and print a message like

```
WHEN AB=3.00 AND BC=4.00 AND CA=5.00,
THE AREA OF TRIANGLE ABC IS 6.00
```

If a, b, and c are the side lengths, then area is $\sqrt{[s(s-a)(s-b)(s-c)]}$, where s is the half perimeter $(a+b+c)/2$. (The formula is due to Hero, a mathematician of ancient times.)

If the three values in a set couldn't represent the sides of a triangle, print a message like

```
23.37, 9.51, AND   9.37 COULD NOT POSSIBLY
                   BE THE SIDES OF A TRIANGLE.
```

---

a property of Hero's formula: If $s(s-a)(s-b)(s-c)$ is negative, then a, b, and c can't make a triangle.

(Thanks to Rob Kelman, who prefers "Hero" to "Heron," for his help with this problem.)

4. Write a program which READs data containing EPA mileage information. Each data line should have an INTEGER (car identification number) and two REALs (EPA highway gas mileage and EPA city gas mileage). Use a negative car identification number to signal the end of data. Print out the data on each car, plus the average of the two mileage figures. If a car's average is less than 16.0 miles per gallon, print THIS CAR IS A GUZZLER. If its average is greater than 30.0 miles per gallon, print a complimentary message.

5. One Denver Mint Tea tea bag makes one cup of strong, aromatic tea in eight minutes. Leaving the bag in longer than ten minutes has no further effect on the strength of the tea. If we say that strong (eight minute) tea has relative strength 1.0, then the relative strength of tea steeped in a teapot for other lengths of time is

$$\text{number of bags} * \frac{\text{number of minutes}}{\text{number of cups}} * \frac{1 \text{ cup}}{8 \text{ minutes}}$$

if the steeping time is under ten minutes. For steeping times over ten minutes the relative strength is

$$\text{number of bags} * \frac{10 \text{ minutes}}{\text{number of cups}} * \frac{1 \text{ cup}}{8 \text{ minutes}}$$

Write a program which READs several data lines, each containing three values: (1) the number of bags used, (2) the number of cups of water used, and (3) the steeping time in minutes. Have your program compute and print the relative strength of the tea for each data line. If the relative strength is less than 0.5, print HOPE YOU LIKE WEAK TEA, and if it's greater than 1.25, print HOPE YOU LIKE YOUR TEA STRONG.

Program Design Problems

6. Write a program to make daily weather reports. Each data line should contain nine INTEGER values giving the following information: current month, day, and year; high temperature for the day, low temperature for the day; year in which the record high for this day was set; record high temperature; year of record low; and record low temperature. After READing a data line, print a message of one of the following four types, depending on the data.

a.   `10/23/77      HIGH TODAY          52`
     `              LOW TODAY           23`

b.   `10/24/77      HIGH TODAY          71 *`
     `              LOW TODAY           38`
     `     *(BEATS RECORD OF 70 SET IN 1906)`

c.   `10/25/77      HIGH TODAY          73*`
     `              LOW TODAY          -10**`
     `      *(BEATS RECORD OF 68 SET IN 1932)`
     `    **(BEATS RECORD OF -8 SET IN 1918)`

d.   `10/26/77      HIGH TODAY          22`
     `              LOW TODAY          -18*`
     `    **(BEATS RECORD OF -12 SET in 1892)`

7. Write a program to count the votes in an election. There are three candidates; Milton P. Waxley (incumbent), Patricia Rhoder (progressive liberal), and Frederick "Red" Kemmeny (a reluctant candidate who filed at the last minute). Each voter makes his vote by entering a letter: "W" for Waxley, "R" for Rhoder, or "K" for Kemmeny.

At 7:30 P.M. an election official enters a period (".") at the end of all the ballots and submits them as data for your program. Your program should print the election results. (*Note:* Be sure to reject all mismarked ballots.)

This man has supported Milton P. Waxley in the last seventeen elections

8. You have a job in a store on the border and are getting tired of doing money conversions all the time. Write a program that will convert pesos to dollars or dollars to pesos. READ in the daily exchange rate, then READ data that contains either a 'P' followed by an amount in pesos or a 'D' followed by an amount in dollars. The program should do the appropriate conversion and PRINT the original amount and the converted value.

9. The local cable TV company is doing a survey. They need to know which of the four major networks—NBC, CBS, ABC, or PBS—is the most popular. They also want to know the percentage of the total viewing audience watching each network. Write a program that will interpret the survey data. Each data line contains one response in the form of a network name. PRINT out the survey data, the name of the most popular network, and each network's percentage of the total viewing audience.

10. Write a program which READs numbers until a value less than −1,000,000 is entered. Then have your program print the number of values, the largest value, the smallest value, and the range. (The **range** is the difference between the largest and smallest values.)

11. The 324th Annual Pumpkin Growing Contest of the Future Farmers of Grand Fenwick has 16 entries this year. The weights of the pumpkins (in tsernotecs, the traditional measure of weight in Grand Fenwick) are shown below beside the names of the entrants.

Write a program that judges could use to select the winner. Print a
congratulatory message which lists the name of the lucky winner
and tells how many tsernotecs the winning pumpkin weighs.
(Thanks to the late Walter Orvedahl for this problem.

Weight (tsernotecs)	Grower	Weight (tsernotecs)	Grower
60.4	Hans Von Smong	69.4	Katy Klunz
86.1	Karl Schultz	78.8	Hans Von Der Door
63.9	Hans Von Neumann	85.3	Hans Schultz
71.2	Kristina Hampker	50.4	Hans Hanson
105.3	Karl Schmidthorst	67.3	Katy Kleinholter
54.7	Hans Von Laughen	57.9	Hans Bratworst
91.6	Karl Von Hausdorf	94.7	Kris Von Steinholder

8 FORMATS

Special note: This chapter is optional. It may be read piecemeal, as needed, or deferred entirely until after Chapter 11.

8.1 LINE SPACING CHARTS AND OUTPUT FORMATS

The PRINT and READ statements we have been using in the previous chapters fall into the category of **list-directed I/O.** In list-directed I/O, the output list determines the precise appearance of printed lines, and data for list-directed input can be keyed anywhere on the data line (or lines) as long as the order of the individual data matches that of the variables in the input list.

For many applications, list-directed I/O is sufficient. But sometimes we want to have complete control over printed output, or we want to process data which hasn't been keyed with Fortran's list-directed I/O as a guiding influence. It is in these cases that we need to use FORMATs.

If you're writing a program where you're going to be fussy about the appearance of the output, you will want to design the output carefully. The best way we know of to do this is to draw a prototype of the desired output. You can draw these pictures entirely by hand, but it is easier if you use specially prepared forms which mark off and number the character positions of the printed line. The forms we use are known as **line spacing charts.** We buy them at our college bookstore, but there are many types of printed computer forms which work almost as well (Fortran coding forms, for example). What you need is some paper ruled like graph paper with the columns numbered across the top line (see Figure 8.1.1). Their advantage over Fortran coding forms is that coding forms

Figure 8.1.1   Part of a Line Spacing Chart

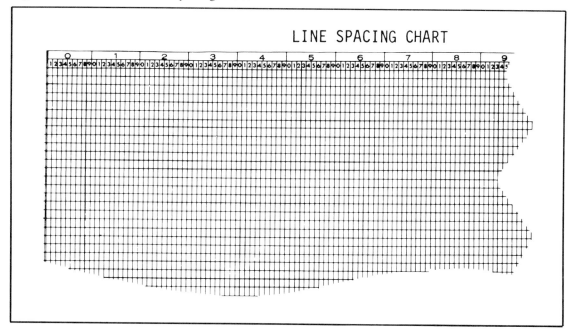

have only 80 columns, and most line printers have more than 80 print positions.

To see how to use line spacing charts in designing output, let's look at an example. Suppose we want to print a loan repayment schedule on a bank loan for the purchase of a Mazda RX-7. We want to compute the new status of the loan after each monthly payment and print the monthly statistics in a tabular format. There are three relevant amounts to compute for each month: old balance, interest, and new balance. Figure 8.1.2 displays a prototype for the output we want.

There are many places in the prototype where we don't know exactly what figures are going to be printed. (If we did, we wouldn't be writing a computer program to make the computation!) In these spots, we just put the Greek letter delta to stand for "digit." (It looks like a backward "6.") The prototype is used to plan where the digits will go, not to figure out exactly which digits they will be.

The prototype is a picture of the output we want. We describe this picture to the Fortran processor through FORMATs. The process of translating a prototype from a line spacing chart into a FORMAT is a mechanical routine and is subject to the pitfalls of any routine process. Sometimes we get bored and our attention wanders and we make trivial mistakes. Hard as it is to do, we have to try to keep our wits about us when we translate prototypes into FORMATs.

Basically, each PRINT statement in the Fortran program will need a separate FORMAT. By now you've probably had enough experience to realize that we'll have four PRINT statements for the first four lines and another PRINT statement (within a loop) to handle the remaining lines of

Figure 8.1.2 A Prototype for the Output of the Loan Repayment Program

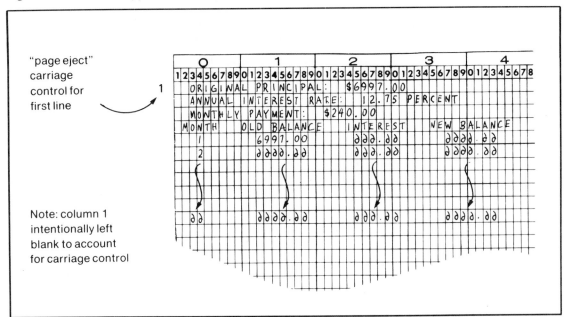

the prototype in Figure 8.1.2. If we were using list-directed I/O, the statements would look something like those below.

```
PRINT *, 'ORIGINAL PRINCIPAL: $', PRINC
PRINT *, 'ANNUAL INTEREST RATE:', RATE, 'PERCENT'
PRINT *, 'MONTHLY PAYMENT:  $', PAYMNT
PRINT *, 'MONTH', OLDBAL, INT, NEWBAL
```

To use FORMATs, we need to change the PRINT statements in two small ways. First, we replace the "*" with a FORMAT statement label, and we put one additional element, known as the **carriage control character,** into the output list. When we do this, the PRINT statements look like the new ones shown below.

```
      PRINT 1001, PAGEJC, 'ORIGINAL PRINCIPAL:  $', PRINC
      PRINT 1002, SNGLSP, 'ANNUAL INTEREST RATE:',
     +                    RATE, 'PERCENT'
      PRINT 1003, SNGLSP, 'MONTHLY PAYMENT:  $', PAYMNT
      PRINT 2000, SNGLSP, 'MONTH', 'OLD BALANCE',
     +                    'INTEREST', 'NEW BALANCE'
      PRINT 2010, SNGLSP, MONTH, OLDBAL, INT, NEWBAL
```

The FORMAT statement label identifies a FORMAT to be used by the PRINT statement. The label can, of course, be any positive INTEGER with up to five digits. The carriage control character is a CHARACTER* (1) value which determines the vertical spacing of the printed lines. A line may be single spaced from the previous line, or it may be double spaced leaving a blank line in between. It may start on a new page, or it may overprint the previous line. (The overprint facility is used to get **boldface** printing or other rarely used special effects.)

To understand the need for carriage control in FORTRAN, you need to realize that the processor doesn't really know that it is dealing with a line printer which can do special operations like controlling vertical spacing. As far as the processor is concerned, when it executes a PRINT statement, it sends a bunch of characters to an output device—any output device. It's up to the *device* to handle details like vertical spacing. (We'll discuss other I/O devices in Chapter 13.)

A line printer is a special kind of output device which, in a sense, has a mind of its own. When the processor sends it a line of characters to print, the printer rips off the first character of the line and uses it to decide on vertical spacing. *It does not print the first character.* It expects the first character to be one of four possibilities: "blank" for single spacing, "0" for double spacing, "1" for page ejection, that is, starting on a new page, or "+" for overprinting.

In our example we want the first line to be printed at the top of a new page and the remaining lines to be single spaced, so we'll put the values '1' and '*b*' (*b* for "blank") in the memory cells PAGEJC (for page eject) and SNGLSP (for single space).

```
CHARACTER*(1)PAGEJC, SNGLSP
PAGEJC = '1'
SNGLSP = ' '
```

Carriage Control Characters

' '	(blank)	move down the page one line before printing	single space
'0'	(zero)	move down the page two lines before printing	double space
'1'	(one)	move to the top of the next page before printing	eject page
'+'	(plus)	overprint the previous line	overprint

It will be easier for us to translate prototypes from the line spacing charts into FORMATS if we always write the necessary carriage control just to the left of the first column on the chart. That'll remind us to include it as the first element in both the PRINT and the FORMAT.

FORMATs tell PRINT statements two things: (1) where to put the data on the line, and (2) the level of accuracy (decimal places) needed to print the numbers. For each element in the output list, we put these two pieces of information in the FORMAT. The first bit of information (the "where" part) is specified with a **tabular adjustment** in the form T*c* where *c* is an integer designating the column on the line where you want the data to begin.

The second bit of information is specified with a **data descriptor.** Different types of data require different data descriptors. We'll study only three in this section—A, I, and F. The "A" data descriptor is used to designate data of the type CHARACTER. If we want to print "RODNEY BOTTOMS" starting in column 25 of the line, we would use the combination T25,A, as shown below.

```
        PRINT 1000, SNGSLP, 'RODNEY BOTTOMS'
1000    FORMAT(A, T25, A)
```

Note that there is a separate data descriptor for the carriage control character. This is because SNGLSP is an element of the output list, and every element of the output list must have a matching data descriptor in the FORMAT. The only difference is that for the carriage control we don't need a tabular adjustment because things begin at the start of the line automatically.

The second data descriptor we'll study in this section, the "I", is used

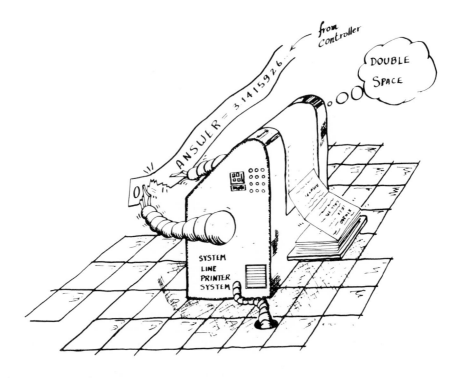

The printer rips off the first character on each line sent by the processor and uses it to decide how far to move the paper before printing.

to designate INTEGER data. It is written in the form Iw, where w—known as the **field width**—is an INTEGER specifying the number of columns to use in printing the data. We didn't need a field width designation with the A descriptor because the width is determined by the number of characters in the corresponding value in the output list. INTEGERs are treated differently. They are always **right-justified** within their fields. If the INTEGER 1979 is to be printed in a six-column field, I6, then it will be printed with two leading blanks in order to fill out the six columns so that the last digit is right-justified into the last column of the field.

"F" data descriptors denote REAL data. They always have the form F$w.d$. As with Iw, the w in F$w.d$ designates field width. It specifies the *total amount* of space to use in printing the number, including the decimal point and an optional " + " or " − " sign. The d determines the accuracy in terms of decimal places. Thus, F7.2 designates a field of the form δδδδ.δδ—two decimal places, seven spaces altogether. One of the spaces is always taken up by the decimal place, and one of them may be taken up by the sign. This is hard to remember and is the source of many frustrating but trivial mistakes.

Using the "A," "I," and "F" data descriptors, we can compose the FORMATs for the example on loan repayment. We simply look at the prototype we drew on the line spacing chart and note the columns in which each item starts. This gives us the tabular adjustment. The data descriptor is determined by the type of data and the accuracy desired in the printout. (This can be easily figured by looking at the prototype and counting columns.)

```
           PRINT 1001, PAGEJC, 'ORIGINAL PRINCIPAL:  $', PRINC
1001       FORMAT(A, T3, A, T26, F7.2)
           PRINT 1002, SNGLSP, 'ANNUAL INTEREST RATE:',
      +                  RATE, 'PERCENT'
1002       FORMAT(A, T3, A, T26, F5.2, T32, A)
           PRINT 1003, SNGLSP, 'MONTHLY PAYMENT:  $', PAYMNT
1003       FORMAT(A, T3, A, T22, F6.2)
           PRINT 2000, SNGLSP, 'MONTH', 'OLD BALANCE',
      +                  'INTEREST', 'NEW BALANCE'
2000       FORMAT(A, T2, A, T10, A, T24, A, T35, A)

           PRINT 2010, SNGLSP, MONTH, OLDBAL, INT, NEWBAL
2010       FORMAT(A, T3, I2, T12, F7.2, T25, F6.2, T37, F7.2)
```

"A" for CHARACTER and"F" for REAL

CHARACTER data used to be called "alphanumeric" data, which is where the "A" data descriptor came from. REAL data used to be called "floating point." (You may be familiar with that term if you've ever shopped for a hand-held calculator.) That's where the "F" came from.

Figure 8.1.3   The Loan Repayment Program

```
          Read PRINC, RATE, PAYMNT.
          Print heading.
          Let OLDBAL = PRINC.
          Set MONTH to 1

          ┌─────────────────────────────────────┐
          │  Exit if OLDBAL < or = zero          │
          │                                      │
          │  Compute interest.                   │
          │  Compute NEWBAL.                     │
          │  Print.                              │
          │  Update OLDBAL and MONTH.            │
          └─────────────────────────────────────┘

          COMMENT:                    AMORTIZING A LOAN
                    CHARACTER*(1) SNGLSP, PAGEJC
                    PARAMETER (SNGLSP = ' ', PAGEJC = '1')
                    INTEGER MONTH
                    REAL PRINC, RATE, OLDBAL, NEWBAL, INT, PAYMNT
                    READ *, PRINC, RATE, PAYMNT
                    PRINT 1001, PAGEJC, 'ORIGINAL PRINCIPAL:  $', PRINC
          1001      FORMAT(A, T3, A, T26, F7.2)
                    PRINT 1002, SNGLSP, 'ANNUAL INTEREST RATE:',
               +                 RATE, 'PERCENT'
          1002      FORMAT(A, T3, A, T26, F5.2, T32, A)
                    PRINT 1003, SNGLSP, 'MONTHLY PAYMENT:  $', PAYMNT
          1003      FORMAT(A, T3, A, T22, F6.2)
                    PRINT 2000, SNGLSP, 'MONTH', 'OLD BALANCE',
               +                 'INTEREST', 'NEW BALANCE'
          2000      FORMAT(A, T2, A, T10, A, T24, A, T35, A)
                    OLDBAL = PRINC
                    MONTH =1
```

The FORMAT statements can be put anywhere in the program without affecting results. They are passive descriptions of printed lines, not executable statements. A PRINT statement finds out which FORMAT to scan via the label, so the physical position of the FORMAT statement is irrelevant on theoretical grounds. We usually put a FORMAT right after the PRINT statement which uses it, but some people prefer to collect all the FORMATs together at the end of the program; others like them at the beginning of the program. You'll have to make up your own mind as to what's best.

Common F Mistake

> F3.1 describes a field of the form $\delta.\delta$ not a field of the form $\delta\delta\delta.\delta$

So that you can see the FORMATs within the context of a complete program, we've put a plan and the program for the loan repayment schedule in Figure 8.1.3. In the next section, we'll discuss more examples and a convenience feature which can save you quite a bit of typing.

```
200        IF (OLDBAL .LE. 0.00) GO TO 300
           INT = OLDBAL * ((RATE/12) * .01)
           NEWBAL = OLDBAL + INT - PAYMNT
           PRINT 2010, SNGLSP, MONTH, OLDBAL, INT, NEWBAL
2010       FORMAT(A, T3, I2, T12, F7.2, T25, F6.2, T37, F7.2)
           OLDBAL = NEWBAL
           MONTH = MONTH + 1
           GO TO 200
300        END
```

Data

```
6997.00    12.75    240.00
```

Output

```
ORIGINAL PRINCIPAL: $  6997.00
ANNUAL INTEREST RATE:  12.75 PERCENT
MONTHLY PAYMENT:  $240.00
MONTH    OLD BALANCE    INTEREST    NEW BALANCE
  1         6997.00       74.34        6831.34
  2         6831.34       72.58        6663.93
  3         6663.93       70.80        6494.73
  4         6494.73       69.01        6323.74
  5         6323.74       67.19        6150.93
  .
  .
  .
 34          490.30        5.21         255.51
 35          255.51        2.71          18.22
 36           18.22         .19        -221.59
```

8.1   EXERCISES

In all exercises, assume that SNGLSP, DBLSP, AND PAGEJC are CHARACTER*(1) memory cells with the values ' ', '0', and '1'.

1. The PRINT statement

```
PRINT 1000, SNGLSP, 12
```

produced the line of output shown below.
col 1
↓
*bbbbb*12

Which of these FORMATS could *not* have been the one used to produce the output?

a. 1000 FORMAT (A, T1, I7)
b. 1000 FORMAT (A, T6, I3)
c. 1000 FORMAT (A, T2, I6)
d. 1000 FORMAT (A, A5, I3)

2. Here's the PRINT statement

    ```
    PRINT 2000, SNGLSP, 1.23
    ```

    which produced this line of output
    col 1

    ↓

    ƀƀƀƀƀ1.23

    Which of these FORMATs could have been the one used?

    a. `2000 FORMAT (A, T1, F9)`
    b. `2000 FORMAT (T1, F3.2)`
    c. `2000 FORMAT (A, T2, F3.2)`
    d. `2000 FORMAT (A, T3, F7.2)`

3. Assume that PAGENO is an INTEGER memory cell with the value 3.
    Which of the FORMATs below could be used with this PRINT state-
    ment

    ```
    PRINT 3000, PAGEJC, 'PAGE NO', PAGENO
    ```

    to put this heading
                col 50

                  ↓

                PAGEƀNOƀƀ3

    at the top of the next page of output?

    a. `3000 FORMAT (A, T1, A, T50, I1)`
    b. `3000 FORMAT (A, T50, A, T57, I3)`
    c. `3000 FORMAT (A, T50, A, T59, I1)`
    d. `3000 FORMAT (T50, A, A, T57, I3)`

8.2 MORE OUTPUT FORMATS PLUS REPEAT SPECIFICATIONS

In this section we'll study a series of problems in output design and their
solutions in terms of FORMATs.

For our first problem, let's suppose that we want to print a table of
seasonal rainfall amounts for the Hoh Valley Rain Forest over the ten-
year period beginning in 1960. One way to lay out the table would be to
print the seasons across the top of the page and list the years down the
left-hand side of the table as shown in Figure 8.2.1. In the program we'll
need two PRINT statements, one for the heading (the list of seasons
across the top), and the other is a loop to print the rainfall, one year at a
time. We can write the two necessary FORMATs by direct transcription
from the line spacing chart.

```
        PRINT 1000, PAGEJC, 'SPRING', 'SUMMER',
      +                     'AUTUMN', 'WINTER'
1000    FORMAT(A, T8,A, T16,A, T24,A, T32,A)
        PRINT 2000, SNGLSP, YEAR, SPRING, SUMMER,
      +                     AUTUMN, WINTER
2000    FORMAT(A, T2,I4,  T8,F6.2, T16,F6.2,
      +                   T24,F6.2, T32,F6.2)
```

Figure 8.2.1   Prototype Output for Rainfall Table

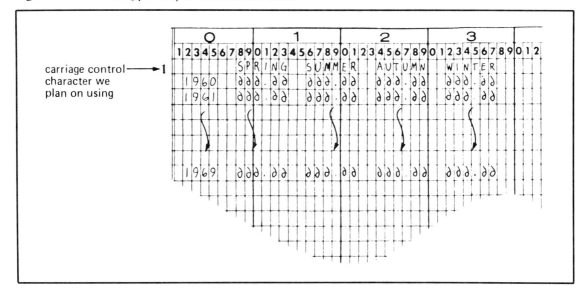

There is nothing difficult in composing these FORMATs. It's just a matter of reading column numbers off the line spacing chart and using them to set the tabular adjustment. However, FORMATs have a tendency to get bulky, as you can see in FORMAT 2000 above. Fortunately, there is a shorthand notation we can use to eliminate some of the bulk.

When a series of numbers are *regularly spaced* and all printed with the *same data descriptor*, as in the rainfall amounts in our example, then we can use a repeat specification on the data descriptor and avoid having to type it several times. As you can see in Figure 8.2.1, the rainfall numbers are each printed in a six-column field preceded by two blanks. Since numbers are always right-justified within their fields, we could view these rainfall fields as four adjacent eight-column fields. When a series of fields is adjacent, we can leave off the tabular adjustment on all of them except the first one. Look at it this way. *The tab placement doesn't need to be adjusted if it's already in the right place.* When printing two adjacent fields, the tab is already in the right place to print the second field as soon as the first field has been printed.

Leaving off the extra tab adjustments, we get the FORMAT below.

```
2000 FORMAT(A,T2,I4,T6,F8.2,F8.2,F8.2,F8.2)
```

Now we have four identical data descriptors in a row. This is where we can use a repeat specification to write an equivalent FORMAT in a shorthand form. Any data descriptor ("A," "I," "F," and others we'll learn about later) may be preceded by an unsigned INTEGER constant known as a **repeat specification.** The effect is as if the data descriptor were repeated in the FORMAT as many times as indicated. Thus, 4F8.2 is precisely equivalent to F8.2, F8.2, F8.2, F8.2. With this new convenience we can write the FORMAT as shown below. We have eliminated all the tabs because all the fields, including the carriage control field and the INTE-

Table 8.2.1   Automobile Performance Statistics

Make and model	0-60 mph (sec)	Fuel econ (mpg)	Cornering (g)	Stop from 80 (ft)	Noise at 70 (dBA)
Alfa Romeo Spider Veloce	11.7	21.0	0.76	288	81
Audi 5000S Turbo	10.6	18.0	0.76	284	71
BMW 325e	8.9	28.0	0.76	258	72
Chevrolet Corvette	6.6	19.0	0.88	245	77
DeTomaso Pantera GT5	5.5	10.0	na	258	84
Ferrari Testerossa	5.3	12.0	na	242	78
Isuzu Impulse	12.9	29.0	0.73	275	73
Jaguar XJ6 Van den Plas	12.3	17.5	0.76	262	69
Lancia Rally	7.1	20.0	0.83	256	78
Lotus Turbo Esprit	6.6	17.5	0.81	280	78
Maserati Biturbo E	6.3	18.0	0.81	286	73
Mercedes-Benz 500SEC	9.0	16.5	0.73	270	70
Nissan 300ZX Turbo	7.4	17.0	0.80	249	73
Pontiac Trans-Am HO	7.9	13.0	0.81	301	76
Porsche 930 Turbo	5.3	16.0	0.83	253	81
Saab Turbo	8.6	22.5	0.76	282	72
Toyota MR2	8.9	25.0	0.82	241	73
Volvo 740 Turbo Wagon	8.4	24.0	0.75	263	69

(Reprinted by permission from *Road and Track*, August, 1985, page 16.)

GER field for the year, are adjacent. Therefore, no tab adjustment is needed.

```
2000 FORMAT(A, I4, 4F8.2)
```

Let's try another example. Suppose we want to tabulate some data on automobiles: make and model, performance, covering, fuel economy, etc.,—as shown in Table 8.2.1. First, we draw a prototype of the output on a line spacing chart, as usual. Then we translate it into FORMATs. Let's ignore the heading on this one and just consider the layout of the numbers.

Next Test—Headroom

Figure 8.2.2   Output Prototype and Formats for Automobile Statistics

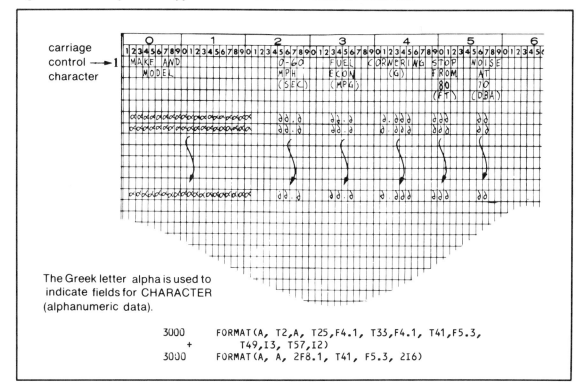

The Greek letter alpha is used to indicate fields for CHARACTER (alphanumeric data).

```
3000        FORMAT(A, T2,A, T25,F4.1, T33,F4.1, T41,F5.3,
  +             T49,I3, T57,I2)
3000        FORMAT(A, A, 2F8.1, T41, F5.3, 2I6)
```

Figure 8.2.2 displays the prototype and two FORMATs which would work. One of them is the direct translation with all the tabular adjustments, and the other is an equivalent FORMAT which has been condensed through the use of repeat specifications and adjacent fields.

This pair of examples should be enough to give you the general idea. What you need is practice. You should be sure to do the exercises at the end of this section and check your answers against the appendix.

There is one more convenience feature we'd like to cover while we're on the subject of repeat specifications. It is possible to repeat groups of FORMAT descriptors by enclosing the group in parentheses and putting a repeat specification in front of it. If we wanted to print an I4 field, then an A field, then an F6.2 field and repeat that pattern three times, we could put the necessary descriptors—I4, A, F6.2—in parentheses with a 3 in front. The prototype and four equivalent FORMATs are shown in Figure 8.2.3. Note that the FORMAT still needs the "A" at the beginning to handle the carriage control. Furthermore, the last two "I" fields are jammed against the preceding "F" fields. We are assuming that the INTEGERs printed will have no more than three digits so that the numbers will be separated by at least one blank because the INTEGERs will be right justified.

The fourth FORMAT in Figure 8.2.3 uses a new FORMAT descriptor known as the *tab-right* (TRc) descriptor. It causes a *relative* tab adjustment two places to the right of the current tab position, leaving two blank spaces on the line.

FORMAT Statement

form
label FORMAT *(flist)*
label is a Fortran statement label
flist is a list of FORMAT specifications separated by commas

meaning
Describes the layout of a printed line

examples

```
1000 FORMAT (A,T22,F10.3,T46,I2,T52,A)
2000 FORMAT (A,T6,3A,T50,3F6.2)
3000 FORMAT (A,4(I6,F6.2,A))
4000 FORMAT (A,3(I6,A),T50,2A,T60,2(2A,I3))
```

Using this tab-right descriptor, we can rewrite the FORMAT for the heading in Figure 8.2.1.

```
1000 FORMAT (A, T8,4(A, TR2))
```

Figure 8.2.3   Repeat Specification on Group

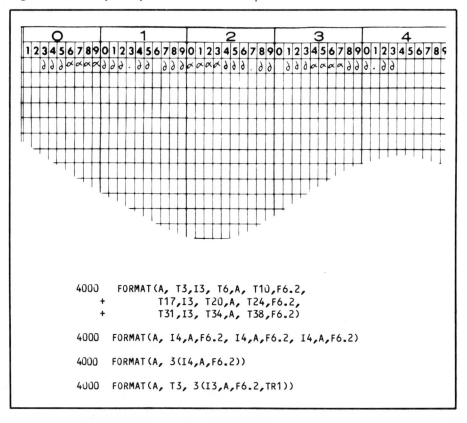

```
4000    FORMAT(A, T3,I3, T6,A, T10,F6.2,
   +           T17,I3, T20,A, T24,F6.2,
   +           T31,I3, T34,A, T38,F6.2)

4000    FORMAT(A, I4,A,F6.2, I4,A,F6.2, I4,A,F6.2)

4000    FORMAT(A, 3(I4,A,F6.2))

4000    FORMAT(A, T3, 3(I3,A,F6.2,TR1))
```

FORMAT Specification

---

forms
rdd
fd
r(flist)
r is a repeat specification (an unsigned INTEGER constant)
   which may be omitted
dd is a data descriptor (e.g., A, I*w*, F*w.d*)
fd is a FORMAT descriptor which is not a data descriptor (e.g.,
   T*c*, TR*c*)
flist is a list of FORMAT specifications separated by commas

8.2   EXERCISES

1. Suppose we want to revise the line spacing chart in Figure 8.2.1 to
    add "underlines" below the season names. We add a line below the
    season headings and put minus signs under each season. What FOR-
    MAT would you use with these added statements?

    ```
    CHARACTER*(6) ULINE
    ULINE = '      '
    PRINT 1900, SNGLSP, ULINE, ULINE, ULINE, ULINE
    ```

    Once you figure out what FORMAT you want, revise it using a TR
    descriptor and a repeat specification (if you didn't use them to begin
    with).
2. Three of these FORMATs have the same effect. Which one is differ-
    ent?

    ```
    1000 FORMAT (A, T1, I3, T4, I3, T7, I3)
    1000 FORMAT (A, 3(T1, I3))
    1000 FORMAT (A, 3I3)
    1000 FORMAT (A, I3, I3, T7, I3)
    ```

3. Devise PRINTs and FORMATs for the first three lines of the output
    prototype in Figure 8.2.2.
4. Can you do exercise 3 using list-directed I/O (i.e., without using FOR-
    MATs)?
5. Write a program which makes a "French flag" out of these basic
    constituents.

    ```
    CHARACTER*(4) RED, WHITE, BLUE
    RED = '++++'
    WHITE = '....'
    BLUE = '****'
    ```

Here's the design:

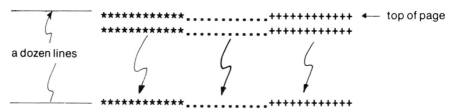

6. Draw the line spacing chart that these statements implement

```
        CHARACTER*(1) SNGLSP, PAGEJC, DBLSP
        PARAMETER (SNGLSP = ' ', DBLSP = '0', PAGEJC = '1')
        CHARACTER*(12) TEAM
        PRINT 1000, PAGEJC,1,2,3,4,5,6,7,8,9, 'R','H','E'
1000    FORMAT(A, T14, 9I3, 3(TR2, A))
        TEAM = 'REDS'
        PRINT 1010, SNGLSP, TEAM, 0,0,1,1,0,0,0,4,0,6,9,0
1010    FORMAT(A, A, T14, 12I3)
        TEAM = 'GIANTS'
        PRINT 1010, SNGLSP, TEAM, 1,2,0,0,0,0,0,0,1,4,7,1
        PRINT 1020, DBLSP, 'W-SEAVER', 'L-BLUE'
1020    FORMAT(A,A, TR2,A)
        END
```

7. Devise the PRINT statements and FORMATs required to produce this line spacing chart.

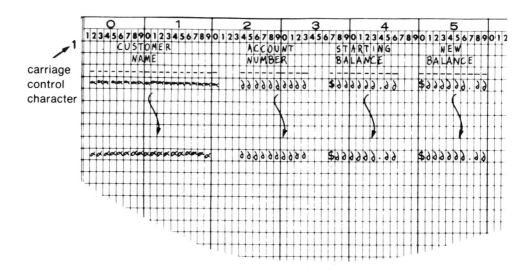

Assume that the program will give appropriate values to these memory cells:

```
CHARACTER*20 CNAME
INTEGER ACCTNO
REAL STBAL, NEWBAL
```

8. Dates look best with no extraneous blanks around the slashes (i.e., 6/

19/84 instead of 6 / 19 / 1984. 6/9/1978 instead of 6 / 9 / 1978). Devise PRINTs, FORMATs, and IF THEN ELSE statement to do this job.

```
INTEGER MONTH, DAY, YEAR
```

8.3   DATA LINE LAYOUT FORMS AND INPUT FORMATS

Suppose you wanted to bring text from a data line into elements of CHARACTER*(1). If you used list-directed READ statements, then the data would have to be keyed as individual characters surrounded by quote marks.

```
CHARACTER*(1) C1,C2,C3,C4,C5,C6,C7,C8,C9,C10
READ *, C1,C2,C3,C4,C5,C6,C7,C8,C9,C10
```

Data

```
'F' 'O' 'U' 'R' ' ' 'S' 'C' 'O' 'R' 'E'
```

This requires a lot of keying which can be avoided by using a FORMAT.

FORMATs for READ statements, like those for output, are made up of lists of FORMAT specifications. We need one data descriptor in the FORMAT for each variable in the input list. In the READ statement above, there are ten variables in the input list, so we need ten data descriptors in the FORMAT. All of them will be "A" descriptors. Hence we can write the FORMAT with a repeat specification, as shown below.

```
     CHARACTER*(1) C1,C2,C3,C4,C5,C6,C7,C8,C9,C10
     READ 1000, C1,C2,C3,C4,C5,C6,C7,C8,C9,C10
1000 FORMAT(10A)
```

Data

```
FOUR SCORE
```

What we have here is ten consecutive and adjacent one-column fields, beginning in column one. (Note that the quote marks in the data aren't used with FORMATs. The data descriptors in the FORMAT tell the processor what type of data will be in what field, so the quote marks aren't needed.)

If we had wanted to start the text in column 5 instead of column 1, we could have used a tab adjustment in the FORMAT.

```
     CHARACTER*(1) C1,C2,C3,C4,C5,C6,C7,C8,C9,C10
     READ 1000, C1,C2,C3,C4,C5,C6,C7,C8,C9,C10
1000 FORMAT(T5, 10A)
```

Data

FOUR SCORE

When the layout of the input becomes complicated, it should be designed as carefully as formatted output. To aid in the design process, we use **data line layout forms**. (You can buy them at the same place you get your line spacing charts.) Once a prototype of a data line is drawn, it can be easily translated into a FORMAT. In addition, the prototype is useful in actually keying the data because it shows where each item of data goes on the line.

To see how this can be done, let's suppose we've written a program to be used as an aid in keeping inventory tallies for the Bach or Rock Record Shop. Each data line for our program will have five pieces of information.

col. 1–20: album title
col. 21–29: label
col. 32–50: artist
col. 51–55: list price
col. 56–60: number of copies in stock

Figure 8.3.1 shows a prototype and FORMAT for data lines with this layout. Just as with output FORMATs, we can do a direct translation using tab adjustments for each field. This is the safest and easiest way to write FORMATs. However, in order to avoid awkwardly long FORMATs, we can take advantage of adjacent fields to eliminate some of the tabs. The second FORMAT in Figure 8.3.1 is based on that technique.

Figure 8.3.1 Prototype and FORMAT for Record Inventory Data

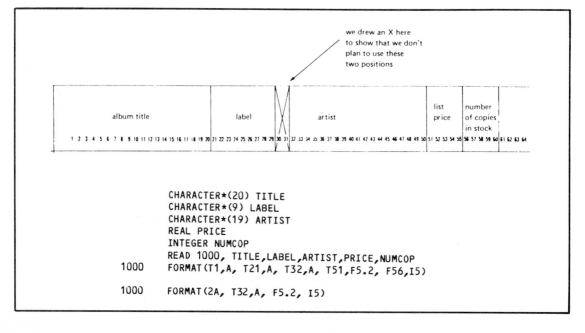

```
            CHARACTER*(20) TITLE
            CHARACTER*(9) LABEL
            CHARACTER*(19) ARTIST
            REAL PRICE
            INTEGER NUMCOP
            READ 1000, TITLE,LABEL,ARTIST,PRICE,NUMCOP
      1000  FORMAT(T1,A, T21,A, T32,A, T51,F5.2, F56,I5)

      1000  FORMAT(2A, T32,A, F5.2, I5)
```

Principles of Input FORMATs

1. One data descriptor in the FORMAT for each element of the input list
2. Width of "A" fields determined by length of corresponding CHARACTER variables
3. Type of variable in input list matches type of corresponding descriptors in FORMAT and matches type of value in corresponding field of data card

8.3 EXERCISES

1. Given this data card (or the equivalent data line on your system),

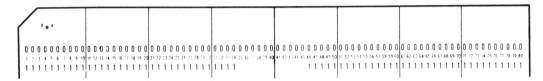

   what will be stored in the CHARACTER*(1) memory cell CHAR by each of the four READ statements below?

```
      READ *, CHAR
      READ 2000, CHAR
2000  FORMAT(A)
      READ 2001, CHAR
2001  FORMAT(T4, A)
      READ 2002, CHAR
2002  FORMAT( T3, A)
```

2. Suppose you keyed a line of data for the program in Figure 8.3.1 that looked like this:

JOHNNY MCLAUGHLIN ELECTRIC GUITARIST COLUMBIA J MCL6.99 15

   What values would be stored in TITLE, LABEL, and ARTIST by the READ statement?

3. Design a FORMAT suitable for use with this data layout

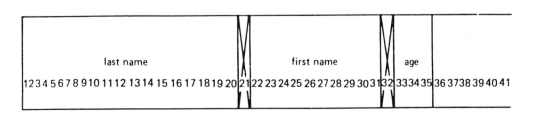

and these statements.

```
CHARACTER*(20) LASTN, FIRSTN
INTEGER POSTN
READ 2500, LASTN, FIRSTN, POSTN
```

4. Draw the data line layout that should be used with these statements.

```
CHARACTER*(10) MAKE, MODEL
REAL BASEPR
INTEGER DOORS
READ 2000, MAKE, MODEL, DOORS, BASEPR
2000 FORMAT(A, TR1, A, TR1, I1, TRI, F9.2)
```

5. When a huge amount of data must be entered, programmers sometimes design the data lines with all values crammed together. The goal is to save a little keying effort, but the effect is often to make the lines harder to check for accuracy. Revise this data line layout so the individual values can be more easily distinguished by the human who has to proofread the lines.

base price	sales tax	commission earned	profit margin	
1 2 3 4 5 6 7 8 9	10 11 12 13 14 15 16	17 18 19 20 21 22 23 24	25 26 27 28 29 30 31 32	33 34 35 36 37 38 39 40 41

The next two exercises refer to the layout in exercise 5. In addition, they assume that the lines will be read using these statements.

```
REAL BPRICE, STAX, COM, PROFIT
READ 3000, BPRICE, STAX, COM, PROFIT
```

6. Design a FORMAT statement that could be used to READ lines in the original (crammed together) FORMAT shown in exercise 5.
7. Design a FORMAT for use with your revised version of the layout in exercise 5.

8.4 DATA DESCRIPTORS

So far we have discussed only three types of data descriptors: A, F$w.d$, and Iw. There are many others including two additional descriptors for REAL data (E$w.d$ and G$w.d$), a modified form for CHARACTER (Aw), and a descriptor for LOGICAL data (Lw). Learning about these new data descriptors is a matter of studying a great many technical details.

The basic principle you must understand is that all I/O involves converting data between an **external representation** (outside the computer's memory) and an **internal representation** (inside the computer's memory). A READ statement causes a conversion from the external to the internal form, and PRINT statements go the other way, from an internal data representation to an external one.

The external form of data for Fortran programs is sequences of characters and is fundamentally the same for all types of computers. However, the internal form is determined by the computer system and varies significantly from one processor to the next. As we have discussed before, data is represented internally as patterns of binary digits, and the processor uses different types of patterns for each type of data. The essence of an I/O operation is to translate between a pattern of binary digits and a string of characters.

We will explain the meaning of data descriptors in terms of the internal/external conversion process. Our external representatives can, and will be, very precise, but we will denote internal representations in a less formal way.

What follows in this section is a long list of technical details. You should view it primarily as reference material: use it when you need it; don't try to remember it all at once.

I/O Operations

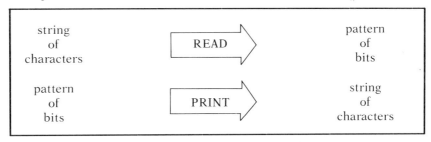

---

b: in picturing printed lines or data lines where spacing is critical, we use the symbol *b* for the blank character.

---

right justified: a string of characters is right justified in a field if the last character is in the rightmost position in the field.

I*w* (INTEGER)

Input

An external string of *w* or fewer digits which may include a preceding sign (+ or −) is converted to an INTEGER constant. No characters other than blanks, digits, or signs are legal. Any blanks in the field will be ignored, except that an entirely blank field is interpreted as zero.

external	I6	internal
bb1042		1042
$bbb-27$		-27
$-27bbb$		-27
$bb+bb6$		6
$-3bb4b$		-34
$bbbbbb$		0
$b-3+44$		illegal
bb3.14		illegal

Output

An internal INTEGER value is converted to a string of w characters. If the value is negative, the digits will be preceded by a minus sign. If the value does not use up all w characters in the field, the number is right justified in the field with blanks to the left. If the value is too large to fit in a field of width w, the field is filled with asterisks.

internal	I6	external
1042		bb1042
-27		$bbb-27$
-27000		-27000
6		$bbbbb$6
-30040		-30040
0		$bbbbb$0
-300400		$******$
3.14		illegal

Fw.d (REAL)

Input

The external character string in the field of width w is interpreted as a REAL constant. As such it may be preceded by a plus or a minus sign and may contain a decimal point. If the decimal point is not present, it is assumed to precede the d rightmost digits in the field (d must be smaller than w). The number may be written in scientific notation (E-notation). Blank characters are ignored, except that an all-blank field is interpreted as zero.

external	F6.2	internal
*bb*3.14		3.14
b − 2.79		− 2.79
+ *b*90.1		90.1
0.1234		0.1234
*bbb*372		3.72
*bb*372*b*		3.72
9001 + 1		900.1
2.1E − 3		0.0021
*bbbbb*5		.05

Output

An internal REAL value is converted to a character string of length *w*. The value is rounded (not truncated) to *d* decimal places (digits beyond the decimal point). If the external value has fewer than *w* characters, including the decimal point and a possible minus sign, then the number is right justified, and the field is filled with blanks to the left. If the number is too large to fit into *w* character positions, the field is filled with asterisks.

internal	F6.2	external
3.14		*bb*3.14
− 2.79		*b* − 2.79
90.1		*b*90.10
$49.2*10^{-3}$		*bb*0.05
$49.2*10^{-6}$		*bb*0.00
482.143		482.14
$49.2*10^{6}$		******
3927		illegal

E*w.d* (REAL)

Input

E*w.d* and F*w.d* are equivalent as input descriptors. If a sign is included with the decimal point shift factors, as in 1.7E − 6, and 4.932E + 8, then the E may be omitted to save room in the data field. In addition, the decimal point may be omitted from the number, but if so, it is implicitly placed *d* digits to the left of the decimal point shift factor. The following examples should clarify the myriad cases.

external	E7.2	internal
bb3.141		3.141
bbb3.14		3.14
$bbbb$314		3.14
3.14E00		3.14
3.14E − 2		.0314
b314E − 2		.0314
bb314 − 2		.0314
314b + 2b		3.14*10²

Output

The REAL value in the corresponding memory cell is output in scientific notation, rounded to d significant digits. THe rightmost four spaces in the output field of width w are used for the decimal point shift factor printed in the form E+xx or E−xx where each x is a single digit. The number is printed in the d + 3 spaces to the left of the decimal point shift factor in the form b0.f or −0.f where f is a d digit unsigned INTEGER. The leftmost w−(d + 7) spaces are left blank. As you can see, w should be at least as large as d + 7 to allow enough room for the number.

internal	E10.2	external
3.168		bb0.32E + 01
.492.1*10 ²³		bb0.49E − 21
− 3987.12		b − 0.40E + 04
.48*10¹⁰⁰		bb0.48 + 100
3749		illegal

Gw.d.   (generalized REAL)

Fw.d and Ew.d specifications are particularly useful when you wish to print out values to a certain number of decimal places, but there are also times when you wish to print out values with a certain number of significant digits. The G specification is designed for that purpose. Its form is

Gw.d

where w is the field width and d is the number of significant digits to be printed rather than the number of decimal places. The Gw.d specification has the pleasant feature that the value will be printed in an F style if that is possible in a field width of w−4. Otherwise it is printed in the E style. E-style numbers are right justified, and F-style numbers are justified to the fifth from the right space of the field, leaving four spaces to the right of the number. Thus, if the same FORMAT is used repeatedly, the digits of the numbers will line up in a column, and the exponents will line up in the rightmost four spaces of the field. However, the decimal points *don't* necessarily line up in a column.

Input

Same as F$w.d$.

Output

The rightmost four spaces in the field of width w are reserved for a decimal point shift of the form E $+$ xx or E $-$ xx (each x is a single digit). If the number rounded to d significant digits will fit in the remaining $w - 4$ leftmost spaces in the field, then the rightmost four spaces are left blank. On the other hand, if the number won't fit into $w - 4$ spaces, then it is written with a decimal point shift factor. In this case the number itself is rounded to d significant digits and is written in the form $bx.y$ or $-x.y$, where x is a single digit and y is a string of $d - 1$ digits.

internal	G11.4	external
-1.7526843		$b-1.753bbbb$
-175268.43		$b-1.753$E$+05$
3.1416		$bb3.142bbbb$
0.000031416		$bb3.142$E-05
0.1234		$b0.1234bbbb$
1.234		$bb1.234bbbb$
12.34		$bb12.34bbbb$
123.4		$bb123.4bbbb$
1234.0		$bb1234.bbbb$

Lw (LOGICAL)

Input

The value .TRUE. is represented in the data field by a character string whose first nonblank character is a "T" or a period followed by a "T." The value .FALSE. is represented similarly with "F" in place of "T."

external	L7	internal
$bbTbbbb$		.TRUE.
TURFbbb		.TRUE.
$bbbbbFb$		.FALSE.
F$bbbbbb$		.FALSE.
bTRUEbb		.TRUE.
FALSEbb		.FALSE.
.TRUE.b		.TRUE.
.FALSE.		.FALSE.

Output

The letter T or F is right justified with blank fill to the left if the value of the corresponding memory cell in the output list is .TRUE. or .FALSE., respectively.

internal	L6	external
.TRUE.		*bbbbb*T
.FALSE.		*bbbbb*F

Aw (character)

The field width *w* may be omitted. If it is, then the number of characters in the external field is determined by the length of the CHARACTER string in the I/O list.

Input

The *w* characters in the data field are placed into the corresponding memory cell in the input list. All characters in the field (blanks and single quotes included) are part of the character string placed into the cell. If the cell isn't large enough to hold all *w* characters, then only the rightmost *w* characters in the data field are placed in the cell. On the other hand, if the cell is large enough to hold more than *w* characters, then the *w* characters are placed into the leftmost part of the cell, and blank characters are put into the remainder of the cell.

We assume in this example that the internal memory space designated in the input list is of type CHARACTER*(4).

external	descriptor	internal
ABCD	A4	ABCD
ABCDEF	A6	CDEF
AB	A2	AB*bb*

Output

The *w* characters in the corresponding memory cell in the output list are written in the *w*-space output field. If the memory cell has more than *w* characters, then only the leftmost *w* characters in the cell are written in the output field. On the other hand, if the cell has fewer than *w* characters, then its characters are right justified in the output field with blank fill to the left.

internal	descriptor	external
ABCD	A4	ABCD
ABCD	A2	AB
ABCD	A6	*bb*ABCD

8.4 EXERCISE

1. Take a FORMAT break.

8.5 MULTIPLE-RECORD FORMATS AND RESCANNING

Most FORMATs describe a single line or a single card. In other words, they describe one **I/O record**. The length of a formatted I/O record is measured in characters. For example, the length of a record for an 80-column card reader is 80 characters. No FORMAT should describe a record longer than the record length for the intended I/O device. However, it is possible for a single FORMAT to describe more than one record. For example, the following statement prints two records (i.e., two lines) as a heading on a page.

> **record:** the basic unit of I/O. Different I/O devices have different types of records. The card reader record is one card (usually 80 characters). The printer record is one line. Different printers have different line lengths; 132 is the line length for many printers.

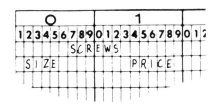

```
         CHARACTER*(1) PAGEJC, SNGLSP
         PAGEJC = '1'
         SNGLSP = ' '
         PRINT 1000, PAGEJC, 'SCREWS', SNGLSP, 'SIZE', 'PRICE'
1000     FORMAT(A, T7,A, / A, T2,A, T14,A)
```

The slash (/) in the FORMAT separates the descriptions of the two records. (Note that each record, being a printed line, has its own carriage control character.) In general, a FORMAT may describe many records, with each record separated from the next by a slash. For example, the following READ statement will read three cards. Two values will be taken from the first card, one value from the second, and two from the third.

```
      READ 2000, A, B, C, D
2000  FORMAT(2F20.0/F30.0/2F15.0)
```

Two consecutive slashes imply a blank record in between. The printer will skip a line because the implied blank line includes a blank character for carriage control. The reader will skip a card when given a // specification.

For the most part, multiple-line FORMATs are used to describe headings for information to be printed in tabular form. Used for other purposes, they have a tendency to get out of hand fast. Try to keep your FORMATs as simple as possible. It's best to work directly from a line spacing chart or data card layout form.

For a final example on FORMATs with slashes, consider the heading in the line spacing chart of Figure 8.2.2. The following PRINT and FORMAT statements handle all four lines of that heading plus the blank line between the heading and the tabulated information under it.

```
      PRINT 1000, PAGEJC, 'MAKE AND', '0-60', 'FUEL',
     +                   'CORNERING', 'STOP', 'NOISE',
     +           SNGLSP, 'MODEL', 'MPH', 'ECON', '(G)',
     +                   'FROM', 'AT',
     +           SNGLSP, '(SEC)', '(MPG)', 80, 70,
     +           SNGLSP, '(FT)', '(DBA)'
1000  FORMAT(A, T2,A, T25,A, T33,A, T39,A, T49,A, T56,A/
     +        A, T4,A, T25,A, T33,A, T42,A, T49,A, T57,A/
     +        A, T25,A, T33,A, T50, I2, T57, I2/
     +        A, T49,A, T56,A/)
```

Carriage Control

Remember! Each line described in a multiple-line output FORMAT must have its own carriage control character.

correct

```
      PRINT 1000, SNGLSP, 'LINE 1', SNGLSP, 'LINE2'
1000  FORMAT (2A/2A)
```

incorrect

```
      PRINT 2000, SNGLSP, 'LINE1', 'LINE2'
2000  FORMAT (A,A/A)
```

An I/O statement may process several records even if the FORMAT describes only one. Here's how that can happen. The PRINT statement below has more values in its list than there are data descriptors in the FORMAT. The computer must print all the values listed, so it simply uses the FORMAT over again, starting a new record when it comes to the end of the specification. This is known as **FORMAT rescanning.**

```
        INTEGER A, BEE, SEA, D
        CHARACTER*(1) SNGLSP
        PARAMETER(SNGLSP = ' ')
        A = 110
        BEE = 60
        SEA = 950
        D = SEA - 5*A
        PRINT 1000, SNGLSP, A, BEE, SNGLSP, SEA, D
1000    FORMAT(A, 2I6)
```

Results

*bbb*110*bbbb*60
*bbb*950*bbb*400

In general, if an I/O statement is not completed when it runs out of data descriptors in the FORMAT, it starts a new record and uses the FORMAT over again. FORMAT rescanning is useful because it lets you describe one record or even several records that you're thinking of as one logical unit and lets you use that description over and over to input or output several sets of data. The following FORMAT describes a pair of data lines, one containing a car name and the other a REAL and an INTEGER. The READ statement READs three pairs of lines, using the FORMAT three times.

```
        CHARACTER*(8) CAR1, CAR2, CAR3
        INTEGER M1, M2, M3
        REAL PRICE1, PRICE2, PRICE3
        READ(5,1000) CAR1, PRICE1, M1,
     +              CAR2, PRICE2, M2,
     +              CAR3, PRICE3, M3
1000    FORMAT(A/F8.0,I7)
```

Data

STE-6000
16000.00*bbbbb*28
CRESSIDA
19500.00*bbbbb*32
MUSTANG*b*
10500.00 *bbbbb*38

FORMAT rescanning gets unbearably complicated if the FORMAT contains groups of descriptors. In this case, the repetition starts from the last top-level group or from the repeat factor preceding it, if it has one. The following PRINT statement illustrates this feature. It assumes the memory cells have the values they were given by the READ statement above.

```
       PRINT 2000,SNGLSP, 'CAR', 'PRICE', 'EPA MILEAGE',
      +          SNGLSP, CAR1, PRICE1, M1,
      +          SNGLSP, CAR2, PRICE2, M2,
      +          SNGLSP, CAR3, PRICE3, M3
 2000  FORMAT(A, T3,A, T13,A, T21,A/
      +        (A, T2,A, T12, F8.2, T25,I2))
```

Output

```
   CAR       PRICE   EPA MILEAGE
   RABBIT   16000.00      28
   FOX      14500.00      32
   DASHER   11500.00      38
```

> **Last top-level group:** the group in a FORMAT which is terminated by the first right parenthesis to the left of the right parenthesis which closes the FORMAT. Got that?

Because the rescanning procedure is so intricate when the FORMAT contains groups, we recommend that you avoid using this feature. When you design a FORMAT to be used with an I/O statement which will cause rescanning, stick with simple, one-record FORMATS with no groups imbedded in them. Then the only rules you have to remember are these:

1. When there are *more* variables in the I/O list than there are data descriptors in the FORMAT, the FORMAT is rescanned until the I/O list is exhausted.
2. When there are *fewer* variables in the I/O list than there are data descriptors in the FORMAT, the extra data descriptors are ignored.

In this chapter we have discussed only a small part of the FORMAT facility. A complete discussion would require at least twice as much space in the text and probably quadruple the study on your part. For your extra effort, you would gain almost nothing which would help you produce the exact output you want. Nor would you gain any information which would significantly help you process data lines. The fact is, experienced programmers avoid complicated FORMATs like the plague.

Getting the data into the computer's memory and getting the results printed in the appropriate way are the hardest parts of many computing problems. It's best to handle the I/O as simply as possible. Use list-directed I/O whenever you can. Write FORMATs only when it's really necessary. When you must write FORMATs, keep them simple. We know a good many excellent programmers who've been successfully designing Fortran programs for a decade and still don't know exactly how FORMAT rescanning works in the more complicated cases. They've never needed to know, and you probably won't need to know either.

8.5   EXERCISES

Assume that SNGLSP, DBLSP, and PAGEJC are CHARACTER*(1) memory cells which have been given the values ' ', '0', and '1'.

1. Which of these PRINT/FORMAT pairs accomplish the astounding feat of causing a blank line to be printed before the line with the day abbreviation?

```
        PRINT 2000, SNGLSP, 'MON'
2000    FORMAT(A,A)

        PRINT 2010, SNGLSP,
     +          SNGLSP, 'TUE'
2010    FORMAT(2A, T1,A)

        PRINT 2020, SNGLSP,
     +          SNGLSP, 'WED'
2020    FORMAT(A/2A)

        PRINT 2030, DBLSP, 'THU'
2030    FORMAT(A,A)

        PRINT 2040, DBLSP, 'FRI'
2040    FORMAT(2A//)
```

2. Here are some pairs of PRINTs with associated FORMATs. Which pairs have the same effect as each other?

```
        PRINT 1000, SNGLSP, 1, 2, 3, '...', 'INFINITY'
1000    FORMAT(A, I2, I2, I2, TR1, A, TR1, A)

        PRINT 1000, SNGLSP, 1, 2, 3, '...', 'INFINITY'
1000    FORMAT(A, TR1, 3(I1, TR1), A, TR1, A)

        PRINT 2020, DBLSP, 'AND LAST BUT LEAST,'
2020    FORMAT(A, T5, A)

        PRINT 2020, SNGLSP, 'AND LAST BUT LEAST,'
2020    FORMAT(A/ T5, A)

        PRINT 2030, DBLSP, '$', 17.95
2030    FORMAT(A, A, F6.2)

        PRINT 2030, SNGLSP,
     +          SNGLSP, '$', 17, '.', 95
2030    FORMAT(A/ 2A, I2, A, I2)
```

3. Which data type and corresponding data descriptor would be most appropriate if you were printing out the following items?
   a. Baseball batting averages
   b. The number of olives in a martini
   c. A list of people's names
   d. The national debt

4. The printed output starts at the top of the page and looks like this:

```
PAGE 1
SYSTEM BUGS

DATE    REPORTED BY              DESCRIPTION
```

The PRINT statement used was

```
PRINT 1600, PAGEJC, 'PAGE', PAGENO,
+            SNGLSP, 'SYSTEM BUGS',
+      SNGLSP, 'DATE', 'REPORTED BY', 'DESCRIPTION'
```

Which of these FORMATS could have been used to produce the output?

```
1600 FORMAT(A, A, I2/ A, A/ A, A, T11, A, T39, A)
1600 FORMAT(A, A, I2/ A, A// A, A, T11, A, T39, A)
1700 FORMAT(F9.2)
1600 FORMAT(2A, I2/ 2A// 2A, TR7, A, T39, A)
```

5. What's wrong with the FORMAT?

```
        READ 1000, A, B, C, D, E, F
1000    FORMAT(6F20.2)
```

6. How should the data be keyed in for the following READ/FORMAT pair?

```
        READ 2000, A, B, C, D, E, F
2000    FORMAT(2F10.2)
```

---

8 PROBLEMS

Practice Problems

1. Take a problem you've already done and redo it using FORMATs. Choose one in which formatting will significantly improve the readability of the output.
2. Write out the ages, heights, and weights for ten of your friends. At the end of the list, print the average age, height, and weight for all those listed.

Input Design:

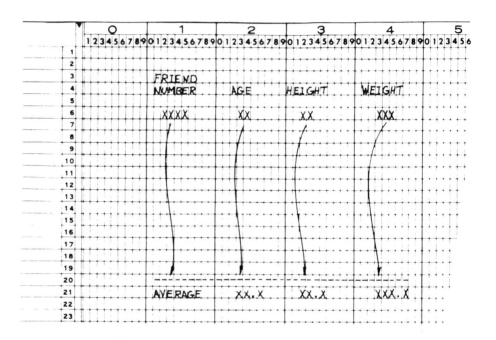

Output Design:

3. As racquetball commissioner, you want to mail out entry forms for the upcoming National Racquetball Association Tournament. Since you were donated 50 cases of address labels of the form shown below, set up your program output accordingly.

Name/Address Labels

Input:

Acct # 1–4	Name 5–28	St # 29–33	Street (P.O. Box) 34–50	Apt 51–54	City 56–72	St 73–74	Zip 75–79

Output:

Print labels form across
Actual label size (1¹/₂″ x 4″)

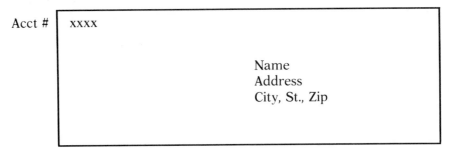

Acct #   xxxx

                                                Name
                                                Address
                                                City, St., Zip

Note: Many printers print 6 lines vertically per inch and 10 characters horizontally per inch.

Program Design Problems

4. Write a computer program which will:
   a. Read lines containing data as shown below.
   b. Summarize the total income, average income, and average number of dependents for each city and print the data as indicated below.
   c. Summarize the average income and average number of dependents for each county.
   d. Summarize the total income, average income, and average number of dependents for all cards.

City and county codes are as follows:

01 Fremont	06 San Lorenzo	11 San Ramon
02 Union City	07 San Leandro	12 Cowell
03 Pleasanton	08 Oakland	13 Drawbridge
04 Livermore	09 Clayton	20 Alameda County
05 Hayward	10 Concord	30 Contra Costa County

Input Data:

data	description
City code	XX
County code	XX
Annual income	XXXXX
Number of dependents	XX

Output Sketch:

```
                         AVERAGE                                    PAGE 1
 CITY   CITY   AVERAGE   NUMBER OF              TOTAL
 CODE   CODE   INCOME    DEPENDENTS             INCOME
  ~      ~    $ ~ . ~      ~                  $ ~ , ~ . ~
  ~      ~      ~ . ~      ~                    ~ , ~ . ~
  ~      ~      ~ . ~      ~                    ~ , ~ . ~

                         ALAMEDA COUNTY                ~
                         AVERAGE INCOME       $ ~ ~ . ~
                         AVERAGE DEPENDENTS            ~
  ─────────────────────────────────────────────────────────
  ~~    ~    $ ~ . ~      ~                  $ ~ , ~ . ~   PAGE 2
  ~     ~      ~ . ~      ~                    ~ , ~ . ~
  ~     ~      ~ . ~      ~                    ~ , ~ . ~

                         CONTRA COSTA COUNTY           ~
                         AVERAGE INCOME       $ ~ ~ . ~
                         AVERAGE DEPENDENTS            ~

                         TOTALS              $ ~ , ~ . ~
                                               ~ , ~ . ~
                                               ~ , ~ . ~
```

5. You and five of your friends are going to Fiesta Lanes to have a weekend bowling festival. Each of you rolls three lines. Print the scores of each game, totals for each person, and averages of each game and total. The winner gets an autographed picture of Dick Weber.

input						output		
		SCORES						
columns	field	GAME 1	GAME 2	GAME 3	TOTAL	NAME		
1–5	ID#	100	150	175	425	Raymond Langsford		
6–8	score 1	192	183	175	550	Henry Hotchkiss		
9–11	score 2	200	100	50	350	Nancy Jimenez		
12–14	score 3	100	200	300	600	Sue Struthers		
20–60	name	147	133	122	402	Tommy Cocco		
		90	80	70	240	Sam Rodriguez		
AVERAGES		138	141	149	428			

6. Archetypal Systems, Inc. has decided to modernize and will promote you from stockroom worker to programmer if you write a program to analyze the inventory on hand. **Extended cost** is the amount on hand multiplied by its cost. Write YES under NEED REORDER if the amount on hand is less than the reorder point.

Input Design:

```
  PART        UNIT   REORDER  AMOUNT
  NUMBER      COST   POINT    ON HAND

 9 9 9 9 9 9|9 9 9 9|9 9 9 9 9|9 9 9 9|9 9 9 9 9 9 9 9 9 9 9 9 9 9 9 9 9 9 9 9 9 9 9 9
 1 2 3 4 5 6 7 8 9 10 11 12 13 14 15 16 17 18 19 20 21 22 23 24 25 26 27 28 29 30 31 32 33 34 35 36 37 38 39 40 41 42 43 44
```

Output Design:

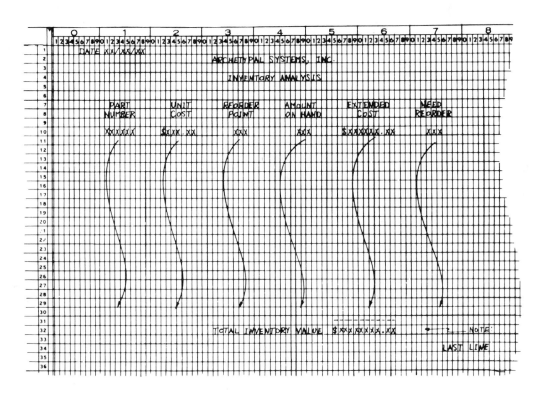

7. Most large purchases involve loans and repayment schedules. Write a program to print out the loan repayment schedule for a number of loans. Interest = principal X rate X time. Rates are usually given as yearly. The monthly rate on a 9 percent loan is 0.09/12.

Input Design:

ACCOUNT NUMBER	MONTH	YEAR	PRINCIPLE	INTEREST RATE	MONTHLY PAYMENT	
9 9 9 9 9 9 9 9 9 9	9 9	9 9	9 9 9 9 9 9 9	9 9 9 9 9	9 9 9 9 9 9	9 9 9 9 9 9 9 9 9 9 9 9 9
1 2 3 4 5 6 7 8 9 10 11 12	13 14	15 16	17 18 19 20 21 22	23 24 25 26 27 28	29 30 31 32 33 34	35 36 37 38 39 40 41 42 43 44 45 46 47 48

Output Design:

8. Programmit Company hires you as a consultant to solve their payroll problem. The previous programmers had botched the job so badly that they were bent, folded, stapled, mutilated, and fired. The information concerning each employee is already keyed, one line per employee, as follows.

data	columns
Social security number	1–9
Employee name	10–20
Hours worked	21–24
Rate of pay per hour	25–28
Tax rate	29–30
Health plan	31

The health plan is coded as follows:

N—doesn't belong
S—$5.34 per week deduction
F—$10.74 per week deduction

The output from the program is to be, for each employee:

a. A paycheck listing gross pay and deductions (tax, health plan, social security, and pension) as well as take home pay.

b. After all the paychecks have been printed, a list giving total gross pay, total tax deduction, total health plan, total social security, and total pension so that the company knows "where the money went."

The output can be computed as follows:

$$
\begin{aligned}
\text{gross pay} &= \text{hours worked} * \text{rate of pay} \\
\text{tax} &= \text{gross pay} * \text{tax rate} \\
\text{health plan} &= \$0, \$5.34, \text{ or } \$10.74 \text{ depending on plan type none,} \\
&\quad \text{single, or family, respectively} \\
\text{social security} &= 6.75\% \text{ of gross pay} \\
\text{pension} &= 6\% \text{ of gross pay} \\
\text{take home pay} &= \text{gross pay} - \text{tax} - \text{health plan} - \text{social} \\
&\quad \text{security} - \text{pension}
\end{aligned}
$$

Run your program with the following test data. Your output should be designed and printed to look like a paycheck (i.e., bank name, address, date, etc.)

532402221	FIELDS	WC	3421	0253	09	S
427556677	RAKE	HIHO	1477	1317	16	F
363407210	FIGMO	FRED	0925	0215	08	N
939721471	CRAFTER	IMA	7500	0876	10	S
874661193	BIG	BUCK	8275	1545	12	F
369452546	DYMO	DINA	4350	0990	11	S

Develop an output design, prepare a plan, and write and execute the program.

9 ARRAYS

CHAPTER
PLAN

- *Identify the need for arrays*
- *Present and give examples of:*
  Declaration of arrays
  Input and output of arrays
  Two-dimensional arrays

9.1 USING ARRAYS

You already have a repertoire of Fortran instructions sufficient to describe all possible computations. Many computations, however, would require programs of unmanageable size if you used only your present stock of instructions. For this reason, all programming languages incorporate some way of referring to a large number of memory cells simply and concisely. In Fortran, **arrays** are provided for this purpose. In this chapter we'll look at several problems in which the use of arrays leads to great simplification.

In the first two examples, we will show how the problem can be solved with or without arrays to demonstrate that it is always possible to avoid using arrays, but it is sometimes easier to use them than to avoid them.

To get started as simply as possible, consider the problem of a lumber company that owns several sawmills and wants to compute its total sales each month. The sawmills are located in pine forests and their output falls into three grades: number 1 (clear) pine, number 2 (construction) pine, and number 3 (shop) pine. The grades are priced (F.O.B. sawmill) at $0.30 per board foot for grade 1, $0.18 for grade 2, and $0.08 for grade 3.

Each mill reports its sales for the month in board feet by grade, and the home office keeps books on the whole operation. To compute the revenue to be collected for one of the sawmills, the home office multiplies the reported board feet in each grade by the appropriate price and

177

sums these amounts to get the total cash for the sawmill. Doing this for each sawmill, the total sales for the company are computed by adding up those for the individual sawmills. A plan detailing this summary is presented in Figure 9.1.1.

Figure 9.1.1   Plan for Lumber Company Bookkeeping

```
Let TOTAL = 0.00

    ┌──────────────────────────────────────────────┐
    │ Fetch sawmill sales figures (bd ft)          │
    │ Exit if termination signal                   │
    │ Compute sawmill sales ($)                    │
    │ Add sawmill sales to TOTAL                   │
    └────────────────────────────────── Repeat

Print TOTAL
```

The following program is a routine implementation of this plan in Fortran using techniques you already know.

```
    COMMENT:              LUMBER COMPANY BOOKKEEPING (WITHOUT ARRAYS)
              REAL G1,G2,G3, SAWMIL, TOTAL, ENDMIL
              PARAMETER (ENDMILL = 0.0)
              TOTAL = 0.00
    100       READ *, G1,G2,G3
                IF (G1 .LT. ENDMIL) GO TO 200
                SAWMIL = 0.30*G1 + 0.18*G2 + 0.08*G3
                TOTAL = TOTAL + SAWMIL
                GO TO 100
    200       PRINT *, 'TOTAL SALES: $', TOTAL
              END
```

Data

```
4285.0    8500.00    15345.0    (sawmill 1)
6400.0   12500.00     9380.0    (sawmill 2)
  -1.0       -1.0       -1.0    (termination signal)
```

Output

```
TOTAL SALES: $8963.50
```

In this program the memory cells G1, G2, and G3 are used for the sales figures reported by a sawmill, G1 for the number of board feet of number 1 pine sold, G2 for number 2 pine, and G3 for number 3 pine. Instead of three individual memory cells, we can use an array for the three sales figures. An array is a collection of memory cells all called by the same name with an INTEGER "subscript" attached to particular cells within the array. Fortran array subscripts are written in parentheses immediately after the array name. In this case we could call the array G, and it would have three memory cells: G(1), G(2), and G(3). The new program, as you can see, is almost identical to the old one except for a minor difference in the declaration statement and in the way the memory cells for the sales figures are denoted: G(1) instead of G1, for example.

```
COMMENT:                   LUMBER COMPANY BOOKKEEPING
            REAL G(3), SAWMIL, TOTAL, ENDMIL
            PARAMETER (ENDMIL = 0.0)
            TOTAL = 0.0
    100     READ *, G(1), G(2), G(3)
              IF (G(1) .LT. ENDMIL) GO TO 200
              SAWMIL = 0.30*G(1) + 0.18*G(2) + 0.08*G(3)
              TOTAL = TOTAL + SAWMIL
              GO TO 100
    200     PRINT *, 'TOTAL SALES: $', TOTAL
            END
```

The program operates exactly the same as before. The only difference is in the way the memory cells are named. There is really no advantage in using the array G in place of the individual memory cells G1, G2, and G3. There is no significant disadvantage either. It's just a different way of doing the same thing. However, later in this chapter we will see examples in which arrays provide more than an alternative notation—they actually simplify the program.

Arrays used in a program must be declared at the beginning. Like memory cell declarations, **array declarations** establish the name and the type of information the array will contain—INTEGER, REAL, or whatever. (An array may contain only one type of data; no single array can contain both INTEGER and REAL numbers, for example.) In addition, an array declaration must specify the number of memory cells in the array by placing that number in parentheses after the array name. This part of an array declaration is known as the **length declarator** and should not be confused with a subscript. A subscript designates a particular memory cell in an array. A length declarator establishes the *number* of memory cells in the entire array.

Array Declarator

> **form**
> *name (len)*
> *name* is a Fortran identifier (up to six characters)
> *len* is a positive INTEGER constant expression
>
> **meaning**
> Establishes an array named *name* with *len* memory cells
>
> **examples**
>
> ```
> INTEGER A, B(12), ARA(103)
> REAL QX(27), BAG, ROT
> ```
>
> These statements establish three arrays (two for INTEGER values, one for REALs). In addition, the types of three simple memory cells are established. Array declarators and memory cell declarators may be mixed in the same declaration statement.

Together, the name and length declarator make up an **array declarator.** Array declarators are placed in type statements (INTEGER statements, REAL statements, and the like) either interspersed with ordinary memory cell declarations or alone.

---

array element: a memory cell in an array

An **array element** (a memory cell in an array) is used in the same ways that other memory cells are used, but each reference to an array element must include both the array name and the subscript. The elements are numbered starting from 1. The last element's subscript, therefore, is the same as the number of elements in the array.

Array Reference

---

form
name(e)
name is an array name
e is an expression whose value is an INTEGER in the range 1 to *len*, where *len* is the number of elements in the array *name*

meaning
designates the *e*th element of *name*

examples
```
A(3) = 47.0*Q
PRINT *, B(3*J-I)
IF ( 4.0*RT(L-2) .LT. T(3)+1 ) GO TO 100
B(L) = B(L-1) + 5.7
A(I+2) = A(J) + A(I)
```

The subscript in an array reference may be an INTEGER constant, as in our sawmill example, or it may be an INTEGER-valued expression involving variables as well as constants. If subscripts had to be constants, then arrays would be simply another way of naming memory cells. Arrays don't realize their full potential for simplifying programs unless variables are used for the subscripts, and we will see how this comes into play in the next section.

9.1 EXERCISES

---

1. Which of the following are legal declarations?
```
REAL A(10)
REAL B(22), C(8), X
INTEGER NUM(K)
INTEGER N, ISLE(22-3)
REAL Y(15.0)
```

2. Rewrite the following program fragment using an array in place of the memory cells.

```
CHARACTER*(4) N1, N2
READ *, N1, N2
IF (N1 .EQ. 'KAT ' .AND. N2 .EQ. 'PAGE') GOTO 200
```

9.2 A PROBLEM THAT CALLS FOR ARRAYS

Let's suppose we have written to the governors of 11 western states inquiring about sales tax. While we are waiting for replies, we will prepare a program to analyze the data we hope to receive. Given 11 data cards, each of which contains the name of a state and its sales tax rate, we want our program to list those states where the sales tax is below average.

We can compute the average from the data easily enough. The problem arises from the necessity to print certain parts of the data after the average is computed and, therefore, after the data lines have all been read. Since there is no way to reread the lines, we must save the information in memory cells. Figure 9.2.1 describes our general strategy. Our program is as follows.

Figure 9.2.1 Strategy for Listing States with Below Average Sales Tax

Get sales tax data.

Compute average.

Print states with below-average sales tax.

```
COMMENT:                    PROGRAM TO LIST THE WESTERN STATES
C                           BELOW AVERAGE TAX RATES
        CHARACTER*(10) S1,S2,S3,S4,S5,S6,S7,S8,S9,S10,S11
        REAL T1,T2,T3,T4,T5,T6,T7,T8,T9,T10,T11,AVE
C
C                    STORE DATA
        READ *, S1, T1
        READ *, S2, T2
        READ *, S3, T3
        READ *, S4, T4
        READ *, S5, T5
        READ *, S6, T6
        READ *, S7, T7
        READ *, S8, T8
        READ *, S9, T9
        READ *, S10, T10
        READ *, S11, T11
C
        AVE = (T1+T2+T3+T4+T5+T6+T7+T8+T9+T10+T11)/11.0
C
        PRINT *, 'STATES WITH BELOW AVERAGE SALES TAX'
        PRINT *, ' '
        IF (T1 .LE. AVE) THEN
          PRINT *, S1
```

(Continued on following page)

```
        ENDIF
        IF (T2 .LE. AVE) THEN
          PRINT *, S2
        ENDIF
        IF (T3 .LE. AVE) THEN
          PRINT *, S3
        ENDIF
        IF (T4 .LE. AVE) THEN
          PRINT *, S4
        ENDIF
        IF (T5 .LE. AVE) THEN
          PRINT *, S5
        ENDIF
        IF (T6 .LE. AVE) THEN
          PRINT *, S6
        ENDIF
        IF (T7 .LE. AVE) THEN
          PRINT *, S7
        ENDIF
        IF (T8 .LE. AVE) THEN
          PRINT *, S8
        ENDIF
        IF (T9 .LE. AVE) THEN
          PRINT *, S9
        ENDIF
        IF (T10 .LE. AVE) THEN
          PRINT *, S10
        ENDIF
        IF (T11 .LE. AVE) THEN
          PRINT *, S11
        ENDIF
        END
```

Data

```
'WASHINGTON'    0.045
'IDAHO      '    0.03
'MONTANA    '    0.00
'OREGON     '    0.04
'WYOMING    '    0.03
'CALIFORNIA'    0.06
'NEVADA     '    0.03
'UTAH       '    0.04
'COLORADO   '    0.03
'ARIZONA    '    0.04
'NEW MEXICO'    0.04
```

Output

```
STATES WITH BELOW AVERAGE SALES TAX

IDAHO
MONTANA
WYOMING
NEVADA
COLORADO
```

As you can see, the program's input section has 11 almost identical statements. So does the output section. Normally, we'd like to make a loop out of each such section, but in this case we have no way of making the statements identical so that we can replace them with a loop. To do so, we'd have to refer to the same memory cells in each READ, and this would continually wipe out previously recorded information. We'd wind up with only one state's sales tax rate in memory. What we need is some way to change the memory cell used by the READ statement without changing the READ statement itself. We can do this by using arrays.

An **array** is a group of memory cells all of which have the same name. They are distinguished by a **subscript** or **index** which is associated with the name. In a program, the name and the subscript are associated by enclosing the subscript in parentheses to the right of the name. In our example, we will need two arrays, each of which is a group of 11 memory cells, one group for the names of the states, and the other for the taxes. Then, instead of dealing with the 11 separate memory cells (S1, S2, S3, etc.) we will use the array S and refer to S(1), S(2), S(3), and so on.

Of course, if our only option were to write S(5) instead of S5 or S(7) instead of S7, nothing would be gained. The advantage is that we can write the subscript as an *arithmetic expression* whose value can change from time to time as the program runs. Instead of writing

```
READ *, S1, T1
```

we will write

```
READ *, S(N), T(N)
```

where N is an INTEGER memory cell whose value will be 1 the first time the computer executes the READ statement, 2 the second time, and so on.

Using arrays, we can rewrite our sales tax program in a simpler way, but still following the strategy of Figure 9.2.1.

```
COMMENT:                 PROGRAM TO LIST THE WESTERN STATES WITH
C                        BELOW AVERAGE SALES TAX RATES
        INTEGER NUMST, LENST
        PARAMETER(NUMST = 11, LENST = 10)
        CHARACTER*(LENST) S(NUMST)
        REAL T(NUMST), AVE
        INTEGER N
```

(Continued on following page)

```
C
C                        STORE DATA
            DO 100 N=1,NUMST
                READ *, S(N), T(N)
    100     CONTINUE
C
    200     AVE = (T(1) + T(2) + T(3) + T(4) + T(5) + T(6) +
        +            T(7) + T(8) + T(9) + T(10) + T(11))/NUMST
C
            PRINT *, 'STATES WITH BELOW AVERAGE SALES TAX'
            PRINT *, ' '

            DO 300 N=1,NUMST
                IF (T(N) .LE. AVE) THEN
                    PRINT *, S(N), T(N)
                ENDIF
    300     CONTINUE
            END
```

Data

```
'WASHINGTON'    0.045
'IDAHO     '    0.03
'MONTANA   '    0.00
'OREGON    '    0.04
'WYOMING   '    0.03
'CALIFORNIA'    0.06
'NEVADA    '    0.03
'UTAH      '    0.04
'COLORADO  '    0.03
'ARIZONA   '    0.04
'NEW MEXICO'    0.04
```

Output

```
STATES WITH BELOW AVERAGE SALES TAX

IDAHO       2.9999999E-02
MONTANA     0.0000000E+00
WYOMING     2.9999999E-02
NEVADA      2.9999999E-02
COLORADO    2.9999999E-02
```

Note the use of named constants to specify the lengths of the arrays and the size of the CHARACTER variables. This clarifies the meaning of the program and makes it easier to modify if need be.

9.2   EXERCISES

1. Under what conditions would B(I) and B(J) refer to the same element of array B?
2. What would the following program print?

```
            INTEGER A(10), I
            A(1) = 0
            A(2) = 1
            DO 100 I=3,10
                A(I) = A(I-1) + A(I-2)
    100     CONTINUE
    200     PRINT *, A(1), A(2), A(3), A(4), A(5)
            PRINT *, A(6), A(7), A(8), A(9), A(10)
            END
```

3. Assuming that B is an array of ten elements and I and J are memory cells with the values 3 and 7 respectively, which of the following statements are legal? For each statement that is not legal, explain why not.

```
B(3)    = B(I)
B(I)    = B(I-1)
B(J)    = B(2*I)
B(4)    = B(J-1) + B(I*J-21)
B(2*I) = B(J+4)
B(1.7) = 0
```

4. Suppose that, instead of wanting to list only the states whose sales tax is below average, we had wanted to make a list of the states and their sales taxes and print the average sales tax at the end of the listings. If the data provided was the same as that of this section, would we need to use arrays to write the program?

5. Which of the following are legal declarations?

```
REAL A(10)
INTEGER A(2-13)
INTEGER A(I)
REAL A(150), BOK(2**10+1)
REAL X(15.0)
LOGICAL QS(23), PS(47)
```

9.3 A MORE USEFUL SOLUTION

We were probably not being realistic when we wrote the program of Section 2 because we assumed that all 11 governors would reply to our letter. A program which would still work with only a partial response would be more useful. Fortunately, such a program is easy to write now that we know about arrays. (Without arrays the program becomes much more difficult—see the exercises.)

   Since we now assume that the data may be incomplete, we can no longer compute the average by summing and dividing by 11. The program itself will have to keep track of the number of responses so that it can divide the sum by the appropriate number. So the program can recognize the end of the input loop, we'll append a special data line containing the string 'END DATA'.

Figure 9.3.1 depicts the general strategy of our revised program. With the exception that it keeps track of the number of data items, our new strategy doesn't differ much from the one in Figure 9.2.1.

Figure 9.3.1   Sales Tax Summary for an Arbitrary Number of States

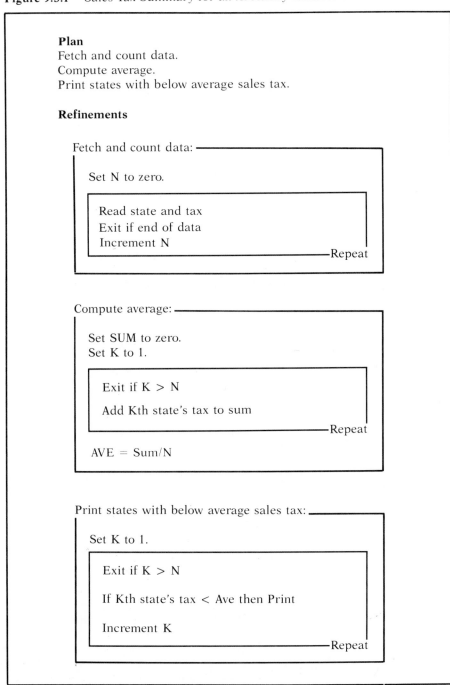

Plan
Fetch and count data.
Compute average.
Print states with below average sales tax.

Refinements

Fetch and count data:

Set N to zero.

Read state and tax
Exit if end of data
Increment N
Repeat

Compute average:

Set SUM to zero.
Set K to 1.

Exit if K > N

Add Kth state's tax to sum
Repeat

AVE = Sum/N

Print states with below average sales tax:

Set K to 1.

Exit if K > N

If Kth state's tax < Ave then Print

Increment K
Repeat

```
COMMENT:                    PROGRAM TO LIST STATES WITH
C                           BELOW AVERAGE SALES TAX
          INTEGER LENST, NUMST
          PARAMETER(LENST = 10, NUMST = 11)
          CHARACTER*(LENST) S(NUMST + 1), ENDST
          PARAMETER(ENDST ='END DATA')
          REAL T(NUMST + 1), AVE, SUM
          INTEGER N, K
C
C                           STORE DATA
          N = 0
  100     READ *, S(N+1), T(N+1)
            IF (S(N+1) .EQ. ENDST) GO TO 200
            N = N + 1
            GO TO 100
C
C                           COMPUTE AVERAGE
  200     SUM = 0.0
          DO 300 K=1,N
            SUM = SUM + T(K)
  300     CONTINUE
          AVE = SUM/N
C
          PRINT *, 'STATES WITH BELOW AVERAGE SALES TAX'
          PRINT *, ' '
          DO 400 K=1,N
            IF (T(K) .LE. AVE) THEN
                PRINT *, S(K), T(K)
            ENDIF
  400     CONTINUE
          END
```

Data

```
'WASHINGTON'    0.045
'IDAHO     '    0.03
'MONTANA   '    0.00
'OREGON    '    0.04
'WYOMING   '    0.03
'CALIFORNIA'    0.06
'NEVADA    '    0.03
'UTAH      '    0.04
'COLORADO  '    0.03
'ARIZONA   '    0.04
'NEW MEXICO'    0.04
```

Output

```
IDAHO       2.9999999E-02
MONTANA     0.0000000E+00
WYOMING     2.9999999E-02
NEVADA      2.9999999E-02
COLORADO    2.9999999E-02
```

Study the new program carefully; it is typical of many that you will write in the future. An important point to notice is that the memory cell

N is used to count the number of state governors who responded to our question. The computer performs the READ statement (statement 100) many times, but it is always true that just before the READ statement is performed, the value of N is the number of governors' responses which have been read. In addition, since N is not increased until after the test for 'END DATA', the value of N when the computer reaches statement 200 is the total number of governors' responses. Thus, the count N does not include the special 'END DATA' line; it counts only response lines. This section's exercises help explain other details of the program.

9.3 EXERCISES

1. Why did we allocate 12 memory cells to the arrays instead of 11?
2. Why does the 'END DATA' line also contain a number?
3. Show how the running sum could be incorporated into the input loop to avoid the loop in the section where the average is computed.
4. If none of the governors responds and we run our program with only the 'END DATA' line, something bad will happen. What?
5. Suppose, by some fluke, we give the program more than 11 responses. What will happen? How can we change the program to avoid this problem? (This is a very important way of making the program more robust.)

> **robust:** a program is more robust if it functions properly given a wider range of input values.

6. What changes need to be made in the program to allow all 50 states to be included in the data?
7. Write a program which does the same thing as the one in this section without using arrays. (*Note:* This is a lot of work. Why not just look at the answer?)

9.4 SOME MISCONCEPTIONS THAT CAUSE BUGS

Arrays confuse many novice programmers. The following list may help you avoid some common mistakes.

1. Don't confuse the *subscript value* with the *array element value*. The value of the element A(5) usually has nothing to do with the number 5.

	A
A(1)	− 4.7
A(2)	192.1
A(3)	3.9
A(4)	485.3
A(5)	− 19.1
A(6)	0.00

2. When a memory cell is used in a subscript, it is only the *value* of that memory cell which is important; its name is irrelevant. At one point in a program, we may refer to A(I), and at another point in the same program, we may refer to A(J). In each case, we are dealing with the same array. In fact, we may even be referencing the same element of the array depending on what the values I and J have at the times of the array references.

3. For the same reason, a program may reference both A(I) and B(I). That is, the same memory cell may be used as a subscript in referencing two (or more) different arrays. Again it is the *value* of the subscript which counts, not its name.

4. Don't use arrays when you don't need them. Profligate use often results in unclear, inefficient, programs (see exercise 9.2.4).

5. In general, Fortran can deal with only one element of an array at a time. For example, if A is an array of ten elements, then the statement

```
IF (A .NE. 0) THEN
   EQZERO = .FALSE.
ENDIF
```

does not test all ten elements of A. In fact, it isn't even a legal statement. If the intention is to set EQZERO to .FALSE. in case some element of A is nonzero, then each element must be tested individually as in the loop below.

```
        EQZERO = .TRUE.
        DO 20 I=1,10
           IF (A(I) .NE. 0) THEN
              EQZERO = .FALSE.
           ENDIF
20      CONTINUE
           .
           .
           .
```

6. Remember: In Fortran the number of memory cells in an array may not be changed in your program. If you don't know exactly how much room you will need (as in the example of Section 9.3), you must declare the array larger than you will actually need, and let your program keep track of how many memory cells it is using.

9.5 ARRAYS OF VARIABLES

In both of the examples you have seen, arrays have been used to store values that never change once they are established. In essence, we have been dealing with arrays of constants. However, array elements are memory cells, and the values stored in memory cells may vary as a computation proceeds. Programs that change the values of array elements are using arrays of variables rather than arrays of constants. In this section we'll look at a program that uses an array of counters, a counter being a variable that keeps track of the number of occurrences of a specific event.

The example problem has been presented before: counting birds in a sanctuary (Section 7.2). The problem was to count the number observations of curlews, egrets, blue herons, and whooping cranes in the Big Thicket.

Whooping Cranes and the Big Thicket

> There aren't any whooping cranes in the Big Thicket, as the data of Section 7.2 attests. Whooping cranes winter in the Aransas National Wildlife Refuge, about 200 miles southwest of the Big Thicket.

In the program, we used four unrelated counters, C, E, H, and W, and selected the appropriate counter to increment with an IF-THEN-ELSE structure. The program is easier to manage if we use an array of four counters, B(1) for curlews, B(2) for egrets, B(3) for blue herons, and B(4) for whooping cranes. A program almost identical to the one in Section 7.2, with array references in place of the variables C, E, H, and W, will count birds in the four categories, just as we did before.

```
COMMENT:                        COUNTING BIRD OBSERVATIONS IN THE BIG THICKET
C                               DATA ENCODING:
C                               'C' STANDS FOR CURLEW
C                               'E' STANDS FOR EGRET
C                               'H' STANDS FOR BLUE HERON
C                               'W' STANDS FOR WHOOPING CRANE
C                               ' ' STANDS FOR NO MORE BIRDS
          INTEGER NUMBRD
          CHARACTER*(1) BIRD, CURLEW, EGRET, HERON, WHOOP, ENDBRD
          PARAMETER(CURLEW = 'C', EGRET = 'E', HERON = 'H',
       +           WHOOP = 'W', ENDBRD = ' ', NUMBRD = 4)
          INTEGER B(NUMBRD)
          B(1) = 0
          B(2) = 0
          B(3) = 0
          B(4) = 0
   100    READ *, BIRD
            IF (BIRD .EQ. ENDBRD) GO TO 200
              IF (BIRD .EQ. CURLEW) THEN
                 B(1) = B(1) + 1
              ELSE IF (BIRD .EQ. EGRET) THEN
                 B(2) = B(2) + 1
              ELSE IF (BIRD .EQ. HERON) THEN
                 B(3) = B(3) + 1
              ELSE
                 B(4) = B(4) + 1
              ENDIF
            GO TO 100
   200    PRINT *, 'CURLEW SIGHTINGS: ', B(1)
          PRINT *, 'EGRET SIGHTINGS:  ', B(2)
          PRINT *, 'BLUE HERON SIGHTINGS: ', B(3)
          PRINT *, 'WHOOPING CRANE SIGHTINGS: ', B(4)
          END
```

Data

```
'H'
'E'
'C'
'C'
'E'
'E'
'C'
' '    (BLANK IS TERMINATION SIGNAL)
```

Output

```
CURLEW SIGHTINGS:        3
EGRET SIGHTINGS:         3
BLUE HERON SIGHTINGS:       1
WHOOPING CRANE SIGHTINGS:       0
```

As you can see, there is virtually no advantage in using the array of counters, B, in place of the four variables, C, E, H, and W. It just changes the names we use. The primary difference between this array and the arrays you've seen before is that these array elements change values as the computation proceeds. The array is used as an *array of variables* rather than an array of constants.

However, just as we did with the sales tax program, we can simplify our bird census program by using a variable for the subscript instead of a constant. We will have an array of variables whose elements are indexed by another variable.

To make the process as simple as possible, we will encode the data differently. Instead of using letters for bird sightings, we will use numbers to match the subscripts of the counters (that is, "1" for curlews, "2" for egrets, and so on). Then we won't need an IF-THEN-ELSE to select a counter to increment. *The subscript will make the selection automatically,* and the program becomes much simpler.

We initialize the counters with a DO-loop that cycles through each subscript and initializes the corresponding counter to zero. This is a minor change from the preceding program and is fairly easy to understand. The other change is in the way the counters are incremented. Each time we read a data line, we have to increment one of the counters. In the first program we had four separate statements to handle the incrementing, but in the new program we will need only one incrementing statement because the counter to be incremented will be selected by a varying subscript instead of a varying statement. In essence we have replaced an "array of statements" with an array of variables. There is no simple notation for an array of statements in Fortran, but there is a simple notation for an array of variables, and this is what simplifies the program.

```
COMMENT:          COUNTING BIRD OBSERVATIONS IN THE BIG THICKET
C                 DATA ENCODING
C                 1 STANDS FOR CURLEW
C                 2 STANDS FOR EGRET
C                 3 STANDS FOR BLUE HERON
C                 4 STANDS FOR WHOOPING CRANE
C                 0 (BLANK) STANDS FOR "NO MORE BIRDS"
```

(Continued on following page)

```
        INTEGER ENDBRD, CURLEW, EGRET, HERON, WHOOP, NUMBRD
        PARAMETER(CURLEW = 1, EGRET = 2, HERON = 3, WHOOP = 4,
     +           NUMBRD = 4, ENDBRD = 0)
        INTEGER BIRD, B(NUMBRD)
        DO 50 BIRD = 1, NUMBRD
          B(BIRD) = 0
50      CONTINUE
100     READ *, BIRD
          IF (BIRD .EQ. ENDBRD) GO TO 200
          B(BIRD) = B(BIRD) + 1
          GO TO 100
        PRINT *, 'BIRD SIGHTINGS IN THE BIG THICKET'
        PRINT *, 'CURLEW', B(1)
        PRINT *, 'EGRET', B(2)
        PRINT *, 'HERON', B(3)
        PRINT *, 'WHOOPER', B(4)
        END
```

Data

```
3
2
1
1
2
2
1
0  (termination signal)
```

Output

```
CURLEW     3
EGRET      3
HERON      1
WHOOPER     0
```

9.5 EXERCISES

1. Simplify the following program fragment by using an array of variables instead of the "array of statements" that you see in the fragment.

```
READ *, XCODE, XPNS
IF (XCODE .EQ. 1) THEN
   FOOD = FOOD + XPNS
ELSE IF (XCODE .EQ. 2) THEN
   CLOTHE = CLOTHE + XPNS
ELSE
   SHELTR = SHELTR + XPNS
ENDIF
```

2. At the end of the bird census program there is a sequence of PRINT statements that are all very much alike, except that they print different bird names. Using arrays containing character values, replace this "array of PRINT statements" by a single PRINT inside a loop.

9.6   A NEW KIND OF LOOP: THE SEARCH LOOP

We simplified our bird census program by using an array of variables instead of an array of statements. However, our simplified program did not operate in exactly the same way as the bulkier one: the data was encoded differently. Instead of using letters to denote the bird sightings, we used numbers. Changes like this are common whenever computers are used because they make programs easier to write. However, such changes place a burden on the people who enter the data. The more unfamiliar the data encoding, the harder it is to check the data for accuracy; and numeric encoding of bird names is certainly less familiar than first-letter encoding, which is what we used before. By adding only a little code to our program, we can go back to the first-letter encodings and make the computer appear to be a little more polite to the people who prepare the data.

What we need to do is to convert a letter ("C", "E", "H", or "W") to a number (1, 2, 3, or 4). We can do this by storing the letters in an array and searching the array for the input letter. If the letters are stored "in order," then the position of the letter in the array reveals the number it should be converted to. For example, the letter "H" will be in position three, and we want to convert "H" to "3".

We can find the position of a particular value within an array with a looping structure that we call an **array search loop.** In general, the purpose of an array search loop is to locate a value that satisfies some "specified properties," which are determined by the nature of the computation

Array Initialization by DATA Statement

---

form
DATA *vlist/clist/*
vlist is a list of variable names, separated by commas.
clist is a list of constants, separated by commas.
note: vlist and clist must have the same length

meaning
Set each variable in vlist to the corresponding value from clist before the program execution begins.

examples

```
DATA N(1),N(2),N(3) /'BROWN','SMITH','JONES'/
DATA C(1),C(2),C(3),C(4) /'B','S','J','E'/
```

usage
PARAMETER statements cannot set up arrays of constants, but DATA statements can be used to obtain a similar effect.

Figure 9.6.1   Skeletal Form of the Array Search Loop

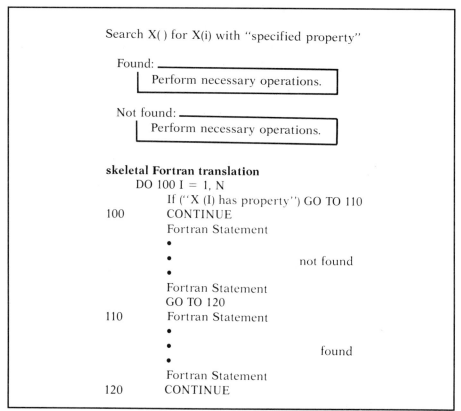

we are trying to carry out. The typical form of such loops is outlined in Figure 9.6.1.

To make it possible to use first-letter encodings in our bird census program, we will put an array search loop after the READ statement to convert the letter from the data into a number to use for a subscript in the statement that increments the appropriate counter. A plan for that loop is shown in Figure 9.6.2. It comes after the exit statement for the READ-loop and before the statement that increments the appropriate counter. You will notice in the plan that we have made the program more robust in the same way that we did in Chapter 7. Our previous program assumed that all birds that were not curlews, egrets, or blue herons must be whooping cranes. The new program will make no such assumption. Instead, all encodings other than "C", "E", "H", or "W" will be lumped into an "other" category. The counter for this "other" category will be a fifth element in the array B( ).

The program has been improved in another way, too. Instead of using a sequence of almost identical PRINT statements to print the results, we use an array to store the names of the birds. The sequence of PRINT statements becomes a DO-loop with one PRINT. The PRINT statement has an extra variable in it to print the name of the bird. Note the use of DATA statements to set up the name and code tables.

Figure 9.6.2   Counting Bird Observations

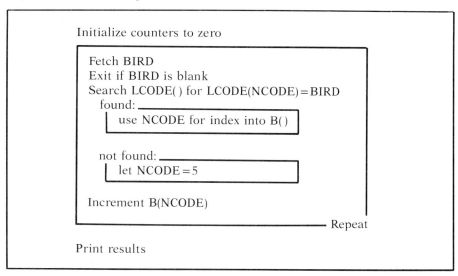

```
COMMENT:                COUNTING BIRD OBSERVATIONS IN THE BIG THICKET
C                       DATA ENCODING
C                       C   STANDS FOR CURLEW
C                       E   STANDS FOR EGRET
C                       H   STANDS FOR BLUE HERON
C                       W   STANDS FOR WHOOPING CRANE
C                       ' ' (BLANK) STANDS FOR "NO MORE BIRDS"
            INTEGER NUMBRD
            PARAMETER (NUMBRD = 4)
            INTEGER B(NUMBRD+1), NCODE
            CHARACTER*(8) NBIRD(NUMBRD+1)
            CHARACTER*(1) LCODE(NUMBRD), ENDBRD, BIRD
            PARAMETER (ENDBRD = ' ')
            DATA LCODE(1), LCODE(2), LCODE(3), LCODE(4) /'C', 'E',
          + 'H', 'W'/
            DATA NBIRD(1), NBIRD(2), NBIRD(3), NBIRD(4), NBIRD(5)
          + /'CURLEW', 'EGRET', 'HERON', 'WHOPPER', 'OTHER'/
            DO 50 NCODE = 1,NUMBRD+1
               B(NCODE) = 0
    50      CONTINUE
   100      READ *, BIRD
            IF (BIRD .EQ. ENDBRD) GO TO 200
C                       (BEGINNING OF SEARCH LOOP)
            DO 110 NCODE = 1,NUMBRD
               IF (LCODE(NCODE) .EQ. BIRD) GO TO 112
   110      CONTINUE
C                       (BIRD NOT IN LETTER CODES)
            NCODE = NUMBRD+1
            GO TO 115
C                       (FOUND BIRD IN LETTER CODES)
   112      CONTINUE
   115      CONTINUE
C                       (END OF SEARCH LOOP)
            B(NCODE) = B(NCODE) + 1
            GO TO 100
C                       (PRINT RESULTS)
   200      PRINT *, 'BIRD SIGHTINGS IN THE BIG THICKET'
```

(Continued on following page)

```
            DO 210 NCODE = 1,NUMBRD+1
               PRINT *, NBIRD(NCODE), B(NCODE)
     210       CONTINUE
               END
```

Data

```
'H'
'E'
'C'
'C'
'E'
'E'
'C'
'D'   (DUCK)
'B'   (RED-WINGED BLACKBIRD)
' '   (TERMINATION SIGNAL)
```

Output

```
BIRD SIGHTINGS IN THE BIG THICKET
CURLEW          3
EGRET           3
HERON           1
WHOOPER         0
OTHER           2
```

A second application of array search loops occurs when you want to put values into arrays from data lines. A READ-loop would be the usual way to handle it, but you have to be careful not to run beyond the end of the array. If there's more data than there is space in the array, then you have to stop READing. The normal exit from this type of loop is the same as in a normal READ-loop: exit on encountering the end of the data. Usually, some special action (error handling) needs to be taken when the array gets filled before the data is exhausted.

The form of these **array READ loops** is fundamentally the same as that of array search loops, but because they are used in a different context, we'll describe them in slightly different terms, as illustrated in Figure 9.6.3.

To illustrate the use of an array READ-loop, let's improve the sales tax program at the end of Section 9.3. The first step was to store the table of sales tax rates (by state) in a pair of arrays.

```
CHARACTER*(10) S(NUMST)
REAL T(NUMST)
```

We used one array for the names of the states and the other for the sales tax rates. The READ-loop placed values in successive array elements until it reached the 'END OF DATA' line. An important assumption we made when writing the program was that there would be no more than 12 data lines, including the one with 'END OF DATA' on it. If there had been more than 12, we would have run out of space in the arrays, and the computer would have attempted to store information in nonexistent memory cells like S(13) and T(13). It is safer to provide an exit from the

Figure 9.6.3   The Skeletal Form of the Array READ-Loop

Read X(I), I = 1, . . . ,N until "end of data"

"End of data" not found: ———

> Number items exceeds N (too much data).
> Use first N items only.
> Perform error handling operations.

Compute number of items read.

skeletal Fortran translation
```
      Do 100 I = 1, N
         Read*X,(I)
         IF ("end of data") GO TO 110
100      CONTINUE
      I = N + 1
      Fortran Statement  ⎫
         •               ⎪
         •               ⎬  too much data
         •               ⎪
      Fortran Statement  ⎭
110      I = I - 1
```

READ-loop on the contingency that we run out of space in the arrays before we run out of data, and we can do this with an array READ-loop. Figure 9.6.4 provides the details. One important point to notice is that the value of N is reduced by one after the array READ-loop terminates. This

Figure 9.6.4   READing the Sales Tax Table

Read S(i) and T(i), i = 1,. . .,N until "end of data"

"End of data" not found: ———

> Print error message.
> Let N = 13

Let N = N - 1

```
      INTEGER N, NUMST
      PARAMETER (NUMST = 12)
      CHARACTER*(10) S(NUMST), ENDST
      REAL T(NUMST)
      PARAMETER (ENDST = 'END DATA')
      DO 100 N = 1, NUMST
        READ *, S(N), T(N)
        IF (S(N) .EQ. ENDST) GO TO 110
100     CONTINUE
      N = NUMST + 1
      PRINT *, 'WARNING—USING ONLY', NUMST, ' STATES'
110     N = N-1
         •
         •
         •
```

is because we use N later in the program to compute the average sales tax. In other words, N must contain the number of states in the sales tax survey. When the array READ-loop terminates, whether by the "end of data" exit or by the "out of space" exit, N will be the number of states in the survey plus one. That's why we have to make the subtraction. We point this out because it is typical of array READ-loops: the DO variable ends up one larger than the number of legitimate data items read.

9.6 EXERCISES

1. Write a DO-loop to double all the elements in an array.
2. Write an array search loop to locate the first pair of numbers in consecutive array elements where the second number is smaller than the first.
3. Write an array READ-loop which will place four-letter words from data lines into an array until it comes to a data line containing the word 'DONE' or until it runs out of space. If it runs out of space in the array, print the values from the remaining data lines without storing them in the array.

9.7 ARRAY DIMENSION BOUNDS

When we are using an array A, we normally want A(1) to be the first element in the array; A(2), the second element; A(3), the third; and so on. Occasionally, however, this numbering scheme doesn't fit the problem. Suppose, for example, we are computing some statistics on soft drink preferences. To be specific, let's assume that a marketing company has circulated a questionnaire to determine the age distribution of people who prefer cola to uncola. The results have been entered on data lines, each of which contains a survey participant's age and preference, 'COLA' or 'UNCOLA'. The ages range from 12 to 65, and we are supposed to find the percentage of people at each age level who prefer cola.

To do this, we'll have to tabulate the data, keeping track of the number of people at each age who prefer cola and the number who prefer uncola. We need two arrays of counters. We could use ordinary arrays, with COLA(1) for counting the number of people at age 12 who prefer cola, COLA(2) for cola lovers age 13, and so on. Similarly we'd have UNCOLA(1) for 12-year-olds who prefer uncola, UNCOLA(2) for 13-year-olds, and finally UNCOLA(54) for 65-year-old UNCOLA lovers. But it would be nicer if we could number the array elements so that they correspond exactly to the ages. In other words, instead of having to start arbitrarily with COLA(1) for 12-year-olds, we'd rather start with COLA(12) for 12-year-olds.

We can arrange for COLA(12) to be the first element in the array by declaring it with a new type of array declaration. Instead of simply listing the length of the array and letting the computer assume we want the usual numbering scheme (1, 2, 3, . . .), we declare both the lower and upper dimension bounds. The **lower dimension bound** is the subscript we desire for the first element in the array, and the **upper dimension bound** is the subscript for the last element in the array.

Array Declarator (Alternate Dimension Bounds)

---

form
a(l:u)
a is an identifier.
l and *u* are INTEGER constant expressions.

meaning
Set up an array named *a* whose first element is *a(l)* and whose last element is *a(u)*

INTEGER constant expressions are defined in Section 3.7.

restriction
The value of *l* must not exceed the value of *u*.

examples

```
REAL A(-47:29), B(0:10), C(-14:-3)
INTEGER LN(489:3472), LSMFT(1945:1958)
```

All we have to do is declare our arrays with both lower and upper bounds on the subscript range:

```
INTEGER COLA (12:65), UNCOLA (12:65)
```

When we read a data line

```
INTEGER AGE
CHARACTER*(6) PREFER
READ *, AGE, PREFER
```

we simply increase the appropriate counter for that age:

```
IF (PREFER .EQ. 'COLA') THEN
  COLA(AGE) = COLA(AGE) + 1
ELSE
  UNCOLA(AGE) = UNCOLA(AGE) + 1
ENDIF
```

The complete program is shown below. Except for this new feature of arrays with arbitrary starting points, there's nothing novel in the program. You've seen counting algorithms many times before.

```
COMMENT:            SOFT DRINK PREFERENCES
          INTEGER YOUNG, OLD
          PARAMETER (YOUNG = 12, OLD = 65)
```

(Continued on following page)

```
          INTEGER AGE, COLA(YOUNG:OLD), UNCOLA(YOUNG:OLD)
          CHARACTER*(6) PREFER, ENDDAT
          PARAMETER (ENDDAT = '      ')
C                      INITIALIZE COUNTERS
          DO 100 AGE = YOUNG, OLD
             COLA(AGE) = 0
             UNCOLA(AGE) = 0
   100       CONTINUE
C                      TABULATE PREFERENCES
   200    READ *, AGE, PREFER
          IF (PREFER .EQ. ENDDAT) GO TO 300
          IF (PREFER .EQ. 'COLA') THEN
             COLA(AGE) = COLA(AGE) + 1
          ELSE
             UNCOLA(AGE) = UNCOLA(AGE) + 1
          ENDIF
          GO TO 200
C                      PRINT RESULTS
   300    PRINT *, '     AGE           COLA          UNCOLA'
          DO 310 AGE = YOUNG, OLD
             PRINT *, ' ', AGE, COLA(AGE), UNCOLA(AGE)
   310       CONTINUE
          END
```

Data

```
12      'COLA'
29      'UNCOLA'
52      'COLA'
12      'COLA'
13      'COLA'
60      'UNCOLA'
52      'COLA'
50      'UNCOLA'
29      'COLA'
30      'UNCOLA'
17      'UNCOLA'
13      'COLA'
29      'COLA'
52      'COLA'
65      '      '
```

Output

AGE	COLA	UNCOLA
12	2	0
13	2	0
.	.	.
.	.	.
.	.	.
28	0	0
29	2	1
30	0	1
.	.	.
.	.	.
.	.	.

9.7 EXERCISES

1. What would happen in our program if one of the data lines had the number 8 in the AGE field?

2. Modify the program so that it will ignore data with ages outside the 12-to-65 range.
3. Declare an array to store estimates of the earth's population for each year from 1000 B.C. to 1980 A.D.

9.8 ARRAYS WITH TWO SUBSCRIPTS

t	w	o								a	y
								r			
d	i	m	e	n	s		r				
					i		a				
					o						
					n	a	l				

Converting first-letter codes to numeric codes in the bird census program was essentially a process of locating the first-letter codes in a table. The table, LCODE, had only four entries, one for each kind of bird involved, and it established a relationship between two entities (first-letter codes and numeric codes). You can think of it as a one-line table with numeric labels across the top and first-letter entries in the table.

first-letter code

Tables are frequently used to present data in an organized fashion so that desired information can be easily retrieved, and they usually have more than one line. For example, there is a phenomenon known as the windchill factor that is commonly reported during the weather portion of the evening news, especially in ski country. Windchill is the cooling effect produced by moving air, and it depends on the speed of movement as well as the temperature of the air. Fast-moving air cools things more quickly than slow-moving air, and this tendency becomes more pronounced as the temperature drops. A windchill table reports the cooling effect of various wind speed/temperature combinations by using still-air conditions as a standard reference point. If you look in a wind chill table under a given temperature and wind speed, you will find the temperature at which still air would produce the same cooling effect as the given wind speed/temperature combination.

In Table 9.8.1 you can see that when the wind is blowing at 15 mph and the air temperature is 10°F, the chilling effect is like that of an air temperature of 4 degrees below zero. In order to write a program which uses this table to print out windchill temperatures when the user enters wind speed and air temperature, it is convenient to use an array with two subscripts. You can think of an array with two subscripts as a table of

Table 9.8.1 Windchill Temperatures

Wind (mph)	Temperature (°F)					
	0	5	10	15	20	25
5	0	5	10	15	20	25
10	−9	−4	1	9	14	18
15	−18	−11	−4	1	9	16
20	−26	−17	−9	−2	5	12
25	−36	−26	−17	−8	0	9

variables with several lines. The number of lines in the table is given by the first whole number in the array declaration. The second number in the declaration gives the number of variables per line.

The statement INTEGER A(3,5) sets up a table of variables like this:

```
A(1,1)  A(1,2)  A(1,3)  A(1,4)  A(1,5)
A(2,1)  A(2,2)  A(2,3)  A(2,4)  A(2,5)
A(3,1)  A(3,2)  A(3,3)  A(3,4)  A(3,5)
```

As you can see, the first subscript says which line the variable is in, and the second subscript says what position on the line it's in.

Windchill

The information in this table was obtained from the work of R. G. Steadman which appeared in the *Journal of Applied Meteorology*, Vol. 10 (1971), pp. 674-683. His figures measure heat loss for a person clothed adequately to maintain thermal equilibrium. For exposed flesh, the windchill temperatures would be considerably lower. Your TV weather personality usually gives the more dramatic "exposed flesh" figures.

The windchill table has five lines and six columns, so we'll need a 5-by-6 array: INTEGER C(5,6). Our only problem is figuring out how to compute the subscripts of the table entry corresponding to given wind speed/temperature combination. Values are given for increments of 5 miles per hour and 5 degrees. For example, the table entry C(3,2) reports the windchill index at a 15 miles per hour wind speed and 5 degrees temperature. Essentially, we have to divide the wind speed by 5 to get the proper line number in the table, and we have to divide the temperature by 5, then add 1 to account for the fact that the temperature entries start at 0 instead of 5. So if W is the reported wind speed and T is the reported temperature, then W/5 and T/5 + 1 are the subscripts to use: C(W/5,T/5+1).

There are two other minor complications. One is that the wind speed or the temperature may not be in "even fives." They may be some in-between values like 13,9 or 22,3. To handle this, we simply need to round off the quotient to the nearest whole number. Fortunately, we've done this before, and we can use a simple statement function to handle it. The statement function below assumes that its argument is an INTEGER and computes the nearest INTEGER to one-fifth of the argument.

```
FIFTH(N) = NINT(REAL(N)/5.0)
```

Using this function, it is easy to locate the appropriate table entry, given a wind speed W and a temperature T: C(FIFTH(W), FIFTH(T)+1). The program below is based on this approach. It simply reads a data line containing a wind speed and a temperature, finds the entry in the wind-chill table corresponding to the given conditions, and prints the windchill factor. (Note that the program is careful to make sure the given conditions are within range. It only has data for wind speeds between 5 and 25 miles per hour and temperatures between 0 and 25 degrees.)

```
COMMENT:                WINDCHILL REPORT
  INTEGER C(5,6), W, T, FIFTH, W5, T5
  DATA C(1,1),C(1,2),C(1,3),C(1,4),C(1,5),C(1,6)/ 0,    5, 10,15,20,25/
  DATA C(2,1),C(2,2),C(2,3),C(2,4),C(2,5),C(2,6)/-9,   -4,  1, 9,14,18/
  DATA C(3,1),C(3,2),C(3,3),C(3,4),C(3,5),C(3,6)/-18,-11, -4, 1, 9,16/
  DATA C(4,1),C(4,2),C(4,3),C(4,4),C(4,5),C(4,6)/-26,-17, -9,-2, 5,12/
  DATA C(5,1),C(5,2),C(5,3),C(5,4),C(5,5),C(5,6)/-36,-26,-17,-8, 0, 9/
  FIFTH(N) = NINT(REAL(N)/5.0)
  READ *, W,T
  W5 = FIFTH(W)
  T5 = FIFTH(T) + 1
  IF (W5.GE.1 .AND. W5.LE.5 .AND. T5.GE.1 .AND. T5.LE.6) THEN
    PRINT *, 'WIND:', W, ' TEMP:', T, ' WINDCHILL:', C(W5,T5)
  ELSE
    PRINT *, 'WIND:', W, ' TEMP:', T, ' WINDCHILL: OFF CHART'
  ENDIF
  END
```

Data

```
20  13
```

Output

```
WIND:     20 TEMP:     13 WINDCHILL:     -2
```

Data

```
35  20
```

Output

```
WIND:     35 TEMP:     20 WINDCHILL: OFF CHART
```

9.8   EXERCISES

1. Which of the following are legal declarations?

```
INTEGER A(100,3), B(3,100), I
REAL QRT(3,49)
REAL P(10), Q(4,2)
REAL X(N,100)
```

2. Assuming the declarations of exercise 1 have been made, which of the following statements are not legal?

```
A(4,3) = 0
B(4,2) = 0
A(3,50) = 0
I = 10
P(8) = Q(3,2)
```

3. What happens if the user of the windchill program enters −10 degrees?

4. Suppose you want to be able to answer questions about the month of May in 1984,—questions of the form "What day of the month does the second Wednesday fall on?" or "What day of the month is the fourth Sunday on?" Explain a way to organize the information that will make these questions easy to answer.

9.9 HIGHER DIMENSIONAL ARRAYS

Fortran arrays may have up to 7 subscripts. Problems in which arrays with several subscripts are handy come up occasionally, but since you are already familiar with one- and two-dimensional arrays, you should have no problem applying your knowledge to arrays with higher dimensions.

Array Declarator

---

form

$a(d_i)$

$a(d_1, d_2, \ldots, d_n)$

a is an identifier

d_i is a dimension specification of the form *len* or of the form *l:u* where *len*, *l*, and *u* are INTEGER constant expressions

notes

$1 \leq n \leq 7$ (no more than seven subscripts)

$l \leq u$

meaning

Set up an array a with n subscripts. If d_i has the form *len*, then the subscript range for the *i*th subscript is $1, 2, \ldots, len$. If d_i is of the form *l:u*, then the subscript range for the *i*th subscript is $l, l+1, \ldots, u$.

examples

```
REAL X(10), Y(3,7:9), Z(-10:10)
CHARACTER*3 A(0:4*12), B(-5:3,2*7+1:3*7)
```

A two-dimensional array is like a multi-line table, and a three-dimensional array is like a multi-page table, each page of which is an ordinary multi-line table. For example, the windchill factor actually depends on the humidity as well as the wind speed and temperature. A table incorporating the humidity into the picture would need a third subscript. Windchill factors would then be located by means of three subscripts, one for the wind speed, another for the temperature, and a third for the humidity.

You can carry this analogy between tables and arrays as far as you like. An array with four dimensions is like a multi-volume table, each volume of which is a multi-page table. Fortran 77 doesn't have a notation for eight-subscript arrays, but there are ways that you can "represent" them, even if your system doesn't directly support them (see Chapter 14).

The primary thing to remember about multi-dimensional arrays is that they provide a way to organize tabular information so that it can be easily retrieved. They are handy as long as the tables have a very *regular* structure: a multi-line table with the same number of entries in each line; a multi-page table with the same number of lines and columns on each page. Ragged tables, such as multi-line tables with lines of varying length, are not so easy to deal with. The more irregular the structure, the more "wasted space" there will be in the array and the more code you will have to write to handle the empty slots as special cases.

9.10 INPUT AND OUTPUT OF ARRAYS

By now you have had a fair amount of experience printing arrays. Perhaps you have noticed that in each PRINT statement you had to know, while writing the program, exactly how many elements of an array you wanted to print. If the number of array elements you wanted to print depended on a computation in the program, you had to write a loop and print one element at a time until you had printed all the appropriate elements (as in the example in Section 9.3). This doesn't cause any particular problems if you want each element on a separate line, but if you want them on the same line, you're in for a lot of work. To eliminate this extra effort, there is an alternative form of the I/O list.

Previously, we said that the list in a READ or PRINT statement must be made up of variable names separated by commas. Until now we haven't really needed anything else. However, the list can be slightly more complicated. In addition to variable names, it can also contain repetitive lists called implied do lists.

An **implied do list** is a list of variable names (possibly subscripted) followed by indexing information which specifies how many times to repeat the variables in the implied do list (that is, how many times to "do" the list) and what values of the index to use in these repetitions. Before we describe the exact form of an implied do list, let's look at an example or two.

Suppose we want to print out all the values in the array A from A(1) to A(N), where N is a memory cell containing some INTEGER. Instead of writing a loop:

```
          DO 50 I = 1,N
             PRINT *, A(I)
50           CONTINUE
```

we can simply put

```
PRINT *, (A(I), I=1,N)
```

This is not only shorter to write and easier to read but has the added benefit of commanding the computer to try to put all the values on one line. If there are too many to fit on one line, the computer will automatically go on to the next. In the case of the loop, each value goes on a separate line because each time the computer performs a PRINT statement, it begins on a new line.

An implied do list doesn't have to be exactly like the one we have written above. The list section can contain more than one element, and the indexing section doesn't have to start the index at 1 and increase by 1 each time; it can start at any value and increase at each stage by any value. What's more, these starting and increment values can be specified by variables instead of constants. Consider the following PRINT statement.

```
PRINT *, (L,A(L),B(L), L=M,N,K)
```

It says to set L equal to M, to print the value of L, then the value of A(L), then B(L), and then to increase L by K and print L, A(L), B(L), and so on. It keeps repeating as long as L isn't larger than N. If we had known while writing the program that M would be 2, N would be 7, and K would be 3, we could have gotten the same result by writing

```
PRINT *, 2,A(2),B(2),5,A(5),B(5)
```

Implied Do List

---

forms
(list,v=s,b)
(list,v=s,b,i)
list is any legal I/O list
v is an unsubscripted memory cell name
s,b, and *i* are arithmetic expressions

meaning
Describes an I/O list consisting of consecutive repetitions of *list* for each value of *v* starting at *s* and incrementing by *i* as long as *v* doesn't exceed *b* (the increment is 1 if *i* is omitted).

examples

```
READ *, (A(I), I=1,10,3)
PRINT *, (A(K-1), K=2,N), (B(K), K=1,N-1)
PRINT *, (NXT,A(NXT),FX , NXT=L,M,INC)
PRINT *, (J, J=1,5)
```

Array Transmission

Entire arrays may be transmitted to output or filled from data lines by placing the array name alone, without subscripts, in an I/O list. The order of transmission is the order in which the array's memory cells are stored in the machine.

```
REAL A, B, C(3)
READ *, A, C, B
```

is
equivalent
to

```
REAL A, B, C(3)
READ*, A, C(1),C(2),C(3), B
```

Implied do lists may also be used in READ statements. They order input variables in the same way that they order output variables. You will get a chance to use some implied do lists in READ statements in the exercises.

So that you can see how implied do lists can be used in the context of a program, consider the problem of summarizing some data in six categories: numbers between 0.0 and 1.0, between 1.0 and 2.0, and so on up to numbers between 5.0 and 6.0. The program should compute the number of values in the data in each category and draw a bar graph. By using implied do lists, we can write a relatively simple program to print bar graphs. Each bar will go horizontally across the page and will be drawn by the character 'X' printed repeatedly across the line.

The program READs in distances, figures out which bar to record the occurrence of each distance in, and eventually leaves the totals for each bar in memory cells BAR(0), BAR(1), . . ., BAR(5). The following statements

```
CHARACTER*(1) XCH
INTEGER COUNT
XCH = 'X'
   .
   .
   .
PRINT *, 'BAR0:', (XCH, COUNT =1, BAR0)
```

will print BAR(0) (the number of distances assigned to that bar) copies of X across the page. If BAR(0) has the value 4, then the PRINT statement will print four X's.

BAR0:XXXX

If BAR(0) is 2, then only two X's would be printed. IF BAR(0) is 0, then no X's would be printed because the starting value for COUNT would be 1, but the ending value would be 0. If the starting value exceeds the ending value, then the implied do list is empty (unless the increment is negative, but we haven't studied that case yet—we're using an assumed increment of one in this implied do list since we didn't specify it explicitly).

```
COMMENT:                    MAKE A BAR GRAPH FROM DISTANCE DATA.
            REAL ENDDAT
            INTEGER NUMCAT
            PARAMETER (NUMCAT = 6, ENDAT = 0.0)
            INTEGER BAR(NUMCAT), NUMB
            REAL DIST
            INTEGER COUNT, THISB
            CHARACTER*(1) XCH
            XCH = 'X'
C                           INITIALIZE BAR HEIGHTS.
            DO 10 NUMB = 1,NUMCAT
              BAR(NUMB) = 0
      10      CONTINUE
C                           READ IN A DISTANCE.  IF IT'S NEGATIVE, THEN
C                           THERE ARE NO MORE DISTANCES IN THE DATA.
      20    READ *, DIST
            IF (DIST .LT. ENDDAT) GO TO 200
C                           CONVERT THE DISTANCE INTO AN INTEGER
C                           (DROP FRACTION)
            NUMB = INT(DIST)
C                           INCREMENT BAR COUNTER.
            IF (NUMB .GE. NUMCAT) THEN
              PRINT *, 'DISTANCE', DIST, ' IS OUT OF RANGE! '
            ELSE
              BAR(NUMB + 1) = BAR(NUMB + 1) + 1
            ENDIF
            GO TO 20
C
C                           PLOT A BAR GRAPH
      200   DO 300 NUMB = 0, NUMCAT - 1
              THISB = BAR(NUMB + 1)
              PRINT *, 'BAR', NUMB, ':', (XCH, COUNT = 1, THISB)
      300   CONTINUE
            END
```

Data

```
3.9
0.4
5.4
0.9
0.9
3.9
17.5
5.6
2.8
4.5
5.8
3.2
5.8
6.9
4.5
3.7
2.9
5.2
-1.0
```

Output

```
DISTANCE   17.50000     IS OUT OF RANGE!
DISTANCE   6.900000     IS OUT OF RANGE!
BAR         0 : X X X
BAR         1 :
BAR         2 : X X
BAR         3 : X X X X
BAR         4 : X X
BAR         5 : X X X X X
```

Note that the general form allows **nesting** of implied do lists. That is, one implied do list can be inside another. The effect of nesting is to cause the inside implied do list to be completely repeated with every repetition of the outside implied do list. The following examples should help clarify the effects of this nesting.

```
PRINT*, C, (B, (A, I=1,3), J=1,2), D
```

is equivalent to

```
PRINT*, C, B, A,A,A, B, A,A,A, D
```

```
PRINT*, ((A(I,J),J=1,3),I=1,2)
```

is equivalent to

```
PRINT*, A(1,1),A(1,2),A(1,3),A(2,1),A(2,2),A(2,3)
```

As you can see in the first example, the *list* section of an implied do list does not need to involve the index. It may or it may not, at your option.

> **nesting:** placing a certain program construct inside a program construct of the same form

---

Implied do lists may also be used in READ statements. They order input variables in the same way that they order output variables. You will get a chance to use some implied do lists in READ statements in the exercises.

9.10 EXERCISES

---

1. Without using implied do lists, write I/O statements equivalent to the following, assuming that M, N, and K have values 4, 12, and 2 respectively.

```
READ  *, (A(J), J=1,4)
PRINT *, (A(J), J=M,N,K)
PRINT *, (A(J), J=K,N,M)
```

2. Using implied do lists, write I/O statements equivalent to the following.

```
PRINT *, A(1), A(2), A(3), A(4), A(5)
PRINT *, A(2), A(4), A(6), A(8), A(10)
```

3. Which of the following I/O statements is illegal, and why?

```
PRINT *, (A(J), J=1,N-1)
READ *, (J, A(J), J=1,N)
PRINT *, (A(J), J=1,C(N))
```

4. What will happen in the bar graph routine if there are more items in a bar than will fit on a line?

5. Use nested implied do lists to construct PRINT statements equivalent to the following.

```
PRINT *, 0+0,0+1,0+2,0+3, 1+0,1+1,1+2,1+3, 2+0,2+1,2+2,2+3
PRINT *, X(1),X(2),Y(1,1),Y(2,1),Y(1,2),Y(2,2),Y(1,3),Y(2,3)
PRINT *, Y(1,1),Y(1,2),Y(1,3),Y(2,1),Y(2,2),Y(2,3)
```

9.11 SUMMARY

Many algorithms would be exceedingly difficult to implement in Fortran without using arrays. They are needed in algorithms which must make several passes through the data, especially when we need to select random data elements to be processed individually. We gain access to an element of data simply by computing its position relative to the other elements and using that position as an index into an array.

Depending on how the data is to be used, the array can be linear (one subscript), two-dimensional (two subscripts), three-dimensional (three subscripts), up to seven-dimensional. Applications for multi-dimensional arrays become more and more rare as the number of subscripts increases, and linear arrays probably account for at least 90 percent of array usage. In fact, it's always possible to use linear arrays in place of multi-dimensional ones by finding a suitable method of indexing. For example, a 3-by-4 two-dimensional array

```
REAL A(3,4)
```

is equivalent to a linear array of 12 elements

```
REAL B(12)
```

when we index B in groups of 3.

```
A(1,1):B(1)  A(1,2):B(4)  A(1,3):B(7)  A(1,4):B(10)
A(2,1):B(2)  A(2,2):B(5)  A(2,3):B(8)  A(2,4):B(11)
A(3,1):B(3)  A(3,2):B(6)  A(3,3):B(9)  A(3,4):B(12)
```

You should choose the number of dimensions and the size of each dimension to fit the problem you are trying to solve. Arrays permit you to organize data in a way which matches the algorithm's needs for access to the data.

The range of array subscripts is normally from 1 up to n where n is the declared dimension. When an alternate range is desirable, it can be specified in the array declaration. Again, this feature is primarily a convenience. The same effect can be obtained by using a suitable method of indexing, but if you choose the subscript range to suit the problem, your program will be easier to write and to understand.

---

9 PROBLEMS

Practice Problems

1. Write a program which prints out a multiplication table. The size of the table should be determined by an INTEGER between 2 and 9 on a data line. Your program should print a table of products up to that number. For example, if the number is 3, your output should look like this:

    ```
    *  1  2  3
    1  1  2  3
    2  2  4  6
    3  3  6  9
    ```

Aging guru radiates potential

2. Over the years, the qualifications for being a recognized guru have become more refined. In one modern certification test, scientists record the potentials induced in a ten-by-ten sheet of polystyrene by the meditations of candidate gurus. If a candidate is able to cause

some point on the sheet to have a voltage greater than twice the average voltage over the ten-by-ten grid, the candidate passes the first phase of the test. Otherwise, the candidate is labeled a sham and sent away in disgrace.

In the second, more rigorous, phase of the test, the pattern of points having above-average potential is plotted, and if the pattern is balanced, with no more large values appearing to the left than to the right, at the top than at the bottom, the candidate is welcomed into the Brotherhood of Enlightened Guhury.

Write a program which carries out the first phase of the test and prints an appropriate message. For candidates who pass the first phase (and for *only* those candidates), print the pattern of voltages they induced. Print a blank at spots which were of average or below average voltage; print a "*" at spots of above average potential.

Make up some data, or perform the measurements yourself on a guru of your acquaintance.

3. Write a program which translates English words into their French equivalents. The idea is to have the corresponding English and French words paired up in DATA statements. The last word should be a sentinel (a value which marks the end of data). Accept an English word from the user, and then use a search loop to find it and its French equivalent. If the word the user entered isn't in your list of words, print an appropriate message. YES↔OUI, NO↔NON, PENCIL↔CRAYON, DOG↔CHIEN, HOUSE↔MAISON.

4. Using three nested DO-loops, print out all possible three-person games of "rock, paper, scissors." Associate an INTEGER value with each symbol—for instance, you could use a CHARACTER*8 array organized like this:

NAMES

1	R	O	C	K			
2	P	A	P	E	R		
3	S	C	I	S	S	O	R	S

When the three DO-loop indices are 2, 2, and 3, that would correspond to player 1 holding out "paper," player 2 holding "paper," and player 3 holding "scissors."

Beside each game, print how many wins each player had in that particular game. Recall that "paper wraps rock," "rock breaks scissors," and "scissors cut paper." In paper, paper, scissors, player 3 would win against both player 1 and player 2.

Sample output:

	GAME			WINS	
PLAYER1	PLAYER2	PLAYER3	PLAYER1	PLAYER2	PLAYER3
ROCK	ROCK	ROCK	0	0	0
ROCK	ROCK	PAPER	0	0	2
SCISSORS	PAPER	ROCK	1	1	1

5. Here are instructions for knitting a scarf:

Using No. 9 needles, cast on 76 sts.
row 1 and all odd rows up to 19: k across
row 2 and all even rows up to 20: p across
rows 21–100: k4, p2 across, end k4
row 101 and all odd rows up to 119: p across
row 102 and all even rows up to 120: k across

Write a program which carries out the knitting instructions by:

a. printing a + for every "knit"
b. printing a − for every "purl"
c. going to a new line for each new row

Use an array of 76 characters to store each "row" as it is "knitted." Then print the entire array each time a row is finished.

6. Write a program to produce a list of students, an honor roll, and a list of suspended students. Each data line will contain a student's name (up to 40 characters) and grade point average on a scale from 0.000 to 4.000 (REAL). The terminating data line will read

'NO MORE STUDENTS'

Your program should print the heading CLASS ROLL followed by a list of all students and their grade point averages, the heading HONOR ROLL followed by a list of students whose averages exceed 3.299, and finally the heading SUSPENDED followed by a list of students whose averages are less than 1.7. Your program may assume that there are no more than 100 students.

7. Write a program using the same data as that in problem 6 but which prints the list of all students with an asterisk (*) beside each student whose average is above the average grade point for all the students. After the list, print the percentage of students above the average.

Program Design Problems

8. The Boss Tweed clothing store has computerized its inventory operations. It sells ten different styles of suits referred to by number. Initially, it has five of each in stock. Each time a salesperson unloads a suit on a customer, a line is keyed with the word SOLD followed by the style number. Each time the manager wants to check on supplies, she types WELL? and the computer prints out the number of suits of each style in stock.

   Write a program to handle Boss Tweed's inventory procedure. Your program should READ data like that described above and update the inventory appropriately, or print the inventory, depending on the type of data. If the number of suits of a particular style becomes less than two, print a message warning the manager to restock that style. Keep READing data until END comes in. Use this data:

'SOLD' 3
'SOLD' 2

(Continued on following page)

```
'WELL?'
'SOLD' 5
'SOLD' 5
'SOLD' 4
'SOLD' 5
'SOLD' 3
'WELL?'
'END'
```

9. Expand the capabilities of the Boss Tweed clothing store's inventory program (problem 8). If a salesperson sells a style of suit that the store is out of, print a message. (Depending on how you think the store should run, either tell the salesperson that there has been some mistake or else that he or she will be considered for a raise.)

   Also, allow for a fourth type of data for restocking:

```
'RESTOCK STYLE' 3 5
```

   Such data will indicate the number of suits of a given style purchased by the store. Make up 15 or 20 data lines which demonstrate the capabilities of your program.

10. Write a program which prints beef price differences in a group of up to 100 cities. Each data line will contain the name of a city (up to 40 characters) followed by the price of a pound of hamburger at a local supermarket. The last data line will be

```
'NO MORE CITIES'
```

   Your program should compute the average price of hamburger over all the cities and print a table of cities, hamburger prices, and the amounts above or below the average price. Thus, each line of the table should contain the name of a city, the price of hamburger there, and the difference between that price and the average price of hamburger (a positive number if the price is above average, and a negative number if it's below average).

11. Add a section to the program of problem 10 to print the lowest and highest of the hamburger prices surveyed along with the corresponding cities.

> Notice: Problem 12 requires some knowledge of mathematics.

12. The year is 1811, and the fame of the pirate Lafitte has spread throughout the islands of the Caribbean and the Gulf of Mexico. In Havana there resides a wealthy soldier of fortune, Captain Hawkbill, who owns a fast gunship and can hire a large crew of tough sailors. He reasons that he can make a fortune if he can capture Lafitte and take his loot. His enterprise would bring him both fortune and favor because Lafitte is universally hated by honest, law-abiding people.

   The captain sails his ship into the Gulf to a point five nautical miles south and five nautical miles east of New Orleans. Then, from his position, he sees Lafitte's ship five nautical miles due west. Fortunately for Hawkbill, Lafitte's crew has just finished robbing a large cargo of gold and furs from a British ship. Lafitte's ship is sailing due north toward New Orleans at nine knots. Hawkbill gives chase immediately. In today's wind, his ship can travel at 13 knots, and he orders his crew to keep the ship at top speed and pointed directly at Lafitte's ship.

knot: a measure of speed equal to one nautical mile per hour.

Write a program that computes each ship's position at one-minute intervals in terms of nautical miles south and east of New Orleans. Assume that the chase is ended if Lafitte reaches New Orleans or is overtaken by Captain Hawkbill. Print out on the line printer a graphic display of the chase in a format similar to the following:

```
X . . . . . . . . . . . . . . . . . . . . . . . . . . . . . . . . . . . . . . . . . .
.
.
.
H
.
L
.
.
.
L
.
.
L   H
.
L      H
.        H
.
L             H   H
```

Note that the chase is over if either Hawkbill's distance east of New Orleans or Lafitte's distance south of New Orleans becomes negative.

13. Write a program which evaluates polynomials. The data should consist of two groups. Group 1 describes the polynomial by giving the coefficients and corresponding powers. That is, each line in group 1 contains a coefficient (REAL) and a power (INTEGER). This group is followed by a termination line with coefficient 0.0 and power -1. The following group of data would describe the polynomial $3x^4 + 2x^2 + 4.7x + 1$.

```
3.0   4
2.0   2
4.7   1
1.0   0
0.0  -1
```

You may assume that there are no more than 51 cards in group 1.

Group 2 is a list of points at which the polynomial is to be evaluated. That is, each line in group 2 will contain a REAL value for the independent variable in the polynomial. The termination line for group 2 will contain 999999.9 (which shouldn't be taken as a value with which to evaluate the polynomial). Your program should print a description of the polynomial and a table of values of the polynomial at the points listed in the group 2 data.

14. Horner's scheme for evaluating polynomials is quicker and more accurate than the straightforward scheme. Write the program of problem 13 so that it uses Horner's evaluation scheme.
    Horner's scheme:

    $$a_n x^n + a_{n-1} x^{n-1} + \ldots + a_1 x + a_0 =$$
    $$(((a_n x + a_{n-1})x + a_{n-2})x + \ldots + a_1)x + a_0$$

    e.g.,

    $$3x^4 + 2x^2 + 4.7x + 1 = (((3x + 0)x + 2)x + 4.7)x + 1$$

15. Design a program which converts kitchen measures. Data lines will look like this:

quantity	current units	desired units
32	'TABLESPOONS'	'GALLONS'
2	'QUARTS'	'TEASPOONS'

    The output should look like this:

    ```
    32 TABLESPOONS MAKE    0.1250 GALLONS
     2 QUARTS       MAKE 384.0000 TEASPOONS
    ```

    Here are some hints on how to proceed. First, create an array which stores the names of the measures you want to deal with and which will allow you to associate an INTEGER with each measure. Suppose this array is a CHARACTER*11 array called NAMES with values as shown below.

    NAMES

1	GALLONS
2	QUARTS
3	PINTS
4	CUPS
5	TABLESPOONS
6	TEASPOONS

    Then the INTEGER 1 will denote gallons; the INTEGER 2, quarts; etc.

    Suppose the second sample data line above is the one we are working on. We find QUARTS in the second element of the array NAMES and associate QUARTS with 2. We'll call the INTEGER associated with this input measuring unit the **source.** We find that TEASPOONS is associated with 6, and we'll call this INTEGER the **destination.**

    We need one more collection of information before we can carry out the conversion. We need to know the number of cups per pint, pints per quart, and so on. We'll put this information in an array called CONV (2:6).

	2	3	4	5	6
CONV	4	2	2	16	3

CONV(i) tells how many units of measure i make one unit of measure $i-1$. Thus CONV(2)=4 because there are 4 QUARTS in a GALLON.

To convert from quarts to teaspoons, first multiply by CONV(3), then by CONV(4), by CONV(5), and finally by CONV(6). To go from teaspoons to quarts, proceed in the other direction, and use division: first divide by CONV(6), then by CONV(5), CONV(4), and finally CONV(3).

16. Suppose a zoologist comes to you with a collection of data. He has made a count of the number of prairie rattlesnakes (*Crotalus viridis viridis*) found on a square mile of land at various altitudes around Fort Collins, Colorado. The data he has gathered is summarized in the table below.

Altitude	Number of snakes
5000′	30
5300′	28
5800′	20
6000′	14
6500′	10
7000′	3

He suspects that the number of snakes s at altitude a can be expressed as a linear function

$$s(a) = Da + M$$

and he asks you to try to determine from his data what would be reasonable values to take for the coefficients D and M.

Naturally, you want to choose values for D and M so that the observed data deviates as little as possible from the values predicted by your coefficients D and M. In other words, you want

$s(5000)$ to be close to 30
$s(5300)$ to be close to 28
$s(5800)$ to be close to 20

One technique that is often used in cases like this is to choose values for D and M which minimize the sum of the squares of the deviations from the observed values. In other words, so that

$$(s(5000) - 30)^2 + (s(5300) - 28)^2 + (s(5800) - 20)^2 + (s(6000) - 14)^2 + (s(6500) - 10)^2 + (s(7000) - 3)^2$$

(where $s(a) = Da + M$)

is as small as possible.

Your job is to write a program which READs an integer n, then READs n measurements a_i, s_i from the following n lines, then calculates values for D and M by solving the following pair of linear equations (which solve the least squares problem posed above).

$$\left(\sum_{i=1}^{n} a_i^2 \right) D + \left(\sum_{i=1}^{n} a_i \right) M = \sum_{i=1}^{n} a_i s_i$$

$$\left(\sum_{i=1}^{n} a_i \right) D + nM = \sum_{i=1}^{n} s_i$$

The output from your program should include the values of D and M as well as the value of the square deviation (for the computed values D and M) divided by n, that is

$$\frac{1}{n} \sum_{i=1}^{n} (Da_i + M - s_i)^2$$

10 CHARACTER STRINGS

CHAPTER PLAN

- *Introduce the notion of operating on CHARACTER strings*
- *Discover what symbols your system makes available*
- *Define and use*
    The CHAR and ICHAR operators
    The Index operator
    Substrings
    Concatenation

10.1 WHAT OPERATIONS MAKE SENSE?

So far, we've used CHARACTER strings and variables in a limited way, primarily for storing, testing, and PRINTing static information like names of things. Fortran provides the capability of operating on CHARACTER data as well. But what kinds of operations make sense on CHARACTER strings? Certainly the arithmetic operators like +, −, *, /, and ** don't make sense with respect to CHARACTER data—who knows what 'RAYMOND' multiplied by 'CHANDLER' would mean? The kinds of operations that we can perform on strings are just those operations you make when you proofread something you've written. That is, we are able to do things like

make a copy,
replace or remove part of a string,
insert something into a string, and
search a string looking for the occurrence of another string.

Up to now, all the CHARACTER strings we've used have been very short, but most computer systems allow the use of long strings. That means it's reasonable to consider writing a program which READs the text of a term paper into one CHARACTER variable; operates on the string, making changes you want and correcting the spacing; and PRINTs your finished product. A typical double-spaced, typewritten page has about 2,000 characters on it (counting spaces between words), so a five-page term paper could be stored in the variable declared here

```
CHARACTER*(10000) TEXT
```

In this book, we use all UPPERCASE letters in all our programs and CHARACTER strings. In fact, the official Fortran alphabet has uppercase letters only. However, within a CHARACTER string you are allowed to use any character your computer system provides. If you're using a modern computer system, this means that you will probably be able to use both upper- and lowercase letters. There are two ways to tell if your printer is capable of printing lowercase letters. One is to run the program which appears below. It makes use of the CHAR operator. The CHAR operator takes one argument, an INTEGER value, and it returns the CHARACTER*(1) value that corresponds to the INTEGER on your particular machine. (The inverse operation is also available—ICHAR takes a CHARACTER*(1) value as an argument and returns the INTEGER value which corresponds to the internal representation of the CHARACTER on your machine.)

```
C         DISCOVER WHAT SYMBOLS THE PRINTER CAN PRINT.
          INTEGER SYMNUM
          PRINT *, 'THE SYMBOLS ARE:'
          PRINT *, (CHAR(SYMNUM), SYMNUM =   0,  63)
          PRINT *, (CHAR(SYMNUM), SYMNUM =  64, 127)
          PRINT *, (CHAR(SYMNUM), SYMNUM = 128, 191)
          PRINT *, (CHAR(SYMNUM), SYMNUM = 192, 255)
          END
```

> *Note:* If your system doesn't provide 256 different characters (hardly any do), several things may happen when you run the program. Perhaps multiple copies of each character will appear in the output. Perhaps all characters will be the blank character (' ') after a certain point. Perhaps you'll get an error message when SYMNUM—the number of characters printed—gets too big. In any event, you will accomplish the goal—getting the printer to print each character it is capable of.

10.1 EXERCISES

1. Well? What characters is your printer able to PRINT?
2. It takes more than one data line to enter the text for a five-page term paper. Does that create trouble?

10.2 SUBSTRINGS

When we look over or edit a text, we automatically focus our attention on small sections of the text at a time. To write programs which do editing tasks, we need some way to specify what precise spot in the text the program should test, change, or PRINT. In Fortran each CHARACTER*(n) string is thought of as n characters in a row, and each position in the string can be referred to by giving a number, called a **character position.** The first position in a string is character position 1, the last in a CHARACTER*(n) string is character position n. By specifying a starting position and a stopping position in a string value, we identify just part of a string, that is, a **substring.** The next example program uses this ability to isolate parts of a string in order to search for occurrences of specific patterns.

Researchers in the field of literature sometimes look for ways to characterize an author's style so that unidentified manuscripts dating from a particular period can be classified as having been written by one author or another. A successful technique for characterizing manuscripts involves counting the frequency of use of certain words or phrases. A simple version of this technique would be to read a sample of an author's work and compute the percentage of the words which are articles: "the," "a," and "an."

Let's assume that a sample of the text is written on a data line and has been cleansed of all punctuation marks so that each word is surrounded by blanks. In order to count the number of articles on the card, we can simply look for patterns of the form 'bTHEb', 'bAb', 'bANb' (where b stands for "blank"). We'll need a way to get at small parts of the whole string, and we can do this in Fortran with the **substring** facility. If S is a CHARACTER*(n) variable, then S(j:k) is a substring within the variable. S(j:k) is the substring starting with the jth character of S and ending with the kth character of S, where j and k are INTEGER values. Of course, k must be greater than or equal to j; otherwise the substring would be empty. In addition, both j and k must be in the range 1,2,. . .,n; otherwise they wouldn't correspond to character positions within the variable.

Substrings

---

form

v(j:k)

v is a CHARACTER*(n) variable (which may be subscripted)

j and k are INTEGER valued expressions

$1 \leqslant j \leqslant k \leqslant n$

meaning

denotes the portion of v beginning at character j and ending at character k. If j is omitted, it is assumed to be 1; if k is omitted it is assumed to be n.

examples

```
CHARACTER*(10) A, B(3), C(5,4)
IF (A(6:9) .EQ. A(1:4)) GO TO 100
A(3*N:3*N+2) = 'CAT'
B(2)(2:8) = A(3:9)
IF (C(2,4)(1:N).NE.C(5,3)(11-N:10)) GO TO 100
```

Figure 10.2.1   Finding the Articles in a Phrase

Fetch phrase.
Set counters THE, A, and AN to zero.

For each character position in the phrase ──────

> **Select matching substring**
>
> "THE" : Let THE = THE + 1
>   "A" : Let A = A + 1
> "AN" : Let AN = AN + 1

Print THE, A, AN.

Using this notation, we can easily count the number of articles in the input phrase. Starting at the beginning of the phrase, we compare substrings of the text to each of the three articles, "a," "an," and "the." If there is a match, we increase the appropriate counter. The program plan is shown in Figure 10.2.1 and written in detail below.

```
COMMENT:              PROGRAM TO COUNT ARTICLES
          INTEGER WIDTH
          PARAMETER(WIDTH = 80)
          CHARACTER*(WIDTH + 4) PHRASE
          INTEGER POS, THE, A, AN
          READ *, PHRASE
          THE = 0
          A = 0
          AN = 0
          DO 100 POS = 1, WIDTH
            IF (PHRASE(POS: POS + 4) .EQ. ' THE ') THEN
              THE = THE + 1
            ELSE IF (PHRASE(POS: POS + 2) .EQ. ' A ') THEN
              A = A + 1
            ELSE IF (PHRASE(POS: POS + 3) .EQ. ' AN ') THEN
              AN = AN + 1
            ENDIF
  100     CONTINUE
          PRINT *, 'THE:', THE
          PRINT *, 'A:  ', A
          PRINT *, 'AN: ', AN
          END
```

Data

```
' THE OWL AND THE PUSSYCAT WENT TO SEA IN A BOAT '
```

Output

```
THE:    2
A:      1
AN:     0
```

There are a few details about the program that need special mention. First, the variable PHRASE is several characters longer than it needs to be to store a phrase written on one line. This is due to a technicality. The words THE, A, and AN all have a different number of letters in them. In searching for '*b*THE*b*' as a substring of the phrase, we can stop when we finally compare it with the substring beginning five characters from the last character in the phrase. However, when we are searching for the substring '*b*A*b*', we can't stop so soon. To avoid having to treat each stopping condition differently, we simply pad the phrase with a few blanks on the end. We'll make a few more comparisons than we need to on "THE", but the program is much less complex without the special cases. Another subtle point is in the way the data is presented. We've padded the phrase on both the left and the right with one blank. Our comparison requires blanks surrounding the article, and if we had left off the leading blank, we wouldn't have counted the article "THE" at the beginning of the phrase.

The above example illustrates the use of substrings as *values*. They can also be used as *variables*. We can assign new values to substrings in the same way that we assign values to CHARACTER variables. We can also put values into substrings with READ statements. In fact, a substring of *n* characters can be used in any Fortran statement where a CHARACTER*(*n*) variable could be used. However, there *is* one restriction (see the **CHARACTER assignment** box). Using this facility, we can manipulate portions of CHARACTER variables in the same ways that we manipulate the whole variable.

In our previous example, we wanted to tabulate the frequency of certain words in a phrase. Suppose instead that we would like to censor certain words. Instead of incrementing a counter when we find a word we're looking for, we want to mark it out. One way to do that is to replace it with asterisks. The program below censors certain obscenities from the input phrase. The structure of the program is almost identical to that of the one which tabulates articles. The primary differences are that it looks for different words, and when it finds them, it *replaces* them instead of counting them.

```
COMMENT:                    CENSOR PROGRAM
          INTEGER WIDTH
          PARAMETER(WIDTH = 80)
          CHARACTER*(WIDTH) PHRASE
          INTEGER POS
          READ *, PHRASE
          DO 100 POS = 1,WIDTH-5
            IF (PHRASE(POS: POS + 5) .EQ. ' HECK '
       +        .OR. PHRASE(POS: POS + 5) .EQ. ' DURN ') THEN
                  PHRASE(POS: POS + 5) = ' **** '
            ENDIF
100       CONTINUE
          PRINT *, PHRASE
          END
```

Data

```
' DURN IT I BURNED THE HECK OUT OF MY DURN FINGER '
```

Output

```
**** IT I BURNED THE **** OUT OF MY **** FINGER
```

CHARACTER Assignment

form
$v=e$
v is a CHARACTER*(n) variable, array, or substring
e is a CHARACTER*(m) expression

meaning
Compute the value of e, and store that value in v; if $n>m$, pad right with blanks, if $n<m$, drop rightmost m-n positions from the value of e.

restriction
None of the character positions being filled in v may be referenced in e.

examples

```
CHARACTER*(32) NAME, WORDS(10)
```

Legal   Illegal

```
NAME(31:32) = '  '              NAME(1:16)=NAME(10:24)
WORDS(5)  = NAME(1:16)
WORDS(1)(1:16)=WORDS(1)(17:32)  WORDS(2)=WORDS(2)(16:32)
```

way around the restriction
You can always get around the restriction by using a temporary variable and an additional assignment. For instance, the second illegal form can be accomplished legally like this:

```
CHARACTER*(32) TEMP
TEMP = WORDS(2)(16:32)
WORDS(2) = TEMP
```

In both example programs in this section, we wanted to find *all* occurrences of specific substrings in a given text string. Therefore, we started looking at character position 1, checked to see if the substring starting there was one we wanted, moved to position 2, checked, moved to position 3, checked, and so on. Each time we discovered one of the substrings we were looking for, we took some action. It happens that there is a built-in operator in Fortran which we can use to do some of the work. In some cases (like the first program in this section), it is most convenient to spell out all the details of moving from character position to character position, testing for the substrings you're looking for. In other cases, (like the censor program), it's a toss-up whether this new operator makes the program simpler. In yet other cases, it is a convenience, as the next example will show. This operator is INDEX. It takes two arguments, both of type CHARACTER, and it returns the character position in the first argument at which the first substring equal to the second argument begins. If there is no substring in the first argument which is identical to the second argument, INDEX returns the value 0.

INDEX('ABCDEFGHIJKLMNOPQRSTUVWXYZ','C') returns 3
INDEX('THEORETICALLY','THE') returns 1
INDEX('THEORETICALLY',' THE') returns 0 because the substring
  ' THE' doesn't occur anywhere in 'THEORETICALLY'
INDEX('A BROWN SHOE AND BROWN LACES','BROWN') returns 3
  (remember, INDEX finds the *first* match only).

Programs used in business applications often have to deal with people's names. Sometimes names are entered in the Last Name, First Middle form, and sometimes in the First Middle Last Name form. A program can tell the difference by checking to see if a comma appears anywhere within the string storing the name. This is an ideal place to use the INDEX operator.

```
INTEGER NAMLEN
PARAMETER(NAMLEN = 32)
CHARACTER*(NAMLEN) NAME
CHARACTER*(1) COMMA
COMMA = ','
READ *, NAME
IF (INDEX(NAME, COMMA) .NE. 0) THEN
   PRINT *, NAME, ' IS IN THE LAST NAME, FIRST MIDDLE FORM.'
ELSE
   PRINT *, NAME, ' IS IN FIRST MIDDLE LAST NAME FORM.'
ENDIF
END
```

Data

  'LANGSFORD, RAYMOND G.'

Output

LANGSFORD, RAYMOND G. IS IN LAST NAME, FIRST MIDDLE FORM

Data

  'RAYMOND G. LANGSFORD'

Output

RAYMOND G. LANGSFORD IS IN FIRST MIDDLE LAST NAME FORM.

10.2 EXERCISES

Assume that the following declarations have been made:

```
CHARACTER*(1) CH
CHARACTER*(80) PHRASE
INTEGER N,I
```

1. What does this program fragment do?

```
        DO 100 N = 80, 1, -1
          IF (PHRASE(N:N) .NE. ' ') GO TO 110
100       CONTINUE
110     PRINT *, N
```

2. What does the program fragment below do to the character string in PHRASE?

```
        DO 200 I = 1, N/2
          CH = PHRASE(I:I)
          PHRASE(I:I) = PHRASE(N - I + 1:N - I + 1)
          PHRASE(N - I + 1:N - I + 1) = CH
200       CONTINUE
```

3. Write Fortran statements to print the first half of the characters in PHRASE on one line and the last half on the next line.
4. Write an assignment statement to replace the middle two characters in PHRASE with plus signs.
5. Write a program which has the same effect as the Last Name, First Middle program but which doesn't use the INDEX operator.

10.3 CONCATENATION

New character strings may be formed by putting one or more old character strings together, end to end. This operation is known as **concatenation** and is denoted by a double slash (//) placed between two character values. In this way, character expressions can be built from CHARACTER constants (i.e., quoted strings), CHARACTER variables and array elements, and substrings. These expressions may be used to form values for assignment to variables, for comparison in relational expressions, or for printing. In this section, we'll develop a program which uses concatenation to adjust strings into a standard form.

In a great number of computer applications, people's names are dealt with as data. In many businesses, account records are organized by customer name. Mailing lists are gathered, analyzed, and sold in computer-readable form. Large organizations and clubs keep membership records by computer, organizing their records by member name. In all these cases, there is a potential problem. A human being looking at the string

```
'LANGSFORD ,   RAYMOND G.'
```

can tell immediately that it refers to the same person as this string

```
'LANGSFORD,RAYMOND G'
```

However, the two strings are not the same. The second form not only has fewer characters than the first—it also lacks one of the characters in the first string, namely, the period. If a person's records were stored under the first version of the name, and someone typed in the second version in an attempt to access them, a program which looked for an exact equality of name strings would be unable to find the entry. Solving the problem *completely* is probably impossible. We can, however, devise algorithms which will do away with much of the problem.

Character Expression

---

form
$c_1 // c_2 // c_3 . . . // c_n$
c_i is a CHARACTER constant, variable, array element, or substring

note
Parentheses may be used to group parts of a character expression, but they do not affect the value of the expression.

meaning
A character string is formed from the components $c_1, c_2, . . . , c_n$ by appending c_2 to c_1, then c_3 to that, and so on.

examples

```
PHRASE = WORD // PHRASE (M:N)
A = B//C//D
IF (A//WORD .EQ. C(1:K)) GO TO 100
F(2) = F(1)//WORD
```

What are the differences between these two strings?

```
'LANGSFORD,RAYMOND G'
'LANGSFORD ,   RAYMOND G.'
```

One difference is the period in the second string. We can solve that by removing all periods from name strings. Other than that, the only differences are ones of spacing.

We can remove differences due to spacing by putting all names into a standard form. Let's use these rules: There should never be more than one blank in a row within a name; there should be no blank *before* the comma; and there should always be one blank *after* the comma.

We want to design a program which will turn both

```
'LANGSFORD,RAYMOND G'
```

and

```
'LANGSFORD ,   RAYMOND G.'
```

into the standard form

```
'LANGSFORD, RAYMOND G'
```

Let's work on the cases one by one. First, let's see how we can remove all periods. To remove a period, first we have to find it. That's easily accomplished using the INDEX operator. INDEX (NAME), '.') will return the character position of the first period in the string name. There might be no periods, as in

```
'LANGSFORD,RAYMOND G'
```

or there might be one, or there might be several, as in

```
'ROBERTS,   TRISTAN D. M.'
```

This state of affairs suggests a pretest loop. Our plan is given in Figure 10.3.1.

The only puzzle remaining is how to remove a character from NAME. The INDEX operator gives us the position of the character we want to remove. We want to replace NAME by the string we get by adding everything up to the first period to everything after the first period. These two statements accomplish that, and they use the concatenation operation to tack the first subpart to the second.

```
TEMP = NAME( :POS-1) // NAME(POS+1:  )
NAME = TEMP
```

In these two lines we've assumed that TEMP (like NAME) is a CHARACTER*33 memory cell (that should be big enough to store any name we're likely to come across) and that POS stores the character position of the first period in the original form of NAME. We need to use the temporary variable TEMP because of the restriction on CHARACTER assignment statements (see the box in Section 10.2).

Figure 10.3.1   Removing All Periods from the Name

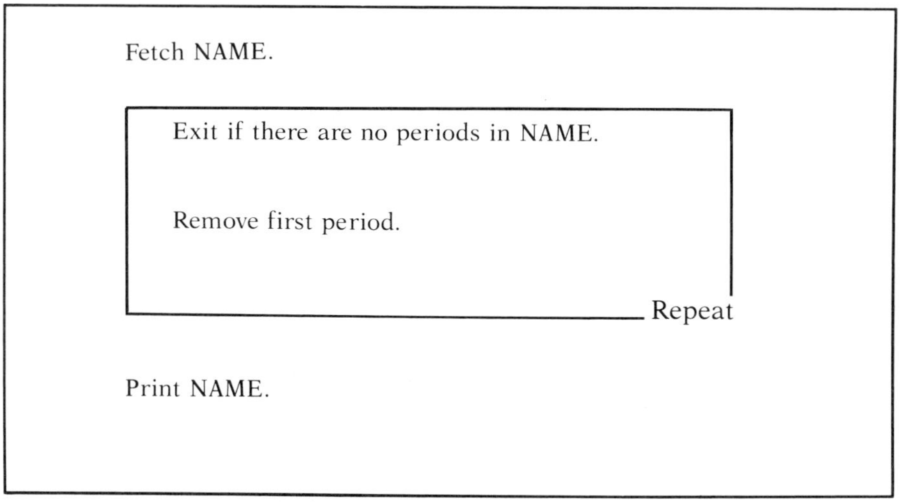

```
Fetch NAME.

    ┌─────────────────────────────────────────────┐
    │    Exit if there are no periods in NAME.      │
    │                                               │
    │    Remove first period.                       │
    └──────────────────────────────────┘ Repeat    │

Print NAME.
```

There is a very important point to understand here. Since NAME has space for 33 characters in it, the total length of the string

```
NAME( :POS-1) // NAME(POS+1: )
```

will be 32—we've left out the character (the period) at position POS. However, since TEMP is of size 33, when the first assignment statement is carried out, a blank will be added to the right of the new form of the name. After carrying out both assignment statements, the total length of NAME will be *unchanged*, even though we've removed a period from the middle. In Fortran, strings never change their length. The number of nonblank characters in a string can change; the numbers of characters you, the programmer, care about can change during the course of a computation; but the size of string stored in a CHARACTER variable is fixed by the declaration statement, which is

```
CHARACTER*(33) NAME, TEMP
```

in this particular example.

So far, our name-standardizer program looks like this:

```
          INTEGER NAMLEN, NOTFND
          PARAMETER(NAMLEN = 32, NOTFND = 0)
          CHARACTER*(NAMLEN + 1) NAME, TEMP
          CHARACTER*(1) PERIOD
          INTEGER POS
          PERIOD = '.'
          READ *, NAME
          POS = INDEX (NAME, PERIOD)
C                      IF POS IS NOTFND, THERE ARE NO PERIODS IN NAME.
    100   IF (POS .EQ. NOTFND) GO TO 200
            TEMP = NAME(:POS-1) // NAME(POS+1:)
            NAME = TEMP
            POS = INDEX(NAME, PERIOD)
            GO TO 100
    200   PRINT *, ' AFTER REMOVING PERIODS, THE NAME IS ', NAME
          END
```

Data

```
'JOE Q. BLOW'
```

Output

```
AFTER REMOVING PERIODS, THE NAME IS JOE Q BLOW
```

The next step in putting NAME in standard form is to remove blanks from within the name. There are two cases. We want to remove a blank if it's immediately before a comma or if it's the first of two consecutive blanks. Convince yourself that deleting the first blank in each pair of blanks within the name guarantees that there will never be more than one consecutive blank within the name.

We can remove a blank which occurs immediately before a comma using the same method we used to remove periods. But we *cannot* use the same method to deal with blanks that occur consecutively. Why not? The method works fine for multiple blanks which occur *within* the name, but if the total name is less than 32 characters long, we'll have multiple blanks at the very end which we can't remove! Let's follow through an example.

Suppose we READ this value into NAME:

```
'FARNSWORTH, CHESTER PROMETHEUS  '
```

— two trailing blanks

Assuming that we've carried out these statements,

```
CHARACTER*(33) NAME, TEMP
CHARACTER*(1) BLANK
INTEGER POS
BLANK = ' '
```

the assignment

```
POS = INDEX( NAME, BLANK // BLANK)
```

will store the value 31 in POS because the first occurrence of the string BLANK // BLANK (i.e., two consecutive blanks) starts at character position 31. Now we attempt to remove the character at position 31.

```
TEMP = NAME( :POS-1) // NAME(POS+1: )
'FARNSWORTH, CHESTER PROMETHEUS'  ' '
```

one blank here

Since the concatenated string on the right of the "=" is total length of 32, but TEMP is a CHARACTER*33 variable, when the assignment is made, a blank is added to the right end of the string. In effect, after we've "removed" the blank, Fortran automatically adds it back in! INDEX (NAME, BLANK // BLANK) will again find a double blank starting in character position 31, and we have an infinite loop.

We can get around this problem by forgetting about using the INDEX operator and doing the work of looking for BLANK // BLANK "by hand," just as we looked for 'A', 'AN', and 'THE' in the program in Section 10.2. Figure 10.3.2 shows our plan.

The final step in standardizing the name is to make sure there's a blank

Figure 10.3.2 Getting Rid of Blanks within NAME

```
For each character in NAME ────────

    If character and succeeding character
       are both blanks or are blank comma

    then ──────────────────────────
         Reform NAME, dropping the first blank.
```

after the comma. All we need do is find the comma (we can do that easily with INDEX), then test the next character. If it's not a blank, we add one. Our completed program appears below.

```
        COMMENT:                  MANIPULATE A NAME INTO STANDARD FORM
                INTEGER NAMLEN, NOTFND
                PARAMETER(NAMLEN = 32, NOTFND = 0)
                CHARACTER*(NAMLEN + 1) NAME, TEMP
                CHARACTER*1 BLANK, PERIOD, COMMA
                INTEGER POS
                BLANK = ' '
                PERIOD = '.'
                COMMA = ','
                READ *, NAME
                PRINT *, 'NAME AS ENTERED=           ', NAME
        C                       REMOVE ALL PERIODS
                POS = INDEX(NAME, PERIOD)
        100     IF (POS .EQ. NOTFND) GO TO 200
                  TEMP = NAME(:POS-1)  // NAME(POS+1:)
                  NAME = TEMP
                  POS = INDEX(NAME, PERIOD)
                  GO TO 100
        200     PRINT *, 'AFTER REMOVING PERIODS= ', NAME
        C                       REMOVE EXTRANEOUS BLANKS
                DO 300 POS = 1, NAMLEN
                  IF    ((NAME(POS:POS+1) .EQ. (BLANK//BLANK))
             +          .OR. (NAME(POS:POS+1) .EQ. (BLANK//COMMA))) THEN
                    TEMP= NAME(:POS-1) // NAME(POS+ 1:)
                    NAME = TEMP
                  ENDIF
        300       CONTINUE
                PRINT *, 'AFTER REMOVING BLANKS=  ', NAME
        C                       ADD BLANK AFTER COMMA
                POS = INDEX(NAME, COMMA)
                IF (NAME(POS+1:POS+1) .NE. BLANK) THEN
                  TEMP = NAME(:POS) // BLANK // NAME(POS+1:)
                  NAME = TEMP
                ENDIF
                PRINT *, STANDARDIZED FORM=           ', NAME
                END
```

Data

```
'LANGSFORD ,   RAYMOND G.
```

Output

```
NAME AS ENTERED=           LANGSFORD,    RAYMOND G.
AFTER REMOVING PERIODS= LANGSFORD,    RAYMOND G
AFTER REMOVING BLANKS=  LANGSFORD, RAYMOND G
STANDARDIZED FORM=         LANGSFORD, RAYMOND G
```

Data

```
'MURRAY ,SIMONE NEIL-FITZIMMONS'
```

Output

```
NAME AS ENTERED=           MURRAY ,SIMONE NEIL-FITZIMMONS
AFTER REMOVING PERIODS= MURRAY ,SIMONE NEIL-FITZIMMONS
AFTER REMOVING BLANKS=  MURRAY,SIMONE NEIL-FITZIMMONS
STANDARDIZED FORM=         MURRAY, SIMONE NEIL-FITZIMMONS
```

10.3   EXERCISES

1. After the assignments have been carried out, what are the length and value of the strings stored in ONE, TWO, THREE, and FOUR?

```
CHARACTER*(4) ONE, TWO, THREE, FOUR
ONE = '+'
TWO = ONE // ONE
THREE = ONE // TWO
FOUR = TWO // (ONE // ONE)
```

> *Warning!* The answer probably isn't what you'd expect.

2. As the name-standardizer program stands now, these two strings do not wind up in the same form.

```
'RUSSELL,LORD BERTRAND'
' RUSSELL     ,LORD BERTRAND'
```

Why not, and how would you alter the program so they do wind up the same?

3. Write a program which READs a name and PRINTs an error message unless the name has exactly one comma in it.

10   PROBLEMS

1. READ a person's name from a data line, and check to see if it's your name. If it is, PRINT an alias (to protect your real identity); otherwise PRINT the name as is. Keep READing lines until you find one with the "name" 'FINISHED'.

2. Write a program to READ a word up to ten characters long from one line, and a sentence from the next line (up to 80 characters, including blanks and other punctuation), then PRINT the word, the sentence, and the number of occurrences of the word in the sentence.

3. Boss Tweed Clothing does tons of direct-mail advertising and has been getting a lot of complaints from people who have received more than one copy of its glossy four-color flyer. Boss Tweed has ˎdiscovered that one of its big problems is that one of the companies it buys mailing lists from records the names like this:

```
'PHILLIP K NERDLY'
```

and the others record them like this:

```
'NERDLY, PHILLIP K
```

Write a program which READs a name (up to 32 characters long) and converts names written in the second form into the first form. If the name is already in the first form (has no comma), leave it be. Watch out for problems with spacing!

4. Telegrams are usually sent with break characters between the words in the message. Write a program that decodes telegrams, i.e. replaces break characters with a blank. Assume the break character is a "/". READ a data line, decode it, then PRINT it. The last data line will be "STOP".

---

palindrome: a word or phrase which reads the same forward as backward

A palindrome: "Madam, I'm Adam."
Not a palindrome: "Able was I ere I saw Chicago."

---

5. Write a program which detects palindromes. Assume that there won't be more than 50 characters. Remember that blanks, punctuation marks, and CapiTaliZations don't count in determining palindromes, so don't enter anything but letters on your data lines. PRINT the input phrase, and follow it by the phrase IS PALINDROMIC or IS NOT, IN FACT, PALINDROMIC, whichever is appropriate. Keep going until a line with '*' on it is read.

   Use these data lines and any others you think up:

   ```
   'RADAR'
   'TOOHOTTOHOOT'
   'ARSMITHIII'
   '*'
   ```

Program Design Problems

6. Redo problem 5, but now include a "preprocessor" which removes punctuation marks and blanks within the phrase before you test to see whether the phrase is a palindrome. You can use some of the ideas in the name-standardizer program (Section 10.3), but you'll have to be careful in how you treat blanks at the very end of the phrase.

   Use these and any others you think up:

   ```
   'TOO HOT TO HOOT'
   'A MAN, A PLAN, A CANAL--PANAMA'
   'WARSAW WAS RAW'
   '*'
   ```

7. Write a program to READ a line containing a sentence. Assume that no punctuation is used other than blanks and commas in the sentence and a period at the end.

   Your program should print the sentence, then compute and print the number of words in the sentence. To do this, you'll have to examine each character separately to look for blanks, periods, and commas, which indicate separations between words.

8. Write a program that keeps track of the number of occurrences of word lengths in a portion of text. Assume there are no words longer

than 30 characters. Your program should PRINT the text and the counts for each word length.

9. Write a program which READs a number of people's names. Keep a list (array) of names seen so far. When each name is READ, PRINT it, convert it to standard form (using the name-standardizer program), then have your program check to see if that name has been seen already (use the **array search loop** from Section 9.6). If it has been seen before, PRINT an appropriate message. If it has *not* been seen before, PRINT a message and add it into the array. Keep going until the name 'END OF NAMES' is READ. Assume there will be no more than 20 names that are really different.

Here are some names to use—add more.

```
'LANGSFORD    ,RAYMOND G.'
'MCDONALD,RONALD'
'MUSEUM, DE YOUNG'
'   LANGSFORD,RAYMOND G'
'LANGSFORD, MARCIA MARY'
'NERDLY   ,   PHILLIP K.'
'MCDONALD   ,   RONALD'
'FARNSWORTH, HECTOR T.'
'LANGSFORD,RAYMOND G.'
'NERDLY, PHILLIP K'
'FARNSWORTH    ,HECTOR T'
'END OF NAMES'
```

10. Write a program which READs in a body of text one line at a time and determines which words appear in the (entire) text and the number of times each word appears. You may assume that not more than 300 different words will appear in the text—if your program finds more, have it give an error message and quite READing lines. Otherwise your program should quit READing lines when it gets one that has the end of the string

```
'END OF TEXT'
```

on it. Once your program has finished READing lines, have it PRINT each different word it found, the number of occurrences of each word, the total number of different words, and the total number of characters READ.

11. After months of searching, you find a job as a programmer for an ad agency. Your first assignment (given to you by your boss, who wears two-foot-wide ties, smokes mentholated cigars, and keeps calling you "baby") is to write a program which arranges ad copy. Your program READs the paragraph from data lines and prints it out in the desired form. Desired forms are:

Rectangle: fit as well as possible within margins n columns side (run your program with $n = 50$, 25, and 12)
Triangle: fit as well as possible in a triangle shape with base at the bottom of the ad

Here is some ad copy to use, written in the triangle form.

```
YOUR
EYES, YOU
SAY? HOW COULD
YOU HAVE - EYE ODOR?
WELL, YOUR EYES ARE SO
CLOSE TO YOUR NOSE THAT YOU
GET USED TO THEIR SMELL. BUT DON'T
TAKE THE RISK OF OFFENDING OTHERS! USE
EYERON-F, THE GENTLE EYE FRESHENER AND
DEODORIZER. AVAILABLE IN THREE SIZES,GIANT,
JUMBO, AND FAMILY. (NOW LEMON-FRESHENED FOR
EVEN MORE PROTECTION.) GET SOME TODAY!
```

12. Write a program that accepts data lines containing names of states or abbreviations of names of states and that returns the official U.S. Post Office abbreviations for each state name. If an abbreviation is undecipherable, print an appropriate message. Unless you feel like doing more, just have your program deal with the 11 western states listed in Section 9.2.

Sample:

input   output

```
NEV.     THE OFFICIAL USPO ABBREVIATION IS NV
MONT.    THE OFFICIAL USPO ABBREVIATION IS MT
C.       SORRY, I DON''T KNOW WHAT STATE YOU MEAN
```

11 Western States

Arizona AZ	New Mexico NM
California CA	Oregon OR
Colorado CO	Utah UT
Idaho ID	Washington WA
Montana MT	Wyoming WY
Nevada NV	

Hint: This problem can be as hard as you want to make it. It would be best to do it in stages. In the first stage, accept only a correctly spelled state name or the official USPO abbreviation. In the next stage, accept those plus anything that matches the first few letters of just one state (i.e., "CAL" matches just "CALIFORNIA," but "C" matches two western states). If you want to go on, start by trying to figure out why "WSHNGTN" seems "closer" to "WASHINGTON" than any other name. Then program your idea.

11 SUBPROGRAMS

CHAPTER PLAN
- *Emphasize hierarchical organization of programs*
- *Introduce the use of*
  SUBROUTINEs
  FUNCTIONs
  Variable-size arrays
- *Explain the differences between formal parameters and local variables*
- *Warn about common bugs in programs using SUBROUTINEs and FUNCTIONs*

11.1 HIERARCHIES AND MODULARITY

Let's do an experiment. Up to this point, we've covered 13 Fortran statements—assignment, INTEGER, REAL, PRINT, READ, END, PARAMETER, LOGICAL, CHARACTER*(n), IF-GO TO, IF-THEN-ELSE, GO TO, and DO. Put this book aside, and try to write down the 13 types of statements.

You probably found it easy to write half a dozen or so of them as fast as you could write, with little mental effort. But you probably found that the rest of the statements, if you could remember them at all, required more mental effort. Perhaps you resorted to some "trick," like thinking back to the programs you've written or trying to group the statements in some way.

Let's try it again, but this time we'll organize the statements into categories.

Read the category names (see box on next page) and the statements in each category aloud a couple times. Then put the book down, and again try to write the 13 types.

This time you probably found it easy—it's easy to remember the four categories: declarations, control statements, I/O statements, and other statements. And once you concentrate on a single category, it's easy to

Fortran Statement Types

Declarations	Control statements	I/O statements	Other statements
INTEGER	GO TO	PRINT	assignment
REAL	IF-GO- TO	READ	
CHARACTER*(n)	IF-THEN-ELSE		PARAMETER
LOGICAL	DO		END

remember the few statements in that category. They just seem to pop into mind.

But notice how strange this is. We've *added* four new items to the list of things to remember, yet we've made the task easier. By imposing a hierarchical organization, we can limit the number of things we have to remember or think about *at each point*.

This appears to be a basic fact about the way the human brain works— we most naturally think, act, and plan in a way that results in about a half dozen ideas, considerations, categories, or possibilities being in mind at once.

---

seven plus or minus two: the classic paper on this remarkable theory of short-term memory was written by G. Miller in 1956 and appeared in *Psychological Review* Vol 63, pp 81-97, under the title "The Magical Number Seven Plus or Minus Two." Most introductory psychology texts discuss the theory.

Let's draw out the two different ways of remembering the statement types. First, we tried this:

```
remember "assignment"
remember "INTEGER"
remember "REAL"
remember "PRINT"
remember "READ"
remember "END"
remember "PARAMETER"
remember "LOGICAL"
remember "CHARACTER*(n)"
remember "IF-GO TO"
remember "IF-THEN-ELSE"
remember "GO TO"
remember "DO"
```

The second method, the organized or **structured** method, looks like this at the top level of the hierarchy:

```
remember the "declarations"
remember the "control statements"
```

remember the "I/O statements"
remember the "other statements"

Then, corresponding to each of the subcategories, there are only a few things to remember. For example, corresponding to

remember the "control statements"

there is something like

control statements:
remember the "GO TO"
remember "IF-GO TO"
remember "IF-THEN-ELSE"
remember "DO"

The psychological fact that thinking, remembering, speaking, and acting are most naturally carried out when the task is hierarchically structured with about a half dozen things to keep in mind at each step is so all-pervasive that most of us aren't even aware of it. And since computers, at least as they are built now, *don't* share this constraint, it is possible to write programs which are acceptable to the computer, but which are incredibly hard for human beings to understand. A program which is hard for humans to understand is very often a program which has errors buried in it, is difficult to debug, may be unwieldy to use, and has caused the programmer grief and wasted time.

Creating long programs can be difficult—we have to make a conscious effort to make things easier for ourselves by giving our programs a clear, understandable organization. Of course, just chopping the problem up into arbitrary subparts isn't enough—you need to learn to choose reasonable organizations. A well-organized program can be thought about in a hierarchical way, so that at any point there are few enough subparts to keep in mind at once. At any point the subparts should be "at the same level" and should correspond to a natural way of dividing up the tasks to be done.

In this chapter, we'll introduce statements which can help you to organize your programs. All our programs in the rest of the book will provide examples of using these organizational ideas. As we'll see in later chapters, the same principles can be used to help organize the way programs interact with their users and the way data is stored. In practice, huge programming projects are divided into subparts (modules) and assigned to programming teams which then use the same organizational principles. The structured, modular approach is used at every level of the professional programmer's world.

There are several convenient ways to give a sequence of statements a simple name. We'll cover two of them, SUBROUTINEs and FUNCTIONs, in this chapter. Both are lumped under the term **subprograms** because they play a *subordinate* role, giving details of computations referred to elsewhere.

FUNCTIONs are appropriate when a single value is returned from the subprogram, and SUBROUTINEs are a better choice when the subprogram returns several values each time it is referenced. We'll deal with FUNCTIONs first.

---

subprogram: a complete and separate program which may be referred to by another program. Subprograms help you break your program into smaller logical chunks. Then you can work on each chunk separately.

---

program unit: the main program or a subprogram. Every Fortran program has at least one program unit. All our programs up to now have had exactly one unit, the main program.

11.2 FUNCTIONs

Fortran includes many intrinsic operations and functions that together provide a simple notation for a great variety of computations, from addition and multiplication through trigonometric and logarithmic operations. When a combination of functions and operations leads to a result we are trying to achieve, as in computing the length of the hypotenuse of a right triangle given the lengths of its legs, we can simplify the notation by using statement functions (see Section 2.4)

```
HYP(A,B) = SQRT(A**2 + B**2)
```

Invoking the HYP function whenever we need to find the length of a hypotenuse is simpler and more direct than writing an expression that computes it from intrinsic operations and functions.

Sometimes an operation we need cannot be described by a single Fortran expression. In such cases, the statement function is inadequate. We need a more general type of facility for defining functions, again for the purpose of simplifying the program as a whole, making it a more direct expression of the computation we want to make. This facility is the external FUNCTION.

An external FUNCTION may be used to specify any sequence of Fortran commands to compute a value needed by a program. It is analogous to the statement function, except that it is not limited to a single expression, and it becomes available from any program unit. (That is, we can invoke it by name from any other FUNCTION or SUBROUTINE, or from the main program unit.)

Consider the following simple example. Suppose we are writing a program to compute areas of irregular polygons by triangulation. Such a program would be useful in computing the amount of material needed to build patios with borders consisting of straight line segments, as illustrated in Figure 11.2.1.

Figure 11.2.1   Patio Triangularization

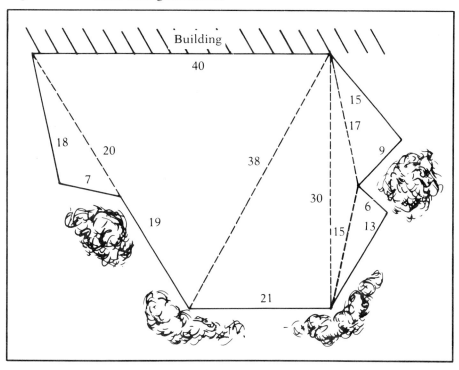

The dotted lines show how the area of the patio can be divided into nonoverlapping triangular regions. We can compute the full area of the patio by adding up the areas of these triangles. A program to compute patio area might consist of a loop that READs the dimensions of a triangular portion, computes the triangular area, and adds this to a running total. Details of this plan appear in Figure 11.2.2.

The Fortran program would be as direct and simple as the plan in Figure 11.2.2 if we had a function that computed the area of a triangle, given the lengths of its sides. We can write such a function based on Heron's formula.

Figure 11.2.2   Patio Area Computation

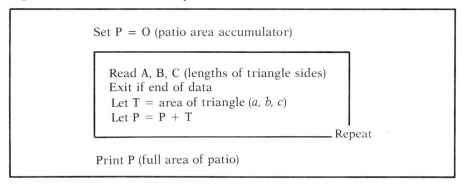

Heron's formula for area of triangle:

$$\text{area} = \sqrt{s(s - a)(s - b)(s - c)}$$

where *a*, *b*, and *c* are lengths of sides and $s = (a + b + c)/2$.

When we express Heron's formula as a Fortran FUNCTION, we have the opportunity to detect some types of errors in measurements that could occur. Specifically, if the product $s(s - a)(s - b)(s - c)$ is negative, then there must be an error in the data, since one of the side lengths exceeds the sum of the other two, and this is impossible for a triangle (the shortest distance between two points is a straight line). If our FUNCTION encounters this condition, it should produce a result that signals the error. Since areas are never negative, we can use negative values for these error signals. The plan for the function, based on these considerations, is shown in Figure 11.2.3.

Figure 11.2.3   Plan for Area-of-Triangle Function

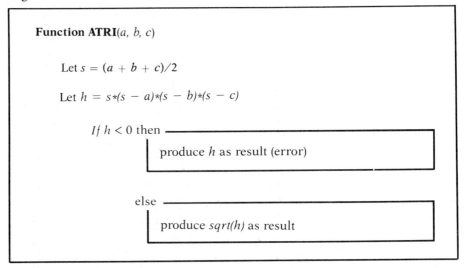

We express the function in Fortran as a sequence of commands, just as in an ordinary program. The only differences are that the function begins with a special statement whose purpose, besides indicating the beginning of a FUNCTION program unit, is to establish the name of the function and the names that will be used to designate its arguments within the definition of the function. This statement begins with a data type indicating the type of the result that the function will produce (INTEGER, REAL, etc.), followed by the keyword FUNCTION, a name for the function, and a list, enclosed in parentheses, of parameter names separated by commas.

After the FUNCTION statement, we specify the data types of the function's parameters. Then we declare any variables needed during the computation (such as *s* and *h* in our plan). After these declarations, the computation is specified as a sequence of ordinary Fortran statements, using the dummy parameter names whenever the value of a parameter is

FUNCTION Statement

forms

type FUNCTION $f(p_1, p_2, \ldots, p_n)$

FUNCTION $f(p_1, p_2, \ldots, p_n)$

type is any data type

f is an identifier (the FUNCTION name)

$p_1, p_2, \ldots, p_n$ (the parameter names) are identifiers

The body of the FUNCTION, that is, the statements between the FUNCTION statement and the corresponding END, must assign a value to the name f.

If *type* is omitted, implicit typing takes over.

If the FUNCTION has no parameters, the list $p_1, \ldots, p_n$ is omitted, but the parentheses must still appear.

meaning

The value the FUNCTION computes when invoked is the value of its name when the END or a RETURN statement in the body of the FUNCTION is executed.

examples

```
REAL FUNCTION F(X)
INTEGER FUNCTION LOCSM(A,N)
FUNCTION G(X,Y,Z)
```

needed. When the result we want has been computed, it is assigned to the function name as if this name were a variable. The last statement in the FUNCTION is the END statement, which is used to delimit the end of all program units. (So far, you've been using it to mark the ends of main programs, but when your programs have several program units, each will have its own END statement.)

```
      REAL FUNCTION ATRI(A,B,C)
      REAL A, B, C
C               COMPUTE AREA OF TRIANGLE
C               A,B,C: LENGTHS OF SIDES
      REAL S,H
      S = (A+B+C)/2
      H = S*(S-A)*(S-B)*(S-C)
      IF (H .LT. 0.0) THEN
        ATRI = H
      ELSE
        ATRI = SQRT(H)
      ENDIF
      END
```

We invoke an external FUNCTION in the same manner as an intrinsic function or a statement function. The only difference is that the data type of an intrinsic function is known to the program using it automatically, but the data type of an external FUNCTION must be declared explicitly within any program unit that invokes the function. For example, if we write a program (based on the plan in Figure 11.2.2) that uses the function ATRI, we will have to include a declaration statement in the program specifying that ATRI produces a REAL value as its result.

```
C                        COMPUTE AREA OF PATIO BY TRIANGULATION
           REAL LEG(3), P, T, ENDDAT
C                        VARIABLES
C                        LEG  -- LENGTHS OF SIDES OF TRIANGLE
C                        P    -- RUNNING SUM OF TRIANGULAR AREAS
C                        (TOTAL AREA OF PATIO, EVENTUALLY)
C                        T    -- AREA OF INDIVIDUAL TRIANGLE
           PARAMETER (ENDDAT = 0.0)
           REAL ATRI
C                        FUNCTION ATRI -- COMPUTES AREA OF TRIANGLE
           P = 0.0
    100    READ *, (LEG(I),I = 1,3)
             IF (LEG(1) .LT. ENDDAT) GO TO 200
             T = ATRI(LEG(1), LEG(2), LEG(3))
             IF (T .LT. 0.0) THEN
               PRINT *, 'BAD DATA:', (LEG(I),I=1,3)
               PRINT *, '  WARNING! INVALID COMPUTATION'
             ELSE
               P = P + T
             ENDIF
             GO TO 100
    200    PRINT *, 'TOTAL AREA: ', P
           END
```

Data

```
18  20   7
40  39  38
38  21  30
30  15  17
17   9  15
15  13   5
-1  -1  -1
```

Output

```
TOTAL AREA:     1216.588
```

11.2 EXERCISES

1. The value of a triangular prism is the area of its (triangular) bases times its height. Write a function that computes the volume of a triangular prism, given its height and the length of the sides of its triangular base.

2. What is wrong with the following FUNCTION definition?

```
REAL FUNCTION R
R = 2.0
RETURN
END
```

3. Since we had all of the lengths of the sides of a triangle stored in a single array in the program of this section, why couldn't we invoke ATRI in this manner: T = ATRI(LEG)?

4. Write ATRI so that it will be invoked as shown in exercise 3.

11.3 FUNCTIONS WITH ARRAY PARAMETERS

The arguments for intrinsic and statement functions are always individual variables (or parts of variables, in the case of substring arguments for INDEX, for example). They are never whole arrays. The only way in Fortran 77 to obtain functions that make computations based on arrays of values is to write external functions. For example, suppose we want to write functions to compute the mean and standard deviation of an array of numbers. These functions are invoked in the following program.

```
C                     COMPUTE MEAN AND STD
C                     DEVIATION OF 10 NUMBERS
      REAL A(10)
      REAL MEAN, STDDEV
      READ *, (A(I), I=1,10)
      PRINT *, MEAN(A,10), STDDEV(A,10)
      END
```

These functions exhibit a characteristic of nearly all functions that have arrays as arguments: the size of an array argument is specified in another argument. This is necessary because the function has no way of knowing the length of an argument array unless it is specified as another argument. (Of course, some functions might operate always on arrays of length 12, say, or some other fixed length, but these are rare. Nearly all useful functions with array arguments will apply equally well to arrays of differing lengths in different invocations.)

To provide for this necessity, Fortran permits declarations of arrays that are dummy parameters to specify the array dimensions by means of additional parameters, as shown in the MEAN function below.

```
      REAL FUNCTION MEAN(X,N)
      INTEGER N
      REAL X(N)
      REAL SUM.
      SUM = 0.0
      DO 100 I=1,N
        SUM = SUM + X(I)
100     CONTINUE
      MEAN = SUM/N
      END
```

It is important to realize that the actual size of the argument array in the invocation does not vary. It is just that, in different invocations of the function, its array argument may have a different length, as illustrated in the program below.

```
REAL A(10), B(100)
REAL MEAN
READ *, (A(I), I=1,10)
PRINT*, 'MEAN A:', MEAN(A,10)
READ *, (B(I), I=1,100)
PRINT *, 'MEAN B:', MEAN(B,100)
END
```

We will discuss this in more detail in Section 11.7, where we present a collection of highly useful routines to aid in plotting graphs and drawings.

All of our examples thus far have invoked functions only in the main program unit, but any program unit can invoke an external function. To illustrate, we will define STDDEV as a function that invokes MEAN to make its computation.

```
      REAL FUNCTION STDDEV(X,N)
      INTEGER N
      REAL X(N)
      REAL MEAN
      REAL SUMSQ
      SUMSQ = 0.0
      DO 100 I = 1,N
         SUMSQ = SUMSQ + X(I)**2
100      CONTINUE
      STDDEV = SQRT(SUMSQ/N - MEAN(X,N)**2)
      END
```

This technique of using functions to help define other functions is an important method of employing a hierarchy to describe algorithms, as we discussed in Chapter 5. Throughout the remainder of the text, you will see this technique used to deal effectively with complex computations.

11.3 EXERCISES

1. Write a function to compute the largest value in a REAL array.
2. Write a function to compute the square of the sum of the base-10 logarithms of the values in a REAL array.
3. What is wrong with the following function?

```
      REAL FUNCTION F(X,N)
      INTEGER N
      REAL X(N)
      REAL MEAN
      REAL A(N)
      DO 100 I = 1,N
         A(I) = (X(I) - MEAN(X,N))**2
100      CONTINUE
      F = MEAN(A,N)
      END
```

4. What is wrong with the expression below, which uses the STDDEV function specified in this section?

```
S = STDDEV(X)*N
```

5. Write a program that uses the function from exercise 1 and the MEAN function of this section to compute the largest deviation from the average value (either Greater Than or Less Than) of 12 numbers on a data line.

11.4 SUBROUTINEs

An important use of subprograms is to avoid having to write the same sequence of statements over and over again. For example, if you are writing a program that generates a long report, you'd probably want to number the pages. To do this, your program needs to keep track of the number of pages printed. Each time a new page is printed, the page counter needs to be updated and its value printed at the upper right-hand corner of the next page of output. In addition, it would be nice to print the title of the report under the page number to insure that different reports don't get scrambled after the pages are burst. This is not a complicated process, but there are several Fortran statements involved. By putting these statements in a SUBROUTINE, we can avoid having to write them at every point in the program where we want to start a new page of output.

> **burst:** to separate continuous-form paper into separate sheets

Like a FUNCTION, a SUBROUTINE is a separate program. It has its own declarations, memory cells, statement numbers, END statement, and so forth. All of these things are **local** to the SUBROUTINE. That is, they are automatically kept separate from their counterparts in other program units. Even if your main program and a SUBROUTINE (or FUNCTION), both have statements labeled 100, the two labels won't be confused. They are local to their own program units. The same goes for memory cells and the other constructs.

In our example we need some way to tell the page-numbering SUBROUTINE what the current page number is so that the SUBROUTINE can update the number and print it. Thus, we need some communication between the main program and the SUBROUTINE. We can transmit a memory cell to the SUBROUTINE via an **argument** in a **CALL statement,** the statement which gets the SUBROUTINE into action. Let's take a look at a typical CALL statement.

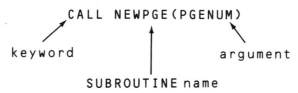

A CALL statement has three parts: (1) the keyword CALL, indicating that a SUBROUTINE is to be invoked; (2) the name of the SUBROUTINE to be brought into action (NEWPGE in our example); and (3) the argument list (there is only one argument, the INTEGER memory cell PGENUM, in our example, but other SUBROUTINEs may have several arguments).

To perform a CALL statement, the processor does three things: (1) it records the place in the program where the CALL occurs (so that control can return to the statement following the CALL), (2) it sets up the arguments to be transmitted to the SUBROUTINE, and (3) it transfers to the beginning of the SUBROUTINE to get its next instruction.

CALL Statement

---

forms
CALL $s(a_1, a_2, \ldots, a_n)$
CALL s
s is a SUBROUTINE name
a_i is an argument (i.e., a memory cell name, array name, constant, or expression)

meaning
Performs the computation described by SUBROUTINE s using the information and/or memory cells specified in the arguments

examples
```
CALL SORT(NAMES, N)
CALL AVG(GRD, N, AV)
CALL PRMESS
CALL CMPT(A, 32.0*CAB+1.0, SQRT(C))
```

Now let's take a look at the SUBROUTINE itself.

```
COMMENT:                WHEN CALLED, INCREMENT PAGE NUMBER AND PRINT IT.
         SUBROUTINE NEWPGE(PAGE)
         INTEGER PAGE
         PAGE = PAGE + 1
C                        LEAVE SOME SPACE BEFORE NEW PAGE
         PRINT *
         PRINT *
         PRINT *
         PRINT *, '                                    ',
        +         '                        PAGE',PAGE
         PRINT *, '                                    ',
        +         'BOOK REPORT--E100'
         PRINT *, '                        ',
        +         'SILAS MARNER, BY GEORGE ELIOT'
         END
```

The first line of a SUBROUTINE, known as the **header** statement, gives the name of the SUBROUTINE and a list of **formal parameters**. Formal parameters are symbols which will be used in the **body** of the SUBROUTINE (the part between the header statement and the END) to stand for

SUBROUTINE Statement

---

forms
SUBROUTINE $s(p_1, p_2, \ldots, p_n)$
SUBROUTINE s
s (the SUBROUTINE name) is an identifier
$p_1, \ldots, p_n$ (the parameter names) are identifiers
The **body** of the SUBROUTINE—that is, the part between the SUB-
ROUTINE statement and corresponding END—must contain at least
one RETURN statement. (The parenthesized list of parameters may be
omitted if the SUBROUTINE neither needs nor delivers outside information.)

meaning
describes an algorithm which may be invoked by a CALL statement

examples
```
SUBROUTINE SORT(A,N)
SUBROUTINE X(U)
SUBROUTINE BUILD(A, C, ROUND)
```

---

the arguments which will be transmitted via a CALL statement. Thus,
they serve the same purpose as formal parameters in FUNCTIONs. Here,
we discuss the idea in more detail.

The name (NEWPGE) of the SUBROUTINE is placed after the key
word SUBROUTINE and is followed by the parenthesized list of formal
parameters (PAGE). After the header statement come the **formal parameter declarations** (INTEGER PAGE). Even though these look like normal
declaration statements, their effect is quite different. Instead of instruct-
ing the compiler to attach names to memory cells or arrays, they tell the
compiler what kind of values or structures to expect the formal parameters to be attached to when the SUBROUTINE is called. The first thing
the processor does when it begins to perform the statements in a SUB-
ROUTINE is to attach the formal parameter names to the arguments
transmitted by the CALL statement. Once that is done, the processor
begins to perform the executable statements in the body of the SUBROU-
TINE. In our example, this amounts to increasing the value of the memory cell attached to the formal parameter PAGE. Our CALL would have
transmitted the memory cell PGENUM from the main program; hence
the first statement would increase the value of PGENUM. Next come the
PRINT statements, which put the page number in the upper right-hand
corner of the next page and the report title underneath. When the processor encounters a **RETURN instruction** (or the END statement), it uses
information recorded by the CALL to return to the statement following
the CALL in the main program. Since every SUBROUTINE is a separate
program unit, the compiler must be instructed when to wrap up the
compilation of a SUBROUTINE. The END statement is used for this pur-

RETURN Statement

---

form
RETURN

meaning
Instructs the processor to go back to the point in the calling program where the subprogram was called.

examples

```
RETURN
IF (X .EQ. Y) RETURN
```

---

pose. It must be the last statement in every program unit. In the program setup, program units are simply placed in sequence, one after the other.

The following program uses the SUBROUTINE NEWPGE.

```
COMMENT:              PROGRAM TO PRINT SILAS MARNER BOOK REPORT
C                     VARIABLES:
C                     PGENUM--CURRENT PAGE NUMBER
C                     (UPDATED BY SUBROUTINE)
C                     REPORT--ARRAY TO STORE CURRENT LINE
C                     LINE--NUMBER OF LINES PRINTED SO FAR ON
C                             CURRENT PAGE
C                     PGELEN--NUMBER OF LINES ALLOWED PER PAGE
      INTEGER PGENUM, LINE, PGELEN
      CHARACTER*60 REPORT, FINIS
      PGELEN = 35
      FINIS = '*END'
C                     TITLE PAGE
      PGENUM = 0
      CALL NEWPGE(PGENUM)
      PRINT *, 'REVIEW OF'
      PRINT *, 'SILAS MARNER'
      PRINT *, 'A NOVEL BY GEORGE ELIOT'
      PRINT *, 'REVIEW BY RODNEY THORPS'
C                     DEDICATION PAGE
      CALL NEWPGE(PGENUM)
      PRINT *, 'THIS REVIEW IS'
      PRINT *, 'GRATEFULLY DEDICATED'
      PRINT *, 'TO MY MOTHER'
      PRINT *, 'AND MY DOG, SPOT'
C                     BODY OF REPORT
      LINE = PGELEN + 1
200   READ *, REPORT
        IF (REPORT .EQ. FINIS) GO TO 300
        LINE = LINE + 1
        IF (LINE .GT. PGELEN) THEN
          LINE = 1
          CALL NEWPGE(PGENUM)
        ENDIF
        PRINT *, REPORT
        GO TO 200
300   END
```

Data

```
'        SILAS MARNER WAS MISER.'
'DUNSTAN CASS STOLE HIS GOLD.'
'EPPIE WAS THE LITTLE BABY.'
'SHE GREW UP AND WAS HAPPY.'
'SO WAS SILAS.'
'  '
'      GEORGE ELIOT WILL GO IN'
'THE ANNALS OF LITERATURE.'
'HE WAS A REAL GOOD WRITER.'
'  '
'        THE END'
'*END'
```

Output

```
                                        PAGE   1
                          BOOK REPORT--E100
                          SILAS MARNER, BY GEORGE ELIOT

REVIEW OF
SILAS MARNER
A NOVEL BY GEORGE ELIOT
REVIEW BY RODNEY THORPS



                                        PAGE   2
                          BOOK REPORT--E100
                          SILAS MARNER, BY GEORGE ELIOT

THIS REVIEW IS
GRATEFULLY DEDICATED
TO MY MOTHER
AND MY DOG, SPOT



                                        PAGE   3
                          BOOK REPORT--E100
                          SILAS MARNER, BY GEORGE ELIOT
        SILAS MARNER WAS A MISER.
DUNSTAN  CASS STOLE HIS GOLD.
EPPIE WAS THE LITTLE BABY.
SHE GREW UP AND WAS HAPPY.
SO WAS SILAS.

      GEORGE ELIOT WILL GO IN
THE ANNALS OF LETERATURE.
HE WAS A REAL GOOD WRITER.



        THE END
```

11.4 EXERCISES

1. Which of the following are legal SUBROUTINE statements? For each statement which is not legal, explain why not.

```
SUBROUTINE APPLE(RED,GREEN)
SUBROUTINE PEAR
SUBROUTINE POMEGRANATE(SEED)
SUBROUTINE PIZZA(SMALL, OR, LARGE(ONE))
```

2. Which of the following are legal CALL statements? For each statement which is not legal, explain why not.

```
CALL APPLE(1,'RED')
CALL PEAR
CALL POMEG(RANATE)
CALL PIZZA(SMALL,OR,LARGE(ONE))
```

3. What would the following program print?

```
INTEGER A, B, C
CALL SQUARE(3,A)
CALL SQUARE(4,B)
CALL SQUARE(5,C)
PRINT *, A,B,C
END

SUBROUTINE SQUARE(NUMBER,SQ)
INTEGER NUMBER, SQ
SQ = NUMBER*NUMBER
END
```

4. What would the following program print?

```
CHARACTER*5 A(3)
A(1) = 'DOG'
A(2) = 'CAT'
A(3) = 'BAT'
CALL CHANGE(A,2)
PRINT *, 'A=',A
END

SUBROUTINE CHANGE(ARRAY,INDEX)
CHARACTER*5 ARRAY (3)
INTEGER INDEX
ARRAY(INDEX) = 'NONE'
END
```

11.5 CAUTION! SUBTLE BUGS WITH SUBPROGRAMS

Because subprograms are completely separate program units, they are often called **externals.** The consequences of this subprogram independence can be confusing at first. Suppose, for example, that you write a SUBROUTINE AREA which has two REAL parameters, but when you CALL AREA you accidentally use an INTEGER argument.

This will cause an error when the computer tries to do the computation in AREA because the INTEGER 2 and the REAL 2.0 are not the same. On most Fortran systems, the pattern of 1's and 0's that represents the INTEGER 2 is very close to the pattern that represents the REAL number 0.0. (See explanation in Section 3.8). This information might help you track down errors of this nature in case your Fortran system doesn't detect them (most don't). Even so, this kind of error can be exceedingly difficult to find. The moral is to make sure the arguments in CALL statements match the corresponding parameter declarations in the SUBROUTINE.

```
CALL AREA(2, S)

SUBROUTINE AREA(R, A)
REAL R, A
```
  • The constant 2 takes on the name R (error! wrong type!).
  •
  •
  •
  •
  •
  • The cell S takes on the name A.
  •
  •
```
END
```

error!

```
REAL S
CALL AREA(2,S)
PRINT *, 'AREA IS', S
END

SUBROUTINE AREA(R, A)
REAL R, A
A = 3.14*R**2
END
```

> **Caution—data type:** The data type of each argument in a CALL statement must match that of the corresponding parameter in the SUBROUTINE.

To illustrate this point further, let's consider a second case. The arguments in CALL statements may be values (that is, arithmetic, CHARACTER, or LOGICAL expressions or constants like 2 in CALL AREA (2,S), or they may be memory cell names or array names. But you must be careful when you write CALL statements. Don't give the SUBROUTINE any arguments that it will try to use in illegitimate ways. For example, suppose we had gotten the data types right in our CALL statement above but had accidentally switched the order of the arguments, as shown on the following page.

```
CALL AREA(S, 2.0)

SUBROUTINE AREA(R, A)
   .
   .
 . The cell S takes on the name R.
 . The constant 2.0 takes on the name A.
   .
   .
   .
   .
   .
   .

A = 3.14*R**2  (Error! constants can't be changed!)
   .
   .
END
```

error!

```
REAL S
CALL AREA(S, 2.0)
PRINT *, 'AREA IS', S
END

SUBROUTINE AREA(R, A)
REAL R, A
A = 3.14*R**2
END
```

Then the A in the SUBROUTINE gets linked to the 2.0 in the CALL. But when the SUBROUTINE tries to perform the assignment statement A = 3.14*R**2, it is actually trying to assign a new value to the constant 2.0—clearly a mistake! The results of such an error vary from one Fortran system to another, but many systems don't give you any warning when this happens, making the mistake very hard to find.

> **Caution—constant arguments:** A SUBROUTINE must not try to change the value of a parameter which is linked to a constant in a CALL statement.

A third way in which CALL arguments and SUBROUTINE parameters must match is in structure. If a SUBROUTINE parameter is declared as an array, the corresponding argument in a CALL must be an array. The two examples in Figure 11.5.1 illustrate the point. In the program on the

Figure 11.5.1   Arguments Must Match Parameters

```
INTEGER A(4)
A(1) = 1
A(2) = 2
A(3) = 3
A(4) = 4
CALL DOUBLE(A(3))
PRINT *, A(1),A(2),A(3),A(4)
END
SUBROUTINE DOUBLE(M)
INTEGER M
M = M+M
END
```

Output   A(3) was doubled

1   2   6   4

```
INTEGER A,B,C,D
A = 1
B = 2
C = 3
D = 4
CALL DOUBEL(A)
PRINT *, A,B,C,D
END
SUBROUTINE DOUBEL(M)
INTEGER M(2)
M(1) = M(1) + M(1)
M(2) = M(2) + M(2)
END
```

Output   B was doubled by mistake *with no warning*

2   4   3   4

top, the SUBROUTINE expects the CALL statement to give it access to a memory cell, and it gets one—the third element in array A. All is well. In the example on the bottom, the SUBROUTINE is expecting an array but gets a memory cell instead. Things will go badly there, possibly without warning—again, a difficult error to eliminate from the program once it creeps in. Be careful when CALLing SUBROUTINEs!

> **Caution—array parameters:** If a SUBROUTINE parameter is declared to be an array, make sure the CALL statement supplies an array for the SUBROUTINE to use.

The matching correspondence between CALL arguments and SUBROUTINE parameters is so crucial that we think one final cautionary example will be helpful. When a SUBROUTINE parameter is declared to be a multi-dimensional array, the corresponding argument in the CALL statement must be an array of the same shape. If it isn't, problems will ensue. You will learn more about these problems in Chapter 14. Until then, avoid problems by being careful in CALL statements.

The two CALL statements in Figure 11.5.2 illustrate what can happen. In the first CALL statement, the array R has a three-by-three arrangement, and the corresponding parameter in the SUBROUTINE is declared to be a three-by-three array, consistent with the argument. The SUBROUTINE puts ones on the diagonal as it was intended to do. In the second CALL, the argument W is again a three-by-three array, but the SUBROUTINE is led to believe its parameter will be a two-by-two array. Instead of getting a diagonal of ones, as expected, we get strange results and no clue as to what went wrong.

The moral is to be careful when CALLing SUBROUTINEs. Know what assumptions the SUBROUTINE will make about its parameters, and make your CALL statements consistent with those assumptions.

> **Caution—multi-dimensional array arguments:** When you put a multi-dimensional array in a CALL statement's argument list, make sure its dimensions are the same as those declared for the corresponding parameter in the SUBROUTINE.

In spite of the difficulties they sometimes cause, SUBROUTINEs are one of the most important and useful features of Fortran. Over the years, people have written programs to do many things. Those that may be applied to many common problems are often written in the form of SUBROUTINEs and saved. At your computer center, no doubt, there is a large collection of SUBROUTINEs already written and available for you to use. Since the means of access to the collection differs from place to place, you will have to consult a local expert. Once you know how to attach these

Figure 11.5.2   Right and Wrong Ways to CALL

```
          INTEGER R(3,3), W(3,3)
          CALL UNITY (R,3)
          CALL UNITY (W,2)
          PRINT *, R(1,1),R(1,2),R(1,3),'        ',W(1,1),W(1,2)
          PRINT *, R(2,1),R(2,2),R(2,3),'        ',W(2,1),W(2,2)
          PRINT *, R(3,1),R(3,2),R(3,3)
          END
          SUBROUTINE UNITY (A,N)
COMMENT:              ONES ON DIAGONAL--ZEROES ELSEWHERE
          INTEGER N, A(N,N)
          INTEGER I, J
          DO 100 I = 1,N
            DO 100 J = 1,N
              A(I,J) = 0
   100        CONTINUE
          DO 200 I = 1,N
            A(I,I) = 1
   200        CONTINUE
          END
```

Output

```
  1   0   0      1   1
  0   1   0      0   0
  0   0   1
```

SUBROUTINEs to your program, you can use them simply by writing CALL statements with appropriate arguments. The availability of pre-packaged SUBROUTINEs, by itself, would be a good reason to learn how to use SUBROUTINEs. This, along with their use as time savers in coding, as in the book report example, should motivate you to become proficient with SUBROUTINEs.

Fortran subprograms are said to be **externals.** As a consequence of this organization, the compiler treats each program unit (i.e., your main program and your subprograms) independently. The END line, which must be the last line of every program unit, tells the compiler to stop compiling one program and to get ready to compile another.

Things to remember about subprograms:

Variable names and statement numbers are not confused between programs.
It is very easy to use subprograms written by someone else.
They can make your program more readable.
You cannot use variables from the calling program merely by using the same names in the subprogram.

11.6 SORTING—AN EXAMPLE OF TOP-DOWN DESIGN

The managers of a marketing and sales research firm have asked us to help them out. Many customers come to their staff with lists of sales figures (usually either monthly or weekly) tabulated over several years. Normally the research firm begins by preparing a year-by-year listing of this data. For each year the sales figures are listed two ways. One is simply a month-by-month (or week-by-week) tabulation of the monthly (or weekly) sales amounts. The other lists the amounts in decreasing order, from the best sales period to the worst. In this way the research firm gets a picture of seasonal effects on the customer's sales.

The research firm's business has grown in recent years and the staff can no longer handle all of it. Consequently they have decided to turn the tabulations over to a computer. The sales figures will be punched on cards, with one group of cards for each year. The first card of each yearly group will have the year and the sales period type (MONTHLY or WEEKLY) punched on it. The remaining cards of the group will have the sales figures (in whole dollars) punched on them. The firm wants us to write a program to print the tabulations in order to save the staff this tedious job.

If you think about it, you will see that this is a relatively simple programming task except for the business of listing the sales figures in order of decreasing sales period. Up to that point it is simply a matter of READing values and printing them. No rearrangement is necessary because they come in chronological order. But to print the sales figures in order of decreasing sales periods, we need to rearrange the data. One way to do that is to put the sales figures into an array and, when necessary, to change the order in which they are stored. We will want the output from the program to look something like the following sample.

```
                      SALES TABULATION

                           1983
                   MONTHLY SALES FIGURES

        CHRONOLOGICAL                   BEST TO WORST
     MONTH       SALES               MONTH       SALES
       1         6472                  12        10428
       2         4103                  10         9342
       3         2001                  11         8497
       4         2422                   1         6472
       5         3501                   6         5402
       6         5402                   7         5117
       7         5117                   8         4322
       8         4322                   2         4103
       9         2173                   5         3501
      10         9342                   4         2422
      11         8497                   9         2173
      12        10428                   3         2001
```

```
                               1983
                        WEEKLY SALES FIGURES

          CHRONOLOGICAL                    BEST TO WORST
      WEEK         SALES              WEEK           SALES
       1           1647                52            2544
       2           1500                49            2544
       3           1399                45            2422
       4           1822                41            2411
       .             .                  .              .
       .             .                  .              .
       .             .                  .              .
      49           2544                10            408
      50           2144                13            385
      51           2066                38            322
      52           2544                11            201
```

Because the line printer can't back up to print the columns under **BEST TO WORST SALES MONTH**, we'll have to store the sales information twice, once in chronological order and once in order of decreasing sales. When we arrange the sales figures in decreasing order, we must also arrange the corresponding month numbers to be printed beside the sales figures. Thus, in addition to the array storing the sales figures in chronological order, we need a pair of arrays to store the monthly numbers

Plan for Sales Report Program

---

1. Determine year of report
2. Determine period of report (weekly or monthly)
3. Process weekly or monthly data (sort and print)
4. Repeat

---

and sales figures in decreasing order. We'll use a SUBROUTINE to arrange the data for the columns on the right. We'll call it SORT since it sorts data into a certain order. It will have three parameters: (1) the array containing the sales figures, (2) the array containing the corresponding month numbers, and (3) the number of elements in the arrays (12 or 52). The first two are both input and output parameters (when SORT is CALLed, the first two arguments will contain information is some order, and SORT will rearrange this information), and the third is an input parameter.

Study the following program. We'll discuss the SORT subprogram once you understand its purpose.

Both of these SUBROUTINEs use the SORT subprogram, but the arguments in the two CALLs are different. Different arrays of different lengths are in the arguments.

Now that the program is written, we must write the SUBROUTINE SORT. The problem of sorting numbers into decreasing order has been studied by many people and there are lots of solutions. Some are better

```
COMMENT:                      THIS PROGRAM MAKES SALES REPORT SUMMARIES
               INTEGER YEAR
               CHARACTER*1 PERIOD
C                            PRINT HEADING
               PRINT *, '                    SALES TABULATION'
C                            GET YEAR AND SALES PERIOD FROM FIRST CARD OF GROUP
      100      READ *, YEAR, PERIOD
                IF (YEAR .EQ. 0) STOP
                PRINT *, ' '
                PRINT *, '                        ', YEAR
C                            CALL APPROPRIATE SUBROUTINE TO HANDLE
C                            WEEKLY OR MONTHLY SALES PERIOD.
               IF (PERIOD .EQ. 'M') GO TO 200
                CALL WEEKLY
                GO TO 100
      200       CALL MNTHLY
                GO TO 100
COMMENT:                      THE SUBROUTINES 'WEEKLY'AND 'MNTHLY' NEED NO
C                            INFORMATION FROM THIS PROGRAM. THEREFORE, THEY'VE
C                            NO ARGUMENTS.  THEY GET THEIR INFORMATION
C                            FROM DATA CARDS AND PRINT THEIR RESULTS.
C                            HENCE, THEY DON'T NEED TO COMMUNICATE VALUES TO
C                            OR FROM THE CALLIN PROGRAM.
               END


               SUBROUTINE      MNTHLY
               INTEGER SALES(12), MN(12), MNSALE(12), I
COMMENT:                      PRINT HEADINGS.
               PRINT *, '                    MONTHLY SALES FIGURES'
               PRINT *, ' '
               PRINT *, '          CHRONOLOGICAL',
     +                  '                    BEST TO WORST'
               PRINT *, '        MONTH      SALES              ',
     +                  'MONTH        SALES'
               READ *, SALES
C                            SAVE SALES FIGURES AND MAKE A LIST OF
C                            MONTH NUMBERS
               DO 100 I = 1,12
                  MNSALE(I) = SALES(I)
                  MN(I) = I
      100      CONTINUE
C                            SORT INFORMATION ACCORDING TO DECREASING SALES.
               CALL SORT(MNSALE, MN, 12)
C                            PRINT REPORT
               DO 200 I = 1,12
                  PRINT *, '   ',I, '      ',SALES(I), '           ',
     +                     MN(I), '         ',MNSALE(I)
      200      CONTINUE
               END


               SUBROUTINE WEEKLY
               INEGER SALES(52), WK(52), WKSALE(52), I
COMMENT:                      PRINT HEADINGS
               PRINT *, '                    WEEKLY SALES FIGURES'
               PRINT *, ' '
               PRINT *, '          CHRONOLOGICAL',
     +                  '                    BEST TO WORST'
               PRINT *, '        WEEK         SALES             ',
     +                  'WEEK        SALES'
C                            READ SALES FIGURES
               READ *, SALES
C                            SAVE SALES FIGURES AND MAKE A LIST OF WEEK NUMBERS
               DO 100 I = 1,52
                  WK(I) = I
```

```
                   WKSALE(I) = SALES(I)
     100           CONTINUE
C                          SORT INFORMATION ACCORDING TO DECREASING SALES.
                CALL SORT(WKSALE, WK, 52)
C                          PRINT REPORT
                DO 200 I = 1,52
                   PRINT *, '    ',I, '       ',SALES(I), '              ',
     +                      WK(I), '          ',WKSALE(I)
     200           CONTINUE
                END
```

than others. The method we describe here has at least two virtues: it is easy to understand, and it clearly demonstrates the use of subprograms.

Briefly, the idea is to locate the smallest of the numbers and put it on the bottom of the list and then to repeat the same process on the remaining unsorted numbers (from the first to the next to last). We keep repeating the process on shorter and shorter lists until finally there are none left. The only tricky part of the process arises from the way in which numbers are stored—in an array. When we find the smallest number and want to put it on the bottom of the unsorted portion of the list, we must do something with the number currently in the bottom position. It must go into the unsorted portion of the list, of course, and the natural place to put it is in the position vacated by the smallest number. In other words, we interchange the smallest number with the number on the bottom of the unsorted portion of the list. Figure 11.6.1 illustrates the method.

The following SUBROUTINE uses a FUNCTION to locate the smallest number in the unsorted part of the array and a SUBROUTINE to interchange the largest with the bottom number. You have already seen techniques for locating the smallest number several times, so the FUNCTION should be easy to follow. Note that the FUNCTION returns the *position* of the smallest value in the array, not the smallest value itself. It's the position that we need to make the interchanges in the sorting algorithm. The actual value doesn't really make any difference. You haven't seen a technique for switching the values in a pair of memory cells, however, and we'll get to that shortly.

As with the MEAN function in Section 11.3, the array declarations have subprogram parameters for length declarators. This clearly illustrates the difference between parameter declarations and true declarations. Since parameter declarations describe already existing objects, the compiler is not required to reserve space for them. Consequently, the length of a subprogram parameter array may be specified by one of the variables in the parameter list. (If the array has more than one subscript, then the range of values for any one or all of the subscripts may be specified by variables in the parameter list.) It is important to realize that this does not mean that any existing array actually has a varying length. All actual array declarations must have a constant length declarator; only parameter array declarations may have variables for length declarators. Furthermore, the value(s) of the parameter(s) declaring the di-

Figure 11.6.1   Sorting a List of Numbers

(a)   original list

(b)   locate largest and switch

(c)

(d)

(e)

(f)   sorted list

mension(s) of the array should not be changed by the subprogram because this would imply a change in the length of the actual array given in the argument list in the subprogram reference. No such change is possible.

Length Declarator for Parameter Arrays

---

form
t p(list)
t is a Fortran data type
p (a parameter array name) is an identifier
list is a list of INTEGER parameter names and/or unsigned INTEGER constants

meaning
The array *p*, which is a parameter in the subprogram being defined, will have the dimensions specified in *list* and the type *t*.

examples

```
SUBROUTINE VARLEN (A, B, N, C, D, M)
INTEGER N, M, A(N)
REAL B(4,N), C(M,N)
```

Figure 11.6.2   A Sorting Algorithm

For BOTTOM = N, N − 1,. . .2 _____

> where N is the subscript of the last element in the list
>
> Let SMLest = the location (array subscript value)
>   of the array element between
>   the first element and the BOTTOM
>   which contains the smallest value.
>
> Interchange the SMLest element with
>   the BOTTOM element.

```
              SUBROUTINE SORT(KEYS, OTHER, N)
              INTEGER N, KEYS(N), OTHER(N)
COMMENT:                ARRANGE THE VALUES IN 'KEYS' AND 'OTHER' INTO
C                       DECREASING ORDER ACCORDING TO 'KEYS'
              INTEGER BOTTOM, SMLEST
              INTEGER LOCSML
              DO 100 BOTTOM = N, 2, -1
C                       FIND SMALLEST NUMBER IN 'KEYS' BETWEEN 1 AND
C                       'BOTTOM'. DECREMENT 'BOTTOM' TO REFLECT NEW
C                       BOTTOM OF UNSORTED PORTION OF ARRAYS.
              SMLEST = LOCSML(KEYS, BOTTOM)
```

(Continued on following page)

```
C                              INTERCHANGE KEYS(BOTTOM) WITH KEYS(SMLEST)
                  CALL SWITCH(KEYS(BOTTOM), KEYS(SMLEST))
C                              TO AVOID MESSING UP THE CORRESPONDENCE BETWEEN
C                              VALUES IN 'KEYS' AND VALUES IN 'OTHER', MAKE AN
C                              IDENTICAL INTERCHANGE IN 'OTHER'.
                  CALL SWITCH(OTHER(BOTTOM), OTHER(SMLEST))
    100           CONTINUE
                  END

                  INTEGER FUNCTION LOCSML(A, TO)
                  INTEGER TO, A(TO)
COMMENT:                       LOCATE THE SMALLEST NUMBER IN 'A' BETWEEN A(1)
C                              AND THE END OF THE ARRAY.
                  INTEGER I
                  LOCSML = 1
                  DO 100 I = 2, TO
                    IF (A(I) .LT. A(LOCSML)) THEN
                        LOCSML = I
                    ENDIF
    100           CONTINUE
                  END
```

The subprogram SWITCH, which interchanges the values in a pair of memory cells, requires explanation. It has three steps: (1) the value in the first cell is copied into a third cell so that it won't be lost in step 2, (2) the value of the second cell is copied into the first, and (3) the value in the third cell is copied into the second. If you think about it, you will realize that a two-step process simply won't work.

```
SUBROUTINE SWITCH(A,B)
INTEGER A, B
INTEGER COPYA
COPYA = A
A = B
B = COPYA
END
```

Please be sure that you understand how this sorting method works by following through a small example. We'll want to use it again.

When our completed program was run using the data lines below, it produced the sales report you saw at the beginning of this chapter.

```
1983 'M'
  6472  4103  2001  2422  3501  5402  5117  4322  2173  9432
  8497 10428
1983 'W'
  1647  1500  1399  1822  1021  1059   987   855   502   408
   201   422   385   638   655   588   574   788   698   755
   802   621  1422  1534  1621  1308  1205  1307  1354  1238
  1104   987   855   445   655   521   411   322  1422  2011
  2411  1955  2134  2111  2422  2031  1902  2032  2544  2144
  2066  2544
     0  ' '
```

11.6 EXERCISES

1. Which of the following parameter declarations are legal and which aren't? For each declaration which is not legal, explain why not.

```
SUBROUTINE ONE(A, N,M)
INTEGER M,N, A(N,M)

SUBROUTINE TWO(A,N)
INTEGER N, A(10,N,4)

SUBROUTINE THREE(A,N)
INTEGER N, A(LENGTH)
```

2. What is wrong with the following SUBROUTINE?

```
SUBROUTINE WRONG(A,N))
INTEGER N, A(N)
N = N + 1
A(N) = 0
END
```

3. What would need to be changed in order to make our SUBROUTINE SORT arrange the numbers into increasing (rather than decreasing) order?

4. What would happen to INTEGER memory cells ONE and TWO if the statement CALL BADWST (ONE, TWO) were executed?

```
SUBROUTINE BADSWT(A,B)
INTEGER A,B
A = B
B = A
END
```

5. What is wrong with the statement CALL BADSWT (1, 2,), given the subprogram in exercise 4?

11.7 PLOTTING—DEVELOPING LIBRARIES OF USEFUL ROUTINES

It wasn't long after the first printed pages came zooming out of the computer line printers that people, perhaps initially attracted by the moving, shifting patterns of program listings, began writing programs which produce two-dimensional patterns for their own sake. Practitioners of **computer graphics** have developed elaborate techniques and can produce a fantastic range of visual effects.

In this section we'll point out a few of the mechanics of plotting—specifically, how to go from an internally stored or generated image to a properly scaled image on the printed page or screen.

All of these routines, as well as others suggested in the problems at the end of this chapter, are useful in many applications. Think of them as a library of canned routines that you can pull out for use in future programs. There are many such libraries of routines that you can invoke from Fortran programs. It is one of the most important advantages of using Fortran that so much is already written in the form of subprograms that you can use to expand the set of operations available to you in the construction of new programs.

Figure 11.7.1 Discretization

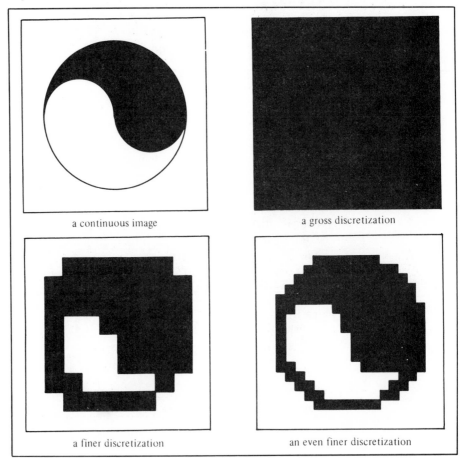

a continuous image

a gross discretization

a finer discretization

an even finer discretization

Your computer center may well have more elaborate devices for plotting which will make it possible to create more elaborate, more finely detailed drawings. Fancy gadgetry is no substitute for imagination, though.

The basic idea we will use to draw pictures on the line printer is **discretization,** which means representing something which is continuously, smoothly changing in terms of a small number of specific values. This is necessary because the printer can't print symbols just anywhere on the page; it is neatly organized to print in columns and rows. We must convert any other sort of image into one which has symbols in column and row positions. Conceptually we lay a grid over our image and let each grid square correspond to a character position on the printed page (i.e., some specific row and column). Then we place a symbol on the page for each grid which covers any dark part of the image. Figure 11.7.1. shows a continuous image and three discrete versions of it at different levels of discretization.

Probably the most convenient way to deal with the print grid is to use a two-dimensional array. If the image grid has H rows and W columns, then we use a W-by-H two-dimensional CHARACTER array to represent the printed page. To begin, we fill the array with blanks. Then we store nonblank symbols (e.g., asterisks) in array positions which correspond to dark spots in the image. The hard part is setting up this correspondence between the image plane and the two-dimensional array. What we need is a way to convert a pair of REAL coordinates, (X, Y) in the image plane to a pair of INTEGER subscripts, (I, J) in the ranges 1 to H and 1 to W, respectively.

First, we'll convert X to I. If the left boundary of the image plane corresponds to X = XMIN and the right boundary to X = XMAX, then (X − XMIN)/(XMAX − XMIN) is a number between 0.0 and 1.0 Consequently, INT(W*(X − XMIN)/(XMAX − XMIN)) + 1 is an INTEGER between 1 and W. This is the conversion formula we wanted (see Figure 11.7.2). Essentially it divides the image plane into W vertical strips of equal width and takes the value I when X is in the Ith strip. Similarly, we convert Y to INT(H*(Y − YMIN)/(YMAX − YMIN)) + 1 where YMIN and YMAX correspond to the bottom and top boundaries of the image plane. Actually, if an image point lies exactly on the top or right boundary, we'll have problems, so we won't allow image points on the top or right boundary. This is easy to do—if there are any troublesome points, just shift the grid a tiny amount by increasing XMAX and YMAX.

We will write three SUBROUTINEs to help plot pictures. One will put blanks in the two-dimensional plotting array, another will put a symbol into the array at a point corresponding to a given point in the image plane, and the third will print the contents of the array. Thus, plotting a picture amounts to CALLing the blank-out routine, then CALLing the point plotting routine once for each dark spot in the image, and finally, CALLing the printing routine. These SUBROUTINEs are written below. The only tricky part is the discretization, that is, converting X to I and Y to J, which we've already discussed.

Figure 11.7.2   Discretizing a Given Number

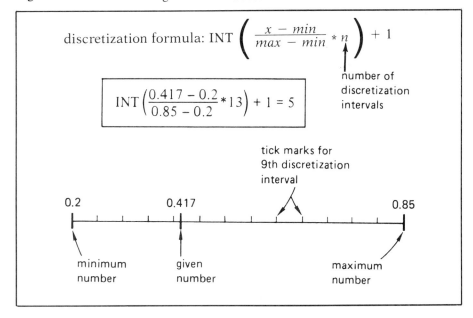

```
COMMENT:                      THIS SUBROUTINE FILLS THE PLOTTING ARRAY 'GRAPH'
C                             WITH BLANKS
          SUBROUTINE BLKOUT(GRAPH, W,H)
          INTEGER W,H
          CHARACTER*(1) GRAPH(W,H)
          INTEGER I,J
          DO 100 J = H,1,-1
            DO 100 I = 1,W
              GRAPH(I,J) = ' '
  100       CONTINUE
          END


COMMENT:                      THIS SUBROUTINE PUTS 'SYMBOL' INTO THE PLOTTING
C                             ARRAY 'GRAPH' AT A POINT CORRESPONDING TO
C                             (X,Y) IN IMAGE PLANE
C                             THE RANGE OF COORDINATES IS ASSUMED TO BE
C                             (XMIN TO XMAX, YMIN TO YMAX)
C                             COORDINATES OUTSIDE THIS RANGE WILL NOT BE PLOTTED
          SUBROUTINE PLOT(X,Y, XMIN,XMAX, YMIN,YMAX,
         +                   SYMBOL, GRAPH,W,H)
          REAL X,Y, XMIN,XMAX, YMIN,YMAX
          INTEGER W,H
          CHARACTER*(1) SYMBOL, GRAPH(W,H)
          INTEGER I,J
C                        DISCRETIZE X AND Y
          I = INT((((X-XMIN)/(XMAX-XMIN)) * W) + 1
          J = INT((((Y-YMIN)/(YMAX-YMIN)) * H) + 1
C                        PUT (X,Y) INTO 'GRAPH' (IF IN RANGE)
          IF (I .GE. 1 .AND. I .LE. W .AND.
         +    J .GE. 1 .AND. J .LE. H) THEN
            GRAPH(I,J) = SYMBOL
          ENDIF
          END
COMMENT:                        THIS SUBROUTINE PRINTS THE PLOTTING ARRAY 'GRAPH'
          SUBROUTINE PRGRPH(GRAPH,W,H)
          INTEGER W,H
          CHARACTER*(1) GRAPH(W,H)
          INTEGER I,J
          DO 100 J = H, 1,-1
            PRINT *, (GRAPH(I,J), I = 1,W)
  100       CONTINUE
          END


COMMENT:                      MAIN PROGRAM -- USE THE SUBROUTINES TO
C                             PLOT THE EXPONENTIAL CURVE
          INTEGER W,H
          PARAMETER(W = 25, H = 15)
          REAL X, EXP
          CHARACTER*(1) G(W,H)
          CALL BLKOUT(G,W,H)
          DO 100 X = -1.0, 1.0, 0.05
            CALL PLOT(X,EXP(X), -1.0,1.0,0.0,2.0,'*',G,W,H)
  100       CONTINUE
          CALL PRGRPH(G,W,H)
          END
```

> J steps "backwards" here because high values of J correspond to
> points at the top of the figure, and the top of the figure must be sent
> to the printer first if we want things right-side up.

Output

When plotting with the line printer, you will get better results if you keep in mind that the distance between characters on a line is less than the distance between lines. That is, the plotting device you are using has sharper resolution in the horizontal direction than in the vertical direction. The ratio of these resolutions is about five to three for most line printers. Therefore, to avoid distorting your picture, you should divide the image plane into about five parts in the horizontal direction for every three parts in the vertical direction. In other words, the ratio w/h of the width to the height of your plotting array should be about 5/3.

Some of the problems at the end of this chapter will give you a chance to use this plotting package we have developed.

11.7 EXERCISE

1. What would you have to change in SUBROUTINE PRGRPH to make it plot the curve x^2 instead of the exponential growth curve?

11 PROBLEMS

Practice Problems

1. Write and test a SUBROUTINE that sums the corresponding values of two arrays and stores the results in a third array. Your SUBROUTINE should work for arrays of any size.
2. Write and test a FUNCTION that finds the median for any number of items in a sorted array. The median is the middle number after the values are sorted in order.
3. Write a FUNCTION that finds the median of the values stored in an array, making no assumptions about what order they are stored in. (*Hint:* use SORT from Section 11.6 and your function from problem 2.)
4. Write and test a SUBROUTINE that accepts an array of people's nicknames and that returns the name which comes first alphabetically and the one which comes last. Don't forget to set up a parameter to input the number of names.

5. Write a LOGICAL FUNCTION called INHERE that has three parameters: (a) an array of people's names, (b) the number of names in the array, and (c) a variable which stores the name of a customer. IN-HERE should return the value .TRUE. if the customer's name appears in the array, and .FALSE. otherwise.

6. Write a FUNCTION called LOG that has two parameters, BASE and X, and return the largest INTEGER, LOG, such that BASE**LOG does not exceed X. For example, L = LOG(2,10) would result in L having the value 3, since $2^3 \leqslant 10$ but $2^4 > 10$.

7. If the numbers produced by your system's random number generator are actually uniformly distributed between 0.0 and 1.0, and if we take a large sample, the average value should be 1/2 and the sample standard deviation should be $\sqrt{1/12}$. Test it to see how close it comes. Use the functions MEAN and STDDEV from Section 11.3. Find out from a local expert how to invoke your system's random number generator or that of RANF in Appendix B.

8. Write and test a SUBROUTINE CONVERT whose input is an INTEGER and whose output is an array of INTEGERs that represent the input number in binary notation.

A number's binary representation can be computed by using the following algorithm, which builds up the binary representation *from right to left.*

Computing the Binary Representation

```
Exit if number = 0
Next binary digit = MOD(number,2)
number = number/2
                              Repeat
```

9. Rewrite SUBROUTINE CONVERT so that it has an additional input parameter, a base to which to convert the input INTEGER's representation.

10. If you are familiar with matrices and use them, here's a problem for you. Write three SUBROUTINEs that manipulate matrices.

SUBROUTINE SCMLT(A,M,N,C)

a. SUBROUTINE SCMLT(A,M,N,C)
   A is an M × N matrix (two-dimensional array) of REAL values and C is a REAL. The SUBROUTINE multiplies matrix A by scalar C and returns the new value of A.

SUBROUTINE ADD(A,B,C,M,N)

b. SUBROUTINE ADD (A,B,C,M,N)
   A and B are two M × N matrices which SUBROUTINE ADD adds together. Their sum is returned in the M × N matrix C.

SUBROUTINE MULT(A,MA,NA, B,MB,NB,C,MC,NC)

c. SUBROUTINE MULT (A,MA,NA,B,MB,NB,C,MC,NC)
   multiplication of the MA × NA matrix A and the MB × NB matrix B, returning the product as the MC × NC matrix C. If A and B are

not compatible (i.e., if NA ≠ MB) issue an error message. Test your routines by verifying some equality like this:

$$2 \times \begin{bmatrix} 100 \\ 010 \\ 001 \end{bmatrix} + 14 \times \begin{bmatrix} 100 \\ 010 \\ 001 \end{bmatrix} = \begin{bmatrix} 400 \\ 040 \\ 004 \end{bmatrix} \times \begin{bmatrix} 200 \\ 020 \\ 002 \end{bmatrix} \times \begin{bmatrix} 200 \\ 020 \\ 002 \end{bmatrix}$$

Program Design Problems

11. One of the methods used for analyzing a set of time series data for periodicity is to calculate an autocorrelation coefficient between values of the variate X_i and the same variate at a constant time lag X_{i+p}. The autocorrelation coefficient for a particular time lag p is given by

$$r_p = \frac{\Sigma(x_i x_{i+p}) - \dfrac{\Sigma x_i \Sigma x_{i+p}}{n - p}}{\sqrt{\left[\Sigma x_i^2 - \dfrac{(\Sigma x_i)^2}{n - p} \right] \left[\Sigma x_{i+p}^2 - \dfrac{(\Sigma x_{i+p})^2}{n - p} \right]}}$$

The summations extend over the range $i = 1$ to $i = n - p$. An examination of r calculated as a function of p indicates those lags or periods over which the data of the time series seem to be correlated. In other words, r will be large for time lags p that are periods of the variate x_i.

Consider the following data, representing the monthly rainfall on a certain watershed between 1901 and 1920. Obtain the autocorrelation coefficients for time lags of 1 to 25 months, printing each value as it is calculated.

Rainfall in Inches

Year	Jan.	Feb.	Mar.	Apr.	May	June	July	Aug.	Sept.	Oct.	Nov.	Dec.
1901	0.14	1.04	1.61	1.63	1.45	1.41	0.01	0.13	0.01	0.05	0.19	0.45
1902	1.42	1.35	1.03	2.05	2.32	0.73	0.06	0.39	0.26	0.21	1.21	0.87
1903	1.31	1.14	1.76	1.85	1.76	1.32	0.11	0.24	0.09	0.37	0.29	1.59
1904	0.32	1.21	2.43	2.10	2.42	1.05	0.02	0.01	0.51	0.19	0.05	1.61
1905	1.07	0.47	1.82	1.92	3.17	1.04	0.03	0.13	0.27	0.26	1.07	0.92
1906	1.06	1.36	1.46	2.31	1.87	0.85	0.07	0.07	0.14	0.62	1.34	0.09
1907	2.04	1.13	2.64	0.95	2.17	1.93	0.09	0.32	0.36	0.32	0.42	1.42
1908	0.41	1.09	1.73	1.74	1.94	0.64	0.10	0.06	0.22	0.73	0.31	0.76
1909	1.71	0.87	1.93	1.42	3.03	1.52	0.00	0.23	0.08	0.93	0.59	1.21
1910	1.41	1.49	2.56	2.09	2.98	1.61	0.00	0.33	0.49	0.24	1.61	0.32
1911	1.33	1.20	0.42	1.67	2.55	1.06	0.13	0.15	0.36	0.15	0.16	1.05
1912	1.32	1.43	2.34	1.76	1.76	1.16	0.07	0.34	0.45	0.84	0.87	1.11
1913	0.95	1.18	1.34	2.04	3.21	1.24	0.10	0.23	0.13	1.01	0.54	0.69
1914	0.42	1.06	1.53	1.82	1.69	0.95	0.31	0.04	0.28	0.36	0.98	1.24
1915	2.61	0.64	1.75	1.94	2.63	1.13	0.05	0.33	0.22	0.09	0.04	0.92
1916	1.42	0.86	1.42	2.15	0.86	0.76	0.09	0.15	0.19	0.37	0.23	1.42
1917	1.17	1.24	2.03	0.61	2.42	0.84	0.13	0.33	0.42	0.19	0.75	0.76
1918	0.76	1.00	2.26	2.21	1.74	0.92	0.00	0.35	0.04	0.75	0.12	0.63
1919	1.61	0.34	1.72	2.20	1.74	1.70	0.21	0.25	0.34	0.27	0.39	1.32
1920	1.27	1.32	1.94	1.23	3.20	1.09	0.17	0.03	0.26	1.21	0.94	0.68

12. Two cars are traveling down the highway at 55 mph, with the second car 70 feet behind the first. The first car suddenly slams on its brakes. Will the second car be able to stop in time to avoid ramming into the first? It will if its driver is able to slam on the brakes before the car has traveled 70 feet (right?). The time it takes the second driver to apply his brakes after seeing the brake lights on the car ahead is called his **reaction time**. People's reaction times depend on a number of factors, such as how tired they are, how distracted they are, how drunk they are, etc., so it seems reasonable to model the reaction time as if it were a random variable.

Assume the driver's reaction time is a (uniform) random number between 0.5 and 1.0 second, i.e., is computed as

react. time = (1.0 + V)/2.0

where V comes from a "random number generator." (See a local expert—many installations provide a function RANF( ) that returns a random number betwee 0.0 and 1.0.) Given the reaction time, you can compute the distance the second car travels and from that, tell whether or not there was a wreck.

Write a program that simulates 100 emergency braking situations and outputs the 100 different distances, the number of wrecks, and the number of "close calls." If the second car stops less than one foot from the first but doesn't hit it, that's a close call.

13. A well-known daredevil stunt man plans to jump a canyon on his motorcycle. Assuming that the air drag is proportional to his velocity (k is the proportionality constant), his position after t seconds is given by the following equations.

$$x = \frac{v_0 \cos \alpha}{k} (1 - e^{-kt})$$

$\quad$ = distance

$$y = \frac{-g}{k}t + \frac{1}{k} (v_0 \sin \alpha + \frac{g}{k}) (1 - e^{-kt})$$

$\quad$ = height

g = 32.2 ft/sec^2
$\quad$ = acceleration due to gravity
v_0 = 330 ft/sec = takeoff speed
α = 45° = angle of takeoff

The canyon is 1000 ft across and 100 ft deep. The ramp is 20 ft high in the front and 20 feet long.

Write a program that writes out his path (x, y, and t) for the cases when k is 0.05, 0.15, and 0.25. Draw the trajectories your program predicts. If he lands on the other side, assume he stops immediately (in a heap).

14. The motorcyclist in problem 13 has a parachute to ease his fall, but the release mechanism is somewhat unstable. When the parachute releases, its effect is to increase the wind resistance factor k.

    Do problem 13 using $k = 0.05$ in the equations before the parachute opens and $k = 0.5$ after. Print his path (x, y, and t) for these three cases:

case	parachute opens after
1	1 second
2	5 seconds
3	20 seconds

> *Note:* The following problems use the plotting ideas of Section 11.7.

15. Improve the output from the motorcyclist problem (problems 13 and 14) by plotting the cyclist's trajectory instead of just printing a numerical summary of his flight. If you feel ambitious, include in the picture a cross section of the canyon and a puff of dust where he lands. You could plot different symbols for the canyon boundary (perhaps +), trajectory (perhaps −), and dust (perhaps *).

16. Write a subroutine CURVE(X, Y, N, XMIN, XMAX, YMIN, YMAX, SYMBOL, GRAPH, W, H) whose arguments are like those of subroutine PLOT in Section 11.7, except that X and Y are REAL arrays of length N.CURVE should use PLOT to draw the points corresponding to (X(i), Y(i)), viewed as coordinate pairs, for i = 1, 2,..., N.

17. Write a subroutine LINE(X, Y, XMIN, XMAX, YMIN, YMAX, SYMBOL, GRAPH, W, H) whose arguments are like those of subroutine PLOT in Section 11.7, except that X and Y are arrays of two elements each. Line should use PLOT to draw the line between the points (X(1), Y(1)) and (X(2), Y(2)).

    Use SUBROUTINE LINE to plot a picture of the path taken by a person caught in the center of an unruly mob. Plot the person's new position each time he or she moves, assuming he or she moves five feet each time, but in a random direction. (You will need access to a random number generator. Most Fortran systems have one called RANF, which delivers a random value between 0.0 and 1.0. You can multiply this by 2π to get a random direction.) Using the random angle, compute the next endpoint, and CALL LINE to fill in the path. Use different SYMBOLs for successive lines so you can follow the unfortunate person's path even though it may cross over itself from time to time.

18. An electric guitar whose A string is plucked puts out this signal:

$$\underbrace{11 \sin(2\pi \times 220t)}_{funaamental} + 3(1 + s)\sin(2\pi \times 440t) + (1/2 + s)\sin(2\pi \times 880t)$$

where $s = 1$ if the switch is set to select the pickup nearest the bridge, and $s = 0$ if the other pickup is selected.

One way to make the guitar sound less "pure" is to run the signal through a fuzz box. The fuzz box works by clipping its input signal.

$$\text{Fuzz output} = \begin{cases} \text{input if } [\text{input}] \leqslant F \\ +F \text{ if input} \geqslant F \\ -F \text{ if input} \leqslant -F \end{cases}$$

where F is the fuzz setting on the fuzz box.

Write a program that prints out the signal every 1.0/4400.0 of a second for a total of 1.0/110.0 of a second (two cycles of the fundamental). Use your plotting routines to draw a graph of the results for each of the four combinations of the two switch settings and the two settings of the fuzz box at $F = 11$ and $F = 15$.

19. Here's an ecological simulation of wolf and rabbit populations. Rabbits eat grass. Wolves eat rabbits. There's plenty of grass, so wolves are the only obstacle to the rabbit population increase. The wolf population increases with the food supply (rabbits). The day-by-day changes in the rabbit population R and the wolf population W can be expressed by the following formulas:

R [tomorrow] = (1 + a)*R − c*R*W [today].
W [tomorrow] = (1 − b)*W + c*d*R*W [today].

a = 0.001	= fractional increase in rabbit population without competition from wolves (0.01 means a 1% increase).
b = 0.005	= fractional decrease in wolf population without rabbits to eat.
c = 0.00001	= likelihood that a wolf will encounter and eat a rabbit.
d = 0.01	= fractional increase in wolf population attributed to a devoured rabbit.

Write a program to calculate the daily population levels of wolves and rabbits over a 1,000-day period. Start with a population of 10,000 rabbits and 1,000 wolves. Plot the population cycle using the routines of Section 11.7, plotting wolves versus rabbits; don't plot the time variable. See what happens when you start with 500 wolves instead of 1,000. Try starting with 2,000 wolves too.

20. Design some SUBROUTINEs to use in conjunction with SUBROUTINEs PLOT, BLKOUT, and PRGRAPH, and use them to produce an interesting series of patterns. Here are some ideas:

    a. SUBROUTINE NEGATE takes an array GRAPH as argument and turns every nonblank square into a blank and every blank into an asterisk.

    b. SUBROUTINE INVERT takes a picture stored in GRAPH and turns it over (rotates 180°).

    c. SUBROUTINE SKLTN takes a picture and turns every square which is completely surrounded by dark squares into a blank.

    d. SUBROUTINE MOVE takes a picture and two INTEGERs DX and DY and shifts everything in the picture along the x-axis DX squares (to the left for negative DX and to the right for positive DX); it also shifts the picture DY squares along the y-axis.

21. Use the line printer to make a graph of the function $\sin(x)/x$ from $x = 0$ to $x = 10$, stepping in increments of 0.1. (*Note:* $\sin(x)/x = 1$ when $x = 0$, and all values of $\sin(x)/x$ are in the range -1 to 1.)

    In plotting graphs like this, it is easier to orient the x-axis down the page rather than across. That way, the program can compute one value of the function, plot it on the current line across the page, and then step to the next value and plot it on the next line, etc.

    The only tricky part might be translating values of the function (which lie between -1 and 1) to positions on the line to be printed (which typically run from column 1 to column 132). To figure out how far across the line to plot a particular value of $\sin(x)/x$ use the discretization formula.

    ```
    I = INT(100.0*(Y+1.0)/2.0) +1
    ```

    where Y is a value of $\sin(x)/x$. Then I will be in the range 1 to 101, and you can plot Y with statements like

    ```
    CHARACTER*1 BLANK, STAR
    BLANK = ' '
    STAR = '*'
       .
       .
       .
    PRINT *, (BLANK, K=1,I), STAR
    ```

    which put an asterisk in the appropriate position across the page.

22. In problem 21 the discretization formula gives the value I if Y is in the range $-1.00 + (I + 1)*0.01$ to $-1.00 + I*0.01$. Use this fact to draw and label the axes of your plot.

23. Draw graphs of other functions using the techniques of problems 21 and 22. The discretization formula will continue to divide the range of values of the function into 100 equally spaced parts if you change the (Y + 1.0)/2.0 expression to (Y − YMIN)/(YMAX − YMIN), where YMIN and YMAX are the smallest and largest values your function can take on.

   Note that you can shrink the plot of your functions by making YMAX larger than the maximum value of the function and YMIN smaller than the minimum.

24. **(Picture enhancement)** Write a program that filters *noise* from a *picture*. A black and white (B & W) picture may be viewed as a rectangular *array of pixels*, each of which may be dark or light. We may represent this array as a rectangular *matrix* with 24 rows and 40 columns. Each element of the array is a 1 (dark spot) or 0 (light spot). We may read in a noisy picture by reading 24 lines, each containing 40 1's and 0's.

   Due to a faulty sensor or a faulty recording medium, what was once a clean picture gets recorded as a noisy picture with extra 1's. (There are no erasures of valid 1's.) These must be removed. We will assume that the picture (whatever it looks like) is composed entirely of segments that look like this locally:

```
1                1                     1
1 1 1    or      1      or            1
  1                1                   1
```

Thus, any valid 1 that is to remain must be part of one of these patterns. All other 1's must be removed.

   Write a program to
   a. Read a noisy picture from 48 data lines (provided), and print it in its original, noisy form.
   b. Remove noise.
   c. Print the cleaned picture, with x's in place of valid 1's (dark spots) and blanks in place of 0's (light spots).
   d. Put a border of *'s around the picture.

   Example: A 4 × 8 noisy picture might do this:

```
    data            output
              * * * * * * * * * * *
  01101101    *   X   X   X   *
  11100110    * XXX   XX      *
  01110110    *  XXX XX       *
  01101111    *   X X   X   *
              * * * * * * * * * * *
```

(Thanks to Rod Oldehoeft for this problem.)

12 PROGRAM DESIGN

12.1 GOOD PROGRAMS DON'T JUST HAPPEN

From the beginning, we have been emphasizing a systematic approach to the design of programs. We first outlined the ideas in The Big Picture of Figure 1.3.1 and followed up with the introduction of design tools like **plans** in the next chapters. Then we discussed **top-down design** and **step-wise refinement** in Chapter 5, where we emphasized the importance of good decomposition of the problem into its component parts. We summarized these points as a series of **steps in program design.**

Steps in Program Design

> 1. Problem statements: State the problem you are trying to solve as precisely as you can.
> 2. Input/output description: Describe in precise terms the input your program will have, roughly what it is to do, and the precise output it will produce.
> 3. Stepwise refinement: Write a plan for your algorithm. Then make more and more detailed descriptions of the complex portions of your algorithm in terminology closer to Fortran operations.
> 4. Fortran coding: Translate the statements in your final refinement from step 3 into Fortran.

You know from experience that the process does not always proceed smoothly. Sometimes problems in coding (step 4) will force you to revise your program design (step 3). Sometimes problems that appear in the final program will force reconsideration of the statement of the problems (step 1) or the desired input/output behavior (step 2). Nevertheless, most programmers find that a systematic approach leads to correct programs more quickly (and more often!) than the helter skelter technique (starting at step 4 instead of step 1).

It is conceivable (but not likely) that you've been able to write all your programs so far without careful planning. If you have found each programming project a struggle, if you tend to write nothing down until a sudden flash of insight makes you start scrawling Fortran statements on a napkin, if you find that you have to run your programs over and over and over to get all the mistakes out, if each programming assignment makes you nervous and irritable, you will be amazed at the difference when you start using the design ideas we've been pushing.

Problem Decomposition

> There are many ways to divide any complex problem into subproblems. A few of these decompositions lead to good solutions, but most lead to hopelessly convoluted programs. The art of top-down design is to perceive fruitful ways of viewing the overall problem as a collection of subtasks. This requires experience, insight, and careful thought.

We hope you'll begin to see that complex problems are more easily solved using the techniques of top-down design and structured programming than they are with the helter skelter technique. The techniques aren't ends in themselves, however. They are methods which help in producing reliable programs, programs that process the input in the desired way to produce correct results. We don't claim that the use of these techniques will automatically produce error-free programs, but we do claim that the debugging process will be shortened. With badly designed programs, debugging often takes longer than writing the original program!

This chapter is practice and review. A few new features will be introduced, but the features themselves are not the important points. They are simple extensions of Fortran statements you already know. The examples are meant to deepen your understanding of the basic principles of program design.

12.2 PUTTING SUBPROBLEMS TOGETHER

Our goal in this section is to write a program which will produce a cross-reference telephone directory. We want our program to print out a list of names and telephone numbers, first in alphabetical order (according to the names) and then in numerical order (according to the phone numbers). To do this, we'll need to rearrange the data, which may come to us with individual phone book listings scrambled in random order.

We have already completed the first step in program design—**statement of the problem**. We want to print a cross-reference telephone directory.

Step 2 is to **describe the desired input and output**. We will assume that the input consists of a collection of data lines, each one containing an individual's phone listing. Both the name and the phone number will be written as character constants. The output should be two copies of the input listings, one copy arranged in alphabetical order by names and the other in numerical order by phone number. Figure 12.2.1 displays a short sample input and the corresponding output.

Figure 12.2.1   Input and Output for Cross-Reference Directory Program

```
Data

'DEERING MOLLIE' '491-5792'
'SEEGERS HOLLY' '221-3748'
'GUSTAFSON JON' '484-2169'
'PORTER GEORGE' '491-7015'
'END OF DATA' 'NONE'

Output

ALPHABETICAL LISTINGS

DEERING MOLLIE 491-5792
GUSTAFSON JON 484-2169
PORTER GEORGE 491-7015
SEEGERS HOLLY 221-3748

NUMERICAL LISTINGS

221-3748 SEEGERS HOLLY
484-2169 GUSTAFSON JON
491-5792 DEERING MOLLIE
491-7015 PORTER GEORGE
```

Finally, we are ready for step 3 in program design: **stepwise refinement**. This is where we begin to design the algorithm which will correctly transform data into the desired output. At the first level, it is pretty clear what we want our algorithm to do. After getting the data, we first must arrange it in alphabetical order. Then we print the alphabetical listing. At that point, we rearrange the individual listings into numeric order by phone number and print the numerical listing. This approach is outlined in Figure 12.2.2.

Figure 12.2.2   Top-Level Design for Producing Cross-Reference Directory

```
Read data.
Arrange according to name.
Print.
Arrange according to phone number.
Print.
```

Subprograms provide a way to make our programs have the same overall structure as our design. Now that we've discovered a way to break our problem into logical components, we can represent the components by separate subprograms. Then, treating each component as a new problem, we will decompose *it* into components, again represented by separate subprograms. In other words, subprograms provide us with a syntactic device within Fortran to represent the various levels in our analysis of problems.

Since the problem involves sorting data in two different orders, at first glance it seems similar to the problem we worked on in Section 11.6, where we produced sales reports in two different formats. There we developed a sorting subprogram that orders a pair of arrays so that they are in order of the values in one of the arrays. Let's look at some of the details here to see if we can use the same subprogram to solve the cross-reference directory problem. Looking at the sample input and output our finished product is supposed to produce (Figure 12.2.1), we can see one difference. In Section 11.6, we were dealing with numerical data and putting it in decreasing order—here we're dealing with text and want it in increasing order. Changing the ordering from decreasing to increasing is easy, so let's not worry about that just yet.

At this point, even though we haven't worked out any of the *details* of the subprocesses, we do know what the subprocesses are supposed to do. That means we can give reasonable names to the subprograms which will carry out the subprocesses, and we can even go so far as to write the program (the **main program**) that will implement the top level of our design.

The main program will consist of declarations and CALL statements. To write it, we'll need to do some thinking about the limits to be placed on our program. We plan to store all the data in arrays, and the length of those arrays will determine the number of listings our program can handle. We've chosen a limit of 500 listings, but the limit can be easily changed (as long as we don't exceed the memory capacity of our computer).

Three different operations need to be performed in our algorithm: input, sorting, and printing. We'll write three SUBROUTINEs to handle these operations. To write the CALL statements for them, we need to think about the input each SUBROUTINE will need and the results it'll produce.

Memory Capacity

> If we tried to modify our program to handle a real phone book of, say, a half-million listings, most computer systems would choke on our declarations. In writing programs to handle large quantities of data, the size of the computer's memory plays a crucial role. The data must be segmented into pieces which will fit into memory, and the pieces have to be processed separately with the results merged together by other programs. Techniques for doing this are covered in Chapter 13.

The SUBROUTINE for bringing data into memory will need to have access to arrays for storing the data and will need to know how much data space is available. These parameters are the **input** to the SUBROU-TINE. In addition, it should report back how many individual listings are to be in the phone book. This number and the information stored in the arrays are the **output** from the SUBROUTINE. Its job is to store and count the data.

The SUBROUTINE for rearranging the data will need to know which part of the listing (name or phone number) to use to determine the order-ing. It will need access to the other half of the listing, too, because when-ever one half of a listing is moved to a new spot, the other half must be moved to the same spot so we don't lose track of which phone number goes with which name. Finally, this routine will need to know how many listings there are.

The SUBROUTINE for printing the listings will need to know what heading to print ("alphabetical" or "numerical"), will need access to the data, and will need to know how many listings to print.

SUBROUTINE INPUT

---

purpose
Stores listings in memory

input
Array for names
Array for phone numbers
Capacity of arrays

output
Number of individual listings
Names and phone numbers stored in array

SUBROUTINE SORT

---

purpose
Rearrange listings in correct order

input
The part of the listings to be used in deciding on arrangement
(names or phone numbers)
The other part of the listings
The number of listings

output
Rearranged arrays

SUBROUTINE OUTPUT

---

purpose
Print listings

input
Heading (''alphabetical'' or ''numerical'')
Array of names
Array of phone numbers
Number of listings

output
Listings printed out
Note: No values need to be communicated back to CALLing
program through arguments

Now that we've completed steps 1 and 2 in the design of the SUBROU-
TINEs, we can write the main program.

```
COMMENT:              PROGRAM FOR CROSS REFERENCE DIRECTORY
          INTEGER MAXLST, NAMLEN, PHLEN
          PARAMETER(MAXLST = 500, NAMLEN = 25, PHLEN = 25)
          CHARACTER*(NAMLEN) NAME(MAXLEN)
          CHARACTER*(PHLEN) PHONE(MAXLEN)
          INTEGER NUMLST
          CALL INPUT(NAME, PHONE, MAXLST, NUMLST)
          CALL SORT(NAME, PHONE, NUMLST)
          CALL OUTPUT('ALAPHBETICAL', NAME, PHONE, NUMLST)
          CALL SORT(PHONE, NAME, NUMLST)
          CALL OUTPUT('NUMERICAL', PHONE, NAME, NUMLST)
          END
```

Note that the first two arguments are interchanged in the two CALLs to
the sorting routine. This matches our input/output plan; the first argument is the one to be used to determine the arrangement of the listings.
The CALL statements for the OUTPUT routine differ, too, in order to
specify different headings for the two parts of the directory and to ensure
that the names be printed first on each line of the alphabetical directory
and the phone numbers first in the numerical directory.

The two SUBROUTINEs for INPUT and OUTPUT are very straightforward. The INPUT routine consists of an array READ-loop with a warning
message in case there are more data lines than the program is set up to
handle. The OUTPUT routine is a simple array processing loop.

Both of these SUBROUTINES use a new kind of parameter declaration: **assumed length** for CHARACTER parameters and **assumed dimensions** for arrays. The number of CHARACTERs in the array elements for
names and phone numbers is established in the main program. By putting an asterisk in place of the length specification for the CHARACTER

Assumed Length for CHARACTER Parameters

---

form
CHARACTER*(*) *list*
list is a list of subprogram parameter names.

meaning
Whenever the subprogram is called, each variable or array in *list* takes on the length of the CHARACTER variable or array given as the corresponding argument in the calling program.

restriction
None of the variables or arrays in *list* can be used in concatenation operations within the subprogram.

examples
```
CHARACTER*(*) A,B,C
CHARACTER*(*) X(100), Y(10,10)
```

---

parameters in the SUBROUTINEs, the parameters automatically take on the length of the corresponding arguments in the CALL statement. In this way we avoid having to communicate explicitly the length information to the subprogram, and we provide for some flexibility. In different CALL statements, arguments may be CHARACTER variables of differing lengths.

Figure 12.2.3   The INPUT Routine

Plan

Read name and phone arrays and exit if end of data

Failure _____
| Print warning message. |

Computer number of entries.

```
        SUBROUTINE INPUT(NAME, PHONE, MAXLST, NUMLST)
        INTEGER MAXLST, NUMLST
        CHARACTER*(*) NAME(MAXLST), PHONE(MAXLST)
        INTEGER N
        DO 100 N =1,MAXLST
           READ *, NAME(N), PHONE(N)
           IF (NAME(N) .EQ. 'END OF DATA') GO TO 110
100        CONTINUE
        PRINT *, 'TOO MUCH DATA--WILL USE FIRST', MAXLST
110     NUMLST = N-1
        END
```

A similar facility can be used with array parameters. An asterisk in place of a dimension declaration indicates that the array parameter in the subprogram is automatically to assume the number of elements of the array in the CALL statement.

Warned of the appearance of this slight extension to parameter declarations in subprograms, you should have little trouble following the development of the INPUT and OUTPUT routines in Figures 12.2.3 and 12.2.4.

Using Assumed-Length Arrays

When a subprogram has an array for a parameter, the subprogram will sometimes need to know the dimension of the array; sometimes it won't need to know the dimensions. For example, SUBROUTINE INPUT needs to know how long the arrays are because it contains an array READ-loop which terminates if the arrays get filled up. On the other hand, SUBROUTINE OUTPUT needs to know only how much information is stored in the arrays. The total capacity of the arrays is irrelevant to the goal of SUBROUTINE OUTPUT—printing the phone book listings. Therefore, we use **assumed-length declarators** for the array parameters in SUBROUTINE OUTPUT and **variable-length declarators** for the arrays in SUBROUTINE INPUT.

Figure 12.2.4   The OUTPUT Routine

Plan
Print heading.

For each listing, K = 1,2,...NUMLIST.
    Print Kth listing.

Fortran translation

```
      SUBROUTINE OUTPUT(HEAD,A,B,N)
      INTEGER N
      CHARACTER*(*) HEAD, A(*), B(*)
      INTEGER K
      PRINT *
      PRINT *
      PRINT *, HEAD, 'LISTING'
      PRINT *
      DO 100 K=1, N
        PRINT *, A(K), ' ', B(K)
100     CONTINUE
      END
```

Basically, SUBROUTINE SORT will be the same as in Section 11.6. We have to make a few changes so that the values will be put into increasing (instead of decreasing) order, and so the routine will handle assumed-length arrays. Let's go through the changes. The main routine, SORT, is conceptually identical to the version in Section 11.6

```
            SUBROUTINE SORT(KEY, OTHER, N)
            INTEGER N
            CHARACTER*(*) KEY(*), OTHER(*)
COMMENT:              ARRANGE VALUES IN 'KEY' AND 'OTHER' INTO
C                     INCREASING ORDER ACCORDING TO 'KEY'.
            INTEGER K, BOTTOM, LOCBIG
            DO 100 BOTTOM = N, 2, -1
C                     FIND LARGEST NUMBER IN KEY
C                     BEWTEEN 1 AND 'BOTTOM'.
        K = LOCBIG(KEY, BOTTOM)
        CALL SWITCH(KEY( BOTTOM), KEY(K))
        CALL SWITCH(OTHER(BOTTOM), OTHER(K))
    100     CONTINUE
            END
```

Assumed Dimension for Array Parameters

---

forms

type a (d,,d,,. . . ,*)

type a $(d_1, d_2 \ldots, b:*)$

type is a Fortran data type

a is a subprogram parameter name

d, is a dimension declaration

b is a lower bound specification

note

The asterisk takes the place of the upper bound in the last dimension specification for the array.

meaning

The subprogram assumes that all references to the array *a* will use subscripts within the space provided by the corresponding argument array in the calling program.

restriction

The array *a* may not be used in whole array I/O in the subprogram.

examples

```
REAL X(*), Y(3,7,*), Z(0:*), T(100,-10:*)
INTEGER A(10,5,*), B(*)
```

We're almost done with the SORT module (**module** is another word for subprocess). The only other change we have to make is to turn our old FUNCTION LOCSML into LOCBIG.

```
            INTEGER FUNCTION LOCBIG(A,N)
            INTEGER N
            CHARACTER*(*) A(*)
            INTEGER K
```

(Continued on following page)

```
COMMENT:              FIND THE (FIRST OCCURRENCE OF) BIGGEST
          LOCBIG = 1
          DO 100 K = 2, N
            IF (A(K) .GT. A(LOCBIG)) THEN
              LOCBIG = K
            ENDIF
100         CONTINUE
          END
```

Our old SUBROUTINE SWITCH requires a minor change. The details are spelled out in Figure 12.2.5. To make a copy of the value in a CHAR-ACTER variable, we need a memory cell to put the copy in. The declaration statement for that variable must specify its length. (We can't use the assumed-length feature. That works only for parameters, not for local variables.) It won't hurt us to use a variable which will hold more characters than the value we're copying, but too few characters will hurt. It would cause our program to drop letters off the ends of names.

We can solve the problem by using a CHARACTER*(25) local variable

Figure 12.2.5   Interchanging Two Values

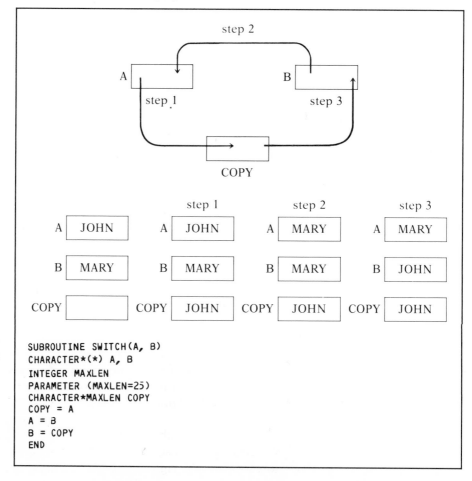

because we know that the main program (the original source of the data for the subprogram SORT) has no variables with more than 25 characters. However, any user of the sorting routine should be warned that the local variable in SWITCH may need to be changed to handle longer character strings in case the declarations in the main program are changed to handle longer names. That's why we put the comment in the main program.

Finally, we have reduced the whole problem to Fortran. The overall task of printing a cross-reference directory is a relatively complex one, but when we look at it in small pieces, taken one at a time, it doesn't seem so bad.

```
COMMENT:                   PROGRAM FOR CROSS REFERENCE DIRECTORY
            INTEGER MAXLST, NAMLEN, PHLEN
            PARAMETER(MAXLST = 500, NAMLEN = 25, PHLEN = 25)
            CHARACTER*(NAMLEN) NAME(MAXLST)
            CHARACTER*(PHLEN) PHONE(MAXLST)
            INTEGER NUMLST
C                          WARNING:  SUBROUTINE SWITCH, CALLED FROM
C                          SORT, LIMITS NAMES TO MAXNAM CHARACTERS
            CALL INPUT(NAME, PHONE, MAXLST, NUMLST)
            CALL SORT(NAME, PHONE, NUMLST)
            CALL OUTPUT('ALPHABETICAL', NAME, PHONE, NUMLST)
            CALL SORT(PHONE, NAME, NUMLST)
            CALL OUTPUT('PHONE-ETIC', PHONE, NAME, NUMLST)
            END
```

12.2 EXERCISES

1. In all, we divided the cross-reference directory program into six modules (subprocesses): the main program, INPUT, OUTPUT, SORT, LOC-BIG, and SWITCH. Draw a diagram that shows the relationships among modules. The higher-level modules should be at the top, and a line should connect two modules if one is used by the other. Do you think a diagram like this would be helpful if you were trying to explain the program to someone? Do you feel that we caused you untold grief by not putting a diagram like that in this section?

2. Here's a list of values
      123
      597
      642
      125
      121
      700

    Using the sorting method covered in this section, but doing it by hand, put the list in order of the digits in the leftmost column. Then take that result, and put it in order of the digits in the middle column. Then take that result and put it in order of the rightmost column. What do you have?

3. Start with the list of numbers given in exercise 2. Using the sorting method described in this section, but doing it by hand, put the list in order of the digits in the rightmost column. Then take that result, and

put it in order of the digits in the middle column. Then take that result, and put it in order of the leftmost column. What do you have?

4. Look carefully at the first Comment statement in the new version of FUNCTION LOCBIG. The fact that it finds the "FIRST OCCURRENCE OF" the biggest value is very important to the success of the column-at-a-time sorting method.

   a. How would you change FUNCTION LOCBIG so that it finds the *last* occurrence of the smallest value?

   b. Why would this change foul up our cross-reference directory? (*Hint:* Follow through exercise 3, paying special attention to the eventual fates of the values 121, 123, 125.)

5. In which cases below would assumed-length arrays be appropriate? For which would variable-length arrays be better?

   SUBROUTINE ZEROS (A,N)   to put zeros in array A, which has exactly N elements.

   SUBROUTINE ONES (B,M)   to put M ones in array B, which has at least M elements.

   SUBROUTINE THRESH (A,M,N,T) to count the number of values in array A, which exceed T. Array A is an M-by-N array.

   SUBROUTINE INIT(STATES)   to put the names of the 50 United States into the array STATES, which has 50 elements.

12.3 STEPWISE REFINEMENT

Our goal in this section is to write a program which converts INTEGERs into roman numerals. If the input to our program is the number 7, the output should be the roman numeral VII. The input 9 should be converted to IX. You probably remember from your grade school days that this conversion process is not as easy as it sounds. We'll have to analyze it carefully to write the program. In fact, we'll see that by the time we've figured out what the problem really involves, we'll have almost written the program.

> **rough problem statement:**
> Print numbers as roman numerals.

To get a firm grasp on what we want our program to do, let's try to describe the output we want for a given class of inputs. You hardly ever see roman numerals these days except as dates on movies or buildings (used so it's hard to tell how old they are) and as page numbers in book prefaces. Therefore, it's unlikely that we'd need roman numerals for numbers of more than four digits. We'll write our program with this in mind.

Input/Output Description

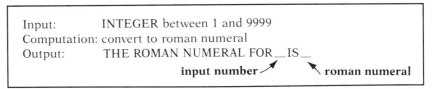

Input: INTEGER between 1 and 9999
Computation: convert to roman numeral
Output: THE ROMAN NUMERAL FOR __ IS __
                      input number ↗   ↖ **roman numeral**

To get a feeling for how the process works, let's look at a few conversions.

1	I
3	III
8	VIII
48	XLVIII
109	CIX
1066	MLXVI
1492	MCDXCII
1984	MCMLXXXIV

You can look at the conversion as a digit-by-digit process. To write the roman numeral for 1896, we first convert the first digit, the 1 in the thousands place, to the corresponding roman numeral M. The next digit, the 8 in the hundreds place, leads to the roman numeral DCCC. Now we have MDCCC, with two digits to go. The 9 in the tens place gives XC; the 6 in the units place, VI; and we end up with MDCCCXCVI. Of course, a 0 in any position adds nothing to the roman numeral: 105 becomes CV, the 0 in the tens place having no effect.

step-by-step conversion
1896 → M 896
          ↓
    M DCCC 96 → M DCCC IX 6
                      ↓
              M DCCC IX VI
    105 → C05 → C5 → CV

The conversion of 105 to CV brings up an interesting point. To make the process seem consistent with the digit-by-digit conversion of 1896, we actually went through an extra step: C05 to C5 is extra because the 05 part has a *leading zero*. We could have gone directly from 105 to C5, then on to CV, skipping the zero digit, but we have a feeling it will be easier to write the program if we treat leading zeros in the same way that we treat other digits. Since none of our numbers will have more than four digits, we can treat *all* inputs as if they had *exactly* four digits, viewing 105 as 0105 and 48 as 0048. Doing this, we get a first stab at a conversion algorithm, as shown in Figure 12.3.1.

In converting a digit, there are, of course, ten possibilities, one for each digit from 0 through 9. Each of these produces a pattern of roman symbols, and the roman symbols used depend on the position of the digit in the number (thousands, hundreds, tens, or units position). A zero digit is easy to handle. It produces no roman symbols, no matter what position it's in. The other patterns are more complicated. Study the accompanying table of digit conversions (Table 12.3.1). Notice the three different symbols involved in the conversion list for each digit position. The units place uses the symbols I, V, and X; the tens place uses X, L, and C; the hundreds place, C, D, and M; and the thousands place, M, V, and X. Fortunately, the three symbols involved are used consistently in each column. If we call the three symbols *a*, *b*, and *c*, then each column of the table is the same. We can condense the table (Table 12.3.2).

Figure 12.3.1   Conversion Algorithm

input:

INTEGER *between* 1 *and* 9999

output:

pattern of roman symbols

Start with empty pattern.
Convert thousands digit and add to pattern.
Convert hundreds digit and add to pattern.
Convert tens digit and add to pattern.
Convert units digit and add to pattern.

Table 12.3.1   Table of Digit Conversions

Thousands place	Hundreds place	Tens place	Units place
0 (nothing)	0 (nothing)	0 (nothing)	0 (nothing)
1 M	1 C	1 X	1 I
2 MM	2 CC	2 XX	2 II
3 MMM	3 CCC	3 XXX	3 III
4 M$\overline{\text{V}}$	4 CD	4 XL	4 IV
5 $\overline{\text{V}}$	5 D	5 L	5 V
6 $\overline{\text{V}}$M	6 DC	6 LX	6 VI
7 $\overline{\text{V}}$MM	7 DCC	7 LXX	7 VII
8 $\overline{\text{V}}$MMM	8 DCCC	8 LXXX	8 VIII
9 M$\overline{\text{X}}$	9 CM	9 XC	9 IX

Now we're getting somewhere! To convert a digit, no matter what its position, we need to know both which digit it is (0 through 9) and the three necessary symbols. Digit conversion is then simply a matter of looking up an entry in the condensed table of digit conversions (Figure 12.3.2).

Now we have a way to produce a correct pattern of roman symbols given a digit and its position in the INTEGER being converted. We can put four of these digit conversions together and get a complete coversion. We still need a way to figure out which digit is in which position given a Fortran INTEGER. It comes to us in one piece, and we have to take it apart. Fortunately, there is a built-in Fortran FUNCTION which will help us out: MOD. MOD gives us the remainder in the division of its two INTEGER arguments. If we give MOD the arguments 492 and 10, it returns the remainder 2 ($492 \div 10 = 49$ rem 2). The remainder in a division by ten is the last digit in the dividend. That's how we get the units digit. To get other digits, we simply shift them over to the units place by means of INTEGER division (remember, it's truncated) and pluck them off.

---

digit selection algorithm

units digit: MOD (I, 10)
tens digit: MOD (I/10, 10)
hundreds digit: MOD (I/100, 10)
thousands digit: MOD (I/1000, 10)

If you need to review the use of MOD, see Section 3.3.

Looking back over the pieces of our algorithm so far, we see that we have found techniques for converting each digit of the input number to the correct pattern of roman symbols, but we haven't yet decided how to add that pattern to the roman numeral. Suppose we decide to store the symbols of the roman numeral in an array, one symbol to each element. We can keep track of the number of symbols in a separate INTEGER memory cell, N, by updating the value of N each time we add some symbols to the roman numeral.

Table 12.3.2   Condensed Table of Digit Conversions

Thousands place	Hundreds place	Tens place	Units place
a = M	a = C	a = X	a = I
b = V	b = D	b = L	b = V
c = X	c = M	c = C	c = X
1 a	4 ab	7 baa	0 *nothing*
2 aa	5 b	8 $baaa$	
3 aaa	6 ba	9 ac	

Furthermore, the value of N will tell us where to put the symbols to be added each time we convert a digit of the input INTEGER.

Now that we've developed a plan and understand each of the subproblems, we're finally ready to write some Fortran code. We'll use a SUBROUTINE named DIGIT to do the digit conversion so the main program will look very much like the conversion algorithm we originally described. The inputs to SUBROUTINE DIGIT will be the digit to be converted (an INTEGER), the three relevant roman symbols (characters), the array in which the roman numeral is being accumulated (an array of characters), and the current length of that array (an INTEGER memory cell). DIGIT will update the input array and its length in the appropriate way.

Figure 12.3.2   Digit Conversion Algorithm

input:

digit d (0,1,2,3,4,5,6,7,8, or 9)
symbols a,b, and c

output:

pattern of symbols (possibly empty)

```
Select digit
    0: output nothing
    1: output a
    2: output aa
    3: output aaa
    4: output ab
    5: output b
    6: output ba
    7: output baa
    8: output baaa
    9: output ac
```

The program emerges from the development so naturally that it should be easy to understand the lightly annotated version which follows. We've used W for the symbol $\overline{V}$ and Y for $\overline{X}$. We've established 16 as the length of the array which stores the roman numeral. No roman numeral for a four-digit number can have more than 16 symbols. (The digit 8 has the longest roman equivalent, 4 symbols. Thus, 8888 would generate 16 symbols. Nothing could be longer.)

There is one final point before you read the program. The digit conversion algorithm has to make a selection among ten different alternatives. We could implement this selection in Fortran by writing a series of IF statements, but there is a cleaner way to do it.

The situation is made to order for a special kind of statement that you don't know about yet: a multiple-branch transfer of control called the **computed GO TO**. This GO TO statement, instead of specifying one place to go, specifies many possible destinations. One of them is selected based on the value of an INTEGER selector which is part of the statement. If the value of the selector is 1, then the program jumps to the first statement in the list; if it is 2, to the second statement; and so on.

Computed GO TO Statement

---

form

GO TO $(s_1, s_2, \ldots, s_n), k$

GO TO $(s_1, s_2, \ldots, s_n) k$

s_i is a statement label

k is an INTEGER expression

the comma before the expression k is optional

meaning

Control is transferred to the kth statement in the list

$s_1, s_2, \ldots, s_n$.

If $k < 1$ or if $k > n$, control passes to the next statement.

examples

```
INTEGER N, JMP, CASE
GO TO (85, 10, 100, 453),N
GO TO (465, 700, 25),JMP
GO TO (200, 100, 100, 200, 100, 400) CASE
```

Here's our completed program for roman numerals:

```
COMMENT:              ROMAN NUMERAL PROGRAM
C                     INPUT:  INTEGER
C                     OUTPUT:  INPUT INTEGER AND ITS ROMAN EQUIVALENT
C                     VARIABLES:
C                             I--INPUT INTEGER
C                             R--ARRAY TO STORE ROMAN NUMERAL
C                             N--CURRENT NUMBER OF SYMBOLS IN R
          INTEGER I, N, J
          CHARACTER*(1) R(16)
          READ *, I
          IF (I .GT. 0 .AND. I .LT. 10000) THEN
C                     START WITH EMPTY ROMAN NUMERAL
            N = 0
C                     CONVERT THOUSANDS, HUNDREDS, TENS, UNITS
          CALL DIGIT(MOD(I/1000,10), 'M', 'W', 'Y', R, N)
          CALL DIGIT(MOD(I/100 ,10), 'C', 'D', 'M', R, N)
          CALL DIGIT(MOD(I/10  ,10), 'X', 'L', 'C', R, N)
          CALL DIGIT(MOD(I     ,10), 'I', 'V', 'X', R, N)
          PRINT *, 'ROMAN NUMERAL FOR', I,' IS ', (R(J),J=1,N)
          ELSE
            PRINT *, 'CANNOT CONVERT', I
          ENDIF
          END

          SUBROUTINE DIGIT(D, A,B,C, R,N)
          INTEGER D, N
          CHARACTER*(1) R(16), A, B, C
```

(Continued on following page)

```
COMMENT:                  INPUT:
C                         D--NUMBER BETWEEN 0 AND 9
C                         A,B,C--ROMAN SYMBOLS
C                         R--ARRAY TO STORE ROMAN NUMERAL
C                         N--CURRENT NUMBER OF SYMBOLS IN R
C                         OUTPUT:
C                         R,N--UPDATED BY CONVERTING D TO ROMAN SYMBOLS
          GO TO (100,101,102,103,104,105,106,107,108,109), D + 1
C                         INPUT D=0, OUTPUT PATTERN= NOTHING
     100     RETURN
C                         INPUT D=1, OUTPUT PATTERN=A
     101     R(N+1) =  A
            N = N + 1
            RETURN
C                         INPUT D=2, OUTPUT PATTERN=AA
     102     R(N+1) = A
            R(N+2) = A
            N = N + 2
            RETURN
C                         INPUT D=3, OUTPUT PATTERN=AAA
     103     R(N+1) = A
            R(N+2) = A
            R(N+3) = A
            N = N + 3
            RETURN
C                         INPUT D=4, OUTPUT PATTERN=AB
     104     R(N+1) = A
            R(N+2) = B
            N = N + 2
            RETURN
C                         INPUT D=5, OUTPUT PATTERN=B
     105     R(N+1) = B
            N = N + 1
            RETURN
C                         INPUT D=6, OUTPUT PATTERN=BA
     106     R(N+1) = B
            R(N+2) = A
            N = N + 2
            RETURN
C                         INPUT D=7, OUTPUT PATTERN=BAA
     107     R(N+1) = B
            R(N+2) = A
            R(N+3) = A
            N = N + 3
            RETURN
C                         INPUT D=8, OUTPUT PATTERN=BAAA
     108     R(N+1) = B
            R(N+2) = A
            R(N+3) = A
            R(N+4) = A
            N = N + 4
            RETURN
C                         INPUT D=9, OUTPUT PATTERN=AC
     109     R(N+1) = A
            R(N+2) = C
            N = N + 2
            RETURN
          END
```

Data

```
3649
```

Output

```
ROMAN NUMERAL FOR    3649 IS MMMDCXLIX
```

The digit conversion SUBROUTINE seems long and bulky for such a simple idea, but it would be even worse if we had implemented it with IF statements. About the only way to shorten it is to leave out the comments, and that's dangerous. If you leave them out and later misplace the documentation you did on the program while developing it, you'll have a hard time maintaining the program in the future. You'll have to do most of the design work over again to figure out how the program works.

In case you were surprised to find the error message (ELSE branch) in the main program (we hadn't discussed it earlier), we're sure you realize that it's never a good idea to trust your input to be correct. It's always best to test the input for consistency with the assumptions your program makes about it. Sometimes this is very hard to do, but in our case, we assume only that the input is an INTEGER between 1 and 9999, and we can easily test for that.

12.3   EXERCISES

1. What are the four steps in program design?
2. Did we follow the four steps in sequence here? Which parts of this section correspond to which steps in top-down design?
3. Write computed GO TO statements that do the same as
   a.
   ```
   IF (K .EQ. 1) GO TO 10
   IF (K .EQ. 2) GO TO 20
   IF (K .EQ. 3) GO TO 30
   ```

   Assume K is 1, 2, or 3.
   b.
   ```
   IF (I .GT. 2 .AND. I .LT. 5) GO TO 100
   IF (I .LE. 6) GO TO 200
   ```

   Assume I is positive.
4. Why is the expression in the computed GO TO in SUBROUTINE DIGIT D + 1 instead of just D?
5. A computed GO TO statement has an "array of statement labels." Often, all of the statements indicated in the computed GO TO list ("array") are similar, and in these cases the program can usually be simplified by using an "array of variables" instead of a computed GO TO. Simplify the roman numeral program by using ordinary arrays to take the function of the computed GO TO in the version of the program in this section.

12.4 TRADE-OFFS AND DESIGN ALTERNATIVES

In this section, our goal is to show that two programs that do the same thing can have important differences between them. Once we accept that fact, we have to accept that to develop a really good program we'll have to consider several alternative methods and weigh each against the others to decide which is most suited. And, since no one wants to go to all the work of writing and debugging two or three versions of the same thing, the weighing of alternatives should be done in the planning stages, before very many (if any) actual lines of Fortran are written.

We'll go through four different ways of solving what is essentially the same problem. We'll compare things like the amount of storage space required, the relative speed, and convenience of each tentative solution. The problem itself sounds simple—at first.

Problem Statement

> Maintain a list of items, where each item consists of an account name and an entry. Provide these options:
>> Store a new item
>> Retrieve the entry of an existing account
>> Change the entry of an existing account

We've stated the problem in a very general way, because it won't be until we get to specific details that we can choose among the methods we'll show. For now, imagine that the items are airline reservations and the entries are flight numbers, or that the account names are phone numbers and the entries are the names of agents responsible for tapping each phone, or the account names are title of books in a library and the entries show who has each book checked out, or. . . .

We want to concentrate on the schemes themselves, not on the details of the application, so we'll consider the problem in a simple form. Specifically, we'll assume we'll have about 1,000 items, that the account names are numbers between 1 and 999999999 (that's the range of social security numbers), and that the entries are numbers. If we could manage to solve this form of the problem, we would be able to use our solution to solve any specific application. For instance, we could change from an account number to a person's name, and we could add even more arrays to store an ''entry'' giving quite detailed information about that person. Or, if the application involved a huge number of items stored on an external storage device like a disk, we could adapt the methods so that the ''entry'' was a record number, which would then be used to get the appropriate complete information from disk.

All our methods use the same basic scheme, namely arrays. That is, we'll store the information in specific array elements and use elements with different subscript values for different items (see Figure 12.4.1).

Figure 12.4.1

	ACCT( )	ENTRY( )				
1	276407576	1200				
2	114552332	123				
3	500646565	1796				
4	721469870	92				
5	633371207	888				
NAME( )		BAL( )	TYPE( )	STATUS( )	LIMIT( )	DATE( )
1 PORTER GEORGE		321.75	0	300	1000	30208
2 DEERING POLLY		−2.17	1	200	1000	71485
3 GUSTAFSON JON		12.72	1	200	5000	20383
4 DEERING HOLLY		512.65	7	300	750	121282

On the top, a typical collection of items. The second item has the account name ACCT(2) = 114 55 2332 and entry ENTRY (2) = 123. On the bottom, a more realistic "data base," which can be manipulated using the same basic techniques.

So far, when we've used arrays, we've always "looked things up" in them by specifying the subscript value of the item we want. Why are we even bothering with account numbers here? So far, if we want to know the entry for account number 47, we'd just do something like

```
PRINT *, ' ACCOUNT NUMBER 47  ENTRY=',ENTRY(47)
```

Let's consider this method, which we'll call **direct access**, as the first way of solving our problem. In terms of programming, it's by far the simplest. The plan is shown in Figure 12.4.2. And it has the advantage that we don't even need an array to store account numbers—they're just the subscript values for the array of entries. Assume we know that no legal entry value could ever be less than −1000000. Then we can solve all the steps of our main problem in the following manner.

Initially fill the entire array of entries with the (illegal) value EMPTY.

```
       EMPTY = -2000000
       DO 10 HERE = 1,999999999
         ENTRY(HERE) = EMPTY
10       CONTINUE
            .
            .
            .
```

Then, to add a new item, all we need to do is call SUBROUTINE ADD.

```
       SUBROUTINE ADD(NACCT, NENTRY, ENTRY, LEN, SUCCSS)
       INTEGER NACCT, NENTRY, LEN, ENTRY(LEN), SUCCSS
       INTEGER EMPTY
       PARAMETER (EMPTY = -2000000 )
       IF (ENTER(NACCT) .NE. EMPTY) THEN
         PRINT *, '***ACCOUNT ',NACCT, ' ALREADY EXISTS****'
         SUCCSS = 0
       ELSE
         ENTRY(NACCT) = NENTRY
         SUCCSS = 1
       ENDIF
       END
```

To remove an item, all we need to do is store EMPTY as its entry. To change an entry for account number NACCT, all we need do is assign the new value to ENTRY (NACCT). Very simple. Of course, there's one big problem with the direct-access method that makes it *hopelessly* impractical. Remember, we're assuming that we'll have around 1,000 items to store and retrieve. But the account numbers can vary from 1 to 999999999. To use the direct-access method, we'd need 999,999,999 elements in the array ENTRY ( ).

    INTEGER ENTRY (999999999)

Obviously, the direct-access method is extremely wasteful of memory space. In fact, on most computer systems, its not just wasteful, it's impossible. There's just not that much room available for a Fortran array. The direct-access method is very simple to program, and (if it were possible at all) would be very fast to add, delete, or change entries, but it's not practical.

In the direct access scheme, to store 1,000 items, we'd use 1,000 memory locations in the array and leave 999,998,999 memory locations empty. Surely there's a better way. Suppose we use two arrays, one to store the account number and one for the entry. Then we could find the entry value for a given account number by this simple scheme. Look at the contents of

Figure 12.4.2   The Direct-access Method

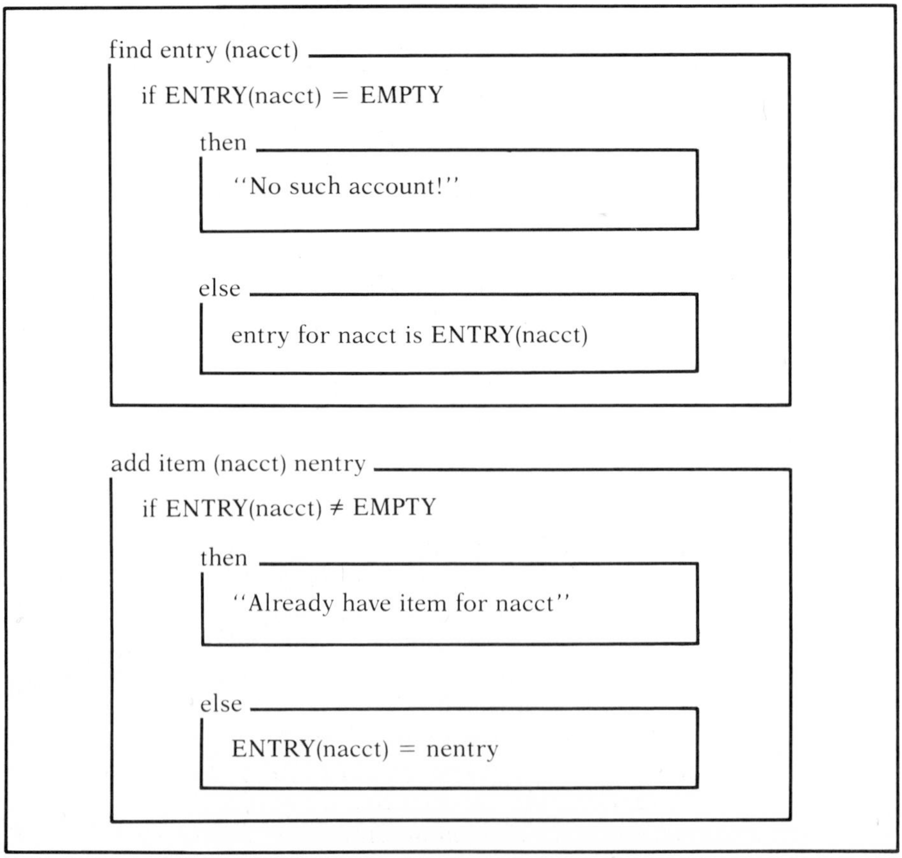

ACCT(1), and see if that's the one we want. If so, we're done. If not, look at ACCT(2), and so on. We'll call this scheme **sequential search**.

We've solved only part of the problem—finding the entry for a given account number. Let's back up a minute and see how we can do the other parts of the problem. Assume that the variable NITEMS stores the number of items currently being stored. To add a new item, we just add one to NITEMS and stick the new account number and new entry value at the end of the current items. To change an entry, we use the "look up" process to find the position in the array, and then assign the new entry value to ENTRY (that position).

The sequential-search method is relatively simple, but it does have one potential problem. Let's consider how long it takes to look up an item. Since the items are in no particular order, the item being sought is equally likely to be in any position. So, if there are NITEMS items, on the average it will take NITEMS/2 steps to locate the item we want. If there are 1,000 people on a company's payroll, it would take about

$$1,000 \quad * \quad 1,000/2 = 500,000 \text{ steps}$$

number of employees   average search for each employee

to compute all the paychecks.

The first method, direct access, is extremely efficient for searching (namely, one step to find any item) but very inefficient in memory usage. The second method, sequential access, shown in Figure 12.4.3, is very efficient in memory usage, but inefficient for looking things up. Are any methods reasonably efficient at both tasks? Yes, but of course you can't expect something for nothing—you have to pay in one way or another, whether it's in terms of the length and complexity of the program or in terms of the efficiency in seaching or in adding new or removing old items.

The third method we'll look at has a flair of gambling to it. In this method (called **hashing**), we try to get the best properties of the first two methods most of the time. Figure 12.4.5 illustrates this method. Even though the account names run from 1 through 999999999, maybe we can still use the direct-access method by shrinking the names. That is, instead of using the entire account name to look the item up, maybe there's a way of deriving a smaller number from it that will still uniquely identify the item. Suppose, for example, that we take the first digit, the middle digit, and the last two digits of the account name and multiply them together in such a way that we get a number between 1 and 10000. Then we divide that by (say) 5 to get a number between 1 and 2000. Finally, we'll look for the item at that array position. Figure 12.4.4 shows some examples.

Here's the idea. We hope that most of the account names will have different hash numbers. If they all did, we'd have all the advantages of the direct-access scheme. If most of them do, we get most of the benefits of it. Since we know that some accounts that are actually different will have the same hash number, we have to take that into account. We'll store both the account name and the entry for each item. We'll initialize the array storing account names to the (illegal) value 000000000 so we can

Figure 12.4.3 The Sequential Access Method

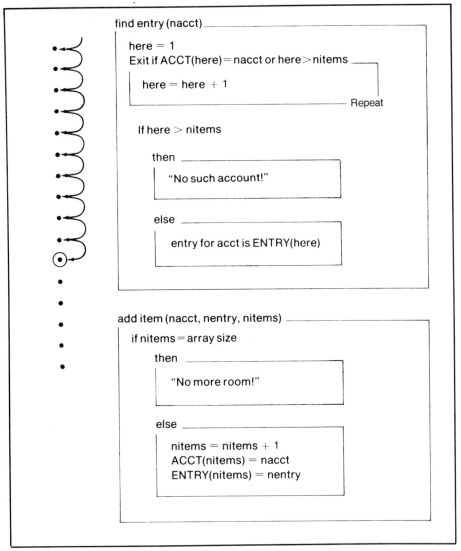

tell if a particular position has an item in it yet. To look up an item, we compute the hash number and look at the account number stored at that position. If the account number stored there matches the one we're looking for, we've found it and we're done. If the account number at that position is zero, we know the item we sought isn't in the array at all. But what do we do if the account number we d doesn't match the one we're looking for? (Obviously, this will happen sometimes when two different account numbers have the same hash number.) Here's what we'll do. We'll just keep looking at succeeding positions in the array until one of two things happens. Either we find the account number we're looking for (and now know where its entry is), or else we come to an empty spot (an account number of 000000000). In the latter case, we know that the account number we wanted to find isn't in the array at all.

Figure 12.4.4   Hashing Examples

Given account names which are nine digit numbers: $d_1 \, d_2 \, d_3 \, d_4 \, d_5 \, d_6 \, d_7 \, d_8 \, d_9$

Hash function: $[(d_1 + 1)*(d_5 + 1)*(d_8 + 1)*(d_9 + 1) - 1]/5 + 1$

account name   hash number

276	40	7576	34	$= (3*1*8*7 - 1)/5 + 1$
114	55	2332	29	
500	64	6565	252	
721	46	9870	90	
633	37	1207	90	

```
        INTEGER FUNCTION HASH(ACCT)
        INTEGER ACCT
C       CONVERT ACCT TO A HASH NUMBER IN THE
        RANGE 1 THRU 2000.
C       HASH = PRODUCT OF 1ST, 5TH, 8TH AND 9TH
C               DIGITS DIVIDED BY 5.
        INTEGER DIG1, DIG5, DIG6, DIG9
        DIG1 = MOD(ACCT/100000000,10)
        DIG5 = MOD(ACCT/10000,10)
        DIG8 = MOD(ACCT/10,10)
        HASH = ((DIG1+1)*(DIG5+1)*DIG8+1)*
                (DIG9+1)-1)/5 +1
RETURN
```

The hash numbers corresponding to several account names. Each hash number is guaranteed to be in the range from 1 to 2000, but (unfortunately) the hash numbers aren't guaranteed to be unique. The last two account names give rise to the same hash number.

If most items' hash numbers are different (this can happen with good planning, luck, and/or the provision of enough memory space so that the arrays aren't very full), this scheme does combine the good features of direct access and sequential search. Not much memory is wasted, and for most look-ups, the desired item will be at the first place the program looks. However, if most items ''hash'' to the same location, the hashing scheme degenerates into sequential search.

The final scheme, shown in Figure 12.4.6, also combines some of the good features of direct access and sequential search. Specifically, it wastes no memory space (like sequential search), and it guarantees that you'll always be able to find an item after a relatively small number of tries (even if you're unlucky).

It is called **binary search**, and you use something very much like it all the time. Suppose you're trying to find someone's phone number in the phone book. If the phone book listings were in no particular order (like

Figure 12.4.5   Access Through Hashing

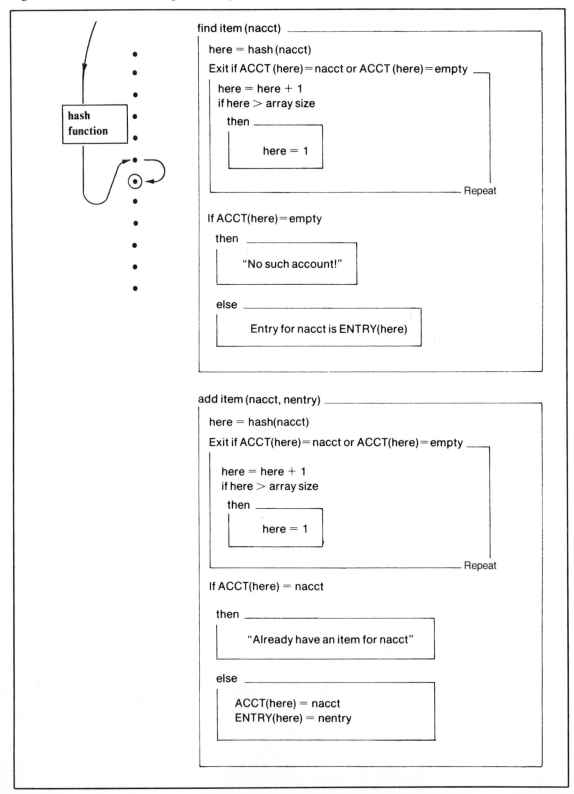

Figure 12.4.6 Binary-search Access Method

```
find item (nacct, nitems)
    low = 0
    hi = nitems + I
    Exit if low > hi − 1 or ACCT(low + hi)/2) = nacct
        If nacct < ACCT((low + hi)/2)
            then
                low = (low + hi)/2
            else
                hi = (low + hi)/2
                                                    Repeat
    If low > hi − 1
        then
            "No such item!!"
        else
            Entry for nacct is ENTRY( (low + hi)/2)

add item (nacct, nentry, nitems)
    low = 0
    hi = nitems + 1
    Exit if low > hi − 1 or ACCT((low + hi)/2) = nacct
        If nacct > ACCT( (low + hi)/2)
            then
                low = (low + hi)/2
            else
                hi = (low + hi)/2
                                                    Repeat
    If ACCT((low + hi)/2) = nacct
        then
            "Already have item for nacct"
        else
            If nitems = array size
                then
                    "No more room!"
                else
                    nitems = nitems + 1
                    For here = nitems, nitems − 1, down to hi + 1
                        ACCT(here) = ACCT(here − 1)
                        ENTRY(here) = ENTRY(here − 1)

                    ACCT(hi) = nacct
                    ENTRY(hi) = nentry
```

Table 12.4.1 Comparison of the Techniques

operation	method			
	direct access	sequential access	hashing	binary search
Looking up	1 step	NITEMS/2	1 step in best case, NITEMS/2 in worst	Log_2 (NITEMS) in worst case
Adding new item	1 step	1 step	1 step in best case, NITEMS/2 in worst	NITEMS + Log_2 (NITEMS) in worst case
Memory usage	ridiculous	NITEMS	NITEMS*2 or so	NITEMS
Size of programs	smallest	small	relatively small	moderate

The time required to change an item is the same as the time for look up. For times to delete an item, see exercise 12.4.6

the sequential-search case), or if you needed to know a code (like the hashing scheme), you'd have a terrible time. Fortunately, the phone company has had the good sense to put the listings in alphabetical order. You open the book somewhere and look at a name. If the name you want comes after that name, you look toward the back of the phone book. If the name you want comes earlier, you look toward the front of the book. We could follow that idea to find items in our arrays, *if they were in order.*

Let's assume the arrays are in increasing order of the account numbers. Then we can use the binary-search method. We'll use two variables, one called LOW, which stores an array index value that we know is lower than the place we want, and one called HIGH, which is higher than the place we want. Before we look anywhere, we know that 0 is lower than the place we want and NITEMS + 1 is higher. Now we start looking. Since we don't have any information yet, the natural thing is to look at the middle item, guessing that the place we want is just as likely to be in the first half of the arrays as in the last half. The account number of the item in the middle position is ACCT((LOW + HIGH)/2). Maybe that's the one we wanted. If so, we're done. If not, we can tell if the value we wanted is before the middle or after the middle by comparing the value we're seeking, NACCT, with the value ACCT((LOW + HIGH)/2). Depending on the outcome of the test, we change either LOW or HIGH and continue the same process. If LOW and HIGH ever get so close together that there are no entries between them, we know that NACCT isn't there at all. This method is called a binary search because at each step about half of the alternatives (positions) are eliminated.

Since we eliminate about half of the alternatives each time around the loop, after one time there are about NITEMS/2 alternatives left. After two times there are NITEMS/(2*2) left, and after n times there are NITEMS/2^n left. We stop if there is only one (or fewer) alternatives left, that is, when NITEMS/$2^n \leqslant 1$. Solving for n we find that the most steps the process could ever take is $n = \log_2$ (NITEMS). Using this method to compute the payroll for a company of 1,000 employees would take no more than

$$1000 \quad * \quad \log_2(1000) \cong 9900 \text{ steps}$$

which is many, many fewer than the number of steps required by the sequential search method.

There are yet more methods for searching arrays, but we hope we've shown enough to convince you that programs that appear to do the same thing can be quite different when you look at all the details and implications of the methods used (see Table 12.4.1). It is especially important to realize that the analysis of the benefits (and shortcomings) of a method you propose to use can be carried out without going all the way to Fortran. That is, the plans themselves are sufficient for decision making.

12.4 EXERCISES

1. We covered four different methods of organizing a collection of "items." Which method would be best for:
   a. an airplane reservation program, where account names are people's names, speed is the most important consideration, and lots of memory space is available?
   b. keeping track of the business expenses of a basketball team using a microcomputer without much memory and where the account names are players' names?

2. Explain the conditions under which two "account names" will be given the same hash number by the hash function shown in Figure 12.4.4.

3. The plans for the hashing method are incomplete. What happens if the arrays are completely full and you try to add another item? What would you do to avoid this problem?

4. Following the plan shown in Figure 12.4.5, write a Fortran SUBROUTINE that FINDs the entry for account NACCT.

5. Try the old number guessing game to convince yourself of the speed of the binary-search strategy. Pick a number between 1 and 1000. See how many guesses a friend makes before he or she gets the number if after each wrong guess you tell him or her "high" or "low." The binary-search method guarantees that, at most, ten guesses are needed.

6. Consider the problem of deleting an item. To delete an item in the hashing scheme, just replace the account number by a special value that means "deleted." In the other schemes, actually remove the item. Make a plan for each case, and give an indication (in the spirit of Table 12.4.1) of the time required for each.

---

12 PROBLEMS

Practice Problems

1. Write a program which READs in 20 people's names, stores them in an array, PRINTs·them out, reverses the array by making repeated CALLs to SUBROUTINE SWITCH (from Section 11.2), and finally PRINTs the reversed array.

2. Design and write a program which READs a year number and determines whether that year was (or will be) a leap year.

   Although this won't be a lengthy program, it will require you to make a careful plan to express the necessary selection in a clear, correct manner. Here are the rules for leap years: If a year is evenly divisible by 4, then it's a leap year unless it's also divisible by 100. If it's evenly divisible by 100, it's *not* a leap year unless it's evenly divisible by 400, in which case it *is* a leap year. For example, 1984 is a leap year; 1900 was not a leap year; 2000 will be a leap year.

3. Construct a SUBROUTINE ARAB which accepts an array containing a number in roman notation and returns the equivalent INTEGER. (*Note:* This is an easier problem than it would be the other way around.)

4. Write a program which performs addition, subtraction, multiplication, and division of roman numerals. Organize the program using SUBROUTINEs which split up the work as shown below. (You'll need SUBROUTINE ARAB from exercise 3.)

> **problem statement**
> Perform arithmetic on roman numerals.

First refinement:

> Get roman numerals and operator.
> Convert roman numerals to INTEGERs.
> Perform the operation on the INTEGERs.
> Convert the result to a roman numeral.
> Print resulting roman numeral.

Notice that the module
> Convert roman numerals to INTEGERs.

can be quickly refined to
> Use SUBROUTINE ARAB to convert
> first roman numeral.

> Use SUBROUTINE ARAB to convert
> second roman numeral.

While the program you wind up with will be fairly large and does a rather complex task, by using the top-down, successive refinement method, it is constructed quickly from small, manageable modules, many of which you already know how to write programs for.

Samples:

input	output
X + X	X+X=XX
X / L	X/L IS NOT REPRESENTABLE AS A ROMAN NUMERAL
IX * XI	IX*XI=XCIX
IV − XIII	IV−XIII IS NOT REPRESENTABLE AS A ROMAN NUMERAL

5. READ a value for *m* (the number of grades for each student). READ in *m* grades for each student, compute each student's average, and store the average grades in a one-dimensional array. Arrange the array of average grades in descending order, and write out the ordered array. Finally, calculate and PRINT (with appropriate labeling) the number of average scores which fall in each of the percentile groups 1 to 10, 11 to 20,..., 91 to 100.

6. Compare the sorting method of Section 11.2 with the **bubble sort** (described below) by generating 1,000 random numbers, sorting them each way, and counting how many times each routine compares pairs of numbers.

    The bubble sort works like this: Go through the array element by element, comparing the current element with the next and reversing their order if the first is larger than the second. Keep doing this until you have gone completely through the array. Repeat until you complete one entire pass with no reversals. At that point you're finished—the array is in order.

    PRINT the original numbers, the sorted numbers, and the number of comparisons made by the two different sorting methods. Each sorting method should be expressed as a SUBROUTINE.

7. Each of the following data lines has three pieces of information: the name of a football player, his number, and his weight. Write a program to read and print the arrays in four different orders: <u>first</u>, in the original order; <u>second</u>, in alphabetical order using the players' last names; <u>third</u>, in order of their numbers; and <u>fourth</u>, in order of their weights.

Data	#	WEIGHT
	1⁹	2	3
'SQUARE,JOHNNY'	27	170
'DUDA,PAUL'	31	200
'JULIANA,PAT'	9	180
'BLACKFORD,BOB'	5	183
'WILSON,MIKE'	25	197
'CASWELL,GERALD'	95	240
'DRISCOLL,MARK'	8	175
'BABICH,FRED'	80	220
'BATTLE,GREG'	46	195
'MONTGOMERY,CHARLES'	63	255
'ST.CLAIR,STEVE'	87	195
'STEWART,GUY'	18	170
'MOSS,JESSE'	19	190
'O'ROURKE,DAN'	22	190

8. Write a program which creates and keeps track of bank accounts for up to 20 people. For each person, keep track of (a) the person's name, (b) the account balance, and (c) the number of withdrawals or deposits. A deposit will correspond to a data line such as

```
'MARY MOONY'              +303.02
```

and a withdrawal will correspond to a card like

```
'CAPT. BEEFHEART'        -2.00
```

Each time your program reads a line, check to see if there is an account for that person, and if not, create a new entry. If there already is an account, add or subtract the deposit or withdrawal and add 1 to the number of transactions. After there is no more data to read, your program should print the information it has compiled about each account.

```
'FRANK FEEBLES'          +  100.00
'RALPH WILLIAMS'         +1901.74
'RALPH WILLIAMS'         +2794.25
'BETTY FURNACE'          +     3.01
'RALPH WILLIAMS'         +  470.00
'HARRY IGNAZ'            +    25.00
'FRANK FEEBLES'          -    35.00
'JESS UNRUH'             +    11.00
'HAROLD STASSEN          +  342.00
'RALPH WILLIAMS'         -  400.00
'JESS UNRUH'             -5243.00
'MINNEY MOOS'            +    35.75
'RALPH WILLIAMS'         +7500.00
'WAYNE ASPINALL'         -      .06
'BETTY FURNACE'          +     3.01
```

Hint:
Use several one-dimensional arrays to keep track of the accounts so that after the first three lines have been read, the arrays look like the following:

	NAME	BAL	TRANS
1	'FRANK FEEBLES'	100.00	1
2	'RALPH WILLIAMS'	4695.99	2
3			
4			

Program Design Problems

9. You are a programmer for a progressive college town that has a great deal of bicycle thievery. The town council decides to require

bicycle registration by all bike owners so that there will be some chance of returning captured stolen bikes. Your job, should you decide to accept it, is to write a program which maintains and searches the data on bicycles. Your program must accept data lines of two different types:

new registrations

'NEW'	owner's name	brand of bicycle	serial number

sample:

'NEW'	'MILTON P. WAXLEY'	'SCHWINN'	'M34257Q'

(If the serial number is scratched off, leave it blank.)

found bicycles

'OLD'	brand of bicycle	serial number	dummy

Obviously, if a 'NEW' line comes in, you just add the information. If an 'OLD' line comes in, there are two different situations. First, if the serial number of the recovered bike is known, you search the data and, if such a bike has been registered, print the owner's name (for later notification). Second, if the serial number has been scratched off, print the names of everyone who owns that type of bike so they can be asked if the recovered bike is theirs. (Do not assume that the 'NEW' and 'OLD' lines have been separated.)

10. Suppose you own a travel service and your policy is to book your customers with a direct flight if possible. You have a list of the direct flights for which you may schedule passengers. That is, each line contains a departure point and time, an arrival point and time, and the name of an airline, e.g.,

flight description line:

`'KANSAS CITY' '10:00AM' 'DENVER' '11:00AM' 'TWA'`

You have a second list which contains the customer's name, point of departure, and destination, e.g.,

customer request line:

`'CLIFFORD TREASE' 'CHICAGO' 'SAN FRANCISCO'`

You are to write a program which stores the flight description in memory and then tries to find a direct flight to fill each customer request. If the program finds a direct flight, it should print out the customer's name, departure point and time, arrival point and time, and airline. Otherwise, it should print the customer's name and a message to the effect that there is no direct flight available for the customer between the requested departure and arrival points.

Your program may *not* assume that the data has been counted, so you will need some sort of termination line at the end of the two lists so that it can test to see when it has stored all the flight descriptions and when it has taken care of all the customers. You may assume that there are no more than 100 flight descriptions, but your program should not depend *in any way* upon the number of customers.

11. Write a program to make airline reservations. Assume that the airline you work for has seven flights with the number of seats given in the table below.

flight	seats available
101A	147
237	83
208	6
505	21
110	122
650	62
810B	3

Your program should reserve seats on these flights on a first-come, first-served basis. Each data line will contain a customer's name (up to 40 characters) and the desired flight number (4 characters). The termination line will contain the phrase NO MORE CUSTOMERS in place of the name. Make no assumptions about the number of customers.

For each request, print the name of the customer and a message indicating whether or not the reservation is confirmed.

12. Write a program to solve a more general version of problem 11. The program should first READ the flight information data. Each flight description will be on a separate line with the flight number (4 characters) followed by the number of seats available (INTEGER). The termination line for the flight descriptions will be

'++++'

The rest of the data will be customer requests, as in problem 11. As before, make no assumptions about the number of customers, but assume that the airline has no more the 100 flights.

The advantage of this version is that the airline can still use the program if it adds or deletes flights or changes to planes of different capacities.

13. For people who really like factorials: Write a program that can compute $n! = n*(n - 1) * (n - 2)* \ldots *2*1$ for values of n that are so large that the answer can't fit in a single INTEGER memory cell.

$$25! = 15{,}511{,}210{,}043{,}330{,}985{,}984{,}000{,}000$$

One way to do this is to use an array to store the answer (and partial results) using one memory cell in the array per digit. Thus, $12! = 479{,}001{,}600$ would be stored like this:

	9	8	7	6	5	4	3	2	1
...	4	7	9	0	0	1	6	0	0

Now to find 13!, multiply each memory cell by 13 (taking care to move carries) to get

	11	10	9	8	7	6	5	4	3	2	1
...		6	2	2	7	0	2	0	8	0	0

14. Use the idea for storing huge numbers (problem 16) to print out a table of powers of 2 from 2^0 to 2^{160}.

15. Write a program to list all the prime numbers between 1 and 1000. To compute these numbers, use the algorithm below, which is known as **Eratosthenes' sieve.**

   a. Make a list of all the consecutive integers you are interested in, starting from 2.

   b. Mark off all the multiples of 2 (they can't be primes).

   c. Find the next integer remaining in the list beyond the one whose multiples you just marked off, and mark off *its* multiples (they can't be primes).

   d. Repeat step c unless the integer whose multiple you just marked off is the square root of the largest integer in the list, that is, the square root without its fractional part. (This termination condition depends on the two factors in a product not both exceeding the square root of the product.

   One way to keep track of which numbers are still on the list is to initialize a logical array of 1000 elements to .TRUE. (for "on the list") and cross the number *n* off the list by changing the *n*th element of the array to .FALSE.

16. Compute all the prime numbers less than 59^2 (see problem 12.15 for an algorithm to use). Then plot the primes in the following way. Number a 59 × 59 grid of squares from the center out in a spiral. To figure the appropriate (I,J) subscript in the 59 × 59 array given a number *n*, use SUBROUTINE COORD below.

```
            SUBROUTINE COORD(N, I,J)
            INTEGER N, I,J
COMMENT:              THIS ROUTINE COMPUTES THE ARRAY SUBSCRIPT (I,J)
C                     CORRESPONDING TO THE NUMBER N IN THE SPIRAL
C                     NUMBERING OF THE LATTICE POINTS IN THE PLANE
            INTEGER SQRTN, R, CNR, RES, RESRES, QUAD, SR
            INTEGER RSGN(4), DSGN(4), ISIGN, OFFSET
            RSGN(1) = -1
            RSGN(2) = +1
            RSGN(3) = +1
            RSGN(4) = -1
            DSGN(1) = +1
            DSGN(2) = +1
            DSGN(3) = -1
            DSGN(4) = -1
C
```

(Continued on following page)

```
C                           ARRAY DIMENSIONS:  2*OFFSET-1 BY 2*OFFSET-1
            OFFSET = 30
C
C                           N=1 GOES IN CENTER
            IF (N .LE. 1) THEN
              I = OFFSET
              J = OFFSET
            ELSE
C                          FIND THE NUMBER 'R' SUCH THAT 'N' IS IN THE R-TH
C                          CONCENTRIC SQUARE ABOUT THE ORIGIN
              SQRTN = SQRTN - 1
              IF ((SQRTN - 1)**2 .EQ. N) THEN
                SQRTN = SQRTN - 1
              ENDIF
              R = SQRTN/2
C                          FIND THE SPIRAL NUMBER OF THE LOWER LEFT
C                          HAND CORNER OF THE R-TH CONCENTRIC SQUARE
              CNR = (2*R - 1)**2 + 1
C                          FIND THE NUMBER OF STEPS, COUNTING
C                          COUNTERCLOCKWISE ALONG THE CONCENTRIC SQUARE
C                          FROM THE LOWER LEFT HAND CORNER
              RES = N - CNR
C                          DETERMINE EDGE NUMBER OF SQUARE (QUAD) AND
C                          DIRECTION FROM ORIGIN (SIGNED RADIUS)
              QUAD = RES/(2*R)
              SR = ISIGN(R,RSGN(QUAD + 1))
C                          FIND SIGNED DISTANCE ALONG EDGE (RESRES)
              RESRES = DSGN(QUAD + 1)*(MOD(RES,2*R) - R)
C                          COMPUTE COORDINATE
              IF (MOD(QUAD,2) .NE. 0) THEN
                I = SR + OFFSET
                J = RESRES + OFFSET
              ELSE
                I = RESRES + OFFSET
                J = SR + OFFSET
              ENDIF
            ENDIF
            END
```

22	21	20	19	18
23	8	7	6	17
24	9	1	5	16
25	2	3	4	15
10	11	12	13	14

etc.

17. If you are familiar with vectors, write a program to convert a given vector to a unit vector in the same direction. Assume each line contains the dimension (i.e., number of components) of the vector (INTEGER) followed by the components of the vector (REALs). You may assume the dimension is less than 100. The termination line will contain the vector 0.0 of dimension 1. (Don't try to convert it to a unit vector!

The unit vector in the same direction as $(x_1, x_2, \ldots, x_n)$ is $(u_1, u_2, \ldots, u_n)$, where

$$u_k = x_k/r \text{ and } r = \sqrt{(x_1^2 + x_2^2 + \ldots + x_n^2)}$$

Print the vector and the corresponding unit vector.

18. Write a program to compute the cosine of the angle between two given vectors. Assume that each data line will contain the dimension of the two vectors involved (INTEGER), followed by the components of the one and then the components of the other. Assume the dimension is less than 100. The termination line will contain 1,0.0, 0.0. If $(u_1, \ldots, u_n)$ are $(v_1, \ldots, v_n)$ are the unit vectors in the same direction as the given vectors x and y, respectively, then the cosine of the angle between the two given vectors is $u_1 v_1 + u_2 v_2 + \ldots + u_n v_n$. A formula in problem 17 shows the relation between a given vector and the corresponding unit vector.

19. Write a program to do the matching for a computer dating service. The dating service's questionnaires have statements, and the applicant indicates his or her degree of agreement with each statement on a scale of one to five. Thus, each data line will contain the applicant's name (up to 28 characters), sex (M or F), and responses to the questionnaire (20 INTEGERs). The last data line will contain the phrase NO MORE APPLICANTS. You may assume there are no more than 100 applicants.

    Match each person with the two most compatible people of the opposite sex. As a measure of compatibility, use the cosine of the angle between their two response vectors; the larger the cosine, the more compatible the couple (see problem 18 for a way to compute the cosine). Your program's output should be a list of the applicants along with the names of their two guaranteed dates, e.g.,

```
JOHN DOE            DATES MARY SLATE
                    AND ALICE HILL

JANE FLUG           DATES ROGER WHIMSBY
                    AND JOE THORNTOR
```

20. Problem 19 has a feature which wouldn't be acceptable to a real computer dating service. If one person is compatible with many others, he or she will receive the names of two dates, but may be listed as a good date on *many* people's lists. The whole thing could get out of balance with almost everybody trying to date a few people. Do problem 19 so that no one person is listed for more than six other people. Print *all* the dates a person is involved in, not just the two optimal matches as before. Now another problem arises. You may have to refund some participants' money because in some cases there may not be enough suitable matches to go around. Print a polite apology to those who come up short.

Problems 21 through 24 assume that your computer system has a built-in function which produces a random REAL number between 0.0 and ..0 each time you call it. On many systems, the built-in function RANF serves this purpose. If your system doesn't provide RANF, use the one in Appendix B.

21. Write a program which produces an array of shuffled cards, represented as the INTEGERs 1, 2,..., 52. If you establish an appropriate correspondence between INTEGERs and cards, you can compute the card's suit and denomination with expressions like (Card − 1)/13 and MOD(CARD, 13).

    Write the shuffling algorithm as a SUBROUTINE, and use it to shuffle a deck of cards. PRINT the shuffled deck one card at a time. If the jack of any suit comes up, print SLAP on the same line.

```
KING OF CLUBS
TEN OF HEARTS
SEVEN OF HEARTS
FOUR OF SPADES
JACK OF CLUBS—SLAP
NINE OF SPADES
QUEEN OF SPADES
   •
   •
   •
```

Plan

For each DECK(i) ────────
    DECK(i) = i

For N=52, 51,..., 3, 2 ────────

Let R be a random number between 1 and N.
Swap the Rth and the Nth values in DECK( ).

Shuffle Algorithm

22. Design and write a program which deals a random bridge hand and displays it in the usual bridge notation.

NORTH
S: K J 3
H:
D: A Q 7 4
C: K Q 10 9 4 2

WEST
S: A 5 4
H: 8 7 4 3 2
D: K 9 6
C: A 7

EAST
S: Q 10 7 6
H: 10 5
D: J 10 5 3 2
C: 6 3

SOUTH
S: 9 8 2
H: A K Q J 9 6
D: 8
C: J 8 5

Use SUBROUTINE SHUFFLE from problem 12 to shuffle the deck.

23. Write an INTEGER FUNCTION GOREN which takes a bridge hand as an argument (i.e., an array of 13 INTEGERs that represent cards, as in problems 21 and 22 above) and returns the Goren point value of the hand.

24. Suppose you are running a pizza parlor and you want to figure out how many waitresses/waiters you should hire. If you have too few,

then customers will have to wait a long time to be served and you'll lose business, but if you have too many, you'll lose money paying them. You decide to simulate the process. You estimate that every minute the odds are 50/50 that a new customer will come in and that it takes three minutes of a waitresses's time to serve each customer. Your program should simulate the arrival of 1,000 customers and should PRINT the total amount of time customers spend waiting and the amount of time waitresses/waiters spend waiting. Try your program with one, two, and three waitresses/waiters to see how many it would be best to have. Here are some hints about how you could write the program:

a. Have one main loop which corresponds to what happens each successive minute.

b. Have memory cells which keep track of the following things:

How many customers are waiting: CWAIT
How many waitresses/waiters are idle: WWAIT
How many waitresses/waiters have just started waiting on a customer: WWAIT0
How many waiters/waitresses have been waiting on a customer for one minute: WWAIT1
How many waiters/waitresses have been waiting on a customer for two minutes: WWAIT2
How much (total) time customers have spent waiting: CTIME
How much (total) time waitresses/waiters have spent idle: WTIME

Initialize all variables.

Plan

If there's a new customer this minute
then _____
> | Add 1 to CWAIT.

Update waitress state, i.e.
WWAIT = WWAIT2
WWAIT2 = WWAIT1
  etc.

If there are any customers waiting
then _____
> Wait on as many as possible,
>   i.e., WWAIT0 = minimum of customers
>   waiting and idle waitressess.
> CWAIT = CWAIT − #waited on.

Let CTIME = CTIME + CWAIT
Let WTIME = WTIME + WWAIT

_____ Repeat if not closing time

Print CTIME, WTIME.

25. We got this problem from Professor Wm. M. McKeeman. We'll use a square two-dimensional array of INTEGER memory cells to represent a patch of skin. Each element in the array is *sick, immune,* or *healthy.* To operate, the program needs three numbers. The first, an INTEGER which we'll call SICK, tells how many time steps a skin spot remains sick once it has been infected. The second, an INTEGER called IMMUNE, tells how many time steps a skin spot remains immune after it is through being sick. The third, a REAL named RATE, tells the odds (probability) that a sick spot will infect a neighboring healthy spot during the current time step.

    To represent a healthy spot of skin, store a 0 in the corresponding array location. To start things off, make the whole patch of skin healthy except for the spot in the very center. Store a 1 in the location representing a skin spot when that spot becomes sick. For each time step, sweep through the entire array.

    > **ringworm:** a contagious disease caused by a fungus. Help end the heartbreak of ringworm. Do problem 25.

    In the first sweep through the array, each healthy spot (zero value) stays healthy, and each sick or immune spot (nonzero value) gets updated to reflect the passage of time. Update a sick or immune cell by adding 1 to its current value. If its new value goes beyond the sick/immune cycle (that is, if the new value is greater than SICK + IMMUNE, then set it back to the healthy state, zero).

    After the first sweep through the array, make a second sweep to handle newly infected cells. Stop at each sick cell, and check each neighbor separately using the random number generator. If the number generated is less than RATE, then the healthy neighbor should be set to the sick state (1).

    You will need an auxiliary array so that the states of affairs at time steps t and $t + 1$ don't get confused. You can convert INTEGERs into characters to make the output nice. We suggest a blank for healthy spots, an asterisk for sick spots, and a period for spots in the immune state.

    By trying different values of the three numbers SICK, IMMUNE, and RATE, you can observe a variety of "diseases"—ringworm, blotches, measles, infestations that die out (cure themselves), and infestations that continue reinfecting recovered skin. *Note:* The computation time increases rapidly with the size of the array of cells. Write the program so that you can easily change the size of the array in case you have a time limit. Start with a 20 × 20 patch of skin.

13 FILES

13.1   FILES, RECORDS, AND I/O DEVICES

There are three parts of the Fortran computer—**processor, memory,** and **I/O devices.** So far, we have dealt with just two sorts of I/O devices—a card reader or keyboard for input to the computer and a printer or screen for receiving output from it. For programs which don't tax the computer's resources very much, having just those two I/O devices is fine. In Section 12.2 we wrote a program to produce a cross-reference directory of phone book listings. Except for very small towns and very large computers, that program will not be practical because there will not be enough room in memory to store all the names and phone numbers at once. The program uses 25 characters for each name and 8 for each phone number, so a directory for a town of 100,000 people would consume 3.3 million characters just for the data. However, there are computers all over the world with nowhere near that memory capacity doing problems like the cross-reference dictionary every day. The way it's done is by breaking the problem into chunks and using special I/O devices to store the partial results. Only a small part of the data is brought into memory at a time. For this we need an I/O device which is both machine readable and machine writable, one capable of serving as both an input device and an output device.

Most computer systems have at least one such I/O device. There are many possibilities: magnetic tape, disk, cassette tape, floppy disk, magnetic drum, magnetic bubble devices, paper tape units, etc. None of these devices provides a suitable medium for communication between people and computers—they are used to store information in computer-readable form. They can be thought of as extensions of the computer's memory. Typically, such storage devices provide many times the information storage capacity of the computer's main memory at a fraction of the cost. Of course, there are disadvantages—it may take a thousand or even a million times as long for the computer to retrieve a data value from an I/O device as it would take to fetch a value from main memory. Some of these I/O devices provide an additional benefit—they provide a convenient, inexpensive means of transferring large amounts of data from one computer installation to another.

From the Fortran point of view, all information for input or output is organized in files. A **file** (strictly speaking, an **external file**) is a collection of values written on some I/O medium—paper, cards, magnetic tape, disk, etc. Files reside on I/O devices and may be **connected** for processing by a Fortran program. The programs we've written have dealt with only two files. One of them, the **input file,** has been processed with READ statements; the other, the **output file,** has been processed with PRINT statements.

All files are made up of **records,** which are the smallest pieces of information that can be processed by a single Fortran I/O statement. In the input file, each card or line is a record, and each READ statement reads at least one card or line. In the printed output file, each line is a record, and each PRINT statement prints at least one line. These two I/O statements automatically refer to special files. To deal with other files, we need new I/O statements, and because the number of different files a program may process is unpredictable, we can't expect to have special I/O statements for each different file. We need general-purpose I/O statements which designate the file to be used.

To use an I/O device from within a Fortran program, you need to specify a few things. First, your program must inform the computer system which I/O device (and which file on that device) it wants to use. All Fortran programs are assumed to need an input file and an output file, so those are provided automatically. In other cases, you gain access to a file by associating an **external file name** with a **unit number.** The first step in doing that is to figure out the appropriate **external file name.** Different computer systems provide different ways of giving names to files—see your friendly local expert. In some cases, file names have several parts, and you must choose each part appropriately. For example, the file name

'MT2:RAT.DAT'

refers to a file named 'RAT' (we chose that to remind us of what was on the file), of type 'DAT' (DATa), on Magnetic Tape drive number 2. In other cases, the file name is simpler, and the specification of which I/O device the file is on is specified by special job control statements which appear before your actual Fortran program. In still other cases (for example, if the computer system has only one I/O device used for files) the computer system itself figures out what device the file will be on. In this chapter, we'll assume that any string of characters is a legal file name, but the rules on your system will be more restrictive.

A **unit number** is an INTEGER value (greater than or equal to zero). After your program gains access to a file (i.e., after the external file name has been associated with a unit number), all further references to the file are made by giving the unit number. The association between the external file name and a unit number can be made in several ways, depending again on your specific computer system. In this chapter, we'll make the association by using an OPEN statement. In other cases, the association will be made by using special job control statements before your Fortran program. In still other cases the association is automatic (for example, some computer systems automatically associate a card punch file with unit number 7).

The next piece of information you must specify is the **access method** you will use. Some devices (like paper tape readers and punches, card readers and punches, and most magnetic tape drives) store and retrieve values **sequentially,** that is, one after the other. If your program has stored a value at the front of a tape, and you need to retrieve it, the tape machine can't just jump back to the spot you want; typically, the tape must be rewound. Other devices (like disks, drums, and magnetic bubble devices) provide for **direct access.** That is, your program can store and retrieve information at any location in any order.

There is still more information to be specified. The data stored in a file may be **formatted** or **unformatted.** All of the I/O operations we have done so far have been **formatted;** that is, each value has been treated in a special way, depending on its type (INTEGER, REAL, LOGICAL, CHARACTER$*(n)$). In some cases, when your program is using a file to extend the computer's memory to store temporary values, your program may run faster if you allow the computer system to choose the way the temporary values are stored. This is done by selecting the **unformatted** option and not specifying any FORMAT for the data. Since this results in a storage format that is peculiar to your brand of computer, it is not a suitable method for producing a file you intend to send to someone else to use on their system.

The next three sections in this chapter provide details of using **sequential files, direct-access files,** and **unformatted files**. In all cases, we need a method to set up access to a file, that is, to connect it. This is usually done with an OPEN statement. In all cases, we need a method to terminate our program's use of a file. This can be done with a CLOSE statement. And in all cases, we need means of getting values transmitted from a particular record in a file into memory cells and vice versa. These operations are done with generalized READ and WRITE statements.

Here we'll describe those parts of the OPEN, CLOSE, READ, and WRITE statements that are common to all the cases.

An OPEN statement specifies the unit number to be associated with the file, the **name** of the file, and various properties of the file. In addition, the OPEN statement specifies the file's **status**.

The STATUS of a file may be NEW, OLD, SCRATCH, or UNKNOWN. A NEW file is one which has not yet been created—in other words, a file for information you intend to produce with the current program. An OLD file is one which already exists and will be processed by the current program. A SCRATCH file is one which will be created and used *only* by the current Fortran program. A SCRATCH file will be wiped out at the end of the program. When a file's status is specified as UNKNOWN, the processor will determine the STATUS property automatically using its own methods.

OPEN Statement

form
OPEN (*speclist*)
speclist is a list of specifiers separated by commas.
Possible specifiers are listed below.

UNIT = *u*   required
             u is the unit number.
FILE = *f*   optional
             f is a CHARACTER expression giving the file name.
ACCESS = *a*   optional
             a is a CHARACTER expression whose value is either SEQUENTIAL or DIRECT. If omitted, SEQUENTIAL is assumed.
FORM = *fm*   optional
             fm is a CHARACTER expression whose value is either FORMATTED or UNFORMATTED.
RECL = *len*   required if ACCESS = 'DIRECT' is specified; not allowed if ACCESS = 'SEQUENTIAL'.
             len is an INTEGER expression whose value is greater than zero, indicating the record length.
STATUS = *s*   optional
             s is a CHARACTER expression with the value NEW, OLD, SCRATCH, or UNKNOWN. If omitted, UNKNOWN is assumed.

restrictions
Allowable values for *u* and *f* are set by your local computer system.
If STATUS = 'SCRATCH', then no FILE name may be given.

meaning
Associate the specified file with unit *u*. From now on, in any part of the program, the file may be referenced by giving the unit number *u*.

examples

```
 OPEN(UNIT = 9, FILE = 'RAT.DATA', STATUS = 'OLD')
 OPEN(UNIT = 0, FILE = 'FAMILY', ACCESS = 'SEQUENTIAL',
+     FORM = 'FORMATTED', STATUS = 'NEW')
 OPEN(UNIT = 2, FILE = 'SYSSTATS', ACCESS = 'DIRECT',
+     FORM = 'FORMATTED', RECL = 20*4, STATUS = 'OLD'
```

Once a file has been connected to a unit number, it can be processed with READ and WRITE statements which refer to that number. These I/O statements work exactly like the READ and PRINT statements you are accustomed to except that the files they deal with are different. In addition, the statement syntax is modified to accommodate the unit specifier and other control information.

There may seem to be a bewildering array of options in the READ and WRITE statements. However, once you know the access method you will be using (SEQUENTIAL or DIRECT) and whether you will use the FORMATTED or the UNFORMATTED technique, the forms you may use are fixed. If the file is SEQUENTIAL, you must not include the REC = rn specifier. If it is DIRECT access, you must. If the file is UNFORMATTED, you must not include the FMT = s specifier. If it is FORMATTED, you must include it.

After a file has been processed, whether it has been newly created or is an old file, it should be closed by the program. This is done with a CLOSE statement of the form

CLOSE (UNIT = u)

where u has the usual meaning. (However, any connected files which aren't explicitly closed in the program will be automatically closed when the program terminates.) Files opened with a NEW or OLD status will be available for reconnection and processing after they are closed, but SCRATCH files are deleted from the system automatically when they are closed. NEW or OLD files can be **deleted** (wiped out) by closing them with a statement of the form.

CLOSE (UNIT = u, STATUS = 'DELETE')

After a file has been closed, the unit number which was associated

CLOSE Statement

---

form
CLOSE(UNIT = u, STATUS = c)
u is a unit number
c is a CHARACTER expression whose value is KEEP or DELETE

meaning
Disconnect the file which is currently connected to unit u. If c is 'DELETE', wipe the file out. If c is 'KEEP', then keep the information in the file, so it can be accessed later. If the file currently connected to u was OPENed as a SCRATCH file, the c = 'KEEP' option is not allowed.
The STATUS = c part is optional. If not present, the statement has the same effect as if c is 'KEEP' unless the file is a SCRATCH file.

examples
```
CLOSE( UNIT = 1)
CLOSE(UNIT = 3, STATUS = 'DELETE' )
```

General Purpose READ/WRITE

form

READ(UNIT = *u,controllist*) *list*

WRITE(UNIT = *u,controllist*) *list*

u is an INTEGER expression designating a connected file or

u is an asterisk (which automatically designates the system input or output file).

controllist is a list of control specifiers separated by commas.

Some of the legal control specifiers are given below:

FMT = *s*   required if the file connected to unit *u* is FORMATTED.

may not appear if the file is UNFORMATTED.

s is the statement label of a FORMAT statement.

REC = *rn*   required if the file is DIRECT.

may not appear if the file is SEQUENTIAL.

rn is an INTEGER expression whose value is greater than zero, indicating the number of the record to be processed. (See Section 13.3. for details.)

END = *e*   optional in a READ if the file is SEQUENTIAL.

may not appear if REC = *rn* option appears.

e is the statement label of an executable statement.

list is an input list (for READ) or an output list (for WRITE), and is optional.

meaning

READ: bring information from the file connected to *u* into the variables in *list*. If the file is FORMATTED, use the FORMAT *s* in making the translation from external to internal form. If the file is the DIRECT access type, take the information from record number *rn;* otherwise take the information from the next record on the file. The END = *e* part is optional. If present, it means that control is to be transferred to statement *e* if the READ statement encounters the end of the file.

WRITE: send information from the elements of *list* to the file connected to *u*. If the file is FORMATTED, use the FMT = *s* statement to find the FORMAT statement to be used. If the file is the DIRECT-access type, send the information to record number *rn;* otherwise put the information into the next record on the file.

examples

```
READ (UNIT=9, FMT=1000) A, B, C
READ (UNIT=0, FMT=2000, END=120) (Y(K), K=1,100)
READ (UNIT=2, FMT=3000, REC=N+1) MESS, COUNT
WRITE (UNIT=9, FMT=1000) A, B, C
WRITE (UNIT=NUMB, FMT=2500) 'LANGSFORD, RAYMOND G.'
WRITE (UNIT=2, FMT=3300, REC=24) 'OUT OF RANGE', 33
WRITE (UNIT=SC) TEMP1
```

with it may be used in another OPEN statement for connecting a different file. Furthermore, most computer systems charge for "connect-time" on files, and you can save money by disconnecting files your program no longer needs. Finally, there may be a limit on the number of files, which may be simultaneously connected to your program. If so, you will have to CLOSE a file before you can connect another one if your program is manipulating too many files.

13.1 EXERCISES

1. Which properties do the input and output files you normally use have?
   a. Formatted, direct access
   b. Unformatted, direct access
   c. Formatted, sequential access
   d. Unformatted, sequential access

2. What I/O devices are available on your system which can be used for storage of information in machine readable form?

13.2 SEQUENTIAL FORMATTED FILES

While fads in computer technology have come, gone, and been reborn in slightly different forms, tape drives have been around through it all. They are hardly dying out—the first I/O device for machine readable storage that caught on for home/personal computers was the cassette tape recorder. Sequential access is the most natural method for storing files on tape: you WRITE or READ one record after another until you come to the end of the file. Except with more sophisticated tape drives, the only way to re-access a given record is to rewind the tape, then "play" it, record by record, until you come to the one you want. Of course, tape isn't the only medium with which we can use sequential formatted files but it's the most common.

To set up access to a sequential formatted file, we use an OPEN statement, as with other kinds of files. However, since sequential formatted files are so common, if you don't include the ACCESS and FORM specifiers, Fortran will assume that you want a sequential formatted file.

With sequential files the concept of the **end of file** is an important one, and there is a special statement which places a special end-of-file record on the file. Your programs should place this record at the end of every sequential file. The ENDFILE statement has this form

ENDFILE(UNIT = u)

The special end-of-file record is detected when read, and the END = *e* specifier in the generalized READ statement can be used to select some action when the end of a file has been reached.

A sequential file can be extended by READing to the end, backspacing, then WRITEing additional records (thus overwriting the end-of-file record) and finally putting in a new end-of-file record. Backspacing is performed by the statement BACKSPACE(UNIT = *u*), which positions the file back one record.

If your program needs to go through a sequential file several times, it can start at the beginning again by carrying out a REWIND statement. The REWIND statement has the form

REWIND (UNIT = *u*)

Here's a simple example of using a sequential formatted file.

Suppose you have been handed several boxes of data cards which contain weather statistics collected over the past year by forest rangers in Rocky Mountain National Park. Each card contains the date, amount of precipitation (in inches), type of precipitation (rain, snow, or hail), average wind speed (mph), and level of sunshine (sunny, partly sunny, partly cloudy, or cloudy). You are supposed to summarize these statistics in terms of a number of measured parameters, including autocorrelation, covariance, and several others you've never heard of.

Figure 13.2.1 Data Card Layout Forms for Weather Statistics

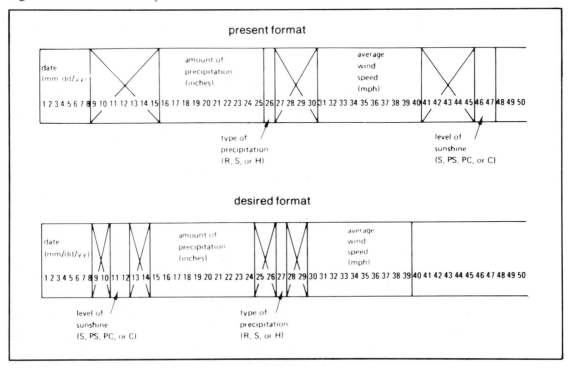

Figure 13.2.2 Reformatting the Weather Statistics

```
Open file for reformatted data.

    ┌─────────────────────────────────────────────┐
    │  Read card                                   │
    │  Exit if no more cards                       │
    │  Write reformatted record.                   │
    └─────────────────────────────────────── Repeat
Write endfile record.
Close reformatted data file.
```

Fortran translation

```
COMMENT:                   TRANSFORM THE DATA
          CHARACTER*(10) PRECIP, WIND
          CHARACTER*(8) DATE
          CHARACTER*(2) SLEVEL
          CHARACTER*(1) PTYPE
          OPEN(UNIT = 1, FILE = 'WEATHER STATISTICS',
     +         FORM = 'FORMATTED',ACCESS = 'SEQUENTIAL',STATUS = 'NEW')
  100     READ(UNIT=*, FMT = 1000, END = 200) DATE, PRECIP, PTYPE,
     +                                   WIND, SLEVEL
  1000      FORMAT(A, T16, A, A, T31, A, T46, A)
            WRITE(UNIT=1, FMT= 1010) DATE,SLEVEL,PRECIP,PTYPE,WIND
  1010      FORMAT(5(A, TR2))
            GO TO 100
  200     ENDFILE(UNIT = 1)
          CLOSE(UNIT = 1)
          END
```

Fortunately, you have found a program which performs the desired statistical analyses. It was written last year as part of a similar project. Unfortunately, last year's forest rangers recorded the data in a different way, and this year's data is arranged on the cards in an incompatible format. Either the program will have to be changed, or the new data will have to be reformatted to be compatible with the program. We choose the reformatting alternative.

As you can see in Figure 13.2.1, the problem is simply a matter of rearranging the data. The program is detailed in Figure 13.2.2.

The program begins by OPENing the file. We specified STATUS = 'NEW' because our program is going to create a new file, one which we want the computer system to keep for later use (STATUS = 'SCRATCH' would create a new file, but wipe it out at the end of our program). Notice that we've used a generalized READ statement to READ the cards from the card reader, and that the END = e option will transfer control to statement 200 after the last card is read (i.e., when we reach the end of file of the card reader file). The generalized WRITE statement puts the five CHARACTER values on the next record of our new file each time it is carried out, according to FORMAT 1010.

Carriage Control?

> Notice that no carriage control characters are included in the statements which WRITE to the file. Carriage control characters are used only by the printer—they are not a necessary part of the output process. If we had included a carriage control character, it would be written on the file along with the other data.

After the last card has been read and the last record written by the WRITE, our program tries to READ another card. Since the card reader is at the end of the file of data cards, control passes to statement 200, where the end-of-file record is put on the file. If at this point in the program we had wished to READ, say, the fifth record in the file we had just created, we could do so by adding statements like these.

```
      REWIND(UNIT = 1)
      DO 300 COUNT = 1,5
         READ(UNIT = 1, FMT = 1010)
    +                  DATE, SLEVEL, PRECIP, PTYPE, WIND
300      CONTINUE
```

Notice that to get the fifth record, we had to READ the first four.

13.2 EXERCISES

1. Which of these statements would be appropriate if we intend to connect a sequential formatted file which already exists, is named 'SYSTEM STATS', and is on a tape which will be mounted on a tape drive which the computer system calls unit 3?

   ```
   a.  READ(UNIT = 3, FMT = 'SYSTEM STATS')
   b.  OPEN(UNIT = 3, FILE = 'SYSTEM STATS', STATUS = 'OLD',
       +                 FORM = 'FORMATTED', ACCESS = 'SEQUENTIAL')
   c.  OPEN(UNIT = 3, FILE = 'SYSTEM STATS', FORM = 'FORMATTED',
       +                 ACCESS = 'SEQUENTIAL', STATUS = 'SCRATCH')
   d.  OPEN(UNIT = 'SYSTEM STATS', STATUS = 'NEW')
   ```

2. Which of these statements would be appropriate if we intended to read the next record from a file which was connected with this OPEN statement?

   ```
         OPEN(UNIT = 1, FILE = 'RAT.DAT', STATUS = 'OLD',
       +                 FORM = 'FORMATTED', ACCESS = 'SEQUENTIAL')
   a.  READ(UNIT = 1, FMT = 1000) NEXT
   b.  READ(UNIT = 'RAT.DAT', FMT = 1000) NEXT
   c.  OPEN(UNIT = 1, FILE = 'RAT.DAT', STATUS = 'READ')
   d.  READ(UNIT = 1, FMT = 1000)
   ```

3. Which of these statements would be appropriate if we intended to disconnect a file which was OPENed like this

   ```
   OPEN(UNIT = 1, FILE = 'RAT.DAT', STATUS = 'OLD')
   ```

   with the intention of reconnecting the file for further use at a later date?

```
a. CLOSE(UNIT = 'RAT.DAT', STATUS = 'DELETE')
b. CLOSE(UNIT = 1, STATUS = 'DELETE')
c. CLOSE(UNIT = 1, STATUS = 'KEEP')
d. CLOSE(UNIT     = 1)
```

13.3 DIRECT-ACCESS FILES

Some I/O devices (for instance, disks, magnetic bubble devices, and charge-coupled devices) make it possible to access any one record in a file in about the same length of time as any other record. When this is true, there's no need to go through the laborious rewinding and record-skipping process required to find a particular record on a sequential file—your program can get at the record it wants directly. If your problem requires the file to be manipulated in some complex way, with records being switched around, your program will be easier to write if you can use a DIRECT-access file.

When a file has been OPENed for DIRECT access, its records are accessed by **record number** rather than in sequential order. We can think of the file as an array of records, the record numbers corresponding to array subscripts.

The OPEN statement for a DIRECT-access file must specify ACCESS = 'DIRECT' and must give the desired record length. For example,

```
OPEN(UNIT=4,FILE='BIRD.DOC', STATUS='OLD', FORM='FORMATTED',
+     ACCESS ='DIRECT', RECL = 80)
```

opens an existing file named BIRD.DOC for DIRECT access. All READs and WRITEs on the file will use FORMATs.

The record length for formatted files is always measured in characters, so the RECL = 80 specifier sets the record length at 80 characters. Your program may fill a record with values of any data type, just as long as no more than 80 characters are required. On some computer systems, extra characters are introduced between values and at the end of each record (so that files created by Fortran programs can be manipulated by text editors and other systems programs). In such cases, you will have to increase the record length to provide extra room. In any case you can tell how many characters *you* are putting in a record directly from the FORMAT. If you use an I10 format descriptor to WRITE an INTEGER value, then that will always write 10 characters (some of which will be blanks if the value is less than 10 digits long).

When your program WRITEs to or READs from a FORMATTED DIRECT-access file, you must always use a FORMAT, and you must always indicate the record number, using the REC = *rn* specifier in the READ or WRITE. You may WRITE records in any order, and you may READ in any order, as long as each record you READ has been written at some time since the file was originally created. If we think of a DIRECT-access file as an array of records, with the record number being analogous to an array subscript, then we can think of a WRITE as analogous to the left part of an assignment statement, since it stores values into a specific record.

To illustrate the use of FORMATTED DIRECT-access files, we'll redo parts of the cross-reference directory program from Section 12.2. Be sure to refer to Section 12.2 as you look over our new version. Instead of using the arrays NAME( ) and PHONE( ) to store the data, we'll place the values in a DIRECT-access file. Since once a file has been OPENed, any program unit can refer to it, we have no need for subroutine arguments to pass in the data. To indicate to the subprograms which values (name or phone number) are the sort keys, we'll pass in a CHARACTER value of 'NAME' or 'PHONE' to SUBROUTINE SORT. Here's the new version of the main program.

```
COMMENT:                    PROGRAM FOR CROSS REFERENCE DIRECTORY
            INTEGER NUMLST
            OPEN(UNIT=1, FILE='DIRECTORY', FORM='FORMATTED',
     +      ACCESS='DIRECT', RECL=36, STATUS='SCRATCH')
            CALL INPUT(NUMLST)
            CALL SORT('NAME', NUMLST)
            CALL OUTPUT('ALPHABETICAL', NUMLST)
            CALL SORT('PHONE', NUMLST)
            CALL OUTPUT('NUMERICAL', NUMLST)
            CLOSE(UNIT=1)
            END
```

SUBROUTINE INPUT will READ data consisting of names and phone numbers, just as before. Instead of storing the values in arrays, however, it will WRITE them as successive records on the file we OPENed in the main program.

```
            SUBROUTINE INPUT(NUMLST)
            INTEGER NUMLST
            INTEGER NAMLEN, PHLEN
            PARAMETER(NAMLEN = 25, PHLEN = 8)
            CHARACTER*(NAMLEN) NAME, ENDDAT
            PARAMETER(ENDDAT = 'END OF DATA')
            CHARACTER*(PHLEN) PHONE
            INTEGER RECORD
            RECORD = 1
100         READ *, NAME, PHONE
            IF (NAME .EQ. ENDDAT) GO TO 110
                WRITE(UNIT=1, FMT=1000, REC=RECORD) NAME, PHONE
1000            FORMAT(A, A)
                RECORD = RECORD + 1
                GO TO 100
110         NUMLST = RECORD
            END
```

SUBROUTINE SORT will follow the same algorithm as before, but some of the details are changed. Now the FUNCTION called LOCBIG will return the record number of the record with the largest value, and SWITCH will be told which records to interchange. Since a given record stores *both* a name *and* a phone number, we'll need only one call to SWITCH.

```
            SUBROUTINE SORT(WHICH, NUMLST)
            CHARACTER*(*) WHICH
            INTEGER NUMLST
```

```
        INTEGER K,M
        DO 100 M = NUMLST, 2, -1
          K = LOCBIG(WHICH, M)
          CALL SWITCH(M, K)
100       CONTINUE
        END
```

In FUNCTION LOCBIG, we need to READ data values from the file. Accessing a file typically takes from a thousand to a million times as long as getting a value from main memory, so we'll want to change the algorithm a little to avoid unnecessary READs. Specifically, we'll keep track of the largest value seen so far in addition to its position (record number). Also, since sometimes LOCBIG is supposed to look for the largest name and sometimes for the largest phone number, we store both the name and phone number in a single array and use the variable KEYPOS (for KEY POSition) to select the desired one.

```
        INTEGER FUNCTION LOCBIG(WHICH, N)
        CHARACTER*(*) WHICH
        INTEGER N
        INTEGER NAMLEN, PHLEN
        PARAMETER(NAMLEN = 25, PHLEN = 8)
        CHARACTER*(NAMLEN) NAME, BIGNAM
        CHARACTER*(PHLEN) PHONE, BIGPH
        LOGICAL NEWBIG
        INTEGER K, KEYPOS
        IF (WHICH .EQ. 'NAME') THEN
          KEYPOS = 1
        ELSE
          KEYPOS = 2
        ENDIF
        LOCBIG = 1
        READ(UNIT=1, FMT=1000, REC=LOCBIG) BIGNAM, BIGPH
1000    FORMAT(A, A)
        DO 100 K = 2, N
          READ(UNIT=1, FMT=1000, REC=K) NAME, PHONE
          GO TO (10,20), KEYPOS
10          NEWBIG = (NAME .GT. BIGNAM)
            GO TO 30
20          NEWBIG = (PHONE .GT. BIGPH)
30          CONTINUE
          IF (NEWBIG) THEN
            LOCBIG = K
            BIGNAM = NAME
            BIGPH = PHONE
          ENDIF
100       CONTINUE
        END
```

SUBROUTINEs SWITCH and OUTPUT need slight alterations too.

13.3 EXERCISES

1. Which of these statements would be appropriate if we intend to create a FORMATTED DIRECT-access file named 'BILLS' with unit number stored in INTEGER memory cell U?

```
      a.   OPEN(UNIT=1, FILE='BILLS', STATUS='SCRATCH',ACCESS='DIRECT')
      b.   CREATE(UNIT=U,FILE='BILLS',ACCESS='DIRECT',FMT='FORMATTED')
      c.   OPEN(UNIT=U,FILE='BILLS',ACCESS='DIRECT',FORM='FORMATTED',
         +      STATUS='NEW')
      d.   OPEN(UNIT=U, FILE='BILLS', STATUS='NEW', ACCESS='DIRECT')
```

2. Here's a partially completed version of SUBROUTINE SWITCH for use with our revised cross-reference directory program that uses files. What should be filled in in place of *****A*****, *****B*****, and *****C*****?

```
      SUBROUTINE SWITCH(REC1, REC2)
      INTEGER REC1, REC2
      CHARACTER*(25) CNAME, NAME
      CHARACTER*(8) CPHONE, PHONE
      *****A*****, FMT=1000, REC=REC1) CNAME, CPHONE
      *****B*****, FMT=1000, REC=REC2) NAME, PHONE
      WRITE(UNIT=1, FMT=1000, REC=REC1) NAME, PHONE
      *****C*****
1000  FORMAT(A, A)
      END
```

13.4 UNFORMATTED FILES

The input and output statements we have been dealing with have always involved a *conversion*. As we have used them so far, input statements convert character strings (taken from our data lines or from a file) into INTEGERs, REALs, or whatever type is specified in the FORMAT. An output statement performs the reverse conversion from a representation of data in memory to a character string. The I/O device stores the information in a form very different from the way it would be stored in memory cells. This is quite natural, of course, because we have been using I/O devices primarily as a means of communication between human and computer.

However, I/O devices can be used as an extension of the computer's memory as well as a means of communication. When an I/O device is used for this purpose, the information on the I/O device might just as well be stored in essentially the same form as it would be stored in memory cells, since that would avoid the conversion process. This is the reason for **unformatted files.** We use the word *unformatted* to mean that the form in which the data is stored in the I/O device is left up to the computing system being used and hence is not specified by a FORMAT statement. Most computing systems choose a form essentially like the one used in representing data in memory cells, so the I/O process involves very little computation.

READ and WRITE statements for unformatted files are like those for ordinary (formatted) files except that the FMS = *s* specifier is omitted. In addition, FORM = 'UNFORMATTED' must be specified in the OPEN statement that connects the file.

The UNFORMATTED option may be used with SEQUENTIAL or with DIRECT files. Like FORMATTED files, an UNFORMATTED file consists of a number of records.

As with FORMATTED SEQUENTIAL files, records are processed one after the other in UNFORMATTED SEQUENTIAL files. Here, however, each unformatted I/O statement processes *exactly one* record. (A formatted I/O statement may process more than one record if the FORMAT contains slashes or if it is rescanned.) In fact, we may define an **unformatted record** as a block of information which has been written by a single unformatted WRITE statement.

Just as with FORMATTED SEQUENTIAL files, the ENDFILE (UNIT = u) statement is used to place an end-of-file record in the file. The REWIND (UNIT = u) statement can be used to start at the beginning of the file again. In addition, the statement

BACKSPACE(UNIT = u)

can be used to move back to the immediately preceding record. READ statements with the input lists omitted may be used to move the file forward to the next record.

When an unformatted READ statement has fewer list elements than there are in the record being processed, the excess values in the record are skipped. However, the input list must not be longer than the number of values in the record, and the values must match the data types of corresponding variables in the input list.

UNFORMATTED DIRECT-access files are dealt with in the same way as FORMATTED DIRECT-access files except that the FMT = s specifier is omitted from READs and WRITEs. In addition, the meaning of the RECL = *len* specifier is dependent on your computer system. RECL = 10 may make the record length equivalent to the space required to store ten INTEGER values instead of ten characters. Check with a local expert.

There is one potential source of trouble—if a CHARACTER constant to, say, length 8 is written to an unformatted file, it must be read back into a CHARACTER*(8) variable. Thus, more changes than just removing the FORMATs and FMT = s specifiers would be needed to convert our example in the previous section to the UNFORMATTED case.

Roughly, the choice between FORMATTED and UNFORMATTED files comes down to these two considerations: If you intend to send a copy of a file to someone else for use on another system, the odds are much better that this person will be able to use it if it is FORMATTED. If you are running a program on just one system, and want it to run as fast as possible, try UNFORMATTED files.

13.5 INTERNAL FILES

In Fortran, a given memory cell has a fixed type. You can't treat a REAL variable as a CHARACTER even though in some cases you might want to. For instance, if someone using your program enters $2.85 for the rate of pay, and your program tries to READ that value into a REAL variable, bad things happen. In cases like that you'd like to be able to READ the data item as a CHARACTER string, have your program go through it to make sure it's in acceptable form, remove any leading dollar sign, and then convert the result to a REAL value. There are ways to do it using just the Fortran statements we've seen so far, but they're awkward. One way we could convert a CHARACTER value to a REAL value is by writing the CHARACTER string to a formatted scratch file, rewinding the file, and reading the value back into memory as a REAL value. If that roundabout process seems clumsy to you, it is. It's time consuming, too. **Internal files** provide a way to eliminate the middleman (the scratch file) and make conversions between CHARACTER type and other data types directly within memory.

Internal files aren't like the other files we've seen in this chapter. What they are is a way to use the FORMAT facility to transform values right in memory. They involve no I/O devices, even though we'll be using versions of READ and WRITE statements. It's just for consistency that they're described as a sort of file. If you try to think of them in the same terms as the (external) files we've covered so far, you may be confused. Keep reminding yourself that "internal files" are CHARACTER-valued memory cells whose values can be interpreted in different ways, depending on the FORMATs used.

An **internal file** is a CHARACTER variable, substring, array element, or array. An internal file of the last category, the CHARACTER array, has as many records as the array has elements. Each record is *len* characters long, where *len* is the declared size of the elements of the CHARACTER array. An internal file of any other category (CHARACTER variable, substring, or array element) has exactly one record whose length is the declared length of the variable or array element or the number of characters in the substring.

Writing information into an internal file amounts to converting the information from its present data type to CHARACTERs. Reading information from an internal file goes the other way, from CHARACTERs to another data type. I/O statements dealing with internal files designate the files to be processed with the UNIT specifier.

UNIT = *internal file*

For example, the WRITE statement below puts a CHARACTER string representation of the REAL number in X into the CHARACTER variable CHX.

```
        REAL X
        CHARACTER*(10) CHX
        X = 123.725
        WRITE(UNIT=CHX, FMT=1000)X
1000    FORMAT(F10.1)
```

The contents of CHX after the WRITE would be *bbbbb* 123.7, where *b* stands for blank.

Each record in an internal file which is modified by a WRITE statement is filled out with blanks in parts of the record not explicitly altered by the WRITE. If the FORMAT above had been F8.1 instead of F10.1, then the value of CHX after the WRITE would have been *bbb*123.7*bb*.

Each record of the internal files acts like a printed line when written. It's possible to write values from several variables into the same record.

```
          INTEGER M, N
          CHARACTER*(12) CH
          M = 24
          N = 144
          WRITE(UNIT=CH, FMT=2000)M, N
2000      FORMAT(2I5)
```

After the WRITE statement above, the value of the one-record, internal file CH is *bbb24bb144bb*.

Writing into more than one record of a multiple-record internal file is like writing several printed lines.

```
          CHARACTER*(6) C(100)
          INTEGER M, N
          REAL X
          M = 24
          N = 144
          X = 123.725
          WRITE(UNIT=C, FMT=3000)M, N, X
3000      FORMAT(I6/I6/F6.2)
```

After the WRITE statement above, the first three records of the internal file C (i.e., the elements C(1), C(2), and C(3) of the array C) would have the values *bbbb*24, *bbb*144, and 123.73. The remaining elements in C would remain unchanged.

FORMAT rescanning falls into the same pattern as for printed lines. The program fragment below puts values in the first four records of the internal file D by rescanning the FORMAT and moving to a new record with each rescan.

```
          CHARACTER*(8) D(10)
          INTEGER M,N,P,Q
          M = 12
          N = 24
          P = 100
          Q = 3172
          WRITE(UNIT=D, FMT=4000)M,N,P,Q
4000      FORMAT(I6)
```

After the WRITE, D(1), D(2), D(3), and D(4) have the values *bbbb*12*bb*, *bbbb*24*bb*, *bbb*100*bb* and *bb*3172*bb*.

One example where writing into internal files comes in handy is in printing tables of numbers where blanks are to be written in places where data is not available. If the data is stored in a 5-by-5, two-dimensional array, where negative entries indicate data not available, then devising a program to write out the table inserting blanks in place of negative values is a formidable task—without internal files. But with internal files it's relatively easy. The idea is to write the information for one line of the table into an internal file using an ordinary numeric data descriptor in the FORMAT. Then, go through and change to blanks each entry which corresponds to negative data. Figure 13.5.1 elaborates the details.

Figure 13.5.1 Printing a Table of Numbers with Some Blank Entries

Read data for table.

For each line _____

Write line into internal file.
Change "unavailable" entries to blanks.
Print line.

Fortran translation

```
          REAL DATA(5, 5)
          CHARACTER*(10) TABLE(5)
          INTEGER LINE, ENTRY
          READ *, ((DATA(LINE, ENTRY), ENTRY=1,5), LINE = 1,5)
          DO 120 LINE=1, 5
            WRITE(UNIT=TABLE, FMT=1000)
     +           (DATA(LINE, ENTRY), ENTRY=1,5)
 1000       FORMAT(F10.2)
C             CHANGE UNAVAILABLE ENTRY
            DO 110 ENTRY=1,5
              IF (DATA(LINE,ENTRY) .LT. 0.0) THEN
                TABLE(ENTRY) = '          '
              ENDIF
  110       CONTINUE
C             PRINT LINE
            PRINT *, (TABLE(ENTRY), ENTRY = 1,5)
  120       CONTINUE
          END
```

Data

```
  4.57  -3.92   1.28   1.91  -7.07
 -6.11   4.02   8.36   9.42   1.86
  5.21  -5.67   2.17   3.14   7.00
  0.00   4.62  -9.90   2.71   5.77
  6.29   6.38   0.17  -6.44   3.69
```

Output

```
  4.57            1.28   1.91
          4.02    8.36   9.42   1.86
  5.21            2.17   3.14   7.00
  0.00    4.62           2.71   5.77
  6.29    6.38    0.17          3.69
```

READing values from internal files is like getting values from data lines: CHARACTERs are converted to numbers or other types of data. For example, if the CHARACTER*(5) variable C has the value 12345, then the statement

```
          READ(UNIT=C, FMT=1000)M
 1000     FORMAT(I5)
```

puts the INTEGER 12345 into the memory cell M. The READ statement

```
       READ(UNIT=C, FMT=1000)M,N
2000   FORMAT(I3,I2)
```

would put the numbers 123 and 45 into the memory cells M and N.

Multiple-record internal files are treated like multiple data lines. The READ statement below takes values from two records of the internal file D and ignores the remaining records.

```
       INTEGER M,N
       CHARACTER*(5) D(100)
       D(1) = '  427'
       D(2) = ' 1982'
       READ(UNIT=D, FMT=3000)M,N
3000   FORMAT(T3,I3/T2,I4)
```

One situation in which READing from an internal file is useful occurs when you want your program to allow a value to be input in several different forms. For example, if your program will be used by people who know little about computers, you may want to allow them to enter dollar figures either with or without a dollar sign. The program fragment below illustrates this. First, the value is READ as a CHARACTER string. Then it is searched (using the INDEX operator—see Section 10.2) for a dollar sign. If one is found, it is replaced with a blank. Finally, a READ statement which treats the CHARACTER variable PAYCH as an internal file is used to convert the resulting value into a REAL for use in the rest of our program.

```
           .
           .
           .
       CHARACTER*(80) PAYCH
       INTEGER SPOT
       REAL PAYVAL
           .
           .
           .
       READ *, PAYCH
       SPOT = INDEX(PAYCH, '$')
       IF (SPOT .GT. 0) THEN
         PAYCH(SPOT:SPOT) = ' '
       ENDIF
       READ(UNIT=PAYCH, FMT=1000) PAYVAL
1000   FORMAT(F80.2)
           .
           .
           .
```

13.5 EXERCISES

1. Which of these statements accomplishes the task of converting the REAL value stored in X into the equivalent CHARACTER value in XCH? Statement 1500 looks like this:

```
1500 FORMAT(F10.2)
```

a. `READ(UNIT=XCH, FMT=1500) X`
b. `WRITE(UNIT=XCH, FMT=1500) X`
c. `WRITE(UNIT=X, FMT=1500) XCH`
d. `READ(UNIT=X, FMT=1500) XCH`

2. Which of the statements in exercise 1 has the effect of converting the CHARACTER value stored in XCH into the equivalent REAL value in X?

3. What statements could you add to the last program fragment in this section so that all characters which are neither periods nor digits are replaced by blanks?

---

13 PROBLEMS

---

1. Complete the cross-reference directory program which uses files (Section 13.3), and use it to generate a directory of your friends' phone numbers.

2. Write a program which makes a **concordance** from a text read in as data. Gather the basic data as in problem 6 in Chapter 10. Then sort the resulting file and print it.

> **concordance:** an alphabetical list of all the words in a text along with the number of occurrences of each word.

3. Suppose two files contain sorted entries.

file1:$r_1 r_2 \ldots r_n$ where $r_i \leqslant r_{i+1}$
file2:$s_1 s_2 \ldots s_n$ where $s_i \leqslant s_{i+1}$

Then we can merge the two files into one file of $n + m$ sorted entries by the procedure shown on the next page.

Using this type of merge and four files, we can sort as many entries as we like without using much computer memory. (Recall that the sorting technique we discussed in Chapter 12 required all the entries to be stored in an array.) This type of **external sorting** method is known as a **balanced merge.** We use four files and assume that two of them contain an equal number of "sections," a section being a collection of sorted entries. We make a first pass by merging the first section of one of the files with the first section of the other file and writing the merged result on a third file. Then we merge the second section of one file with the second section of the other file and write the result on file 4. We keep merging sections with sections, alternating where we WRITE the newly merged sections between files 3 and 4, until we run out of sections. (If one file contains more sections than the other, we simply split the remaining sections: half go onto file 3 and the other half onto file 4.)

Read A (first entry on file 1).
Read B (first entry on file 2).

Exit if end of file 1 or if end of file 2
If A ≤ B **then**
    Write A on file 3.
    Read A (next entry on file 1).
  else
    Write B on file 3.
    Read B (next entry on file 2).
                                                    Repeat
If file 1 or 2 contains additional entries
  then
      copy them onto file 3.

At the next stage we repeat the same process, but this time we are reading from files 3 and 4 and writing onto files 1 and 2. As we continue this merging process, alternating the READ-files and the WRITE-files, the sections get longer and longer until, finally, all the entries are merged into one section which is the sorted file.

Implement a balanced merge and test it on two files which, at the beginning, each have 100 sections of one entry per section.

4. Use the program of Section 12.2 to generate an alphabetical directory in a sequential file. This will be the master file. Then design and write a program that will update the master file. Updating a file involves three procedures: adding new items to the file, deleting items from the file, and changing existing information in the file. The items for updating will be in a specific file called a transaction file and must be in sequential order. You will need a code to indicate the type of transaction for each update item, e.g., A = add, D = delete, C = change. Don't forget to check the validity of each transaction. PRINT the updated master file at the end of the update.

14 ARRAYS AS DATA STRUCTURES

14.1 DATA STRUCTURES

Throughout this book we have been emphasizing the idea of breaking down the problem you are trying to program so that it will be easier to understand (more clearly organized) and hence easier to work with. In this chapter, we will deal with an organizational idea which makes programming easier by making the details of your program directly analogous to the details of the problem you want to solve. The idea is to recognize some of the structure (relationships among subparts) of your problem and, after you feel you understand the structure of the problem, to assemble units of information in the computer memory into that structure. We call such assemblages of memory words **data structures.** Every program you have written has used memory cells in some way, so you have been using data structures all along. This is the first time that we will be very conscious of relationships among memory cells, however. Let's look at an example.

> **data structure:** A group of memory cells organized in some manner

Figure 14.1.1 displays the same information in two ways. Take a look at them. Which one is better? If your problem is "How many mothers

Figure 14.1.1 (a) Tree Structure. (b) List Structure

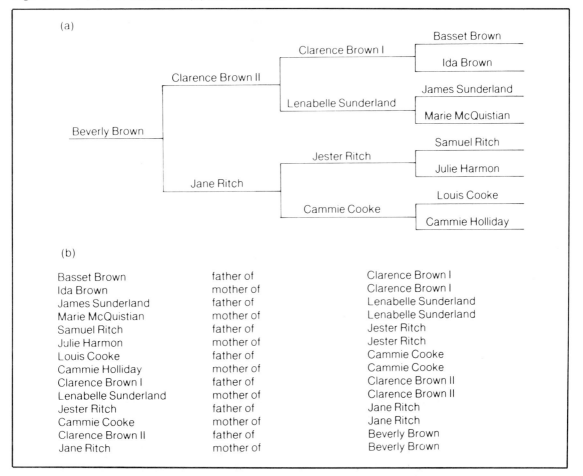

are there?"then the list is probably best. However, if you must determine more complex family relationships among people, then the family tree seems easier to use. Different organizations of the same data may be best suited to different problems.

What is it about the family tree that makes it conducive to answering questions about relationships? One thing is that, the closer two names are in the tree, the closer the relationship between them; but there is no way to rearrange the list so that this is true. In the tree, names along the same vertical line tend to be of the same generation, but this is obviously not true in the list. These and other reasons seem to make it easier to find your way around in the data when it is represented as a tree. More effort has gone into organizing the data in the tree than in the list, but this effort can pay off when the time comes to use the data.

This chapter deals with the organization of data as an important part of programming. Often, spending some time and thought organizing your data can result in a program which is not only easier to write and understand but also more efficient.

Of course, organizing the data in this way takes some careful thought. We hope that once you have studied these data structures, you will be able not only to apply them to problems you encounter, but also to make up new organizations of data suited to whatever problem is at hand.

14.2   MULTI-DIMENSIONAL ARRAYS

We have used individual memory cells to store several different kinds of data. Fortran automatically maintains an internal organization for each memory cell. This internal organization is different for different types of data. For instance, REAL numbers are stored in a very different way from INTEGERs. Because of this internal organization, each memory cell alone could be considered a data structure, but people usually reserve the term **data structure** for organizations which involve a number of memory cells. We have used such organizations already. When we have had several related items of information, we have stored the items in an array. An array is a data structure consisting of several memory cells grouped together and referred to under the same name. A subscript appended to the name distinguishes one item of the group from another: MEMBER(3) refers to the third memory cell in the array called MEMBER. Because Fortran includes a special notation for arrays (the subscript notation), they are very easy to use.

Memories in almost all computers are organized like one-dimensional arrays. Thus, all other more complex data structures are constructed from one-dimensional arrays. Fortran automatically does this additional organizing for us in the case of multi-dimensional arrays, but beyond that we're on our own.

Suppose, for a moment, that Fortran hadn't provided two-dimensional arrays. How could we organize the data in a one-dimensional array so that we could use it as if it were a two-dimensional array? There are many answers to this question, but the one we describe here is the most common—it's the one used by the Fortran compiler.

---

why bother?
There are two good reasons for going into the details of using one-dimensional arrays to represent two-dimensional arrays. First, it's a good introduction to the more complex techniques which follow. But more important, there are times when it is very helpful to know the details of the Fortran representation of two-dimensional arrays. For example, it determines the order of the elements when whole arrays are transmitted in I/O statements

---

If the array is to have m rows and n columns, then we need to use $m*n$ memory cells to represent it. Therefore, we declare a one-dimensional array (which we call TWODIM in our illustration) with $m*n$ memory cells. We organize this block of cells into n sections, each section having m cells in it. The first section of m cells represents the first column of the

Figure 14.2.1 Using a One-Dimensional Array to Represent a Two-Dimensional Array

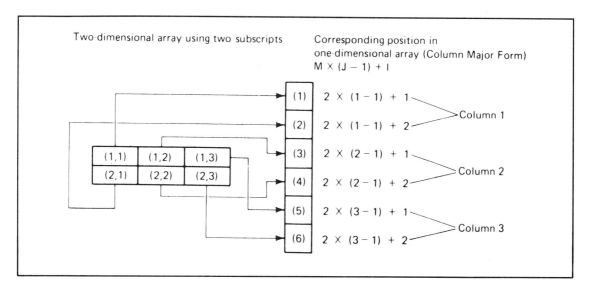

two-dimensional array we are creating, the second section represents the second column, and so on (see Figure 14.2.1). Remember, since there are m rows, each column has m elements in it.

If we want to find the place in the array TWODIM which represents the two-dimensional array element in the Ith row and the Jth column, we skip down to the Jth section and pick the Ith element in that section. This means that TWODIM(M*(J − 1) + I) is the memory cell representing the two-dimensional array element normally designated by the pair of subscripts (I,J). Figure 14.2.1 shows the details for an array with two rows and three columns.

This method of organizing a two-dimensional array is often called the **column major form;** we say that we are storing the array "by columns."

Fortran stores two-dimensional arrays by columns. It can be helpful to know this when you are using them. For example, suppose you have declared an array REAL A(3,2) in the main program and you CALL a SUBROUTINE with that array and its dimensions as parameters: CALL SUBR (A, 3, 2). If the SUBROUTINE starts out like this, using N as the *first* length declarator,

```
SUBROUTINE SUBR(B, M,N)
REAL B(N,M)
    .
    .
    .
```

then you would have problems because the SUBROUTINE will place a different organization on the array than does the main program. The diagram below shows the memory cell names as they are in the main program on the left, and their temporary names when the SUBROUTINE is CALLed on the right. You can see that the subscripting is entirely different. It pays to know what you're doing when you use two-dimensional arrays as arguments to subprograms.

```
A(1,1)  ┌─────────┐  B(1,1)
        │         │
A(2,1)  ├─────────┤  B(2,1)
        │         │
A(3,1)  ├─────────┤  B(1,2)
        │         │
A(1,2)  ├─────────┤  B(2,2)
        │         │
A(2,2)  ├─────────┤  B(1,3)
        │         │
A(3,2)  └─────────┘  B(2,3)
```

14.2 EXERCISES

1. Draw a figure similar to Figure 14.2.1 showing the representation of a three-by-four array.

2. In setting up the column major representation of a two-dimensional array with m rows and n columns, what is the role of m? What is the role of n? Why is m more important than n? Could you set up the representation if you knew m precisely, but knew only that n was, say, smaller than 100? Will Barbara marry Jason? Will Jason leave Toni? Will Toni find happiness in the arms of Willard? And what about the dog?

3. There is a similar representation of a two-dimensional array called the **row major form.** In this representation, an array with m rows and n columns is again represented by a one-dimensional array with $m*n$ memory cells. The array is divided into m sections, each section containing n memory cells and representing one row. Work out a formula which, given a subscript pair (I,J) designating the element in the Ith row and Jth column of the matrix, computes the place in the one-dimensional array which corresponds to the (I,J)th element of the matrix. In this row major representation is it more important to know the number of rows or the number of columns?

4. Where do the 1's go?

```
          INTEGER A(4,4)
          CALL ZAPDIA(A,2)
          END
          SUBROUTINE ZAPDIA(B,M)
          INTEGER M, B(M,M)
          INTEGER I
COMMENT:                 PUT ONES ON DIAGONAL
          DO 10 I=1, M
   10       B(I,I) = 1
          RETURN
          END
```

5. Throughout this section we have been dealing with arrays whose subscripts were numbered from 1 up to the upper limit. Devise the formula you think Fortran uses to represent the array below as a one-dimensional array with subscripts numbered from 1 up.

```
REAL X(L:M, K:N)
```

14.3 ODD-SHAPED ARRAYS

It is easy to generalize from the two-dimensional case to see how to represent a three-dimensional array.

Suppose we want to represent an m-by-n-by-l three-dimensional array. The first subscript varies between 1 and m; the second, between 1 and n; and the third, between 1 and l. Therefore, we need $m*n*l$ memory cells to represent the array, and we declare a one-dimensional array THREE with $m*n*l$ memory cells. We divide the array into l sections, each section having $m*n$ memory cells. In each of the sections we organize an m-by-n two-dimensional array in column major form. That is, we divide each of the l sections into n subsections, each subsection having m memory cells. To refer to the (I,J,K)th element of the three-dimensional array, we go to the Ith memory cell of the Jth subsection of the Kth section. Then conceptual array element (I,J,K) corresponds to

```
THREED(M*N*(K-1)+N*(J-1)+I)
```

The M*N*(K − 1) term moves us to the Kth section of the array, the N*(J − 1) term moves us to the Jth subsection of that section, and the I term moves us to the Ith element of that subsection.

> ANSI Fortran allows arrays of up to seven dimensions.

Perhaps you can begin to see a general scheme here for representing multi-dimensional arrays. Try to write down the formula for the four-dimensional case, given the range of each subscript.

The two-dimensional array we represented is rectangular in shape. That's just one of many possibilities. Think of the problem faced by a traveling pharmaceuticals salesman in West Texas. His district includes the towns of El Paso, Van Horn, Odessa, Big Spring, Midland, Abilene, Pecos, Lubbock, Amarillo, and Wichita Falls. He lives in Pecos, and since he must travel his route once every month, he wants to plan it carefully so that it will be as economical as possible. In other words, he wants to choose the shortest route, starting and ending in Pecos, which visits all ten of the towns in his district. Fortunately, the corner gas station has a table of intertown distances (Figure 14.3.1).

We want to write a program to find the shortest route. Obviously, our program needs to know the intertown distances. How should we arrange the data from the table in the computer's memory cells? The table from the gas station looks like a normal two-dimensional array with a missing part. We will call it a **triangular array**. To represent the triangular array, we can use an idea from our representation of rectangular two-dimensional arrays. One method of storing a rectangular two-dimensional array is the row major method (see exercise 14.2.3); that is, storage "by rows." We divide the array into sections, one section for each row. In the rectangular case, each row is the same length, so it's easy to find the beginning of each section in the array. In this new triangular case, each row has a different

Figure 14.3.1 Distance Table

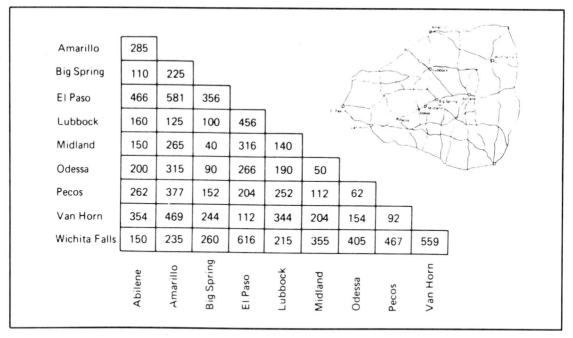

	Abilene	Amarillo	Big Spring	El Paso	Lubbock	Midland	Odessa	Pecos	Van Horn
Amarillo	285								
Big Spring	110	225							
El Paso	466	581	356						
Lubbock	160	125	100	456					
Midland	150	265	40	316	140				
Odessa	200	315	90	266	190	50			
Pecos	262	377	152	204	252	112	62		
Van Horn	354	469	244	112	344	204	154	92	
Wichita Falls	150	235	260	616	215	355	405	467	559

length, and this complication makes it slightly more difficult to locate the beginning of each section.

Let's look at the details. The first row has one member; the second row has two members; the third, three; and so on up to the ninth row, which has nine members. Thus, the first section of our one-dimensional array representing this triangular array should have one memory cell; the second section, two memory cells; and so on. To find the fourth section, we have to skip over the first three. That means skipping over the first row (length one), the second row (length two), and the third row (length three). Altogether we skip over $1 + 2 + 3 = 6$ memory cells.

In general, to find the beginning of the kth section, you must skip over $1 + 2 + 3 + \cdots + (k - 1) = k*(k - 1)/2$ memory cells.

$$
\left.
\begin{array}{l}
1 \;+\; 2 \;\;+\; 3 \;\;+ \ldots + k \\
+ k + (k - 1) + (k - 2) + \ldots + 1
\end{array}
\right\} = 2 \times (1 + 2 + 3 + \ldots + k)
$$

$$
\begin{array}{cccc}
\| & \| & \| & \| \\
(k + 1) + (k + 1) + (k +) + \ldots + (k + 1)
\end{array}
$$

$$
= k \times (k + 1) \qquad \frac{k \times (k + 1)}{2} = 1 + 2 + \ldots + k
$$

Thus, the conceptual triangular array element (I,J) corresponds to

```
TRIANG(I*(I-1)/2+J)
```

where I, of course, may never be smaller than J. It is interesting that, unlike the case for rectangular arrays, here we don't need to know either the number of columns *or* the number of rows in order to refer to an element in the triangular array. Thus, the triangular array offers a surprising advantage over the rectangular structure.

To set up and use a triangular array, all you need to do is declare an array with as many memory cells as you need, that is, $n(n+1)/2$ memory cells if the array is to have n rows. For our example, since there are ten towns, we need a nine-row triangular array, 45 memory cells in all.

Listing all ten towns both vertically and horizontally would result in the chart having ten unnecessary zeros in it.

The problem we are concerned with is to find the route of shortest length which visits all the towns and which starts and ends in Pecos. We will take a straightforward approach. (This, the **traveling salesman problem,** has been much studied, and there are more efficient solutions, but we're looking for a simple solution rather than efficiency.)

What we're going to do is look at a road map of west Texas and pick three or four routes that look about as short as possible. Then we'll have the program figure out which one is the shortest. This doesn't mathematically guarantee us that we've found the shortest route, but we can be pretty sure. Most of the routes are easy to reject.

Figure 14.3.2 is an outline of our program. It's really just an elaborate version of the algorithm we used in Section 12.2 in the "sorting" example.

The program itself appears below. It uses a couple of FUNCTIONs which look complicated but are actually very simple in concept. The

Figure 14.3.2 Finding the Shortest Route

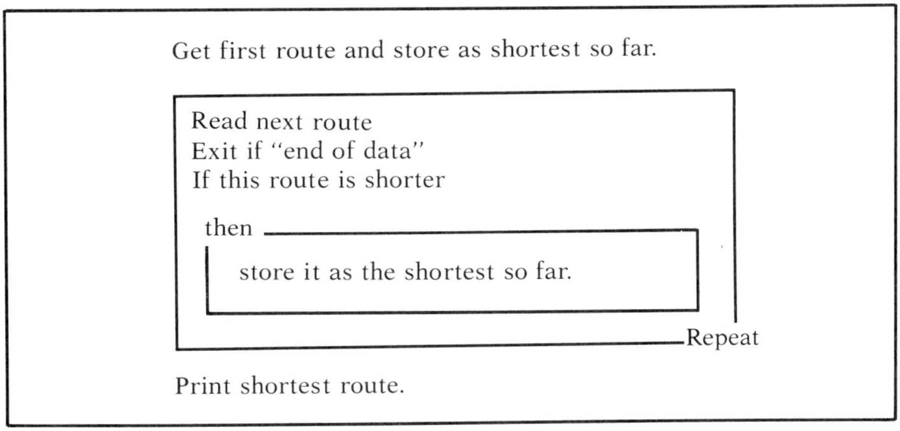

Get first route and store as shortest so far.

Read next route
Exit if "end of data"
If this route is shorter

then

store it as the shortest so far.

Repeat

Print shortest route.

function LENGTH computes the length of a route. In order to index into the distance chart, it has to encode the names of the towns as numbers to use for subscripts in the triangular array. For this reason each town name in the route is converted to a number by a table LOOKUP procedure before the LENGTH function is called.

The LOOKUP procedure simply locates the position of a given entry in a table. There are many ways of doing this, but we take the simple-minded approach. We just scan down the table until we find it.

```
COMMENT:                    FIND SHORTEST WEST TEXAS ROUTE
            INTEGER TLEN, TNUM
            PARAMETER(TLEN = 13, TNUM = 10)
            CHARACTER*(TLEN) TOWNS(10), NEXTR(TNUM + 1)
            INTEGER ROUTE(TNUM + 1), SHORTR(TNUM + 1)
            INTEGER DIST(TNUM*(TNUM-1)/2), I, J
            INTEGER BTWEEN, LENGTH, T
            READ *, (TOWNS(I), (DIST(BTWEEN(I,J)), J=1,I-1), I=1, TNUM)
            READ *, NEXTR
            CALL STORE(NEXTR, SHORTR, TOWNS, TNUM)
100         READ *, NEXTR
              IF (NEXTR(1) .EQ. 'END OF DATA') GO TO 200
              CALL STORE(NEXTR, ROUTE, TOWNS, TNUM)
              IF (LENGTH(ROUTE,DIST,TNUM) .LT.
        +         LENGTH(SHORTR,DIST,TNUM)) THEN
                DO 110 T=1, TNUM + 1
                  SHORTR(T) = ROUTE(T)
110             CONTINUE
              ENDIF
            GO TO 100
200         PRINT *, 'SHORTEST ROUTE (',LENGTH(SHORTR,DIST,TNUM),
        +                          ' MILES):'
            DO 210 T = 1, TNUM + 1
              PRINT *, TOWNS(SHORTR(T))
210         CONTINUE
            END


            INTEGER FUNCTION LENGTH(R, DIST, N)
            INTEGER N, R(N + 1), DIST(N*(N-1)/2)
            INTEGER BTWEEN, I
            LENGTH = 0
            DO 100 I=1,N
              LENGTH = LENGTH + DIST(BTWEEN(R(I), R(I+1)))
100         CONTINUE
            END


            INTEGER FUNCTION BTWEEN(TOWN1, TOWN2)
            INTEGER TOWN1, TOWN2
COMMENT:                    COMPUTE INDEX INTO TRIANGULAR ARRAY
C                           ROWS: 2,3,4... -- COLUMNS: 1,2,3...
C                           2,1
C                           3,1  3,2
C                           4,1  4,2  4,3
C                            .         .
C                            .         .
C                            .           .
            INTEGER MAXT, MINT
            MAXT = MAX(TOWN1, TOWN2)
            MINT = MIN(TOWN1, TOWN2)
            BTWEEN = (MAXT-2)*(MAXT-1)/2 + MINT
            END
```

```
              SUBROUTINE STORE(NEXTR, R, TOWNS, N)
              CHARACTER*(*) NEXTR(N+1), TOWNS(N)
              INTEGER R(N+1)
              INTEGER T, LOOKUP
              DO 100 T=1,N+1
                  R(T) = LOOKUP(NEXTR(T), TOWNS, N)
    100       CONTINUE
              END

              INTEGER FUNCTION LOOKUP(TOWN, LIST, N)
              CHARACTER*(*) TOWN, LIST(N)
              INTEGER T
              DO 100 T=1,N
                  IF (TOWN .EQ. LIST(T)) GO TO 110
    100       CONTINUE
              PRINT *, 'NO SUCH TOWN AS ', TOWN
              LOOKUP = 0
              GO TO 120
    110       LOOKUP = T
    120       CONTINUE
              END
```

Data

```
'ABILENE'
'AMARILLO'        285
'BIG SPRING'      110 225
'EL PASO'         446 581 356
'LUBBOCK'         160 125 100 465
'MIDLAND'         150 265  40 316 140
'ODESSA'          200 315  90 266 190  50
'PECOS'           262 377 152 204 252 112  62
'VAN HORN'        354 469 244 112 344 204 154  92
'WICHITA FALLS'   150 235 260 616 215 355 405 467 559
 'PECOS' 'ODESSA' 'BIG SPRING' 'ABILENE' 'WICHITA FALLS'
 'AMARILLO' 'LUBBOCK' 'MIDLAND' 'VAN HORN' 'EL PASO' 'PECOS'
 'PECOS' 'VAN HORN' 'EL PASO' 'AMARILLO' 'WICHITA FALLS'
 'ABILENE' 'LUBBOCK' 'BIG SPRING' 'MIDLAND' 'ODESSA' 'PECOS'
 'PECOS' 'EL PASO' 'VAN HORN' 'ODESSA' 'MIDLAND' 'LUBBOCK'
 'AMARILLO' 'WICHITA FALLS' 'ABILENE' 'BIG SPRING' 'PECOS'
 'END OF DATA'         ' '     ' '     ' '     ' '     ' '
       ' '     ' '       ' '       ' '       ' '
```

Output

```
    SHORTEST ROUTE (       1432 MILES):
    PECOS
    ODESSA
    BIG SPRING
    ABILENE
    WICHITA FALLS
    AMARILLO
    LUBBOCK
    MIDLAND
    VAN HORN
    EL PASO
    PECOS
```

14.3 EXERCISES

1. Why not store triangular arrays "by columns"?
2. How would you store an array shaped like this?

```
 .  .  .  .  .
    .  .  .  .        (upside-down
       .  .  .        triangular array)
          .  .
             .
```

14.4 STACKS AND QUEUES

The data structures we've seen so far have been fixed in size. The data has been collected and manipulated, but the amount of data stored in the structures remains static once it has been collected. In this section, we want to study some data structures that are useful when the amount of data varies dynamically during the computation. To implement these data structures in Fortran, we'll simply use auxiliary variables to keep track of what parts of a large fixed-length array are currently occupied. But before jumping into the details, let's look at a problem in which dynamic data structures are useful.

You may have noticed that railroad cars have small colored bars on their sides. These bars form an identification code for the cars, a code which can be read by machine and transmitted to a computer. The computer can be used to automate some parts of the railroad operation. Let's write a program which figures out how to do the switching operation that goes on in a classification yard. "Classification yard" is the railroad term for the places where switch engines "classify" cars according to their destination. The switch engines move the cars around and hook them together to make trains heading for particular destinations. We are going to write a program to automate the classification process for a certain classification yard in Durham, North Carolina. Our program will use the bar markings on the sides of the cars, along with information communicated from central control giving the destination of each car, to print out explicit directions for the crew operating the switch engine.

---

problem statement: Automate the procedure for putting trains together at Durham.

---

classify: To put a car on the correct train.

Figure 14.4.1 Durham Yard

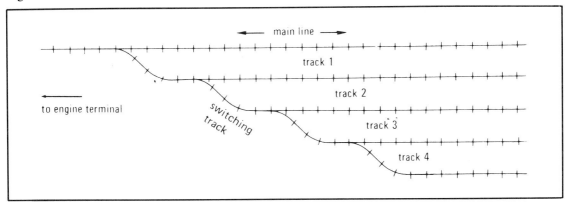

Figure 14.4.1 shows the track layout of Durham, a small classification yard. Trains arriving at Durham leave their cars on track 1.

There are three trains a day which leave Durham for three different destinations: Norfolk, Roanoke, and Portsmouth. Incoming trains include cars for all three destinations, and must be broken up so that each car can be put into the proper train. Every morning the head office sends Durham a list of the cars which will be arriving and which trains (1, 2, or 3) they are to go out on. We'll write a program to print detailed instructions which tell the crew working the switch engine how to classify all the cars in the yard. When the yard crew is finished with the classification, all three trains should be properly assembled: the Norfolk train on track 1, the Roanoke train on track 2, and the Portsmouth train on track 3.

Input/Output Description

> **input:** A list of arriving car identification codes and the destination for each car.
>
> **output:** A list of instructions for the yard crew.

The classification technique used by the yard crew is well known to all railroad men, but it is outlined in algorithmic form in Figure 14.4.2 so that we non-railroaders will know what's going on.

Looking at the plan in Figure 14.4.2, you will see that the innermost box contains explicit instructions for the yard crew. (In a fully automated yard, they would be commands to the switch engine control system.) To prepare a sequential list of detailed instructions, our program can follow the classification algorithm, printing out an instruction each time it makes one of the selections in the innermost box. A typical list of

Figure 14.4.2 The Classification Algorithm

Exit if track 1 is empty.

Move onto track 1 and couple first car to switching train.

If this car's destination isn't Norfolk
then

Select destination

Roanoke: Pull out and move onto track 2.
Portsmouth: Pull out and move onto track 3.
Unknown: Pull out and move onto track 4.

Uncouple car and pull back onto switching track.

Repeat

Move onto track 1 and uncouple all cars on switching train.

Pull engine into terminal.
Relax.

instructions might be: Back onto track 1 and couple first car. Pull out of track 1 onto track 3. Uncouple last car and pull out. Back onto track 1 and couple first car . . . .

Classification Program Plan

1. Store list of car-ID, train-membership pairs.
2. Record ID's of incoming cars (in order) as they go onto track 1.
3. Follow the classification algorithm, printing instructions as they come up.

We can think of track 1 as a dynamic data storage device. All the cars start out there and are removed and put back one at a time from the open end of the track. Because there is only one open end, the last car to go on will be the first car to come off the track. The last-in, first-out nature of track 1 puts it in a class of data storage devices known as **stacks** (also called **push-down stacks** and **LIFO** (last-in, first-out) **devices**).

Conceptually, a stack is a storage device in which elements may be added to or removed from the top only. Traditionally, adding a new element to the top is called **pushing** the stack, and removing the top element is called **popping** the stack. We implement a stack by using an array (declared to be as large as our estimate of the greatest number of items that will ever be on the stack at one time) and a simple INTEGER memory cell (traditionally called the stack **pointer**) which stores the index (i.e., array subscript) of the current top element.

Durham Yard isn't really all that big. Only 200 cars will fit on track 1. That means that we can get by with 200 elements in the array we use to implement the stack representing track 1.

```
INTEGER MAXTRN
PARAMETER(MAXTRN = 200)
INTEGER TRACK1(MAXTRN), FRONT1
```

When a train bringing cars to be classified backs onto track 1, the automatic scanner reads the car identification numbers and flashes them to the computer (we'll simulate that process by READing data lines). As each car passes the scanner, we want to push its identification number onto our stack.

```
        INTEGER MAXTRN
        PARAMETER(MAXTRN = 200)
        INTEGER TRACK1(MAXTRN), FRONT1
        INTEGER IDNO
          .
          .
          .
100     READ *, IDNO
          .
          .
          .
        CALL PUSH(IDNO, TRACK1, FRONT1, MAXTRN)
          .
          .
          .
```

Before going on with the program, let's resolve the problem of pushing a new value onto the stack. This amounts to putting the new value in the next available spot in the array and changing the pointer so that it indicates the new top element.

```
COMMENT:              STACK MANIPULATION ROUTINE:
C                     PUSH AN ELEMNT ON THE STACK
C                        (IF THERE'S ROOM)
        SUBROUTINE PUSH(ELEMNT, STACK, TOP, DEPTH)
        INTEGER ELEMNT, DEPTH, STACK(DEPTH), TOP
        TOP = TOP + 1
        IF (TOP .LE. DEPTH) THEN
          STACK (TOP) = ELEMNT
        ELSE
          PRINT *, 'STACK OVERFLOW WHILE PUSHING', ELEMNT
          STOP
        ENDIF
        END
```

STOP Statement: Terminates Execution of Program

If the ELSE branch in the PUSH routine above is selected, the computer PRINTs a message (stack overflow) and STOPs. It never returns to the program which called PUSH. STOP is used primarily to terminate programs when an unrecoverable error condition occurs within a SUBROUTINE.

Looking at the classification algorithm, you can see that we'll also need a way to simulate the removal of cars from track 1. Cars are removed one at a time from the front. This corresponds to popping the stack, and we may as well use a SUBROUTINE named POP to do it. The input to POP will be the stack array and its stack pointer, and the output will be the value of the top element and an updated stack and pointer to reflect the removal of the top element.

```
COMMENT:                      STACK MANUPULATION ROUTINE:
C                             POP THE TOP ELEMNT OFF THE STACK
C                             (UNLESS THE STACK IS EMPTY)
        SUBROUTINE POP (ELEMNT, STACK, TOP)
        INTEGER ELEMNT, STACK(*), TOP
        IF (TOP .GT. 0) THEN
          ELEMNT = STACK (TOP)
          TOP = TOP -1
        ELSE
          PRINT *, 'STACK IMPLOSION!'
          STOP
        ENDIF
        END
```

Looking back over what we've put together, it appears that we've refined the steps of our program plan carefully enough to write the program. In reading the program below, refer often to the program plan and the classification algorithm to understand what's going on.

```
COMMENT:                      PROGRAM TO CLASSIFY TRAINS AT DURHAM YARD.
C                             INPUT (DATA CARDS):
C                             GROUP1:  ONE CARD FOR EACH AVAILABLE CAR
C                                      CAR-ID:  INTEGER
C                                      TRAIN MEMBERSHIP:CHARACTER.
C                                      TERMINATED BY A LINE WITH A NUMBER
C                                      AND 'END GROUP1'
C                             GROUP2:  ONE CARD FOR EACH ARRIVING CAR
C                                      CAR-ID:  INTEGER
C                                      TERMINATED BY A LINE WITH A ZERO
        INTEGER MAXTRN, IDLEN
        PARAMETER(MAXTRN = 200, IDLEN = 10)
        INTEGER TRACK1 (MAXTRN), FRONT1
        INTEGER NXTCAR, CAR(MAXTRN),N
        CHARACTER*(IDLEN) TRAIN(MAXTRN)
C                             STORE INFO ON DESTINATION OF CAR
        DO 100 N=1, MAXTRN
          READ *, CAR(N), TRAIN(N)
          IF (TRAIN(N) .EQ. 'END GROUP1') GO TO 110
100       CONTINUE
        PRINT *, 'PROGRAM CAN HANDLE ONLY', MAXTRN, ' CARS'
110       CONTINUE
C                             START WITH TRACK1 EMPTY
200     FRONT1 = 0
C                             RECORD CAR-ID'S AS THE CARS ARRIVE
C                             AND ARE PUT ON TRACK1
210     READ *, NXTCAR
          IF (NXTCAR .EQ. 0) GO TO 300
          CALL PUSH(NXTCAR,TRACK1,FRONT1,MAXTRN)
          GO TO 210
C                             CLASSIFY CARS
300     CALL CLSSFY(CAR,TRAIN,N,TRACK1,FRONT1)
        END
```

```
          SUBROUTINE CLSSFY(CARS,TRAINS,N,TRACK1,FRONT1)
          INTEGER CARS(*),N,TRACK1(*),FRONT1
          INTEGER CAR,PTR
          CHARACTER*(*) TRAIN(*)
          INTEGER IDLEN
          PARAMETER(IDLEN = 10)
          CHARACTER*(IDLEN) TRAIN, FNDTRN
          LOGICAL EMPTY
          IF (LEN(TRAIN) .LT. LEN(TRAINS(1))) THEN
            PRINT *, 'IDLEN= ', IDLEN, '...TOO SMALL IN SUBROUTINE
     +               CLSSFY...SHOULD BE AT LEAST', LEN(TRAINS(1))
            STOP
          ENDIF
          EMPTY(PTR) = PTR .EQ. 0
C                   FOLLOW CLASSIFICATION ALGORITHM, PRINTING
C                   INSTRUCTIONS FOR YARD CREW.
C                   NAME USAGES--
C                   EMPTY:  STATEMENT FUNCTION TO TEST FOR EMPTY TRACK
C                   TRACK1, FRONT1:  TRACK 1 SIMULATION STACK
C                   CARS, TRAINS:  ARRAYS CONTAINING TRAIN ASSIGNMENT
C                   FOR EACH CAR
C                   N:  NUMBER OF CARS IN THE YARD
C                   CAR: CURRENT CAR BEING SWITCHED
C                   TRAIN:  TRAIN ASSIGNMENT FOR CURRENT CAR
C
C                   PROCEED WITH CLASSIFICATION
 100      IF (EMPTY(FRONT1)) GO TO 200
            PRINT *, 'MOVE ONTO TRACK 1, COUPLE ONE CAR, ',
     +             'AND PULL OUT'
            CALL POP(CAR,TRACK1,FRONT1)
            TRAIN=FNDTRN(CAR,CARS,TRAINS,N)
            IF (TRAIN .NE. 'NORFOLK') THEN
              IF (TRAIN .EQ. 'ROANOKE') THEN
                PRINT *, 'MOVE ONTO TRACK 2'
              ELSE IF (TRAIN .EQ. 'PORTSMOUTH') THEN
                PRINT *, 'MOVE ONTO TRACK 3'
              ELSE
                PRINT *, 'MOVE ONTO TRACK 4'
              ENDIF
              PRINT *, 'UNCOUPLE CAR AND PULL BACK ONTO ',
     +               'SWITCHING TRACK'
            ENDIF
          GO TO 100
 200      PRINT *, 'MOVE ONTO TRACK 1 AND UNCOUPLE CARS'
          PRINT *, 'MOVE ENGINE INTO TERMINAL'
          PRINT *, 'DONE FOR THE DAY'
          END


          CHARACTER*(*) FUNCTION FNDTRN(CAR,CARS,TRAINS,N)
          INTEGER CAR,CARS(*),N
          CHARACTER*(*) TRAINS(*)
COMMENT:           FIND THE DESTINATION OF 'CAR'
C                  PARAMETERS--
C                  CAR: ID OF CAR
C                  CARS, TRAINS:  ARRAYS GIVING CAR DESTINATION.
C                  N: NUMBER OF CARS IN ENTIRE YARD.
          INTEGER I
          DO 100 I=1, N
            IF (CAR .EQ. CARS(I)) GO TO 110
 100      CONTINUE
          FNDTRN = 'UNKNOWN'
          GO TO 120
 110      FNDTRN = TRAINS(I)
 120      CONTINUE
          END
```

(Continued on following page)

Data

```
423 'ROANOKE'
147 'ROANOKE'
232 'ROANOKE'
976 'NORFOLK'
225 'NORFOLK'
227 'NORFOLK'
322 'NORFOLK'
999 'PORTSMOUTH'
361 'PORTSMOUTH'
882 'PORTSMOUTH'
  0 'END GROUP1'
322
232
361
147
999
423
225
882
227
976
  0
```

Output

```
MOVE ONTO TRACK 1, COUPLE ONE CAR, AND PULL OUT
MOVE ONTO TRACK 1, COUPLE ONE CAR, AND PULL OUT
MOVE ONTO TRACK 1, COUPLE ONE CAR, AND PULL OUT
MOVE ONTO TRACK 3
UNCOUPLE CAR AND PULL BACK ONTO SWITCHING TRACK
MOVE ONTO TRACK 1, COUPLE ONE CAR, AND PULL OUT
MOVE ONTO TRACK 1, COUPLE ONE CAR, AND PULL OUT
MOVE ONTO TRACK 2
UNCOUPLE CAR AND PULL BACK ONTO SWITCHING TRACK
MOVE ONTO TRACK 1, COUPLE ONE CAR, AND PULL OUT
MOVE ONTO TRACK 3
UNCOUPLE CAR AND PULL BACK ONTO SWITCHING TRACK
MOVE ONTO TRACK 1, COUPLE ONE CAR, AND PULL OUT
MOVE ONTO TRACK 2
UNCOUPLE CAR AND PULL BACK ONTO SWITCHING TRACK
MOVE ONTO TRACK 1, COUPLE ONE CAR, AND PULL OUT
MOVE ONTO TRACK 3
UNCOUPLE CAR AND PULL BACK ONTO SWITCHING TRACK
MOVE ONTO TRACK 1, COUPLE ONE CAR, AND PULL OUT
MOVE ONTO TRACK 2
UNCOUPLE CAR AND PULL BACK ONTO SWITCHING TRACK
MOVE ONTO TRACK 1, COUPLE ONE CAR, AND PULL OUT
MOVE ONTO TRACK 1 AND UNCOUPLE CARS
MOVE ENGINE INTO TERMINAL
DONE FOR THE DAY
```

The problems at the end of this chapter suggest other applications for stacks. Use the POP and PUSH routines we've developed here.

Stacks provide a way to store a variable number of items when items enter and leave from the same place (last in, first out). There are many situations in which items enter one place and leave another. For example, Figure 14.4.3 shows people standing politely in line. People enter the line at the BACK and receive their tickets when they get to the FRONT.

Figure 14.4.3   A Queue

As time goes on, the line (or **queue**) shrinks and grows, depending on the rates at which people enter and leave.

The most obvious way to represent a queue is a simple extension of the way we handled stacks. We'll just declare an array big enough, and now, instead of having just one variable keeping track of the top, we'll have *two*, one for the FRONT and one for the BACK.

We start FRONT and BACK off with the value 0 to represent an empty queue. To add an item VALUE (at the back), we can use the statements

```
BACK = BACK + 1
QUEUE(BACK) = VALUE
```

and to remove an item (from the front), we use

```
FRONT = FRONT + 1
VALUE = QUEUE(FRONT)
```

Unfortunately, this scheme doesn't work all that well in practice. Suppose we put on one element, then take it off, then put it on, take it off, and so on. Even though at any point in time the queue is either empty or else has just one value in it, we will need an infinite number of memory locations. Not very practical.

A cure for this problem is to make the array circular. Study SUBROU-
TINE QADD to see what we mean. Statement 10 turns the array into a
circle by making QUEUE(1) come after QUEUE(500).

```
COMMENT:                    QUEUE MANIPULATION ROUTINE.
           SUBROUTINE QADD(QUEUE, FRONT, BACK, VALUE, N)
           INTEGER QUEUE(N), FRONT, BACK, VALUE
C                           FIND SPACE AT BACK OF QUEUE
C                           (WRAP AROUND IF NECESSARY)
   10      BACK = MOD(BACK, N) + 1
C                           INSERT VALUE (IF THERE'S ROOM)
           IF (BACK .NE. FRONT) THEN
             QUEUE(BACK) = VALUE
           ELSE
             PRINT *, 'QUEUE OVERFLOW WHEN ADDING', VALUE
           ENDIF
           END
```

Often you will want to store more than one value in each queue element. For example, if you were writing a simulation of a supermarket
and were using queues to represent shoppers waiting at the checkout
stands, you might need to store three things for each shopper: the time
the shopper entered the queue (so you could tell how long the shopper
had to wait), the number of groceries (so you could tell how long it would
take to get checked out), and whether or not the shopper had Tide-XK (so
you could tell whether the shopper would be accosted by the people
shooting TV commercials in the parking lot).

The solution is simple—just declare an array for each queue you need
and use the same FRONT and BACK values for all of the queues.

```
REAL TIME(QLEN)
INTEGER THINGS(QLEN), FRONT, BACK
LOGICAL TIDE(QLEN)
```

To add a shopper to the queue, just step BACK and insert the appropriate values into TIME(BACK), THINGS(BACK), and TIDE(BACK). The (en-
larged) queue would look like this:

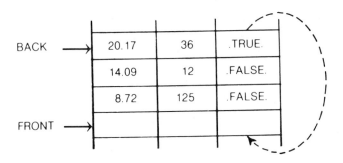

The dotted line is to remind you of our trick for more efficient use of
memory space.

14.4 EXERCISES

1. If the elements you want to store in a stack are REAL NUMBERS, what would you change?
2. Write a SUBROUTINE REMOVE (QUEUE, FRONT, BACK, VALUE, N) which removes the element at the front of QUEUE of length N, puts its value in VALUE, and incorporates the "wraparound" usage of the array called QUEUE.
3. Add a test for an empty queue into your SUBROUTINE REMOVE. (If the queue is empty, there's nothing to be removed.)

14.5 LISTS

In this section, we will study a data structure with a great deal of flexibility. In this new data structure, even the units of information can vary both in size and in their relationship with other units of information. Each unit is called a **list** (or **linked list**) and is made up of data items, each of which contains information about how to find neighboring data items. Thus, it is possible to change not only the number of data items, but also the relationships between data items. In all the data structures we've studied before, the relationship between data items has been fixed (as in one-dimensional arrays, multi-dimensional arrays, stacks, and queues).

Lists are useful in many applications, but an especially important type of application arises when a program needs to maintain several tables of information, each of which changes frequently in size, growing larger, then smaller, then larger again as the program executes. If we use arrays in an ordinary way in cases like this, then we have to allocate enough space for the maximum expected size of each table. This may require more memory than we can obtain from the computer system. By using lists instead of separate arrays for each table, we can make more efficient use of space. Essentially we estimate the maximum *total* size of the tables at any given point in time and store them all in one array. To do this, we have to devise a way to keep track of which elements are currently occupied by which table, a way to obtain extra space if a table grows larger, and a way to release space if a table shrinks. (The released space can be used for another table.)

The example below illustrates techniques for solving these space-management problems.

A great number of predictions have been made about the use of computers in the home. Whether they come true or not will depend to a large extent on whether people can come up with really useful things for home computers to do and then can write programs to carry them out. Let's do some preliminary work on a system which keeps track of grocery supplies and generates shopping lists.

Each item of information will consist of the name of a grocery product and a number. For example, BEANS, REFRIED 2 would stand for two cans of refried beans. The number will stand for the number on hand, the number purchased, or the number used, depending on the context in which we find the data item.

---

problem statement: Develop an automated grocery inventory manager for the home.

What we have in mind here is a computer program which will automatically keep track of the groceries on hand, itemized by grocery product, and print shopping lists of items needed. To keep track of supplies, the program will need to be informed, via data entry (READ), when items are used or purchased. The program will be inconvenient to use because the user will have to enter the data for every purchase and every time a product is used. Maybe by the time home computer systems become commonplace, scanners like those used in automated checkout stands at supermarkets will be cheap enough to be used in the home. These scanners read the machine-coded labels **(universal product code)** on grocery products. With the availability of scanners, the program will be easy to use. Instead of keying in the data, containers can be passed over a scanner built into the kitchen counter before putting them on the shelf (or throwing them out, in case of empties), and the computer can get its information on supplies from the scanner. This kind of a home computer product scanner system will probably become practical in the near future, so it isn't too soon to start designing the programs to control it. In fact, looking a little further into the future, it may become practical to connect your home computer to computers in supermarkets via telephone lines and have your computer automatically shop around for the best prices and place orders for delivery to your door.

We want our program to READ data lines containing information like that shown below.

```
USED          WHEATIES,10 OZ.      1
BOUGHT        BEER,CAN             6
USED          MILK,HALF GAL.       1
SUPPLIES
SHOP
```

Treating each line as a command, the program should respond by deleting or adding items to the list of supplies or the shopping list or by printing the current list of supplies or the shopping list. The plan in Figure 14.5.1 makes the ideas more explicit.

The most complicated parts of the program will be those that manipulate the various lists. From a conceptual point of view, there's little difference between the lists we'll be using and one-dimensional arrays. Lists are made up of elements, one after another in sequence, like arrays. The primary differences are

1. We have direct access to the first element in a list only (in an array we have direct access, via the subscript, to any element).
2. The number of elements in a list can change (the number of elements in an array is fixed, once declared).
3. Elements can be added to or deleted from any part of the list without rearranging the rest of the list (in arrays this can be done only at the tail end).

The first property above is a disadvantage. To get to the fourteenth element in a list, we have to start at the top and move from element to element until we get to the fourteenth one. We'll put up with this undesirable feature in order to have the second property. We need the second property in our grocery inventory program because we have two lists, the list of supplies and the shopping list, which are constantly changing in size. Of course, we could use two arrays to store the lists, but we'd have to declare their (fixed) lengths in the beginning, and many elements would end up unused most of the time. Worse yet, there would be no dynamic flexibility. Unused elements in the shopping list array couldn't be used for the list of supplies, even if the shopping array was almost empty at the same time the list of supplies was full. (Note that this situation occurs frequently. When the shelves are stocked, the shopping list is small.)

Each element in a list has two parts, a **data part** and a **pointer part**. The data part contains the information the element stores. The pointer part tells how to find the next element in the list. Figure 14.5.2 is a diagram of a typical shopping list and a list of supplies (kitchen list). The pointer part is represented by an arrow. The first element in the shop-

Figure 14.5.1 Algorithm for Managing Grocery Inventory

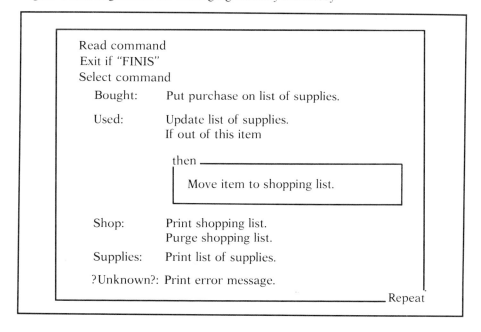

```
Read command
Exit if "FINIS"
Select command
    Bought:     Put purchase on list of supplies.

    Used:       Update list of supplies.
                If out of this item

                    then
                        Move item to shopping list.


    Shop:       Print shopping list.
                Purge shopping list.

    Supplies:   Print list of supplies.

    ?Unknown?:  Print error message.
                                                    Repeat
```

Figure 14.5.2 Some Lists

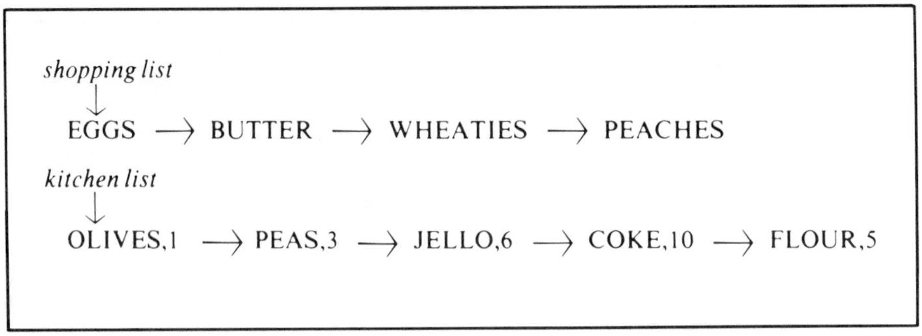

shopping list
↓
EGGS —→ BUTTER —→ WHEATIES —→ PEACHES

kitchen list
↓
OLIVES,1 —→ PEAS,3 —→ JELLO,6 —→ COKE,10 —→ FLOUR,5

ping list contains the entry EGGS; the second, BUTTER; and so on. There is also a pointer to the first element. It is called the **list pointer** and is the only route of access to the list. This is why we can get at only the first element directly.

It's all very well to draw pictures of data values connected by arrows—but how can we implement this organization in Fortran? The key is to see what is constant in a given list structure. The answer is the shape of each list element. In our problem, each list element consists of a word, or a word and a number, and an arrow which points to another element. Although the number of elements on a particular list may vary so that individual lists shrink and grow, the total amount of memory available to your Fortran program is fixed. That means that the total collection of elements is a fixed-size collection of fixed-shape objects—an array of some sort.

We want to store an item description, a number, and a pointer in each list element. We'll need three memory cells per element: one for the description, one for the number, and one for the pointer. Therefore, we'll need three arrays, one for each of the three memory cells per element.

```
CHARACTER*(LENITM) GROC(MAXITM)
INTEGER QUANT(MAXITM), NEXT(MAXITM)
```

A subscript value between 1 and 1000 identifies one spot in each of the three arrays, altogether making a single list element. A pointer, then, is just a subscript. Given a particular element, the value in the array NEXT at that position gives the subscript value of the succeeding element. A pointer value of 0 (not a legitimate subscript value) will mean "end of list." The only other thing we need is a memory cell which stores a pointer to the beginning of the list. Study Figure 14.5.3 to see how the two lists as drawn on the left half of the figure are stored in the arrays on the right.

Now that we have the basic idea of how lists are implemented, let's follow through our grocery list program piece by piece, pausing to inspect specific examples of list manipulation—creation of lists, searching, adding elements, and so forth.

Figure 14.5.3

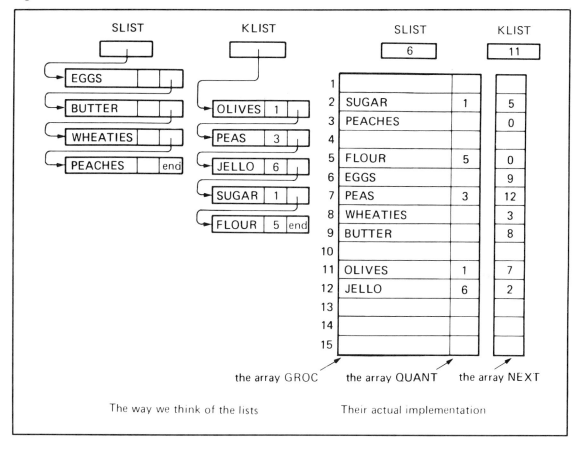

The way we think of the lists   Their actual implementation

Here's our main program:

```
COMMENT:              ORGANIZE AND MAINTAIN AN INVENTORY OF GROCERIES.
C                     GENERATE A SHOPPING LIST
C                     INPUT:  THERE ARE 5 DIFFERENT FORMS OF INPUT CARD
C                     1 'BOUGHT' CARDS SPECIFY NEWLY
C                       PURCHASED ITEMS
C                     2 'USED' CARDS SPECIFY SUPPLIES THAT HAVE
C                       BEEN USED
C                     3 'SHOP' CARDS REQUEST A SHOPPING LIST
C                       TO BE PRINTED OUT
C                     4 'SUPPLIES' CARDS REQUEST A PRINT OUT OF
C                       THE STOCK ON HAND
C                     5 'FINIS' CARDS TERMINATE PROCESSING
C                     OUPUT:  THE PROGRAM ISSUES SHOPPING LISTS AND/OR
C                     INVENTORY LISTS ON COMMAND
C
C                     DATA STRUCTURES:  THE LISTS ARE IMPLEMENTED AS
C                               LINKED LISTS, MADE UP OF ELEMENTS
C                               WHICH HAVE 3 SUBFIELDS:  1 FOR A
C                               DESCRIPTION OF THE ITEM, 1 FOR
C                               QUANTITY, 1 TO INDICATE THE NEXT
C                               ELEMENT ON THE LIST.
              INTEGER LENITM, MAXITM, LENCMD
```

(Continued on following page)

```
                    PARAMETER(LENITM = 16, MAXITM = 1000, LENCMD = 8)
                    CHARACTER*(LENITM) GROC(MAXITM)
                    INTEGER QUANT(MAXITM), NEXT(MAXITM), END
                    INTEGER KLIST, SLIST, FREE, COMAND, CASE, Q
                    CHARACTER*(LENITM) ITEM
                    CHARACTER*(LENCMD) C
                    CHARACTER*(1) PAGEJC, SNGLSP, DBLSP
                    PAGEJC = '1'
                    SNGLSP = ' '
                    DBLSP = '0'
                    PRINT 2000, PAGEJC, 'KITCHEN SYSTEMS, INC.'
      2000          FORMAT(A, T12, A///)
                    END = 0
      C                         SET UP FREE LIST
                    DO 100 FREE = 0, MAXITM - 1
                      NEXT(FREE + 1) = FREE
      100           CONTINUE
      C                         TO BEGIN WITH BOTH 'KLIST' & 'SLIST'
      C                         ARE EMPTY
      200           KLIST = END
                    SLIST = END
      COMMENT:                  PROCESS INPUT COMMANDS.
      300           READ 3000, C, ITEM, Q
      3000          FORMAT(A, T10, A, T30, I4)
                    CASE = COMAND(C)
                    GO TO (310, 320, 330, 340, 350, 360), CASE
      C                         'BOUGHT' A NEW ITEM.
      310           CALL RESTCK(ITEM, Q, FREE, KLIST,
           +                         QUANT, NEXT, END, GROC)
                    PRINT 3100, SNGLSP, 'BOUGHT', Q, ITEM
      3100          FORMAT(A,A,TR1,I3,TR2,A)
                    GO TO 300
      C                         'USED' SOME STUFF
      320           CALL USED(ITEM, Q, KLIST, SLIST,
           +                         QUANT, NEXT, END, GROC)
                    PRINT 3100, SNGLSP, 'USED', Q, ITEM
                    GO TO 300
      C                         'SHOP'-PING LIST WANTED
      330           PRINT 3300, DBLSP, 'HERE IS YOUR SHOPPING LIST'
      3300          FORMAT(2A)
                    CALL PRNLST(SLIST, 0, NEXT, END, GROC)
                    PRINT 3300, DBLSP
      C                         FLUSH SHOPPING LIST
      C                         IF LIST IS ALREADY EMPTY, NOTHING TO DO
                    IF (SLIST .EQ. END) GOTO 339
      335           IF (NEXT(SLIST) .EQ. END) GO TO 338
                      CALL MOVE(SLIST, NEXT, FREE)
                      GO TO 335
      C                         SPECIAL CASE FOR FIRST ELEMENT ON SLIST.
      338           NEXT(SLIST) = FREE
                    FREE = SLIST
                    SLIST = END
      339           GO TO 300
      C                         'SUPPLIES' LISTING WANTED
      340           PRINT 3300, DBLSP, 'SUPPLIES ON HAND'
                    CALL PRNLST(KLIST, QUANT, NEXT, END, GROC)
                    PRINT 3300, DBLSP
                    GO TO 300
      C                         'FINIS'--BAIL OUT
      350           GO TO 400
      C                         WHO KNOWS WHAT COMMAND WE GOT
      360           PRINT 3600, DBLSP, C, 'IS NOT A COMMAND.',
           +                         ' WHAT DID YOU HAVE IN MIND?'
      3600          FORMAT(3A/T10, A)
```

```
              GO TO 300
  400         END

              INTEGER FUNCTION COMAND(C)
COMMENT:                CONVERT COMMAND WORDS INTO NUMBERS
C                         'BOUGHT'   = 1
C                         'USED'     = 2
C                         'SHOP'     = 3
C                         'SUPPLIES' = 4
C                         'FINIS'    = 5
              CHARACTER*(8) WORDS(5), C
              WORDS(1) = 'BOUGHT'
              WORDS(2) = 'USED'
              WORDS(3) = 'SHOP'
              WORDS(4) = 'SUPPLIES'
              WORDS(5) = 'FINIS'
              DO 100 COMAND = 1, 5
                IF (C .EQ. WORDS(COMAND)) GO TO 110
  100         CONTINUE
C                         INVALID COMMAND
              COMAND = 6
  110         END
```

As you can see from its comments, the main program is a direct implementation of Figure 14.5.1. The only addition is the initialization section which sets up the free list (explained shortly) and the other two lists. We'll discuss this section first.

The statements up to statement 300 set up the lists. There will be three lists altogether. You already know about the kitchen list and the shopping list, but the other list, the **free list,** is new. The purpose of the free list is to keep track of currently unused list elements. Most of the time there will be some elements on the kitchen list and some on the shopping list, but the total number of elements on those two lists together will not exhaust the list space (hopefully). It is these leftover elements that we keep on the free list. When we need to add an element to one of the other lists, we simply take an element off the free list, put appropriate values in it, and add it to the other list. When we delete an element from the kitchen list or shopping list, we put it on the free list for later use.

In the beginning, all of the list elements are unused, so they all go on the free list. To put all the elements on the free list, we link them all together and set the head pointer FREE so that it points to the first element. The kitchen list and the shopping list, on the other hand, are empty in the beginning, so we set their head pointers KLIST and SLIST to "end of list" (END = 0).

Once a list has been constructed (either the kitchen list or the shopping list), printing it out is just a matter of repeatedly checking to see if we're at the end of the list and, if not, printing the description and quantity fields, then moving on to the next element.

---

finding the next list element: If NEXT is the array containing the pointers to the next list elements, and we are currently looking at the element in array position N, then NEXT (N) is the subscript of (pointer to) the next element in the list.

```
COMMENT:                    PRINT OUT ALL ITEMS ON 'LIST'.
                SUBROUTINE PRNLST(LIST, QUANT, NEXT, END, GROC)
                INTEGER LIST
                INTEGER QUANT(*), NEXT(*), END
                CHARACTER*(*) GROC(*)
                INTEGER CUREL
                CUREL = LIST
100             IF (CUREL .EQ. END) GO TO 200
                   PRINT 1010, GROC(CUREL), QUANT(CUREL)
1010            FORMAT (T7,A,I6)
                   CUREL = NEXT(CUREL)
                GO TO 100
200             END
```

SUBROUTINE ADD puts new elements on lists. First, it fills in the item description and quantity parts of the list element at the front of the free list, and then it rearranges pointers to cut the element off the free list and install it at the front of the new list (whose head pointer is denoted by LIST in the SUBROUTINE). Figure 14.5.4 shows the necessary pointer changes pictorially. If you study it in conjunction with SUB-ROUTINE ADD, you should be able to figure out what's going on.

```
COMMENT:                    CREATE A NEW ELEMENT BY REMOVING  THE FIRST
C                           ELEMENT OF THE 'FREE' LIST, FILLING IT WITH
C                           'ITEM' AND 'Q', AND INSERTING IT INTO 'LIST'.
                SUBROUTINE ADD(ITEM, Q, FREE, LIST,
         +                     QUANT, NEXT, END, GROC)
                CHARACTER*(*) ITEM
                INTEGER Q, FREE, LIST
                INTEGER QUANT(*), NEXT(*), END
                CHARACTER*(*) GROC(*)
                INTEGER SAVE
                IF (FREE .NE. END) THEN
                  GROC(FREE) = ITEM
                  QUANT(FREE) = Q
                  SAVE = FREE
                  FREE = NEXT(FREE)
                  NEXT(SAVE) = LIST
                  LIST = SAVE
                ELSE
                  PRINT *, 'OUT OF ROOM ON FREE LIST. SORRY!'
                  STOP
                ENDIF
                END
```

Note: the STOP statement terminates execution in case we run out of storage space. ⟶

When a grocery item is used up, we want to remove its list element from the kitchen list and put it on the shopping list. After the shopping list has been printed, we move the elements on it to the free list for later use. Both movements involve the same pointer manipulations. In both there are two cases, determined by whether the element to be moved is the first element of its list or not. If the element is the first element, we must alter the head pointer of the list. If it's not the first element, we must alter the pointer field (NEXT) of the previous element. Look back at the main program. Statements 335 up to (but not including) 340 use SUBROUTINE MOVE to handle elements which are *not* at the front of the shopping list (SLIST), and the three statements starting with 338

Figure 14.5.4 ADDing a New Element to KLIST

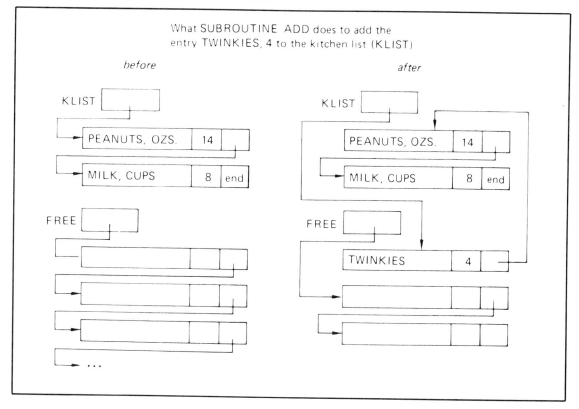

MOVE elements which *are* at the front. If it's not clear to you what's going on, try drawing pictures like those in Figure 14.5.4.

```
COMMENT:                MOVE THE ELEMENT DESIGNATED BY NEXT(PRED) TO
C                       THE FRONT OF LIST
          SUBROUTINE MOVE(PRED, NEXT, LIST)
          INTEGER PRED, NEXT(*), LIST
          INTEGER ELEMNT
          ELEMNT = NEXT(PRED)
          NEXT(PRED) = NEXT(ELEMNT)
          NEXT(ELEMNT) = LIST
          LIST = ELEMNT
          END
```

When we buy something at the grocery store, we enter it into our kitchen inventory by sending the program a BOUGHT command. We need a SUBROUTINE to handle the restocking process. To enter a purchased item on the list of supplies, we search the list to see if we have any such items in stock. If so, we add the quantity purchased to the present quantity. If not, we insert the new item into the list of supplies. Figure 14.5.5 explains the process in more detail. SUBROUTINE RESTCK below follows the plan in the figure.

Figure 14.5.5 Restocking a Grocery Item

Start at front of KLIST.

Search KLIST for desired item.

Not found: Put the purchase into a new KLIST item.

Found: Add quantity purchased to amount on hand.

```
COMMENT:              IF ITEM IS ALREADY IN STOCK, JUST ADD TO QUANT.
C                     OTHERWISE, CREATE A NEW ITEM AND STICK IT ON 'LIST'
          SUBROUTINE RESTCK(ITEM, Q, FREE, LIST,
     +                  QUANT, NEXT, END, GROC)
          CHARACTER*(*) ITEM
          INTEGER Q, FREE, LIST
          INTEGER QUANT(*), NEXT(*), END
          CHARACTER*(*) GROC(*)
          INTEGER LOOK
          LOOK = LIST
100       IF (LOOK .EQ. END) GO TO 200
C                   FIND IT YET?
           IF (ITEM .EQ. GROC(LOOK)) GO TO 300
           LOOK = NEXT(LOOK)
           GO TO 100
C                   IT'S NOT IN THE LIST--ADD IT
 200      CALL ADD(ITEM, Q, FREE, LIST,
     +                  QUANT, NEXT, END, GROC)
          GO TO 400
C                   FOUND IT
 300      QUANT(LOOK) = QUANT(LOOK) + Q
 400      END
```

The body of SUBROUTINE RESTCK is very much like the array search loops we discussed in Section 9.6. What we have here could be called a **list search loop.** All of the loops introduced in Section 9.6 have analogous constructs in dealing with lists: **list processing loops** go through each element of a list and perform the same process on each element; **list READ-loops** fetch values from an I/O device for each element of a list. In fact, loops of these types may be used to deal with the elements of any data structure—arrays, one-dimensional or multi-dimensional, stacks, queues, lists, or any other data structure you can devise.

The bookkeeping we must perform when an item has been used up is very similar to the process of restocking. We search for the item, find it, and subtract the quantity used from the quantity listed. If the subtraction exhausts the supply, we move the item to the shopping list.

This amounts to another list search loop as shown in Figure 14.5.6.

```
COMMENT:              SEARCH FOR 'ITEM' ON KLIST (KITCHEN LIST)
C                     IF FOUND, SUBTRACT Q (QUANTITY USED)
C                          FROM QUANTITY IN STOCK.
C                     IF ALL OF THAT ITEM IS USED UP,
C                          THEN MOVE ITEM TO SLIST (SHOPPING LIST).
```

Figure 14.5.6 What to Do to Account for Using an Item

Start at front of KLIST.

Search KLIST for desired item.

  Not found: Print error message.

  Found: Subtract quantity from amount on hand.

```
              SUBROUTINE USED(ITEM, Q, KLIST, SLIST,
       +                    QUANT, NEXT, END, GROC)
              CHARACTER*(*) ITEM
              INTEGER Q, KLIST, SLIST
              INTEGER QUANT(*), NEXT(*), END
              CHARACTER*(*) GROC(*)
              INTEGER LOOK, PRVIUS, SAVE
C                     FIRST ELEMENT OF LIST MUST BE HANDLED SEPARATELY
              IF (ITEM .EQ. GROC (KLIST)) THEN
                QUANT(KLIST) = QUANT(KLIST) - Q
                IF (QUANT(KLIST) .EQ. 0) THEN
C                       PUT ITEM ON SHOPPING LIST
                  SAVE = KLIST
                  KLIST = NEXT(KLIST)
                  NEXT(SAVE) = SLIST
                  SLIST = SAVE
                ELSE IF (QUANT(KLIST) .LT. 0) THEN
                  PRINT *, 'MUST BE SOME MISTAKE--USED MORE ',
       +                  ITEM, ' THAN WE HAD'
                ENDIF
C                       SEARCH DOWN INSIDE THE KITCHEN LIST
              ELSE
                PRVIUS = KLIST
                LOOK = NEXT(KLIST)
 100            IF (LOOK .EQ. END) GO TO 120
                  IF (ITEM .EQ. GROC(LOOK)) GO TO 110
                  PRVIUS = LOOK
                  LOOK = NEXT(LOOK)
                GO TO 100
C                       FOUND IT. UPDATE KITCHEN LIST
 110            QUANT(LOOK) = QUANT(LOOK) - Q
                IF (QUANT(LOOK) .EQ. 0) THEN
C                       WE'RE OUT OF ITEM--PUT IT ON SHOPPING LIST
                  CALL MOVE(PRVIUS, NEXT, SLIST)
                ELSE IF (QUANT(LOOK) .LT. 0) THEN
                  PRINT *, 'MUST BE SOME MISTAKE--USED MORE ',
       +                  ITEM, ' THAN WE HAD'
                ENDIF
                GO TO 130
C                       NOT FOUND--WHOOPS!
 120            PRINT *, 'MUST BE SOME MISTAKE--USED ', ITEM,
       +              ' WE DIDN''T HAVE'
 130          CONTINUE
              ENDIF
              END
```

At this point you've seen routines for doing all the list manipulation we need for the grocery inventory problem. Below, you can see what happened when we ran the program.

Data

```
BOUGHT    SPAN OLIVES,JAR        3
BOUGHT    RIPE OLIVES,CAN        5
BOUGHT    TORTILLAS,FLOUR       24
BOUGHT    CHEESE,JACK,OZS       30
BOUGHT    HOT CHILIES,CAN        1
BOUGHT    REFRIED BNS,CAN        3
SUPPLIES
USED      CHEESE,JACK,OZS        6
BOUGHT    TOMATO SAUCE,CAN       2
BOUGHT    BEER,CAN              12
BOUGHT    ALKA SELZER           1
BOUGHT    PINTO BEANS OZS       16
BOUGHT    TWINKIES              4
BOUGHT    LETTUCE,OZS           5
BOUGHT    HOT CHILIES,CAN       1
BOUGHT    MILK,CUPS            8
BOUGHT    SPAGHETTI,OZS        12
BOUGHT    PEANUTS,OZS          14
USED      BEER,CAN             1
USED      TORTILLAS,FLOUR      6
USED      SPAN OLIVES,JAR      2
USED      HOT CHILIES,CAN      1
USED      REFRIED BNS,CAN      1
USED      CHEESE,JACK,OZS     12
USED      LETTUCE,OZS          2
USED      BEER,CAN             1
USED      PEANUTS,OZS          1
USED      BEER,CAN             1
USED      PEANUTS,OZS          4
USED      BEER,CAN             2
USED      PEANUTS,OZS          6
USED      BEER,CAN             4
USED      PEANUTS,OZS          3
USED      BEER,CAN             3
USED      SPAN OLIVES,JAR      1
USED      ALKA SELZER          1
USED      TWINKIES             1
BOUGHT    HOT CHILIES,CAN      2
BOUGHT    BREAD, WHL WHT       1
SHOP
SHOP
SUPPLIES
SLURP
FINIS
```

Output

```
            KITCHEN SYSTEMS, INC.


BOUGHT    3    SPAN OLIVES,JAR
BOUGHT    5    RIPE OLIVES,CAN
BOUGHT   24    TORTILLAS,FLOUR
BOUGHT   30    CHEESE,JACK,OZS
BOUGHT    1    HOT CHILIES,CAN
BOUGHT    3    REFRIED BEANS,CA

SUPPLIES ON HAND:
          REFRIED BEANS,CA         3
```

```
                    HOT CHILIES,CAN           1
                    CHEESE,JACK,OZS          30
                    TORTILLAS,FLOUR          24
                    RIPE OLIVES,CAN           5
                    SPAN OLIVES,JAR           3

    USED    6   CHEESE,JACK,OZS
    BOUGHT    2    TOMATO SAUCE,CAN
    BOUGHT   12    BEER,CAN
    BOUGHT    1    ALKA SELZER
    BOUGHT   16    PINTO BEANS OZS
    BOUGHT    4    TWINKIES
    BOUGHT    5    LETTUCE,OZS
    BOUGHT    1    HOT CHILIES,CAN
    BOUGHT    8    MILK,CUPS
    BOUGHT   12    SPAGHETTI,OZS
    BOUGHT   14    PEANUTS,OZS
    USED    1    BEER,CAN
    USED    6    TORTILLAS,FLOUR
    USED    2    SPAN OLIVES,JAR
    USED    1    HOT CHILIES,CAN
    USED    1    RIPE OLIVES,CAN
    USED    1    REFRIED BEANS,CA
    USED   12    CHEESE,JACK,OZS
    USED    2    LETTUCE,OZS
    USED    1    BEER,CAN
    USED    1    PEANUTS,OZS
    USED    1    BEER,CAN
    USED    4    PEANUTS,OZS
    USED    2    BEER,CAN
    USED    6    PEANUTS,OZS
    USED    4    BEER,CAN
    USED    3    PEANUTS,OZS
    USED    3    BEER,CAN
    USED    1    SPAN OLIVES,JAR
    USED    1    ALKA SELZER
    USED    1    TWINKIES
    BOUGHT    2    HOT CHILIES,CAN
    BOUGHT    1    BREAD, WHL WHT

    HERE IS YOUR SHOPPING LIST
                    ALKA SELZER              0
                    SPAN OLIVES,JAR          0
                    BEER,CAN                 0
                    PEANUTS,OZS              0

    HERE IS YOUR SHOPPING LIST  ◄───────
```

Notice that the previous command flushed this shopping list

```
    SUPPLIES ON HAND:
                    BREAD, WHL WHT           1
                    SPAGHETTI,OZS           12
                    MILK,CUPS                8
                    LETTUCE,OZS              3
                    TWINKIES                 3
                    PINTO BEANS OZS         16
                    TOMATO SAUCE,CAN         2
                    REFRIED BEANS,CA         2
                    HOT CHILIES,CAN          3
                    CHEESE,JACK,OZS         12
                    TORTILLAS,FLOUR         18
                    RIPE OLIVES,CAN          4

    SLURP      IS NOT A COMMAND.  WHAT DID YOU HAVE IN MIND?
```

14.5 EXERCISES

1. We declared each of the arrays used for list elements to be 1,000 cells long. What restriction does this place on the total number of grocery items our program can deal with?

2. Redraw Figure 14.5.3 showing all unused list elements tied together on a list pointed to by memory cell FREE.

3. What (few) changes would need to be made so that there is also a command ADD that lets you add new items to the shopping list without using up items from the shelves?

14 PROBLEMS

Practice Problems

1. Verify that Fortran stores two-dimensional arrays using column major form. Declare a one-dimensional array

   ```
   INTEGER TEST(16)
   ```

   in your main program. In each memory cell TEST(i), store i. Now send TEST as an argument to a SUBROUTINE VERIFY which lists a two-dimensional array

   ```
   INTEGER A(4,4)
   ```

   as a parameter. Within VERIFY, print the values in A, column by column. They should come out 1, 2, 3, 4, 5, 6, 7, . . . , 16.

2. Redo problem 1, only this time include a number N as one of SUB-ROUTINE VERIFY's parameters. Use N as a variable dimension, i.e.,

   ```
   INTEGER A(N,N)
   ```

   Then CALL the SUBROUTINE several times, giving N different values. Within VERIFY, print out the values in the array, and study how it is arranged in each case.

3. Use our traveling salesman program (Section 14.3) on a problem of interest (or practical value) to you. For example, go to a company that makes deliveries of some sort and find out the route their truck takes. Then get a map and find the distances between all stops they must make. See if the route they use really is the shortest.

4. Change the grocery inventory program of Section 14.5 to make it easier to check the shopping list from time to time before making the decision to go grocery shopping. As it is, the program deletes all the items from the shopping list after printing, assuming the person requesting the list will now go shopping. In practice, the list may be short and shopping unnecessary. In cases like this, the shopping list should be retained. One way to alleviate this problem would be to have the program print the question, GOING SHOPPING? after

printing the shopping list. If the answer is yes, the shopping list should be dropped as before. If no, then it should be retained.

5. Another odd-shaped array that is sometimes useful is the **polar array.** By computing the subscript properly, a one-dimensional array may be organized into the form shown below.

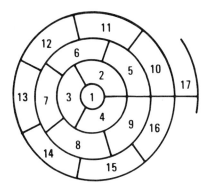

We've chosen this form so that the area that corresponds to each memory cell is about the same. The area of the ring between radius R − 1 and radius R is proportional to

$$R^2 - (R - 1)^2 = 2R - 1$$

Thus, we've placed 2R − 1 locations in each ring of radius R (1 for R = 1, 3 for R = 2, 5 for R = 3, etc.).

We will refer to memory cells in the polar array by giving one value for the radius R and one for the angle THETA. When THETA is 0, to find our way to the memory cell corresponding to the radius R, we must skip over the first R − 1 rings; thus, we must skip over 1 + 3 + 5 + . . . + (2R − 3) locations. The next location will then correspond to the memory cell at radius R and angle 0. Hence the formula for computing the appropriate array subscript for this cell is

$$(R - 1)^2 + 1$$

Amazing, but true: the sum of the first n odd numbers is n^2.

Now all we need is a term to account for nonzero THETAs. Since the ring at radius R has 2R − 1 values for the THETA term, the THETA term is

```
((2*R-1)*THETA)/360
```

We have carefully parenthesized the expression so that INTEGER division helps us out.

Thus, given a value R (1 or greater) and a value THETA (0 to 359), we use the memory cell whose subscript is

```
(R-1)**2+1+((2*R-1)*THETA)/360
```

Figure out how many memory cells must be in the array when we want to have a polar array whose maximum radius is **RMAX**. Write a FUNCTION to convert (R, THETA) values into the appropriate array subscripts. Write a program which implements a polar array and test it by first storing values at various (R, THETA) positions and then printing out the array to verify that the values you stored went into the correct positions.

 If you feel like it, write a FUNCTION CONVRT that will accept values for THETA in any range and return a value in the proper range (0 to 359). For example,

and
> CONVRT (710) returns 350
> CONVRT (− 90) returns 270

6. Devise a scheme for going from (R, THETA) values to array subscripts which organizes a one-dimensional array into a polar array of the form shown below.

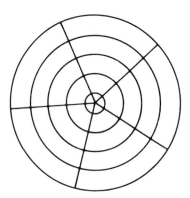

7. A great many board games use a hexagonal grid (early American settlers played Agon on a hex grid, and the majority of the hundreds of battle-simulation board games use hex grids). The reason is simple—unlike on a square grid, the distance from a given cell to each of its neighbors is the same. Some people like hexagonal grids just because they look prettier than square grids.
    Write a collection of subprograms which implement a hexagonal array, including
    a. LOGICAL FUNCTION ISNBR(H1, H2, K2), which returns .TRUE. if hex cells (H1, K1) and (H2, K2) are neighbors.
    b.   SUBROUTINE NBR(H1,K1,NUMB,H2,K2), which, given hex cell (H1,K1), returns in (H2,K2) the NUMBth neighbor of (H1,K1).

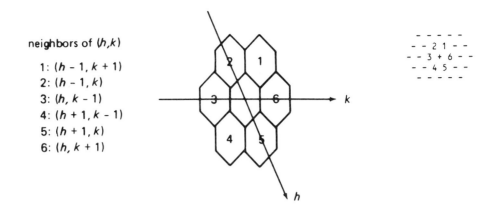

neighbors of (h,k)

1: $(h - 1, k + 1)$
2: $(h - 1, k)$
3: $(h, k - 1)$
4: $(h + 1, k - 1)$
5: $(h + 1, k)$
6: $(h, k + 1)$

Program Design Problems

8. One of the most unpleasant features of the kitchen system in Section 14.5 is that if you don't type the product description exactly the same way each time, the system doesn't know it's dealing with the same item and will proliferate list entries. Character-by-character equality is too strict a criterion for telling whether two items' descriptions match.

   Devise and test several more-lenient matching schemes. Here are a few ideas:
   a. Ignore all punctuation marks.
   b. Ignore position on the line (i.e., " cheese" and "cheese " are surely the same item).
   c. Ignore vowels (is this too extreme?).

9. Do problem 12.24 (ringworm) using polar arrays or hex grids.

10. Suppose you are running a supermarket and you have four checkout counters. You would like to run one of them as an "express lane," but you're not sure where to set the limit which determines who may use the express lane. You decide to write a computer simulation and compare the effects of different limits on how quickly 200 shoppers (who buy a random amount of groceries and come to be checked out at random times) get checked out. Use your system's random number generator, or RANF, Appendix B.

    Here's the strategy of the program: Let the current time be T. For each shopper, generate two random numbers. The first, TENTER, gives the time the shopper arrives at the checkout area; the second, TOUT, gives the length of time it will take for the checker to check the shopper out (once the process starts). For each checkout counter, keep track of the shoppers waiting by using a queue. If there is some shopper already at the head of one of the lines who will be checked out before TNEXT = T + TENTER, check him out (so that T is now T + TOUT). Keep testing until there are no more to be checked out up to time TNEXT. Then enter the shopper who has arrived (thus making T = TNEXT), using the following strategy:

    If the TOUT value is below the LIMIT, the shopper may enter the express lane if he chooses. Otherwise, the shopper should be put in the lane with the fewest people waiting.

Optional: Decide which line the next shopper goes to on a more elaborate basis—perhaps on how many people in a line *and* the TOUT associated with the last person in that line (as if the shopper is also estimating how many groceries the people already in line have).

Print the results of your simulation in a form that makes it easy to compare the results. Run the program for several different values of LIMIT.

11. Write a program which creates and maintains a list of people's names and their telephone numbers. Your program should maintain the links in the list so that the names are in alphabetical order. A list element should have the general structure shown below.

name	phone number	link
JOHNSON, JAMES E.	415-321-2300	———▶

The input for your program should be data lines in one of two types:
a. new entry:
b. ALPHABETICAL LISTING

If your program sees a line of a type **a,** it should add the name and phone number to the list in the appropriate place. If it sees a line of type **b,** it should print out all the names and phone numbers in its list in alphabetical order.

12. Alter the program of problem 11 so that it maintains a doubly linked list. The first link will be the same as in problem 11, and the second link will order the list according to increasing phone number.

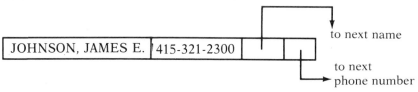

Now your program should accept one more kind of input:
c. NUMERICAL LISTING

If your program sees a line of type **c,** it should print a listing of names and phone numbers in order of increasing phone number (thus creating a cross-reference phone book).

13. A **graph,** for the purposes of this problem, is a number of nodes together with a set of line segments connecting some of those nodes.

A **path** in a graph is a set of its line segments connecting one node to another. A graph is called **connected** if there is a path between each pair of nodes. In the drawing below, (a) and (b) are connected graphs, but (c) is not connected. Write a LOGICAL FUNCTION which decides whether a graph described by its parameters is connected or not.

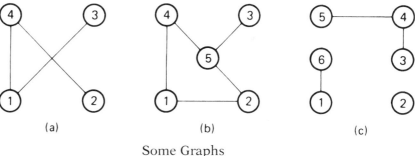

Some Graphs

An easy way to describe a graph is by using a triangular array containing LOGICAL values. The value .TRUE. indicates that a line segment is present between the two nodes determined by the row and column number of that entry in the array; .FALSE. indicates the absence of a connecting segment. Graphs (a), (b), and (c) correspond to triangular arrays (a), (b), and (c). Your LOGICAL FUNCTION should have two parameters: (1) a triangular array describing a graph, and (2) an INTEGER indicating the number of nodes of the graph. The FUNCTION should return the value .TRUE. when the graph is connected and .FALSE. otherwise.

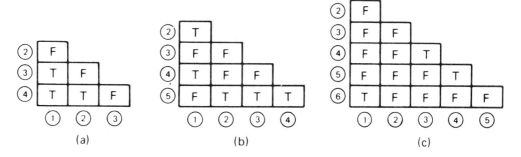

The Same Graph as Triangular Arrays

Use the following algorithm to determine connectedness.

INITIALIZE: Initialize a stack of nodes by placing node 1 on it.
HOOK: Add to the stack all nodes which are connected to the top element on the stack by a path consisting of a single line element.
DECIDE: (a) If the stack contains all nodes, return the value .TRUE..
        (b) If no nodes were added in the HOOK step, return the value .FALSE..
        (c) Otherwise, repeat from HOOK.

14. Devise a data structure with internal links to describe your graphs. Rewrite the algorithm of problem 13 so that it uses your new data structure rather than the triangular array representation of a graph.

15. Make up a data structure of your own, basing it on some complex, real-world problem you are interested in. Write down a precise description of how your data structure works. See if you can explain it to someone else in the class. If you can, write the Fortran statements necessary to implement it. If you can't, your description must not be detailed enough, so try again.

16. Write a program which carries out the logic for the following traffic light system.

   The s's in the drawing represent sensors, and the lights should obey the following rules. If no sensors are on, cycle the lights the same as if all sensors were on. If only one sensor is on, let that car go (give it a green light). Traffic on College has priority, so if sensors on College and on Prospect stay on, let more time pass with green for College than green for Prospect. Cars going straight have priority over cars turning.

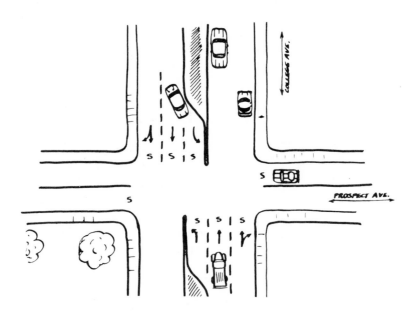

Make up a number of data lines, each of which represents a car, and have on the line some representation of which way the car wants to go and what time it arrives at the light. You may ignore yellow lights. Each time the light changes, print out the current situation, e.g., if at time 10.0, the lights on Prospect are green, three cars are waiting to proceed north on College, and one is waiting in the left turn lane to turn west onto Prospect, then print:

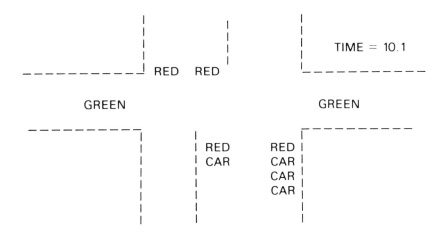

Select an appropriate data structure to store cars which are in the intersection. Queues or list would do.

17. Write a program to print random sentences. Begin by writing a number of rules for generating sentences, using a period at the beginning to distinguish words that are part of the rules from words which may appear in sentences.

Example:

Rule 1	.sentence	= .nounph	.verb	
Rule 2	.sentence	= .nounph	.verb	.nounph
Rule 3	.nounph	= .article	.noun	
Rule 4	.nounph	= .noun		
Rule 5	.verb	= BIT		
Rule 6	.verb	= JUMPED		
Rule 7	.verb	= SWALLOWED		
Rule 8	.article	= THE		
Rule 9	.noun	= HORSE		
Rule 10	.noun	= COW		
Rule 11	.noun	= PILL		

Algorithm for forming sentences:

a. Start a stack with *.sentence*.

b. Find the first rule in the stack (i.e., the first word in the list which starts with a period) and replace it by the definition of that rule (e.g., the definition of the rule .article above is THE). If there is more than one definition for the rule, then choose at random *one* of these definitions.

c. If there are no more words in the stack which start with a period, print out the sentence. Otherwise repeat step 2.

You may want to use two stacks, DONE and WORKIN, to store the partially completed sentences, as shown in the example below:

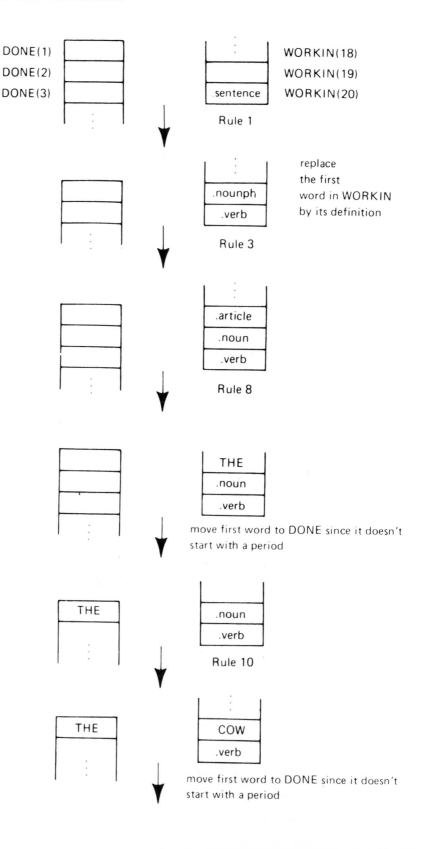

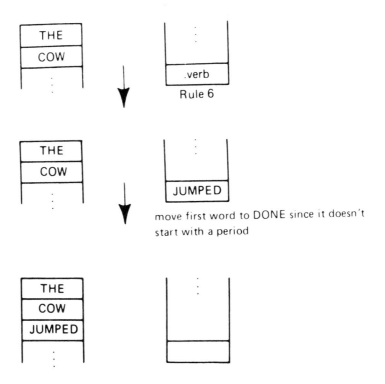

18. In Morse code, each letter is coded into a group of dots and dashes. To represent a Morse code message as data, we can use periods (.) for dots and minus signs (−) for dashes. The letters in the coded message can be separated by one space and the words by two spaces. The end of the message can be signified by a slash (/). For example, the following is a message containing two words:

    . . .b − − −b . . . bb . . . b.b − /

    The data lines may be considered contiguous. That is, words or letter codes may be continued from one line to the next.

    Write a program which READs a coded message from data lines and prints it out in letters. (The message should be written in International Morse Code—see any encyclopedia or Boy Scout manual for a description of it.) Try to write the program in such a way that it makes *no* assumptions about the length of the message. To do this, you will probably find the following subprograms helpful. One of them delivers the next character in the coded message, no matter what line or where on the line the character comes from. The other "prints" the message, one character at a time. Actually, it saves its input characters until it has a whole line and prints them all at once. For this reason it has two arguments. The second argument should be .FALSE. until the last CALL. Then it should be .TRUE. to tell the routine to print the characters it's been saving even if the whole line isn't full. This is necessary to avoid losing the contents of a partially filled last line.

> **buffering:** The technique of saving parts of an output record in memory until a whole record is accumulated is known as **buffering** the output. The array used to save the partial records is called a **buffer**. Input can be handled similarly when partial records are needed in sequence. The SUBROUTINEs GETCH and PRNCH are input and output buffering routines.

```
COMMENT:                    'CH' IS ASSIGNED THE VALUE OF THE NEXT CHARACTER
C                           IN THE INPUT STREAM.
          SUBROUTINE GETCH(CH, CURSOR, CARD)
          CHARACTER*(1) CH
          CHARACTER*(*) CARD
          INTEGER CURSOR
C                           CURSOR IS AN INTEGER VARIABLE WHOSE VALUE SHOULD
C                           BE SET TO ZERO BEFORE YOUR FIRST CALL TO GETCH
C                                     --LEAVE IT ALONE AFTER THAT
C                                 CARD IS THE BUFFER ARRAY
          IF (CURSOR .EQ. 0) THEN
C                           GET NEXT RECORD IF BUFFER IS EMPTY.
            READ 1000, CARD
     1000    FORMAT(A)
            CURSOR = 1
          ELSE
C                           PUT NEXT CHARACTER IN 'CH' AND INCREMENT 'CURSOR'
            CH = CARD(CURSOR:CURSOR)
            CURSOR = MOD(CURSOR + 1, LEN(CARD))
          ENDIF
          END

COMMENT:                    'CH' IS PLACED IN THE LINE TO BE EVENTUALLY
C                           PRINTED.  THE LINE IS PRINTED IF IT IS FULL AND
C                           WE ARE AT A WORD BOUNDRY (SPACE).
C                           IF 'DUMP' IS .TRUE., LINE IS PRINTED REGARDLESS.
          SUBROUTINE PRNCH(CH,DUMP, CURSOR,LINE)
          CHARACTER*(1) CH
          LOGICAL DUMP
          INTEGER CURSOR
          CHARACTER*(*) LINE
          INTEGER MARGIN
          PARAMETER(MARGIN = 60)
C                           CURSOR IS AN INTEGER VARIABLE WHOSE VALUE SHOULD
C                           BE SET TO ZERO BEFORE YOUR FIRST CALL PRNCH
C                                     --LEAVE IT ALONE AFTER THAT
C                           NOTE:  THIS CANNOT BE THE SAME CURSOR AS IN GETCH
C                                 LINE IS THE BUFFER ARRAY
C                                       PUT 'CH' IN 'LINE'.
          CURSOR = CURSOR + 1
          LINE(CURSOR:CURSOR) = CH
          IF ((CURSOR .GE. MARGIN .AND.
     +                          LINE(CURSOR) .EQ. ' ' .OR.
     +                              DUMP) THEN
            PRINT *, LINE(1:CURSOR)
            CURSOR = 0
          ELSE IF (CURSOR .GE. LEN(LINE)) THEN
C                         LINE IS FULL--PRINT WITH HYPHEN
            PRINT *, LINE, '-'
            CURSOR = 0
          ENDIF
          END
```

19. Add a feature to the grocery inventory program of Section 14.5 that allows the user to maintain stocks of individual items at any desired level. Some people may want to keep an extra sack of flour in the house at all times to avoid running out. Or two extra boxes of Wheaties and a carton of milk. It all depends on the person. What you need to do is add another list which the user can set up in the beginning to specify the extra products and quantities. To decide whether to put a product on the shopping list, the program will have to check for an entry on this new stock maintenance list and compare the amount on hand to the quantity entered there. Some products won't be on the stock maintenance list. Those products should be handled as before (put them on the shopping list only when the present supplies are exhausted).

20. Suppose you are working in the credit department of a lumber yard. There are many contractors with active accounts at the yard. The yard must send bills every month to those contractors who have made purchases. Your job is to automate the process. Design a program to print the monthly statements based on charge tickets accumulated over the month.

    Each charge ticket will correspond to one purchase and will contain the contractor's name and account number, a description of the purchase, and the cost. (Your program will READ one data line with this information on it for each purchase.)

    To print an itemized list for each customer, you'll have to keep a list of charges for each customer making purchases this month. Since the number of customers can vary from month to month, you should keep the head pointers for these lists in yet another list (a list of lists).

21. In problem 20, no provision is made for returning goods. Expand the program to accept return tickets and deduct the cost (less a 10 percent restocking charge) from the bill. Itemize the returns as well as the purchases.

22. Write a program which, given a tic-tac-toe board situation, decides on a subsequent move that will not lose the game, or, if there is none, prints a concession of defeat.

15 GENERALIZATIONS ABOUT PROGRAMMING

CHAPTER PLAN
- *Provide a glimpse of some other programming languages*
- *Provide an overview of computers and programming*
- *Rant and rave about the use of computers in our society*

15.1 OTHER LANGUAGES

Literally thousands of higher-level computer languages have been defined. Hundreds of higher-level languages have been developed far enough that someone has actually used them. The most we can do here is to give brief discussions about a few widely used languages. Our goal is to help you see Fortran in a wider context.

BASIC, a language developed by John Kemeny and Thomas Kurtz in 1965 at Dartmouth University, is widely used on time-sharing computer systems. In BASIC, each line is given a number, and the commands in a BASIC program are carried out in order of their line numbers. This allows BASIC programs to be altered easily. Memory cells are named with either a single letter or a letter followed by a digit. The assignment statement takes the form

> *statement number*   LET *memory cell name* = *expression*
> for example: 20   LET X = 2*Y + 1/3

The IF statement has the form

> *statement number*   IF *relation* THEN *statement number*
> for example: 30   IF X = 0 THEN 500

and means if the relation is true, then transfer control to the listed statement number.

BASIC allows the definition of primitive (one-line) functions and has a very primitive form of SUBROUTINE. BASIC is often used as a beginning language in time-sharing situations where a number of users can be simultaneously writing, checking, and running their programs. It is widely available on home microcomputers.

Here's a sample BASIC program which asks the user for a value for memory cell N and then sums the first N numbers. Statements which begin with REM are comments (REMarks).

```
10   REM    SUM FIRST N NUMBERS.
20          PRINT "GIVE ME A VALUE FOR N";
30          INPUT N
40   REM    SUM SO FAR IS ZERO
50          LET S = 0
60          FOR I = 1 TO N
70             LET S = S + 1
80          NEXT I
90          PRINT "THE SUM OF THE FIRST"; N;
100         PRINT "NUMBERS IS"; S
110         END
```

COBOL is a business-oriented language which was first designed in 1959 by a committee. One of the goals was to create a language that was more like English than Fortran. This was done by using English words to make up commands, but the language is still very much a computer language—a person unfamiliar with COBOL couldn't just sit down and produce a valid program.

COBOL makes file manipulation and the handling of various kinds of data more convenient than they are in Fortran. It also makes it easy to create and manipulate quite complex and useful data structures. In addition, it virtually forces the programmer to produce well-documented (orderly, well-commented) programs. For these reasons, it is widely used in business applications. For many of the same reasons, however, COBOL programs take more time to write (they are more wordy) than Fortran programs, and on many systems they require more computer resources (time and memory). We'll show one sample statement. Variable names are made up of letters, digits, and hyphens and may be up to 30 characters long.

```
IF TIME-SPENT EXCEEDS OVER-TIME OR EQUALS LIMIT
        THEN MOVE PAY TO STORE
```

This is equivalent to the Fortran statement

```
IF (TIMES .GT. OVERT .OR. TIMES .EQ. LIMIT) THEN
   STORE = PAY
ENDIF
```

Algol is a language designed for computing numerical algorithms. It was defined initially by an international committee which started meeting in 1958. That committee, its successors, and other workers have produced Algol 58, Algol 60, Algol W, and Algol 68. One of the nice features of Algol is that legal programs are defined by means of a formal grammar. This at once makes Algol less restrictive in its syntactic form and makes Algol programs more orderly in overall organization (compared to Fortran).

In Algol, any sequence of statements may be made into a syntactic unit by bracketing the statements with the reserved words *begin* and *end*. The program below computes the deviations from the average of a collection of numbers. Note that the array is declared within the body of the program after the proper size has been determined. This isn't possible in Fortran, in which the sizes of all arrays must be determined before execution begins.

```
begin
   integer n;
   read(n);
   begin
     real avg; array a[1:n];
     integer i;
     avg: = 0;
     for i: = 1 step 1 until n do
        avg: = avg + a[i];
     avg: = avg/n;
     for i: = 1 step 1 until n do
        print (a[i] − avg);
   end
end
```

Algol is known as a **block-structured** language because of this ability to make compound statements—or even complete programs—into single syntactic units. Full block structure places severe burdens on many computer systems because of the requirement of generality: the system must be capable of performing any type of operation at any point in the execution of a program.

To reduce the burden on the computer system, some languages have been designed with a partial block structure. In this type of language certain restrictions are placed on the types of program subunits which can be formed into blocks through the use of *begin . . . end* brackets. One such language, **PASCAL,** was designed by Niklaus Wirth in the late sixties and early seventies. PASCAL is available on many microcomputers.

Wirth was originally motivated by a desire to develop a language especially suitable for teaching programming techniques to students at all levels, beginning to advanced. As a result, the language has a very consistent syntax and is generally considered "clean" compared to Fortran. (In Fortran it's often hard to remember where the commas go, but in PASCAL the pattern is more predictable.) In addition, PASCAL, like Fortran, has been designed so that it places a low burden on computing systems which support it. Programs can be compiled and run efficiently on almost any computer system. Partially because of this attention to efficiency, and also because of some elegant data structuring facilities within the language, PASCAL is being chosen for many current projects in systems programming. ("Systems programs" are behind-the-scenes programs like compilers which aid people who are using the computer.)

The PASCAL program below keeps track of bank balances. It makes use of the data structuring facility we mentioned, which is known as the RECORD data type. Using RECORDs, we are able to describe and reference the information needed for a typical bank account in terms which would be familiar to a person using the program.

```
PROGRAM BANKBALANCE(INPUT,OUTPUT);
CONST BLANK = ' ';
      SINGLESPACE = ' ';
VAR ACCOUNT:RECORD NAME: PACKED ARRAY[1..20] OF CHAR;
                   BALANCE:REAL
          END;
    I:INTEGER
BEGIN FOR I:=1 TO 20 DO READ(ACCOUNT.NAME[I]; READLN;
      WHILE ACCOUNT.NAME[1] <> BLANK DO
          BEGIN READ(ACCOUNT.BALANCE); READLN;
              FOR I:=1 TO 10 DO READ(TRANSACTION.KIND[I]);
              READ(TRANSACTION.AMOUNT);  READLN;
              WHILE TRANSACTION.KIND[1] <> BLANK DO
                  WITH ACCOUNT, TRANSACTION DO
                  BEGIN IF KIND = 'CHK         '
                          THEN BALANCE:=BALANCE - AMOUNT
                          ELSE BALANCE:=BALANCE + ANOUNT;
                      FOR I:1 TO 10 DO READ(KIND[I]);
                          READ(AMOUNT); READLN;
                  END;
              WRITE(SINGLESPACE);
              FOR I:=1 TO 20 DO WRITE(ACCOUNT.NAME[I]);
              WRITELN;
              WRITE(SINGLESPACE);
              WRITELN(' NEW BALANCE:',ACCOUNT.BALANCE:
                              10:2   );
              WRITELN;
              FOR I:= 1 TO 20 DO READ(ACCOUNT.NAME[I]);
              READLN;
          END
END
```

Data

```
VERNOR VINGE
            456.32
CHK          22.98
CHK          33.54
DEP         291.55
CHK          54.36
             0.00
JON GUSTAFSON
            332.53
CHK          22.03
DEP         329.41
CHK          22.11
             0.00
```

Output

```
VERNOR VINGE
  NEW BALANCE:    636.99

JON GUSTAFSON
  NEW BALANCE:    617.80
```

> "Algol is Fortran done right."
>
> *—Bruce Knobe, 1973*
>
> "Pascal is Fortran done right."
>
> *—Raymond Langsford, 1980*
>
> "Fortran 77 is Fortran done right."
>
> *—James Ball, 1983*

Modula 2, which is essentially an extension of Pascal and was also designed by Wirth, adds an important feature of Fortran systems to Pascal: externally compiled groups of routines (modules) are included in programs. A typical Modula 2 system keeps track of source-code/compiled-code consistency, which is a great benefit during the development of large programs (and a service rarely performed by Fortran systems). In addition, information from modules may be made selectively available to other modules, which helps to protect data and data operations from incorrect use and to make programs independent of particular data representations. It also adds a loop notation similar to the one we use in our program design plans in this text.

Ada, an Algol/Pascal-based programming language designed under the auspices of the U.S. Department of Defense in the late seventies and early eighties, has a more extensive module facility than does Modula 2. Ada permits modules to be independent tasks. Thus a program may consist of several independently operating processes that communicate at appropriate points by passing messages (ideal for describing Pacman-like games and other real-time control programs). Another feature present in Ada but not in Modula 2 is a way for programmers to write "generic" functions (i.e., functions that can operate on many types of data, like Fortran 77's SQRT function, which can operate on REAL, DOUBLE PRECISION, and COMPLEX numbers), as long as you can deduce the proper case of the function from the data types of its arguments without knowing their specific values.

Smalltalk, the brainchild of Alan Kay and his colleagues at Xerox PARC in the seventies, is the all-time champion of the generic function. In Smalltalk, functions defined within the language can adapt to conditions determined by values of arguments as well as their data types. This carries the generic quality from the compile-time domain into the execution-time domain. Smalltalk also provides a very useful hierarchical structure for data types and operations, enabling one type to be a subclass of another, and to inherit all of its appropriate properties.

PL/I is a language defined and developed by IBM. It arose out of a series of meetings and reports issued from 1963 through 1966. At first the purpose was to define a successor to Fortran IV, but this was abandoned for the more ambitious goal of creating a language which combines and generalizes all the features of Fortran, COBOL, Algol, and JOVIAL (a language not discussed here).

This effort produced a language that has an enormous number of statements and forms and which is useful for an extremely wide range of tasks. It is a rare PL/I programmer who knows and uses all of the features.

PL/I compilers are very complex and elaborate and tend to require a large amount of space and time. This may explain why PL/I has not become more dominant.

The following statement (it is, in fact, syntactically just one statement, although it does have other statements as subparts) may convey a feeling for the possibilities.

```
IF TIME>LIMIT THEN PUT FILE(TWO) LIST(N,3,X+1.0);
  ELSE DO N = 1 TO TOTAL BY NUMB1
    TIME = TEST(TIME,N);
  END
```

SNOBOL is a series of languages developed at Bell Laboratories. The main advantage of these languages is in the creation and manipulation of character strings. It is easy to create strings and search them for occurrences of specific substrings, so SNOBOL has found frequent use by people doing linguistic analyses. The following statements are written in SNOBOL4.

```
SAMPLETEXT     =  "JUST WHAT THE WORLD NEEDS"
GLOBEPATTERN   =  "WORLD" | "EARTH" | 'GLOBE"
SAMPLETEXT       GLOBEPATTERN    :S(FOUND)
```

The first line lets the variable SAMPLETEXT stand for the string "JUST WHAT THE WORLD NEEDS." The second line lets the variable GLOBEPATTERN stand for a pattern which will match either the string "WORLD" or the string "EARTH" or the string "GLOBE." The last line is a **pattern match statement.** If the pattern GLOBEPATTERN matches SAMPLETEXT—that is, if any of the strings "WORLD," "EARTH," or "GLOBE" appear as substrings of the string that is the value of SAMPLETEXT—then the pattern match succeeds (as it does in this example). Since the match succeeds, the statement with the label FOUND is carried out next.

In 1959 a group at MIT led by John McCarthy began work on the language **LISP.** Although it is based on a scheme for representing partial recursive functions, it has seen use in a wide number of symbol manipulation tasks. Many "artificial intelligence" programs have been written in LISP, and it has inspired a number of newer languages (PLANNER, CONNIVER, LISP70, etc.). LISP (as well as SNOBOL) was designed to deal with symbolic rather than numeric information; manipulating numbers is somewhat inconvenient in LISP. The basic structure of LISP is the **list**

structure. Both data and programs have the same structure. Thus, it is easy to write LISP programs which write and alter other LISP programs.

Here is a LISP function which returns the value T (true) if its two arguments (given the names STRUCTURE1 and STRUCTURE2) are identical list structures. It uses these primitive functions:

ATOM   which is True if its argument is an atom (the **atom** is the basic element of LISP, much as a **number** is the basic element of Fortran) rather than a list structure

EQ   which is True if its two arguments are the same atom

CAR   which returns the first element of a list

CDR   which returns the rest of a list (after the first element)

```
(EQUAL                              (LAMBDA
     (STRUCTURE1 STRUCTURE2)        (COND
        ((ATOM STRUCTURE1)     (EQ STRUCTURE1 STRUCTURE2))
        ((ATOM STRUCTURE2)  NIL)
        ((EQUAL (CAR STRUCTURE1) (CAR STRUCTURE2))
             (EQUAL (CDR STRUCTURE1) (CDR STRUCTURE2)))
        (T    NIL)                          )))
```

In slightly less obscure terms, the above program says:

> If STRUCTURE1 is an atom then
> > if STRUCTURE1 and STRUCTURE2 are the same
> > > then T
> > > else False (NIL)

otherwise,
if STRUCTURE2 is an atom, the answer is False (NIL)
> since STRUCTURE1 isn't an atom

otherwise,
if the first element of STRUCTURE1 is EQUAL to the first element
> of STRUCTURE2 then the answer depends on whether or not
> the rest of STRUCTURE1 is EQUAL to the rest of STRUCTURE2

otherwise,
the answer is False (NIL)

If you fought through all that, you will have noticed that the very definition of EQUAL involved references to itself. Thus, LISP allows (in fact, encourages) **recursive** programs. Algol, PASCAL, PL/I, and SNOBOL also allow recursive programs.

One of the most important features of LISP is its convenient notation for complex data structures. If you read Section 14.5, you know how difficult it is to represent list structures in Fortran. (It's almost, but not quite, as difficult to represent lists in Algol, PASCAL, Modula 2, Ada, Smalltalk, PL/I, and SNOBOL.) In LISP the notation for list structures is natural, convenient, and built in. In fact, the whole language is designed around the underlying data structure.

Another language designed around an underlying data structure is **APL.** APL (for A Programming Language) was designed by Kenneth Iverson in the sixties and became widely available on computer systems accessible through dial-up connections over ordinary telephone lines in

1968. The basic data structures of APL are vectors and matrices. (These correspond to the one-dimensional and multi-dimensional arrays of Fortran, but they are much easier to write down and process in APL than they are in Fortran.) There are many built-in operations in APL which can operate on whole arrays as easily as they operate on single numbers. Moreover, the notation for the arrays and the programs which process them is so concise and to the point that it eliminates a whole level of detail required in languages like Fortran, COBOL, Algol, or PASCAL. The APL function below is equivalent to the MEAN function of Section 11.3.

```
[0]  ∇MU←MEAN X
[1]  MU ← (+/X) ÷ ρ X
[2]  →0
[3]  ∇
```

There are many, many more computer languages available. There are whole classes of languages we haven't mentioned. For instance, there are languages designed to help write simulation programs, such as GPSS, SIMSCRIPT, and SIMULA.

Since every higher-level language that has received any kind of wide use is general (i.e., theoretically you can write a program in that language which will compute anything computable), the choice of language is based on convenience. Different languages make solving different types of problems easier (or harder).

We used to think that Fortran's days were numbered—that fairly soon a more modern computer language would come to dominate, that fewer and fewer people would choose to use Fortran. Now we're not so sure. The changes made to produce Fortran 77 from Fortran IV are not revolutionary, but they do remove quite a few of the annoyances. They underscore the really astounding accomplishment of the original designers of Fortran. Who could have foreseen that the conceptual framework the original designers chose would be so fundamentally sound that it would be going strong 30 years later? Fortran is an eminently practical computer language, one perfectly suited to the main line of computer architecture (hardware design) in the past decades. It has aged well.

Furthermore, it appears likely that a new version of Fortran will be standardized in this decade, superseding the current Fortran 77 standard. It will be compatible with Fortran 77, but will incorporate an array notation in the manner of APL, a notation for data structures à la Pascal; a module definition facility similar to that of Modula 2; a mechanism for defining generic functions, but not quite as extensive as that of Ada; and (finally!) a loop notation similar to the one we use in our program plans in this text. This extension of Fortran may provide an evolutionary path along which large systems of existing software can migrate toward modern programming practices and notations. If so, Fortran will have a long future.

If a more modern computer language were to threaten Fortran's dominance, what might it be like? Of course, we can't foresee what breakthroughs in language design lie ahead, but we can try to classify current computer languages in an attempt to get ideas about future possibilities.

It seems reasonable to divide existing programming languages into three categories: **iterative scalar languages** (like Fortran, Algol, COBOL, Pascal, etc.), **iterative vector languages** (like APL and SNOBOL), and **functional languages** (like LISP and its derivatives). There is also a class of **application generators**, such as electronic spreadsheet calculators (Visicalc and other "copycalc" products) and database query languages (e.g., SQL) which, while they are not general-purpose programming languages, are applicable to a sufficiently general class of problems to be considered "near programming languages."

Iterative scalar languages are characterized by their limited data manipulation facilities. The only way significant computations can be programmed in these languages is through iteration (repetition) of statements which transforms small pieces of data (scalars). The basic data items usually correspond to the contents of one memory cell and are identified by naming their physical locations in memory. In other words, the program repeats the manipulation of scalars in various ways until the overall transformation the programmer desires is completed. Fortran was the earliest significant language of this type.

Fortran enabled programmers to move away from detailed command sequences that focused on operations, leaving results described implicitly to be deduced by those who understand the dynamic process involved. In place of these command sequences, programmers were able to use algebraic expressions that specified results explicitly, leaving unstated the particular command sequence needed to compute the result. The advantages were immediately obvious, and the resulting increases in programmer effectiveness were tremendous. We haven't seen anything like it since that time.

Command Sequences vs. Algebraic Expressions

algebraic notation	command sequence	
X = A*B + C*D	L	R1, A
	L	R2, B
Result: explicit	MXR	R1, R2
Operation sequence: implicit	L	R2, C
	L	R3, D
	MXR	R2, R3
	AXR	R1, R2
	ST	R1, X
	Result: implicit	
	Operation sequence: explicit	

More recent iterative scalar languages have offered improved syntax and a few new features but little more than that. There have been a few conveniences added over the years, like the IF-THEN-ELSE statement in Fortran 77 (also available in most other iterative scalar languages except

BASIC), and some flexibility in looping structures. (Fortran 77 has only the DO-loop; but most other languages in this class—again, except BASIC—have built-in notations for pretest and posttest loops.) Also, more recent languages (PASCAL, for example) provide convenient notations for data structures more complex than arrays. None of these languages provide automatic loops for processing the elements in data structure—e.g., search loops.

A primary reason for the continued popularity of iterative scalar languages is that they correspond precisely (and in some cases, transparently) to the underlying structure of computer hardware as it exists today. This structure (the trinity of processor, memory, and I/O devices, with both data and programs stored in memory) is that devised by John Von Neumann and his contemporaries in the late forties, plus a few refinements.

John Backus, the leader of the group which developed the first two versions of Fortran, speaking at the 1978 History of Programming Languages Conference, put it this way:

"While it was perhaps natural and inevitable that languages like Fortran and its successors should have developed out of the concept of the Von Neumann computer as they did, the fact that such languages have dominated our thinking for twenty years is unfortunate. It is unfortunate because their long-standing familiarity will make it hard for us to understand and adopt new programming styles which one day will offer far greater intellectual and computational power." Backus' current work is on the design of languages which fit into the functional category (discussed below).

Iterative vector languages have built-in, convenient, usable notations for vectors, matrices, sets, or other structured collections of individual data elements. Instead of writing statements to handle one element of a collection at a time, it is possible to refer to the entire collection at once in a natural way. For example, in APL the statements

```
A ← 4 7 9 6
B ← 3 12 4 1
C ← A + B
```

add the components of the two vectors (arrays of numbers), giving the vector

```
7 19 13 7
```

as a result, and assign that to the vector C.

The built-in operations of APL, along with this explicit vector denotation, make it possible to write most computations directly without worrying about the details of iterating each element of the vector. This leads to substantial simplifications in the intellectual process of program design. The essential contribution of this notation is that it extends the domain of algebraic expressions to encompass arrays as well as scalars, making it possible to express array results directly rather than implicitly through command sequences.

The primary deficiency of current iterative vector languages is their lack of a convenient notation for data structures other than the ones they are explicitly designed to handle. In a sense, they are overspecialized. If your problem is suited to the particular framework of the language, that is, to the specific data structure the language is designed for, then it is easy to state in that language. If not, you're in trouble.

Functional languages get their name because in them, computations are expressed only as function references. A program in a functional language consists of some number of function definitions and a main-function application. Thus, for instance, there is no such thing as an assignment statement in a purely functional language, and the only "variables" are function parameters.

The primary advantage of the functional style is that it brings algebraic notation to bear on the full range of computational problems, not just scalar results or array results. Entire programs become algebraic expressions, denoting their results directly. There are no command sequences from which the designer (or reader) of a program must deduce the (implicit) result.

Most current functional languages are fairly direct descendants of LISP. KRC (for Kent Recursive Calculator), designed by David Turner at the University of Kent, is one of the most elegant of these languages. It extends functional programming to the realm of I/O. Another functional language, ML (designed by Milner and his associates at the University of Edinburgh) is a more comprehensive language than KRC. It pays more attention to data types and efficiency considerations. Yet another functional language, SISAL (designed by a consortium at Lawrence Livermore National Laboratory, Colorado State University, Digital Equipment Corporation, and the University of Manchester) was patterned after VAL (designed by Jack Dennis at MIT). These languages employ a syntax reminiscent of Pascal, but the programming style is entirely different, of course. SISAL and VAL are very much concerned with efficient computation, especially on parallel processors (i.e., computers with many cooperating processors). Existing implementations of functional languages tend to be inefficient in their use of computer resources, but much research is directed toward efficient use of parallel processors by functional languages. (The advantage of functional programming for parallel processing is obvious: since the entire program is a single expression, the only impediments to parallel computation will be dependencies among data values to be computed, and these can't be avoided.) If this work is successful, perhaps we will see the advantages of direct description of full computational results through algebraic expressions extend even into the domain of Fortran (when the next standardized version appears).

Application generators are special-purpose programming languages that apply to more-or-less specific problem areas. For many years these languages tended to be highly specialized and not especially easy to use. For example, the Statistical Package for Social Sciences (SPSS) falls in this category. It gives people a way to use the computer to carry out a wide range of statistical analyses on just about any kind of data, but it can't be used for much of anything outside statistical analysis. However, some of the new application generators can be used in a very broad range of problems. For example, we know of a woman working for a soft-drink bottler who used Visicalc (which is like a two-dimensional table in which the user can set up relationships between the various table entries by means of arithmetic formulas) to implement a sophisticated inventory control procedure on a computer. She was able to do this in a few weeks, despite having had no previous experience with computers and despite having been told by the data processing manager in the bottling plant that what she needed would require a six-month effort for his programming staff to implement on their computer system. Visicalc (and the other electronic spreadsheets which mimic it) is a very powerful tool that can be applied to a broad range of problems— not quite as broad a range as the general-purpose langauges (Fortran, APL, LISP, etc.), but almost.

Data-base query languages, especially "relational" languages like SQL, are growing in generality and ease of use. It may be that at some point, a clever integration of a query language with an electronic spreadsheet and a functional language will bring general-purpose programming within the reach of the casual, untrained computer user.

15.2   SOME OPINIONATED OPINIONS

This is the computer age, so they say. Man couldn't have gotten to the moon if it hadn't been for computers. Computers are giant brains, capable of making flawless, logical decisions in incomprehensibly small fractions of a second. Computers are controlling us, dehumanizing us. "Computer designed" means "better." Computers never make mistakes and they never go on strike. You put data into a computer and it gives you answers. Computers draw pictures and write music; computers play chess; computers control airplanes and missiles; they keep tabs on your every credit transaction, phone call, and suspicious move. Movie computers respond to spoken requests with smooth tongued, seemingly pragmatic but actually borderline psychotic, logic. Computers are good; computers are evil.

Perhaps these "media" notions about computers seem hopelessly at odds with the view of computers you have seen in this book. At least *we* think that they are different. Perhaps a few words about the way we think of computers will help you come to your own conclusions about what computers are or should be or can be. . . .

We think that computers are (1) useful tools and (2) fun. The second point is, of course, very subjective, and we certainly don't mean to imply that learning the intricacies of Fortran FORMAT statements or reading floods of obscure error messages is particularly enjoyable. We just mean that wracking our brains to describe some process, programming our description, and seeing the consequences of our program is enjoyable. It's fun to play around with programs, seeing large changes in the program's behavior with seemingly tiny changes in its exact form.

We see computers as tools just as people see mathematics as a tool, that is, as something which can be used to help you do something you want to do. Computer programs can be used as models of processes that go on in the real world. For example, an architect could write a computer program to study the effects of wind loads on a building; a linguist could use a computer program to describe a way people might analyze sentences; a neurophysiologist could write a computer program to describe the way a certain part of the nervous system operates. The program doesn't replace the reality of the process under study any more than writing a mathematical equation to describe how electrical current behaves in a resistor replaces a real resistor. A computer program is easier to change and experiment with than a real building or an electrical circuit, but it can't really replace them—it *can* be used to help understand them.

An important side issue here is that if we view computers as tools, then we have no more reason to trust the results we get than we do with any other tool. No theory or analysis becomes more (or less) true because it was done on a computer (or adding machine, slide rule, or abacus).

Where would you put more Xs?

Views of computers		day-to-day living	this book	the media: TV, magazines, etc.
	slave			
	tool		X	
	oppressor			X
	god			X

Sources of views

Yet another side issue is that viewing computers as tools says nothing about their limitations. If you want to ask, "Is it possible for a computer to be the world chess champion?" We would have to say that we don't see why not. Such questions are really questions about algorithms, not computers, because any general-purpose computer can, theoretically, carry out anything that is computable.

Computer programs exist today which play

An unbeatable game of Kalah
An excellent game of backgammon
A very strong game of checkers
A good game of chess
A novice game of bridge
A rancid game of Go

OK. If what we say is true, then why are there troubles? Why are we increasingly discovering that, say, a mistake in our credit card bill can go on unfixed for months, piling up spurious interest charges? Why do we get answers like "I'm really sorry you're having trouble, but your account is on the computer."

No doubt someone you know has had some sort of "computer trouble." We have a friend who signed up for meal plan A in his dorm, but was billed for meal plan B. He finally went to the person in charge of the billing, and she pulled out a huge book of computer printout, leafed through until she found his name, and then announced, "You're on Plan B." He said, "But I have a copy of the form I sent you and it's marked Plan A." She said, "No, you're on Plan B, *it says so right here.*"

Yes, you might say, it's true that the problem shows up when someone in an organization puts too much faith in something just because it came out of a computer, but *if the computer weren't there, it couldn't have happened to begin with.* Hah! *Not so,* we would say.

The thing to fear is not that computers are gods; the thing to fear is people who *think* computers are gods.

We know (second hand) of a nice old person who was designing airplanes just before World War II (not for the winning side, incidentally). Part of the design necessitated solving some sets of differential equations that were so difficult that they could not be solved directly. Today we'd just get a stored program from the computer center and have the machine grind out approximate solutions. This person had no computers. Instead there was a large room full of women (called "computer girls"), each one sitting at a desk with an adding machine. The method for solving the differential equations was to write out a series of instructions for each woman, including instructions saying which other woman to get partial results from. After a week or so, the "computer girls" would produce the desired answers. You don't need a computer to compute.

The point here is *not* just the well-known fact that what the computer does is determined by its program, which was written by a human. Ultimately, it is a human being who is responsible for what happens. The people who are responsible are the ones who set up an organization and determine where their data comes from, how it is to be manipulated, and what is to be done with the results. It doesn't matter that it was a computer that printed out an erroneous credit balance or the wrong meal plan. The same wrong results could have been produced by people; the problem is in the structure of the organization. Perhaps computers have made things worse because they are new, modern gadgets that can be blamed for the errors of a faulty organization. Perhaps computers make it easier to get by with bad manners. But we believe these abuses will gradually diminish.

There are lessons to be learned about good programming from all the bad programming we come into contact with daily. For instance, it should be clear to you that a few simple IF statements could immediately halt such absurdities as sending someone an erroneous utility bill for one million dollars. The only reasonable way to program is to admit that there are going to be errors, and to put in tests for them. In the case of billing programs, any bill that is much different from the average should be detected and set aside for someone to examine.

Another bad practice that arises is using abbreviations where the full word is needed for clarity. Programmers tend to fall into this sort of thing, perhaps because early programming languages (like Fortran) require such short memory cell names. This problem can be circumvented if programmers keep in mind the principle that their programs should be understandable not only to themselves and their computer, but also *to other people.*

I'm going down to SFOF to get an RFP for the EVA PEX," he said clearly.

Sometimes the abbreviated form of a term takes on its own special significance. This happens in many fields, but probably more often in the computer area than any other. For example, there is a way of interpreting data transmissions known in the computer network field as "TCP" for "transmission control protocol." The interesting thing is that "TCP" is, in a sense, a more precise term than "transmission control protocol" because the latter could be taken as a generic term that could apply to any one of several data communication schemes, while the former, "TCP," is never used to refer to any protocol other than *the* "Transmission Control Protocol."

Abbreviations, when they take on an identity of their own, lead to an amusing grammatical phenomenon. Take "rpm," for example, which stands for "revolutions per minute." The term is intrinsically plural, but it is now so thoroughly entrenched in our vocabularies that we often hear people refer to speeds like 6000 rpm's, making a plural out of something that's already plural.

Sometimes it goes the other way. The speed of high-performance computers is often given in "megaflops," which stands for "million floating-point operations per second." For example, a computer capable of doing 100 million floating-point operations per second is rated at 100 megaflops. The term "megaflops," like "rpm," is intrinsically plural. The difference is that "megaflops" sounds plural and "rpm" doesn't. What rating should we give a computer that can do only one million floating-point operations per second? "One megaflops" would probably be the correct term, but "one megaflop" sounds better even though it wouldn't be sufficient to say "one million floating-point operations" (which is what "one megaflop" should stand for).

And so on.

So far computers have been employed extensively by the military, widely employed by technologically sophisticated industries, and used for accounting and record keeping by most other large organizations. Certainly, these sorts of uses of large-scale computing will continue to grow, hopefully to yield such things as automated libraries, energy-saving communication devices (since there will be less need for business trips), and better-scheduled mass transit systems, but the most noticeable new uses of computers have been more personal. In the future we expect computers to make more and more intrusions into our everyday lives. To us, the pocket calculators, video games, and small microcomputers are portents of a dramatic domestication of computers. Now that computers are getting into the hands of the kid on the corner, the crackpot inventor, and the lemonade-stand tycoon, watch out! It will be fun. It is clear that computer hardware will continue to undergo revolutionary decreases in size and cost. What will continue to be necessary are new programs and people with good ideas about what to program. With the understanding of programming concepts you've received from this book, you should be in good shape to cope with and help control computers in the future.

15   PROBLEMS

1. Next time you come up against "the computer" in some way (one of the phone companies, your school, the IRS, a computer dating agency), try to learn something about how computers really fit into their operation. What image of computers do they try to project?

2. Think up some useful, fun, or zany products that could be made using tiny, inexpensive computers. Write a Fortran program that emulates your product. Some suggestions are:

    a. a fishhook that analyzes the fish around it and scares away types you don't want to catch.

b.   a pen that measures the surface it's writing on and makes ap-
     propriate changes in the ink flow rate
c.   a typewriter that checks your spelling.
d.   a pipe that regulates the flow of air so as to produce a smoke of
     just the right temperature
e.   a program that writes Fortran textbooks

Turnabout's fair play. We'd be pleased to hear your opinions.

APPENDIXES

A ADDITIONAL FORTRAN FEATURES

THE DATA STATEMENT AND THE SAVE STATEMENT

There are three different ways to put values in memory cells: the assignment statement, the READ statement, and the DATA statement. The assignment statement computes a value and places the result in a memory cell. The READ statement takes values from data lines outside the program itself and places them into memory cells. Both of these statements are executable; that is, they cause the processor to take some action. The **DATA statement,** however, is *not* executable. It is an instruction to the compiler rather than to the processor. The DATA statement instructs the compiler to put initial values into specific memory cells, so that when the machine language version of your program begins to run, those memory cells will already have values.

For example, if we need a FUNCTION which computes the area of a circle given its radius, the FUNCTION will compute the product of π and the square of the radius. Therefore, the FUNCTION will need to know the value of π. Of course, we can simply write the value of the number of digits of accuracy appropriate to our machine, but then we'll have to go look up the value in a table. That's not so bad, even though it takes time we'd rather spend on something else, but there is another disadvantage—if we give our FUNCTION to someone else whose computer carries a different accuracy in its REALs, he'll have to change the number in the program. Therefore, we decide to let the computer compute π for us to whatever accuracy it's capable of. To do this, we use the fact that $\pi/4 = $ arctan (1). We compute PI using the assignment statement PI = ATAN(1.0) $*$ 4.0. If we put the above assignment statement first in the FUNCTION, it will compute a value for PI every time it is called. To avoid this unnecessary computation, we use a DATA statement to place the value .TRUE. in a LOGICAL memory cell. The first statement of the FUNCTION tests this memory cell. If it has the value .TRUE., its value is changed to .FALSE. and PI is assigned the value ATAN(1.0) $*$ 4.0. If its value is .FALSE. (which it will be on every call to the FUNCTION except the first), then that assignment statement is skipped. Instead of having to compute π every time, the FUNCTION only has to perform a simple test.

DATA Statement

form

DATA $vlist_1/clist_1/,vlist_2/clist_2/, \ldots ,vlist_n/clist_n/$

$vlist_k$ must be of the same form as an input list and, in addition, each subscript and implied DO parameter must be an INTEGER constant expression (which may involve implied DO variables). Values delimiting substrings must be INTEGER constant expressions. The number and order of the variables in the list is determined as for input lists.

$clist_k$ is a list of constants, or **repeated constants** of the form $r*c$, where r is an INTEGER constant having the effect of repeating the constant c, **r** times. The number of constants in $clist_k$ must be the same as the number of variables in $vlist_k$. The name of a constant may be used wherever a constant may be used in a DATA statement.

meaning

The variables in $vlist_k$ become initially defined (before program execution begins) with the corresponding values in $clist_k$. Assignments are made as for assignment statements, including conversion between numerical data types when necessary.

restriction

A DATA statement may not precede any nonexecutable statement except a FORMAT

examples

```
CHARACTER*(5) FST,LST
INTEGER MONOID(3)
REAL X, Y, Z(100)
DATA FST,LST / 'ALPHA', 'OMEGA'/
DATA MONOID/47, 342, -9/
DATA X,Y/4.2, 3.7/, (Z(I), I = 1, 50)/50*0.0/
DATA (Z(I), I = 51, 100)/25*1.0, 25*2.0/
```

```
REAL FUNCTION AREA(RADIUS)
REAL RADIUS
REAL PI
LOGICAL FIRST
SAVE FIRST, PI
DATA FIRST/ .TRUE./
IF (FIRST) THEN
   PI = ATAN(1.0) * 4.0
   FIRST = .FALSE.
ENDIF
AREA = PI * RADIUS ** 2
END
```

$$\pi = 3.14159265358979323846 \ldots \ldots$$

The FUNCTION AREA () contains another new statement, the SAVE statement. This is needed because we want the memory cells FIRST and PI to retain their values from one FUNCTION reference to the next. Normally, you can't depend on the values of local variables in subprograms being defined when the subprogram is called. They must be explicitly defined each time the subprogram is entered. (The only exception is local variables defined through DATA statements and never altered by an executable statement, but this is rare because constants defined by PARAMETER statements would normally be used instead of never-altered variables.)

When we want to require the subprogram to save the values of certain local variables to be used during successive calls, we must list the variables in SAVE statements.

SAVE Statement

forms
SAVE
SAVE *list*
list is a list of local variables (unsubscripted) or local array names in the subprogram.

meaning
Values of variables and arrays listed in the SAVE statement are retained and may be used without redefinition or any call to the subprogram. If the *list* is omitted, all local variables and arrays in the subprogram are SAVEd.

note
A SAVE statement in a main program has no effect.

examples

```
SAVE
SAVE X, Y, Z
SAVE ARRAY
```

COMMON REGIONS

The COMMON statement makes it possible for the programmer to create variables which can be accessed directly by any program unit (main program or subprogram) without having been passed as a parameter. Used properly, COMMON regions provide ways to encapsulate information among a group of related subprograms and hide that information from routines which need not (and usually should not) have access to it. COMMON regions can also be used to save space in memory. Used improperly, COMMON regions can lead to bugs which are incredibly hard to discover. We hope the examples below will guide you to the proper uses and steer you away from the pitfalls.

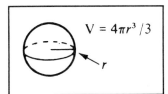 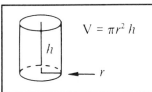 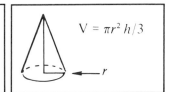

Suppose we want to write three FUNCTIONs; one to compute the volume of a sphere, given its radius; another to compute the volume of a cylinder, given its radius and height; and a third to compute the volume of a cone, given its radius and height. Each of these FUNCTIONs needs to use the value of PI. It would be nice to be able to put that value into some memory cell in the computer and use that memory cell in each of the FUNCTIONs. Of course, we could do this by adding an extra argument to each FUNCTION and supplying the value to the FUNCTION through that argument. The problem with this approach is that including the argument PI in every FUNCTION reference is a nuisance. What we need is an alternative way to allow subprograms to share memory cells.

```
COMMENT:      A CLUMSY WAY TO COMMUNICATE PI TO THREE FUNCTIONS
      REAL PI
      REAL SPHERE, CONE, CYL
      PI = 4.0 * ATAN(1.0)
      PRINT *, 'VOLUME OF SPHERE OF RADIUS 1 =',
     +                               SPHERE(1.0,PI)
      PRINT *, 'VOLUME OF CONE OF RADIUS 1, HT 2 =',
     +                               CONE(1.0, 2.0, PI)
      PRINT *, 'VOLUME OF CYLINDER OF RADIUS 1, HT 2 =',
     +                               CYL (1.0, 2.0, PI)
      END
```

The COMMON statement provides that alternative. Using a COMMON statement, we can set up a part of memory which can be used by any subprogram or program.

Before things get too involved, let's look at the example at hand. We want the three FUNCTIONs, SPHERE, CONE, and CYL, to be able to use a single memory cell whose value is π. To make this possible, we place a COMMON statement in each of the FUNCTIONs. A COMMON statement establishes a region of memory which may be accessed by any program

COMMON Statement

form

COMMON/a_1/$list_1$,/a_2/$list_2$, ... /a_n/$list_n$

a_k is an identifier or blank

$list_k$ is a list of unsubscripted memory cell names or array names separated by commas

If a_1 is blank, the first two slashes may be omitted. An array name in $list_k$ may be followed by a length declarator if its length is not declared elsewhere.

meaning

COMMON storage regions with labels a_k are set up, one area for each distinct label. Within the program unit in which this statement appears, the memory cells in region a_k are given the names in $list_k$ in the order specified by the list. If an array name appears in the list, all of its memory cells are included in the COMMON region. If two of the area names are identical, the effect is the same as if the elements in the second list were placed on the end of the first list.

restriction

If a COMMON region contains any CHARACTER variables, it must consist entirely of CHARACTER variables.

example

```
REAL A(3), B(5), C
INTEGER X(3), Y(2), Z
COMMON /AREA1/ A,X,C, /AREA2/ Y,B,Z
```

sets up regions as follows

AREA 1

	A(1)
	A(2)
	A(3)
	X(1)
	X(2)
	X(3)
	C

AREA 2

	Y(1)
	Y(2)
	B(1)
	B(2)
	B(3)
	B(4)
	B(5)
	Z

unit. We name this region with a unique identifier which, as usual, is a string of six or fewer letters or digits beginning with a letter. We chose the name CONST in this example, as you see below. It is also possible to set up a COMMON region which is nameless; that is, its name may be blank.

```
REAL FUNCTION SPHERE(RADIUS)
REAL RADIUS
REAL PI
COMMON /CONST/ PI
SPHERE = (4.0/3.0)*PI*RADIUS**3
END
```

```
REAL FUNCTION CONE(RADIUS, HEIGHT)
REAL RADIUS, HEIGHT
REAL PI
COMMON /CONST/ PI
CONE = HEIGHT*PI*RADIUS**2/3.0
END

REAL FUNCTION CYL(RADIUS, HEIGHT)
REAL RADIUS, HEIGHT
REAL PI
COMMON /CONST/ PI
CYL = HEIGHT*PI*RADIUS**2
END
```

As you can see, the COMMON statement labels a COMMON region in memory, the label being surrounded by slashes; then it names the memory cells to be included in the COMMON area. It is important to remember that the *label* is the only thing which can be communicated from one subprogram to another. The names of the individual memory cells within the COMMON area are local to the subprogram and *may* differ from one to another, although people usually choose to make them the same in all subprograms.

> **COMMON names:** Each subprogram (or main program) which uses a COMMON region must declare the region with a COMMON statement. A COMMON region is a collection of contiguous storage units. The names referring to these storage units may be different in different subprograms. It is the order of the memory cell and array names in the COMMON statement which determines which names will be associated with which storage units.

> **COMMON safety:** To be safe, for each COMMON region, punch a "COMMON deck" of memory cell and array declarations and a single COMMON statement. Duplicate the deck for each program unit that uses the COMMON region.

In our example of three FUNCTIONs using the COMMON area CONST, we did not include any statements giving PI a value. Of course, it would have to be given a value before any of the FUNCTIONs could be used. This could be accomplished in many ways. We will look at three ways. The first two are essentially different; the third is an embellishment of the second.

The first method is to assign PI a value in the main program before the FUNCTIONs are called.

```
REAL SPHERE, CONE, CYL
REAL PI
COMMON /CONST/ PI
PI = 4.0*ATAN(1.0)
PRINT *, 'VOLUME OF SPHERE OF RADIUS 1 =', SPHERE(1.0)
PRINT *, 'VOLUME OF CONE OF RADIUS 1, HT 2 =', CONE(1.0, 2.0)
PRINT *, 'VOLUME OF CYLINDER OF RADIUS 1, HT 2 =', CYL(1.0, 2.0)
END
```

The disadvantage of assigning PI a value in the main program is that the main program doesn't have any use for the value of PI, so it seems an inappropriate place to even have the memory cell PI around, let alone assign a value to it.

We can instruct the compiler to give values to memory cells located in COMMON areas by using a BLOCK DATA subprogram. Actually "subprogram" is a misnomer here since a BLOCK DATA subprogram contains *no* executable statements, and, therefore, isn't a program at all. The purpose of a BLOCK DATA subprogram is to initialize COMMON regions by means of DATA statements. No executable statements are allowed; only declarations; COMMON statements; and PARAMETER, SAVE, and DATA statements.

In the present example, the BLOCK DATA subprogram would look like the one in the box above. If we put this BLOCK DATA subprogram together with the three FUNCTIONs—SPHERE, CONE, and CYL—the main program no longer needs the COMMON statement because PI is given its value by the BLOCK DATA subprogram.

BLOCK DATA Subprogram

---

form
BLOCK DATA *optional name*
(declarations of memory cells, arrays, and COMMON areas)
(DATA statements)
END

meaning
Instructs the compiler to put values into COMMON areas (may not be used to initialize blank COMMON).

example
```
BLOCK DATA
REAL PI
COMMON /CONST/ PI
DATA PI /3.14159/
END
```

A better way to store the value of π in a memory cell is to let the computer determine its value by using the built-in function ATAN, as you saw in the discussion of DATA statements. Then the value will be computed to as many digits as your computer system can handle in REAL variables. The FUNCTIONs below use this idea along with a LOGICAL variable which becomes .FALSE. as soon as one of the FUNCTIONs has computed the value for PI in order to prevent recomputation. This collection of FUNCTIONs provides an example of how COMMON can be used to hide information within a collection of related routines. The value of PI (and of FIRST) is not accessible except to the three FUNCTIONs which need it. No matter how many other routines there are in the program, none of them can disturb the value of PI unless they too contain the COMMON region named /CONST/.

```
REAL SPHERE, CONE, CYL
PRINT *, 'VOLUME OF SPHERE OF RADIUS 1 =', SPHERE(1.0)
PRINT *, 'VOLUME OF CONE OR RADIUS 1, HT 2 =', CONE(1.0, 2.0)
PRINT *, 'VOLUME OF CYLINDER OF RADIUS 1, HT 2 =', CYL(1.0, 2.0)
END

REAL FUNCTION SPHERE(RADIUS)
REAL RADIUS
REAL PI
LOGICAL FIRST
COMMON /CONST/ PI, FIRST
SAVE /CONST/
IF (FIRST) THEN
  PI = ATAN(1.0) * 4.0
  FIRST = .FALSE.
EDIF
SPHERE = (4.0/3.0)*PI*RADIUS**3
END

REAL FUNCTION CONE(RADIUS, HEIGHT)
REAL RADIUS, HEIGHT
REAL PI
LOGICAL FIRST
COMMON /CONST/ PI, FIRST
SAVE /CONST/
IF (FIRST) THEN
  PI = ATAN(1.0) * 4.0
  FIRST = .FALSE.
ENDIF
CONE = HEIGHT*PI*RADIUS**2/3.0
END

REAL FUNCTION CYL(RADIUS, HEIGHT)
REAL RADIUS, HEIGHT
REAL PI
LOGICAL FIRST
COMMON /CONST/ PI, FIRST
SAVE /CONST/
IF (FIRST) THEN
  PI = ATAN(1.0) * 4.0
  FIRST = .FALSE.
ENDIF
CYL = HEIGHT*PI*RADIUS**2
END

BLOCK DATA
REAL PI
LOGICAL FIRST
COMMON /CONST/ PI, FIRST
SAVE /CONST/
DATA FIRST/ .TRUE./
END
```

(Continued on following page)

Output

```
VOLUME OF SPHERE OF RADIUS 1 =          4.188790
VOLUME OF CONE OF RADIUS 1, HT 2 =      2.094395
VOLUME OF CYLINDER OF RADIUS 1, HT 2 =      6.283185
```

As you can see in the above program, SAVE statements may be used to retain COMMON regions as well as local variables. This is only necessary when the COMMON region is not mentioned in the main program.

There are a few other things you should know about COMMON areas. The first is that the total number of memory cells in a particular COMMON area must be the same in all subprograms in which it is declared. The names of the memory cells in the COMMON area don't have to be the same from one subprogram to the next, but the total length of a COMMON area must be the same from one program unit to another. The one exception is with blank COMMON. The length of the blank COMMON region need not be the same in every program unit. If it's not, the total length of the blank COMMON area is the maximum of its sizes in the various program units where it is declared.

Although COMMON areas are usually used to communicate values from one subprogram to another, they are occasionally used to save memory space. Using them for this purpose is tricky, however, and should be left to the accomplished programmer.

SAVE/COMMON/

When a COMMON region is listed in a SAVE statement, its name is surrounded by slashes. The entire region must be saved. Individual variables or arrays within a COMMON region must not be listed in SAVE statements. All subprograms which reference the COMMON region must SAVE it. (If the COMMON region is declared in the main program, its values are automatically saved throughout the execution of the program. Hence, none of the SAVE statements are needed for the region.)

SUBPROGRAMS AS ARGUMENTS—INTRINSIC AND EXTERNAL

On occasion you may wish to define a FUNCTION or SUBROUTINE which accepts yet another subprogram as one of its arguments. One very common use of this is in subprograms which accept a FUNCTION from your program and then do something useful for you with it. Typical tasks are (1) plotting out its values over some range, (2) finding where your FUNCTION has maxima and minima, and (3) computing the area under your FUNCTION. Subprograms which do these things are no doubt available at your computer center.

Perhaps you recall from Chapter 10 that FUNCTIONs and SUBROU-TINEs are said to be **external** subprograms because their definitions lie wholly outside the program from which they are called and because they are compiled separately and independently from the main program and from each other. This means that when the compiler is dealing with one program unit, it doesn't look at other program units to decide if a partic-ular identifier refers to a memory cell or to another program unit.

Let's examine the problem carefully. Suppose we have a SUBROU-TINE called PLOT which accepts as arguments F (the FUNCTION whose values we want plotted), A and B (describing the range over which values are to be plotted), and DELTA (the stepsize).

SUBROUTINE PLOT below is designed for this task. It uses the dis-cretization technique of Section 11.7 (the plotting section) to map func-tion values from the range −1.0 to +1.0 into INTEGERs in the range 0 to 50. With this INTEGER, it plots function values at appropriate points across the page. The resulting graph will be oriented down the page rather than across, as we normally plot graphs. (Note that function val-ues outside the range −1.0 to +1.0 are plotted along the outside borders of the plotting area.)

```
COMMENT:                PLOT A GRAPH OF THE FUNCTION F:
C                        F(A), F(A+DELTA), F(A+2*DELTA)....., F(B)
          SUBROUTINE PLOT(F, A, B, DELTA)
          REAL F, A, B, DELTA
          REAL X
          INTEGER POINT, I
          REAL LEFT, RIGHT
          INTEGER LEVELS, DSCRET
          PARAMETER(LEFT=-1.0, RIGHT=+1.0, LEVELS=50)
C                        ...STATEMENT FOR DISCRETIZATION
          DSCRET(F) = INT(LEVELS*(F-LEFT)/(RIGHT-LEFT))
C
          DO 100 X = A, B, DELTA
            POINT = DSCRET(F(X))
            POINT = MIN(LEVELS, MAX(0, POINT))
            PRINT *, (' ', I = 1, POINT), '*'
   100    CONTINUE
          END
```

Look at the first statement in the DO-loop. The form of the expression F(X) indicates that F is either an array or a FUNCTION. It can't be an array; if it were, there would be a declaration to that effect. Therefore, F must be a FUNCTION, and when SUBROUTINE PLOT is called, it will be informed of the FUNCTION's name. No problem here.

Now let's go to another program unit and look at a statement which CALLs SUBROUTINE PLOT. Suppose we want to plot the exponentially damped sine wave.

If we have written a FUNCTION to compute the values of this wave—

say the FUNCTION is named DAMP—then we can plot the wave by calling the SUBROUTINE.

```
CALL PLOT(DAMP, 0.0, 2.0, 0.1)
```

Here's where the problem comes up. The name "DAMP," as it's used in the CALL statement, looks as if it could be a memory cell name rather than the name of a FUNCTION. Unless we instruct the compiler otherwise, it will simply assume that DAMP is a memory cell.

It is the purpose of an EXTERNAL statement to inform the compiler which names are the names of subprograms rather than the names of memory cells. We've never needed EXTERNAL before because the meaning of each name was implicit in its context, but in this case the context leaves an ambiguity which the compiler resolves in the wrong way unless we tell it otherwise.

EXTERNAL Statement

---

form
EXTERNAL *list*
list is a list of subprogram names separated by commas.

meaning
Informs the compiler that the names in *list* are subprogram names, not variable names.

examples

EXTERNAL FNC
EXTERNAL GAMMA, BETA, BESSEL

The program below uses PLOT to draw graphs of the exponentially damped sine wave and another function well known to electrical engineers, the ramp wave.

```
EXTERNAL DAMP, RAMP
CALL PLOT(DAMP, 0.0, 2.0, 0.15)
CALL PLOT(RAMP,-1.0, 1.0, 0.15)
END

REAL FUNCTION DAMP(T)
REAL T
DAMP = SIN(3.1416 * T) * EXP(-T)
END

REAL FUNCTION RAMP(T)
REAL T
RAMP = 1.0 - ABS(T)
END
```

Output

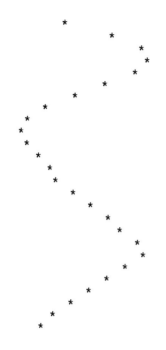

VARIABLE FORMATs

A *variable* FORMAT is a CHARACTER expression or CHARACTER array name used in the FORMAT specifier of an I/O statement. Used in this way, the CHARACTER expression must evaluate to a string starting with a left parenthesis and ending with a right parenthesis enclosing a list of FORMAT specifications like those you might find in an ordinary FOR-MAT statement. (If the variable FORMAT is a CHARACTER array name, then the values of successive elements are treated as if they were concatenated together and the FORMAT specification is scanned from the left parenthesis, which begins the string through the matching right parenthesis.)

The most common use of variable FORMATs is in canned programs which process large quantities of data. So that the user of the program can design his own data line layouts, the program first reads the user's input FORMAT into a CHARACTER variable (or array) and then uses that variable in the FORMAT specifier of the READ statement. A simple example of this process is illustrated below.

```
      CHARACTER*(80) USRFMT
      REAL X(10)
      READ 1000, USRMFT
1000  FORMAT(A)
      READ USRFMT, (X(I), I = 1,10)
```

Variable FORMATs can be used in a more sophisticated way. Instead of READing a user's FORMAT from a data line, it's possible to create the FORMAT through a computational process. This fascinating idea has tantalized many experienced programmers right over the brink of disaster. It is an error-prone process, and we recommend avoiding it. Everything you can do with variable FORMATs you can also do with CHARACTER strings and internal files (see Section 13.5), and you'll probably get into less trouble.

However, just so you'll know what to watch for, consider the following example. Suppose you want to print from one to ten numbers on a line in fields of width five so that, if there are fewer than ten numbers, they appear on the right-hand side of the line. Suppose there is a memory cell N whose value is the number of numbers you want to print on the line and that the numbers are stored in any array A. It would be nice if you could simply put variables in the FORMAT itself. Unfortunately, this is illegal, but with a little more effort we can get the desired effect.

```
          PRINT 1000, SNGLSP, (A(I), I = 1,N)
1000      FORMAT(A, T 5*(11-N), N I5)
```

This FORMAT contains illegal use of variables.

Basically, what we want is a FORMAT like the one shown below, where the empty boxes are filled in with the values 5*(11–N). However, these INTEGER values must be converted to CHARACTER strings because FORMATs can only be made of CHARACTERs.

$$(A, T \boxed{\quad}, \boxed{\quad} I5)$$

We can make this conversion by writing into parts of the variable FORMAT, treating them as internal files. The details are spelled out in the program below.

```
          CHARACTER*(1) SNGLSP
          CHARACTER*(20) VARFMT
          INTEGER K, N
          VARFMT = '(A, TXXX, XXXI5)'
          N = 6
          WRITE(UNIT =   VARFMT(6:8), FMT = 1000) 5*(11 - N)
          WRITE(UNIT = VARFMT(11:13), FMT = 1000) N
100       FORMAT (I3)
          SNGLSP = ' '
          PRINT VARFMT, SNGLSP, (K, K = 1, N)
          END
```

Output

```
1   2   3   4   5   6
```

B INTRINSIC FUNCTIONS

Intrinsic FUNCTIONs, also known as built-in functions, may be used by simply referencing them in your program. The FUNCTIONs shown in the following table are guaranteed to exist in every Fortran 77 system. The advantage to using them should be obvious—if you need to find, say, the square root of some value in your program, it's a lot easier to write

SQRT(X)

than it would be to write a bunch of Fortran statements that compute the square root from scratch!

For a discussion of using these FUNCTIONs, see Section 11.2.

Note: A number of these operators work both with INTEGER values and REAL values. Thus, MAX(1.0, 3.4, − 19.2) gives the REAL result 3.4 while MAX(1, 4, − 19) gives the INTEGER value 4. However, all the arguments must be of the same type, so the expression

MAX(1, 3.4, −19)

is *illegal.* If you need to find the largest of several values, some INTEGER and some REAL, to use the MAX operator, you must convert some of the arguments to make them all the same type. Thus,

MAX(REAL(1),3.4,REAL(− 19))

can be used (and gives the REAL result 3.4).

The following material on intrinsic functions is based on Table 5 of North American Standard FORTRAN X3.9—1978, copyright 1978 by the American National Standards Institute, copies of which may be purchased from the American National Standards Institute at 1430 Broadway, New York, New York 10018.

Class of FUNCTION	Definition	Number of arguments	Name	Type of argument	Type of result	Example use	Value of example
Type of conversion	Conversion to INTEGER (see note 1)	1	INT	INTEGER / REAL	INTEGER / INTEGER	INT(17) / INT(3.1415)	17 / 3
	Conversion to REAL (see note 2)	1	REAL	INTEGER / REAL	REAL / REAL	REAL (3) / REAL (1.0)	3.0 / 1.0
	Conversion to INTEGER (see note 3)	1	ICHAR	CHARACTER	INTEGER	ICHAR('A')	65 ← may differ on your system ↙
	Conversion to CHARACTER (see note 3)	1	CHAR	INTEGER	CHARACTER	CHAR (65)	'A'
Truncation	$int(a)$ (see note 1)	1	AINT	REAL	REAL	AINT(3.1415)	3.0
Nearest whole number	Normal rounding $int(a + 0.5)$ if $a \geq 0$ $int(a - 0.5)$ if $a < 0$	1	ANINT	REAL	REAL	ANINT(3.75)	4.0
Nearest integer	Normal rounding	1	NINT	REAL	INTEGER	NINT(3.74)	4
Absolute value	a if $a \geq 0$ -a if $a < 0$	1	ABS	INTEGER / REAL	INTEGER / REAL	ABS(−2) / ABS(−7.25)	2 / 7.25
Remaindering	$a_1 - int(a_1/a_2) \cdot a_2$	2	MOD	INTEGER / REAL	INTEGER / REAL	MOD(7,4) / MOD(7.0,5.0)	3 / 2.0
Transfer of sign	a if $a_2 \geq 0$ $-a_1$ if $a_2 < 0$	2	SIGN	INTEGER / REAL	INTEGER / REAL	SIGN(2, 2) / SIGN(2.0, − 3.5)	2 / −2.0
Positive difference	$a_1 - a_2$ if $a_1 > a_2$ 0 if $a_1 \leq a_2$	2	DIM	INTEGER / REAL	INTEGER / REAL	DIM(3,2) / DIM(2.0, 3.0)	1 / 0.0

Class of FUNCTION	Definition	Number of arguments	Name	Type of argument	Type of result	Example use	Value of example
Choosing largest value	$\max(a_1, a_2, ...)$ (see note 5)	≥ 2	MAX	INTEGER REAL	INTEGER REAL	MAX(2,3,4,−2) MAX(2.0,3.4, −3.3)	4 3.4
Choosing smallest value	$\min(a_1, a_2, ...)$ (see note 5)	≥ 2	MIN	INTEGER REAL	INTEGER REAL	MIN(2, 3, 4, −2) MIN(2.0, 3.4)	−2 2.0
Length	Length of CHARACTER entity	1	LEN	CHARACTER	INTEGER	LEN('ABC')	3
Index of a substring	Location of substring a_2 in string a_1 (see note 6)	2	INDEX	CHARACTER	INTEGER	INDEX('ABC','B')	2
Square root	$\sqrt{a}$	1	SQRT	REAL	REAL	SQRT(16.0)	4.0
Exponential	e^a	1	EXP	REAL	REAL	EXP(1.0)	2.71828
Natural logarithm	$\ln(a)$	1	LOG	REAL	REAL	LOG(2.0)	0.693147
Common logarithm	$\log_{10}(a)$	1	LOG10	REAL	REAL	LOG10(20.0)	1.30103
Sine	$\sin(a)$ (see note 4)	1	SIN	REAL	REAL	SIN(1.0)	0.841471
Cosine	$\cos(a)$ (see note 4)	1	COS	REAL	REAL	COS(0.0)	1.0
Tangent	$\tan(a)$	1	TAN	REAL	REAL	TAN(0.5)	0.546302
Arcsine	$\arcsin(a)$	1	ASIN	REAL	REAL	ASIN(0.5)	0.523599
Arccosine	$\arccos(a)$	1	ACOS	REAL	REAL	ACOS(0.5)	1.04720
Arctangent	$\arctan(a)$ $\arctan(a_1/a_2)$	1 2	ATAN ATAN2	REAL REAL	REAL REAL	ATAN(0.5) ATAN2(2.0, 0.0)	0.463648 $1.57080(\pi/2)$
Hyperbolic sine	$\sinh(a)$	1	SINH	REAL	REAL	SINH(0.2)	0.201336
Hyperbolic cosine	$\cosh(a)$	1	COSH	REAL	REAL	COSH(0.2)	1.02007

(Continued on following page)

Class of FUNCTION	Name	Number of arguments	Definition	Type of argument	Type of result	Example use	Value of example
Hyperbolic tangent	TANH	1	$\tanh(a)$	REAL	REAL	TANH(0.2)	0.197375
Lexically greater than or equal	LGE	2	$a_1 \geq a_2$ (see note 8)	CHARACTER	LOGICAL	LGE('A','B')	.FALSE.
Lexically greater	LGT	2	$a_1 > a_2$ (see note 8)	CHARACTER	LOGICAL	LGT('A','2')	.TRUE.
Lexically less than or equal	LLE	2	$a_1 \leq a_2$ (see note 8)	CHARACTER	LOGICAL	LLE('A','a')	.TRUE.
Lexically less than	LLT	2	$a_1 < a_2$ (see note 8)	CHARACTER	LOGICAL	LLT('A','B')	.TRUE.

Notes

1. For a of type INTEGER, int$(a) = a$. For a of type REAL, there are two cases: if $a < 1$, int$(a) = 0$; if $a \geq 1$, int(a) is the integer whose magnitude is the largest integer that does not exceed the magnitude of a and whose sign is the same as the sign of a. For example,

$$\mathrm{int}(-3.7) = -3$$

2. For a of type REAL, REAL(a) is a. For a of type INTEGER, REAL(a) is as much precision of the significant part of a as a real datum can contain.

3. ICHAR provides a means of converting from a character to an integer, based on the position of the character in the processor collating sequence. The first character in the collating sequence corresponds to position 0 and the last to position $n-1$. where n is the number of characters in the collating sequence.

The value of ICHAR(a) is an integer in the range: $0 \leq \mathrm{ICHAR}(a) \leq n-1$, where a is an argument of type CHARACTER of length one. The value of a must be a character capable of representation in the processor. The position of that character in the collating sequence is the value of ICHAR.

For any characters c_1 and c_2 capable of representation in the processor, $(c_1$ .LE. $c_2)$ is true if and only if (ICHAR(c_1) .LE. ICHAR(c_2)) is true, and $(c_1$ .EQ. $c_2)$ is true if and only if (ICHAR(c_1) .EQ. ICHAR(c_2)) is true.

CHAR(i) returns the character in the nth position of the processor collating sequence. The value is of type CHARACTER of length one, i is an integer expression whose value must be in range $0 \leq i \leq n-1$.

ICHAR (CHAR(i)) $= i$ for $0 \leq i \leq n-1$.

CHAR (ICHAR(c)) $= c$ for any character c capable of representation in the processor.

4. All angles are expressed in radians.

5. All arguments in an intrinsic function reference must be of the same type.

6. INDEX (a_1, a_2) returns an integer value indicating the starting position within the character string a_1 of a substring identical to string a_2. If a_2 occurs more than once in a_1, the starting position of the first occurrence is returned.

If a_2 does not occur in a_1, the value zero is returned. Note that zero is returned if $len(a_1) < len(a_2)$.

7. The value of the argument of the len function need not be defined at the time the function reference is executed.

8. LGE(a_1, a_2) returns the value .TRUE. if $a_1 = a_2$ or if a_1 follows a_2 in the collating sequence described in ANSI X3.4-1977 (ASCII), and otherwise returns the value .FALSE.

LGT(a_1, a_2) returns the value .TRUE. if a_1 follows a_2 in the collating sequence described in ANSI X3.4-1977(ASCII), and otherwise returns the value .FALSE..

LLE(a_1, a_2) returns the value .TRUE. if $a_1 = a_2$ or if a_1 precedes a_2 in the collating sequence described in ANSI X3.4-1977(ASCII), and otherwise returns the value .FALSE..

LGT(a_1, a_2) returns the value .TRUE. if a_1 follows a_2 in the collating sequence in ANSI X3.4-1977 (ASCII), and otherwise returns the value .FALSE..

If the operands for LGE, LGT, LLE, and LLT are of unequal length, the shorter operand is considered as if it were extended on the right with blanks to the length of the longer operand.

If either of the character entities being compared contains a character that is not in the ASCII character set, the result is processor dependent.

RESTRICTIONS ON RANGE OF ARGUMENTS AND RESULTS

Restrictions on the range of arguments and results for intrinsic functions are as follows:

1. Remaindering: The result for MOD is undefined when the value of the second argument is zero.
2. Transfer of Sign: If the value of the first argument of SIGN is zero, the result is zero, which is neither positive nor negative.
3. Square Root: The value of the argument of SQRT must be greater than or equal to zero.
4. Logarithms: The value of the argument of ALOG and ALOG 10 must be greater than zero.
5. Sine, Cosine, and Tangent: The absolute value of the argument of SIN, COS, and TAN is not restricted to be less than 2π.
6. Arcsine: The absolute value of the argument of ASIN must be less than or equal to one. The range of the result is $-\pi/2 \le \text{result} \le \pi/2$.
7. Arccosine: The absolute value of the argument of ACOS must be less than or equal to one. The range of the result is $0 \le \text{result} \le \pi$.
8. Arctangent: The range of the result for ATAN is: $-\pi/2 \le \text{result} \le \pi/2$. If the value of the first argument of ATAN2 is positive, the result is positive. If the value of the first argument is zero, the result is zero if the second argument is positive and π if the second argument is negative. If the value of the first argument is negative, the result is negative. If the value of the second argument is zero, the absolute value of the result is $\pi/2$. The arguments must not both have the value zero. The range of the result for ATAN2 is: $-\pi < \text{result} \le \pi$.

Some Other Helpful FUNCTIONs.

If you see one you need, copy it whole since these are *not* a part of the ANSI standard library.

```
          INTEGER FUNCTION ROOF(ARG)
          REAL ARG
COMMENT:            "ROOF" RETURNS THE SMALLEST INTEGER WHICH IS NOT
C                   LESS THAN ARG (ROUND UP).
          IF ((ARG .LE. 0.0) .OR. (ARG .EQ. AINT(ARG))) THEN
             ROOF = INT(ARG)
          ELSE
             ROOF = INT(ARG) + 1
          ENDIF
          END

          INTEGER FUNCTION FLOOR(ARG)
          REAL ARG
COMMENT:            "FLOOR" RETURNS THE LARGEST INTEGER WHICH IS NOT
C                   GREATER THAN ARG (ROUND DOWN)
          IF ((ARG .GE. 0.0) .OR. (ARG .EQ. AINT(ARG))) THEN
             FLOOR = INT(ARG)
          ELSE
             FLOOR = INT(ARG) - 1
          ENDIF
          END
```

(Continued on following page)

```
      REAL FUNCTION POS(ARG)
      REAL ARG
      REAL DIM
COMMENT:              IF ARG .GE. 0 THEN ARG, ELSE 0.
      POS = DIM(ARG, 0.0)
      END


      REAL FUNCTION SGN(ARG)
      REAL ARG
COMMENT:              +1, 0, OR -1 ACCORDING TO WHETHER "ARG" IS
C                     .GT., .EQ. OR .LT. ZERO.
      IF (ARG .GT. 0.0) THEN
         SGN = +1.0
      ELSE IF (ARG .LT. 0.0) THEN
         SGN = -1.0
      ELSE
         SGN = 0.0
      ENDIF
      END


         REAL FUNCTION RANF(SEED)
      INTEGER SEED
C RANDOM NUMBER GENERATOR:  0.0 < RANF < 1.0
C    VALUE DELIVERED = SAMPLE FROM UNIFORM VARIATE ON (0,1) INTERVAL
C INSTRUCTIONS: CALL FIRST WITH NON-ZERO SEED
C                    TO START "RANDOM" SEQUENCE
C                 SUBSEQUENT CALLS USE SEED=0
      DOUBLE PRECISION RNGMUL,RNGMOD,RNGNUM
      SAVE RNGMUL,RNGMOD,RNGNUM
      DOUBLE PRECISION DMOD
C  OMIT EXTERNAL DMOD STMT IF YOUR SYSTEM'S DMOD WORKS ON LARGE ARGS
      EXTERNAL DMOD
      IF (SEED .NE. 0) THEN
        RNGMOD = 2.0D0
        N = 1
100     IF (1.0D0+RNGMOD .EQ. RNGMOD) GO TO 200
          N = N+1
          RNGMOD = RNGMOD*2.0D0
          GO TO 100
200     M = N/2
        RNGMOD = 2.0D0**M
        RNGMUL = DBLE(AINT((SQRT(5.0)-1.0)*(REAL(RNGMOD)/8.0) +0.5))
        RNGMUL = RNGMUL - MOD(RNGMUL,8.0D0) + 3.0D0
        RNGNUM = 2*ABS(SEED/2)+1
      ENDIF
      RNGNUM = DMOD(RNGMUL*RNGNUM,RNGMOD)
      RANF = REAL(RNGNUM/RNGMOD)
      RETURN
      END
```

```
      DOUBLE PRECISION FUNCTION DMOD(X,Y)
      DOUBLE PRECISION X,Y
C  VALUE DELIVERED = REMAINDER AFTER DIVIDING X BY Y
C  NOTE: DMOD IS A BUILT-IN FUNCTION, BUT SOME SYSTEMS
C        FAIL TO HANDLE LARGE ARGUMENTS PROPERLY
C  WARNING! BE SURE TO INCLUDE FUNCTION "DINT", DEFINED BELOW
      DOUBLE PRECISION DINT
      EXTERNAL DINT
      DMOD = X - DINT(X/Y)*Y
      END



      DOUBLE PRECISION FUNCTION DINT(X)
      DOUBLE PRECISION X
C  VALUE DELIVERED = X WITH FRACTIONAL PART TRUNCATED
      DOUBLE PRECISION A,B,H,Y, LOG2
      LOG2(Y) = LOG(Y)/LOG(2.0D0)
      Y = ABS(X)
      IF (Y .LT. 1.0D0) THEN
        DINT = 0.0D0
      ELSE
        N = INT(LOG2(Y))
        A = 2.0D0**N
        B = 2.0D0*A
        DO 290 I=1,N
          H = (A+B)/2.0D0
          IF (Y .GE. H) THEN
            A = H
          ELSE
            B = H
          ENDIF
290       CONTINUE
        DINT = SIGN(A,X)
      ENDIF
      RETURN
      END
```

C ANSWERS TO EXERCISES

1.4 ANSWERS TO EXERCISE

1. Making "Pineapple Sliders"—Verbal Description
   Sift together
   - 1 cup all-purpose flour   ¼ tsp. salt
   - 1 tsp. baking powder

   In a separate bowl mix together (with wire whip)
   - 2 eggs   ½ cup brown sugar
   - ½ cup granulated sugar

   Add
   - 1 tsp. vanilla
   - ½ cup chopped walnuts
   - 1 8-oz. can, crushed, unsweetened pineapple (drained)

   Slowly add the flour mixture and blend thoroughly.
   Bake in a slightly greased 8-inch-square aluminum pan for 30 minutes at 350°F.
   Cool on rack for 5 minutes and cut into bars.
   Roll in confectioner's sugar while warm.
   "Pineapple Sliders" courtesy of C.M. Drotos.

   > Thanks to everybody who wrote in telling us how much they liked pineapple sliders.

Put 1 cup all-purpose flour into sifter.
Put 1 tsp. baking powder into sifter.
Put $1/4$ tsp. salt into sifter.
Sift into bowl 1.
Put 2 eggs into bowl 2.
Put $1/2$ cup granulated sugar into bowl 2.
Put $1/2$ cup brown sugar into bowl 2.

> Beat bowl 2 for a while with a wire whip.

Repeat if not mixed

Put 1 tsp. vanilla into bowl 2.
Put $1/2$ cup chopped walnuts into bowl 2.
Put 1 8-oz. can of crushed, unsweetened, drained pineapple into bowl 2.

> Put a little from bowl 1 into bowl 2.
> Blend bowl 2.

Repeat unless bowl 1 is empty

Pour bowl 2 into 8-inch-square pan.
Start baking at 350 °F.

> Wait a while.

Repeat if 30 minutes not up

Cool pan (and contents) on rack for 5 minutes.
Cut into bars.

> Remove a bar.
> Roll it in powdered sugar.

Repeat if more bars in pan

Eat.

1.5 ANSWERS TO EXERCISES

3. **Processor:** executes statements of program.
   Memory: cells in which instructions and data are stored.
   I/O: provides for communication between human and computer.
4. The memory cell is a device which stores information; its name allows us to locate it for purposes of examining or changing its contents; its value is what's in it at a given point in time.

1.6 ANSWERS TO EXERCISES

1. We will need several memory cells: SUM to store the running total of the numbers, N to keep track of the number of numbers, NUM to store the numbers, one at a time, and ST1, ST2, . . . , ST9 in which to store the statements.

card number	memory cell which stores this statement	statement
1	ST1	Store 0 in SUM
2	ST2	Store 0 in N
3	ST3	Remove top card from the card reader stack; copy the number on it into NUM. Discard the card. (If there were no cards, get next instruction from ST7.)
4	ST4	Look at the values in NUM and SUM, add them together, and store the result in SUM.
5	ST5	Look at the value in N, add 1 and store the result in N.
6	ST6	Get your next instruction from ST3.
7	ST7	Look at the values in SUM and N, divide the former by the latter, and store the result in SUM.
8	ST8	Send the string "AVERAGE IS", followed by the number in SUM to the printer.
9	ST9	Stop.
10	none	14
11	none	17
12	none	3
13	none	−4
14	none	8

2. We will need several memory cells: LONGEST to store the longest name seen, NAME to store the names of the cards, one at a time, and ST1, ST2,..., ST6 to store the statements to the program.

card number	memory cell which stores the statement	statement
1	ST1	Remove the top card from the card reader stack and copy the character string on it into LONGEST. Discard the card.
2	ST2	Remove the top card from the card reader stack and copy the value on it into NAME. Discard the card. (If there were no cards on the card reader stack, get your next instruction from ST5.)
3	ST3	Look at the strings in LONGEST and NAME and copy the longer one into LONGEST.
4	ST4	Get your next instruction from ST2.
5	ST5	Send the string "THE LONGEST NAME IS", followed by the value of LONGEST, to the printer.
6	ST6	Stop
7	none	J E Birk
8	none	D E Farmer
9	none	P Das
10	none	P G McCrea
11	none	C C Cheung
12	none	D L Milgram

2.1 ANSWERS TO EXERCISES

1. 23SKIDOO is illegal because it starts with a digit.
SKIDOO 23, TONY THE TIGER, OIL WELL, and FORTRAN are illegal because they have more than six characters.
SALE3, TORQUE, and LIMIT are legal memory cell names.
2. REAL A, 149.2 is illegal because 149.2 is not a memory cell name.
3. `REAL AJAX, FOAM`
4. The REALs are 41.7, 692.0, and − 896.721.

2.2 ANSWERS TO EXERCISES

1. A and B are 10.0 and 2.0, respectively.
2. Memory cell B take on the values 24.0, 3.0, and – 38.0 at successive points in time.
3. −AT = 2.0 and CAT + DOG = FIGHT are illegal because their left-hand sides are expressions rather than memory cell names. CAT + DOG − 3.0, of course, is hopelessly illegal since it doesn't even have an assignment operator.
4. SOUP contains, at successive points in time, the value 15.0, 8.0, 55.0, and 512.0.
5. a. `REAL FIRST`
   `FIRST = 2.0`
   b. `FIRST = FIRST*4.0`
   c. `FIRST = FIRST + 1.0`

2.3 ANSWERS TO EXERCISES

1. Writing a step-by-step plan in English is the first step in writing a program.
2. Revising the plan and making sure it is correct and complete.
3. Translating the plan into Fortran statements.
4. `PRINT *, 'OMAHA POPULATION', POP`

   (The CHARACTER constant isn't strictly necessary, but it makes the output self-explanatory.)
5. ```
PRINT *, 'SCORE'
PRINT *, '   ROCKETS ', HOME
PRINT *, '   BULLDOGS', VISIT
```
6. SINGLE= 74.000 DOUBLE= 148,000

   (The leading spaces in the CHARACTER constant    DOUBLE=' in the PRINT statement keep it from being printed too close to the number 74.)
```

7. Since everything within the "quote marks" is treated *verbatim*, the program produces this line:

```
SINGLE=, M,    DOUBLE=, N
```

which really isn't very useful—we want to know the values of M and N.

2.4 ANSWERS TO EXERCISES

1. X = SQRT(2.0*X)
2. 4.0
3. 2.0
4. D10(X) = (2.0*X) + 10.0
5. AVG3(X,Y,Z) = (X + Y + Z)/3.0
6. INT(ALOG10(X)) + 1.0
7. TAN(X) = SIN(X)/COS(X)

2.5 ANSWERS TO EXERCISES

1. Data

```
182.0
176.0
165.0
```

Output

```
SCORE:  182.000
SCORE:  176.000
SCORE:  165.000
   3,00000 SCORE AVERAGE:  174.333
```

2. The first READ is missing a comma after the asterisk. READ*, A,A + B,2 is illegal because A + B and 2 are values, not memory cell names.
PRINT, A is illegal because the asterisk is missing.

3.
```
REAL A, B, C, D, SUM
READ *, A,B,C,D
SUM = A + B + C + D
PRINT *, SUM
END
```

Data

```
b13.9b1.32b46.8bb1.6    (where b stands for "blank")
```

Output

```
63.6200
```

3.1 ANSWERS TO EXERCISES

1. Gas mileage, gas purchased, and miles traveled: REAL; babies, glasses, and runs: INTEGER.

2. 4.5

3. a, c, and d display pairs that denote the same Fortran constant; in b, 4.92E−1 denotes 0.492, not 4.92.

3.2 ANSWERS TO EXERCISES

1.
```
INTEGER A, B, SUM, DIFF, PROD
READ *, A, B
SUM = A + B
DIFF = A - B
PROD = A * B
```

2. In Fortran, an INTEGER constant cannot contain commas.

3.3 ANSWERS TO EXERCISES

1. The last digit of the number stored in N is MOD(N,10).

2. The hundreds digit of the number stored in N is MOD(N/100, 10)

3. N = N − MOD(N/100, 10)*100

4. N = N − MOD(N/100, 10)*100 + D*100

3.4 ANSWERS TO EXERCISES

1. The expression is evaluated like 0 − 1**4. Exponentiations are performed before subtractions; hence, the result is −1.

2.
```
(MOUSE + (CAT**(DOG**2)))
((S + D) - (R*F) + (A**(B**C))
(DIXIE/MELLOW)/DEE
```

3. Negative values can't be raised to REAL powers.

4. AB is a single identifier in Fortran.

3.5 ANSWERS TO EXERCISES

1.
```
NUM = REAL(N)          NUM = REAL(N)
FRAC = REAL1/M)        DENOM = REAL(M)
```

2. Change the declaration of AVG to "INTEGER AVG"; change the assignment to "AVG = NINT(REAL(TOTAL)/REAL(G)). Then the average score "156" will be printed without a decimal point.

3. SNAFO becomes 2.0, 2.0, 0.0, 4.0, and 4.0, successively.

3.6 ANSWERS TO EXERCISES

1. `WAITFOR RED, THEN WALK`

2. Either add a space before FOR in the PRINT statement, like this:

```
PRINT *, WAIT, ' FOR RED, THEN ', WALK
```

or alter the declaration, like this:

```
CHARACTER*5 WAIT, WALK
```

3. The bottom program must have been the one that produced it because it's the only one which puts a comma in the line of output. Look carefully at the CHARACTER constants in the PRINT statements.

3.10 ANSWERS TO EXERCISES

1. a. (2.8, 7.4)
   b. (− 1.0, 0.0)
   c. The COMPLEX number whose real part is the value contained in A and whose imaginary part is the value of B
   d. The complex conjugate of ZETA
2. In a DOUBLE PRECISION constant, a "D" is used to initiate specification of the decimal-point-shift scaling; an "E" is used in REAL constants.

4.2 ANSWERS TO EXERCISES

1. The first two statements are OK.
   The third statement contains the illegal relation .EG..
   The fourth statement contains the illegal relation .SGT..
   The last statement lacks parentheses and has an illegal comma.
   It should look like this:

```
IF (Y .EQ. 0) GO TO 20
```

2.
```
        REAL S, X, Y
100     READ *, X, Y
        IF (X .EQ. 0.0) GO TO 200
        S = X + Y
        PRINT *, X, ' PLUS ', Y, ' IS ', S
        GO TO 100
200     END
```

3. The program does not reject any scores, even if they are obviously impossible, so 407.0 gets averaged in just like any other score.

4. The goal is to compute the product of the numbers on the data lines. (Do you see the similarity to accumulating a sum as we did in the bowling program? Now we are accumulating a product.)

5.
```
        REAL P, F
        P = 1.0
100     READ *, F
        IF (F .EQ. 0.0) GO TO 200
        P = P * F
        GO TO 100
200     PRINT *, P
        END
```

6.

```
Read amount of purchase
Exit if purchase is negative
Compute tax
Print
                                    Repeat
```

4.3 ANSWERS TO EXERCISES

1. IF (ABS(R**2 - X) .LT. 0.001*X) GO TO 200

2. IF (ABS (R**2 - X) .LT. 0.0005) GO TO 200

3.
```
        REAL X, R, SQRT
        READ *, X
        R = X
100     IF (ABS(R**2 - X) .LT. 0.01*X) GO TO 200
          R = 0.5*(R + X/R)
          GO TO 100
200     PRINT *, 'X=', X, ':APPROX SQRT', R, ':SQRT', SQRT(X)
        END
```

4. If X is negative in the above program, then 0.01*X is also negative. But ABS(R**2 − X) is always positive because any absolute value is positive by definition. This means that the exit test can never come true, and the program loops forever (or until some external force terminates it).

5. Get a value for x

```
Exit if x + x > 100
Let x = x + x
                                    Repeat
```

Print x

6.
```
        REAL X
        READ *, X
100     IF (X + X .GT. 100.00) GO TO 200
          X = X + X
          GO TO 100
200     PRINT *, X
        END
```

4.4 ANSWERS TO EXERCISES

1.
```
        REAL X, P
        INTEGER N
        READ *, X, N
        P = X
100     P = P*X
          N = N - 1
          IF (N .GT. 1) GO TO 100
        PRINT *, P
        END
```

2. The program of exercise 1 computes X raised to the Nth power: X^N.

3. Start with SUM = 0.
Start with N = 1.

Add N^3 to SUM.
Add 1 to N.

Repeat if N ≤ 50

Print SUM.

4.5 ANSWERS TO EXERCISES

1. The statements in the loop would be skipped because the starting value is beyond the ending value. Therefore, only the heading, which is printed before the loop starts, would appear on the output:

```
NUMBER      SQUARED      CUBED
```

2. The increment, if unspecified, is assumed to be + 1. Hence the loop wouldn't be changed.
3. As near as we can tell, two.
4. The IF statement transfers into the middle of the DO-loop. This type of overlapping loop structure is not allowed. DO-loops can be entered only by means of the DO statement at the top of the loop.
5.
```
        S = 0.0
        X = A
        N = MAX(INT((B - A + DX)/DX),0)
        K = 1
100     IF (K .GT. N) GO TO 110
          S = S + X
          X = X + DX
          K = K + 1
        GO TO 100
110     S = S*DX
```

4.6 ANSWERS TO EXERCISES

1. See Figures 4.2.1, 4.3.1, 4.4.1, and 4.5.1 for the structures of the READ-, posttest, pretest, and DO loops.
2. The first Fortran statement of a loop begins in the same column as the statement above it. All the other Fortran statements in the loop are indented to the next level beyond the first statement.

5.2 ANSWERS TO EXERCISES

1. Both the knitting algorithm and the bowling-average program contain nested loops.
2. The program is designed to handle any number of scores per player correctly. Try it!

7.1 ANSWERS TO EXERCISES

1. **Looping** is the repetition of a sequence of statements many times. **Selection** is performing a sequence of statements once, but selecting *which* sequence to perform by testing some condition.

2. (a) looping (b) looping (c) selection (d) selection.

3. Read two numbers, A and B.
    If A > B
    then

    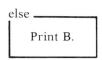

    > Print A.

    else

    > Print B.

4.
```
REAL A, B
READ *, A, B
IF (A .GT. B) THEN
   PRINT *, A
ELSE
   PRINT *, B
ENDIF
END
```

5. It wouldn't affect the operation of the program at all. If you don't say how long the string will be, Fortran assumes you want *1. So

    CHARACTER TYPE

    has exactly the same effect as

    CHARACTER*1 TYPE

6. Since our IF-THEN-ELSE tests to see if the value of TYPE is equal to 'F' and makes no other checks, anything other than 'F' will be treated as if the temperature is in degrees centigrade.

7.2 ANSWERS TO EXERCISES

1. The ducks get added into the whooping crane count.

2. Replace the ELSE by ELSE-IF (BIRD .EQ. 'W') THEN and add an else-block after the W = W + 1 statement:

```
ELSE IF (BIRD .EQ. 'W') THEN
   W = W + 1
ELSE
   OTHER = OTHER + 1
```

    In addition, put OTHER in the list of INTEGER variables in the declaration and put OTHER = 0 in the sequence of initializations at the top of the program.

3. Run your program to see if you were right.

4. Fix it as explained in the answer to question 2.

```
5.  INTEGER DICE
    READ *, DICE
    IF (DICE .EQ. 12) THEN
        PRINT *, 'BOX CARS'
    ELSE IF (DICE .EQ. 3) THEN
        PRINT *, 'CRAPS'
    ELSE IF (DICE .EQ. 2) THEN
        PRINT *, 'SNAKE EYES'
    ELSE
        PRINT *, 'O.K.'
    ENDIF
    END
```

7.3 ANSWERS TO EXERCISES

1. Any of the following will work.

   ```
   IF (X .LT. Y/2.0 .AND. Y .NE. 0.0) GO TO 100
   IF (X .LT. Y/2.0 .AND. .NOT. Y .EQ. 0.0) GO TO 100
   IF (.NOT. (X .GE. Y/2.0 .OR. Y .EQ. 0.0)) GO TO 100
   ```

   There are other possibilities, too numerous to mention. However, if yours is none of these, try it on the computer before you assume it's correct.

2. TWO

3. M = 80   N = 256

4. M = 400 N = 256

5. M = 160 N = 256

7.5 ANSWERS TO EXERCISES

1. SMALL 7.
2. SPREAD would be .TRUE.
3. Eliminate the .AND. PORSCHE from Mary's IF-THEN statement.
4. True, true, false, true, false, true.

8.1 ANSWERS TO EXERCISES

1. b. It would have an extra blank before the 12.
2. d. Notice that b isn't even legal—no FORMAT descriptor matches SNGLSP.
3. b or c.

8.2 ANSWERS TO EXERCISES

1. `1900 FORMAT(A, T8, A, T16, A, T24, A, T32, A)`

   or, using a repeat specification,

```
1900 FORMAT(A, T8, 4(A, TR2))
1900 FORMAT(A, T6, 4(TR2, A))
```

2. a, c, and d have the same effect. b has a strange effect—each time the repeat operation takes place, it tabs back to column 1, overwriting what was there before. (This overwriting takes place internally, not on the printer itself.)
3. Among others, these statements will do the job.

```
      PRINT 1000, PAGEJC, 'MAKE AND', '0-60', 'FUEL'
     +                    'CORNERING', 'STOP', 'NOISE'
1000 FORMAT (A, T2, A, T25, A, T33, A, T39, A, T49,A,T56,A)
      PRINT 1010, SNGLSP, 'MODEL', 'MPH', 'ECON', '(G)',
     +                    'FROM', 'AT'
1010 FORMAT (A, T4, A, T25, A, T33, A, T42, A, T49,A,T57,A)
      PRINT 1020, SNGLSP, '(SEC)', '(MPG)', '80', '70'
1020 FORMAT (A, T25, A, T33, A, T50, A, T57, A)
      PRINT 1030, SNGLSP, '(FT)', '(DBA)'
1030 FORMAT (A, T49, A, T56, A)
```

4. Almost. You can do everything except starting at the top of the page. There's no way to do the PAGEJC carriage control with list-directed I/O. Also, you'd have to be very careful when you entered the data to make sure you had the right number of blanks where they're needed.
5. Here's one solution:

```
      CHARACTER*1 SNGLSP, PAGEJC
      CHARACTER*4 RED, WHITE, BLUE
      INTEGER LINE
      SNGLSP = ' '
      PAGEJC = '1'
      RED = '++++'
      WHITE = '....'
      BLUE = '****'

C                              FIRST LINE GOES AT TOP OF PAGE
      PRINT 1000, PAGEJC, BLUE, BLUE, BLUE, WHITE, WHITE
     +                    WHITE, RED, RED, RED
 1000 FORMAT (A, 9A)
C                    LOOP FOR REST OF THE LINES, USE SAME FORMAT
      DO 100 LINE = 2, 12
         PRINT 1000, SNGLSP, BLUE, BLUE, BLUE, WHITE, WHITE,
     +               WHITE, RED, RED, RED
 100     CONTINUE
      END
```

6.

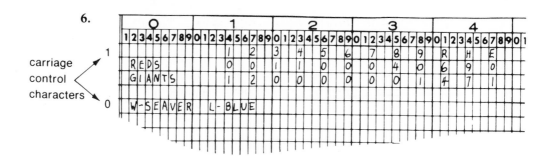

7. For the three lines of the heading, we could use

```
     PRINT 1000,PAGEJC,'CUSTOMER','ACCOUNT','STARTING','NEW'
1000 FORMAT (A, T6, A, T25, A, T38, A, T53, A)
     PRINT 1010, SNGLSP,'NAME','NUMBER','BALANCE','BALANCE'
1010 FORMAT (A, T8, A, T25, A, T38, A, T51, A)
     PRINT 1020, SNGLSP,'_____',
    +          '_____','_____','_____'
1020 FORMAT (A,A, T24, A, T37, A, T50, A)
```

The basic step in printing the lines of data can be accomplished with these statements:

```
     PRINT 1030, SNGLSP, CNAME,ACCTNO,'$', STBAL,'$', NEWBAL
1030 FORMAT (A, A, T24, I10, T37, A, F9.2, T50, A, F9.2)
```

8. Everything is easy except for the day number. If the day number is less than 10, we want to use an I1 descriptor. Otherwise, we want to use an I2. Since variables may not appear in FORMATs, we'll have to use two different FORMATs and choose the right one.

```
                        .
                        .
                        .
         IF (DAY .LT. 10) THEN
             PRINT 2000, SNGLSP, MONTH, '/', DAY, '/', YEAR
2000         FORMAT(A,I2,A,I1,A,I4)
         ELSE
             PRINT 2001, SNGLSP, MONTH, '/', DAY, '/', YEAR
2001         FORMAT (A, I2, A, I2, I4)
         ENDIF
                        .
                        .
                        .
```

8.3   ANSWERS TO EXERCISES

1. a. Results in CHAR having the (length one) value '*'.
    b. Stores a blank in CHAR (the first column on the line is blank).
    c. Has the same end result as a.
    d. Stores an apostrophe (single quote) in CHAR.
2. TITLE will get the value 'JOHNNY MCLAUGHLIN EL'.
    LABEL will get the value 'ECTRIC GU'.
    ARTIST will have the value 'ARISTCOLUMBIA J MCL'.

3. `2500 FORMAT(A, T22, A, T33, I3 )`

    or

    `2500 FORMAT(A, TR1, A, TR1, I3)`

    will work.

4.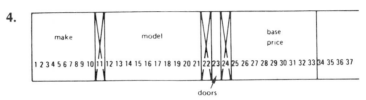

5.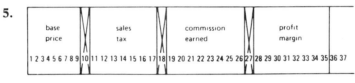

6. `3000 FORMAT (F9.2, F7.2, F8.2, F8.2)`

    or

    `3000 FORMAT (F9.2, T10, F7.2, T17, F8.2, T25, F8.2)`

7. `3000 FORMAT (F9.2, T11, F7.2, T19, F8.2, T27, F8.2)`

    or

    `3000 FORMAT (F9.2, TR1, F7.2, TR1, F8.2, TR1, F8.2)`

8.5   ANSWERS TO EXERCISES

1. c and d.
    Pair b produces a single line that begins with *two* blanks. Pair e skips a line *after* the line with FRI on it.
2. a and c. Unless you have understood FORMATs and carriage control very well, you may be surprised to learn that the two PRINT/FOR-

MAT pairs in b are very close to each other. No carriage control character appears in the PRINT list for the second line here.

```
PRINT 2020, SNGLSP, 'AND LAST BUT LEAST,'
2020 FORMAT (A / T5,A)
```

However, the T5 descriptor makes the second line start with a blank. The printer rips the blank off and treats it as a carriage control command to single space. Since the carriage control character is *not* printed, that leaves just three blanks before the string AND LAST BUT LEAST. Thus, the two PRINT/FORMAT pairs in b have these effects:

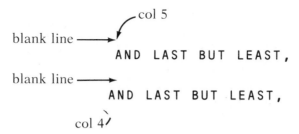

col 5

blank line ⟶

    AND LAST BUT LEAST,

blank line ⟶

    AND LAST BUT LEAST,

col 4

3. a. REAL, F5.3 INTEGER, 13
   b. INTEGER, I1
   c. CHARACTER, A
   d. REAL, F15.2
4. b and d.
5. It describes a data line with 120 columns (most have only 80).
6. On three consecutive lines, with two numbers per line in the two fields, columns 1–10 and columns 11–20.

9.1 ANSWERS TO EXERCISES

1.
`REAL A(10)`	Legal.
`REAL B(22), C(8), X`	Legal.
`INTEGER NUM(K)`	Illegal (length declarator must be constant).
`INTEGER N, ISLE (22-3)`	Legal.
`REAL Y(15.0)`	Illegal (length declarator must be integer).

2.
```
CHARACTER*(4) N(2)
READ *, N(1), N(2)
IF (N(1) .EQ. 'KAT ' .AND. N(2) .EQ. 'PAGE') GO TO 200
```

9.2 ANSWERS TO EXERCISES

1. If the values in memory cells I and J are the same and that value is a legal subscript for B, then B(I) and B(J) denote the same cell.

2.
```
0   1    1    2    3
5   8   13   21   34
```

3.

`B(3) = B(I)`	Legal; but since I has the value 3, nothing is changed.
`B(I) = B(I-1)`	Legal; changes value of B(3) to value contained in B(2).
`B(J) = (2*I)`	Legal; changes value of B(7) to value contained in B(6).
`B(4) = B(J-1) + B(I*J-21)`	Illegal; B(I*J)−21) refers to B(0), which doesn't exist.
`B(2*I) = B(J+4)`	Illegal; B(J+4) refers to B(11), which doesn't exist.
`B(1.7) = 0`	Illegal; REAL subscripts aren't allowed.

4. No arrays would be needed, as shown in the program below.

```
COMMENT:               PROGRAM TO LIST THE WESTERN STATES, THEIR SALES
C                      TAX RATES, AND THE AVERAGE RATE OVER THE WESTERN
C                      STATES.
        INTEGER NUMST, LENST
        PARAMETER(NUMST = 11, LENST = 10)
        CHARACTER*(LENST) S
        REAL T, SUM, AVE
        INTEGER N
C
        SUM = 0.0
        DO 100 N=1,NUMST
           READ *, S, T
           PRINT *, S,T
           SUM = SUM + T
  100   CONTINUE
C
  200   AVE = SUM/NUMST
C
        PRINT *, ' '
        PRINT *, 'AVERAGE WESTERN STATES SALES TAX IS', AVE
        END
```

Data

```
'WASHINGTON'    0.045
'IDAHO'         0.03
'MONTANA'       0.00
'OREGON'        0.04
'WYOMING'       0.03
'CALIFORNIA'    0.06
'NEVADA'        0.03
'UTAH'          0.04
'COLORADO'      0.03
'ARIZONA'       0.04
'NEW MEXICO'    0.04
```

Output

```
WASHINGTON      0.045000
IDAHO           0.030000
MONTANA         0.000000
OREGON          0.040000
WYOMING         0.030000
CALIFORNIA      0.060000
NEVADA          0.030000
UTAH            0.040000
COLORADO        0.030000
ARIZONA         0.040000
NEW MEXICO      0.040000
AVERAGE WESTERN STATES SALES TAX IS      0.034999
```

5.
`REAL A(10)`	Legal.
`INTEGER A(2-13)`	Illegal; the length declarator must have a value greater than zero.
`INTEGER A(I)`	Illegal; no variable allowed in length declarator.
`REAL A(150), BOK(2**10+1)`	Legal.
`REAL X(15.0)`	Illegal; length declarator must be INTEGER.
`LOGICAL QS(23), PS(47)`	Legal.

9.3 ANSWERS TO EXERCISES

1. We need 12 cells in the arrays because the information on the 'END DATA' line will have to be stored somewhere. Since there will be up to 11 responses, we need 12 cells to include the information from the 'END DATA' line.

2. The READ list includes an element of the array T; therefore, the line must contain a value to put into that memory cell.

3. Change the STORE DATA and COMPUTE AVERAGE sections of the program as shown below.

```
C                    STORE DATA
         SUM = 0.0
         N = 0
100      READ *, S(N+1), T(N+1)
           IF (S(N+1) .EQ. ENDST) GO TO 200
           SUM = SUM + S(N+1)
           N = N + 1
           GO TO 100
200      AVE = SUM/N
```

4. Since N will be zero when the computer reaches the COMPUTE AVERAGE section of the program, the computer will attempt to divide by zero, resulting in an error. To avoid this, change the statements between statements 200 and 210 in the program to the ones below and put an ENDIF just before the END statement at the bottom of the program.

```
200      IF (N .EQ. 0) THEN
            PRINT *, 'NO DATA FOR TAX PROGRAM'
            STOP
         ELSE
            SUM = 0.0
            K = 1
```

5. Insert the following statements before GO TO 100 in the STORE DATA section of the program.

```
IF (N .GT. NUMST) THEN
   PRINT *, 'ONLY ', NUMST, 'RESPONSE CARDS ALLOWED'
   PRINT *, 'YOU HAVE INCLUDED TOO MANY'
   STOP
ENDIF
```

6. Change NUMST to 50 in the PARAMETER statement.

7.
```
COMMENT:                   PROGRAM TO LIST THE WESTERN STATES WITH
C                          BELOW AVERAGE SALES TAX RATES
         CHARACTER*10  S1,S2,S3,S4,S5,S6,S7,S8,S9,S10,S11
         REAL T1,T2,T3,T4,T5,T6,T7,T8,T9,T10,T11,AVE
C                          SET ALL TAX RATES TO ZERO SO THAT UNUSED CELLS
C                          WILL NOT CONTRIBUTE TO SUM IN STATEMENT 200
         T1 = 0.0
         T2 = 0.0
            .
            .
            .
         T11 = 0.0
C                          STORE DATA AND ACCUMLATE SUM
         SUM = 0.0
         N = 0
         READ *, S1, T1
         IF (S1 .NE. 'END DATA') THEN
           N = N + 1
           READ *, S2, T2
           IF (S2 .NE. 'END DATA') THEN
             N = N + 1
             READ *, S3, T3
               .
               .
               .
               IF (S11 .NE. 'END DATA') THEN
                 N = N + 1
               ENDIF
               .
               .
               .
           ENDIF
         ENDIF
C
 200     AVE = (T1+T2+T3+T4+T5+T6+T7+T8+T9+T10+T11)/N
C
         PRINT *, 'STATES WITH BELOW AVERAGE SALES TAX'
         PRINT *, ' '
         IF (T1 .LE. AVE .AND. N .GE. 1) THEN
           PRINT *, S1
         ENDIF
         IF (T2 .LE. AVE .AND. N .GE. 2) THEN
           PRINT *, S2
         ENDIF
```

```
          .
          .
          .
     IF (T11 .LE. AVE .AND. N .GE. 11) THEN
        PRINT *, S11
     ENDIF
     END
```

Data

```
'WASHINGTON'    0.045
'IDAHO'         0.03
'MONTANA'       0.00
'OREGON'        0.04
'WYOMING'       0.03
'CALIFORNIA'    0.06
'NEVADA'        0.03
'UTAH'          0.04
'COLORADO'      0.03
'ARIZONA'       0.04
'NEW MEXICO'    0.04
'END DATA'      0.0
```

Output

```
IDAHO
MONTANA
WYOMING
NEVADA
COLORADO
```

Imagine changing this program to handle all fifty states!

9.5   ANSWERS TO EXERCISES

1.
```
   REAL BUDGET(3), XPNS
      .
      .
      .
   READ *, XCODE, XPNS
   BUDGET(XCODE) = BUDGET(XCODE) + XPNS
```

2.
```
       CHARACTER*(8) BNAME(NUMBRD)
       INTEGER B(NUMBRD)
          .
          .
          .
       BNAME(1) = 'CURLEW'
       BNAME(2) = 'EGRET'
       BNAME(3) = 'HERON'
       BNAME(4) = 'WHOOPER'
       DO 210 BIRD = 1, NUMBRD
          PRINT *, BNAME(BIRD), B(BIRD)
210       CONTINUE
```

9.6   ANSWERS TO EXERCISES

1.
```
       DO 100 I = 1,N
          X(I) = 2*X(I)
100       CONTINUE
```

2.
```
            DO 100 I = 1, N-1
                IF (X(I+1) .LT. X(I)) GO TO 110
100             CONTINUE
            PRINT *, ' VALUES INCREASE CONTINUALLY'
            GO TO 120
110         PRINT *, I, X(I), X(I+1)
120         CONTINUE
```

3.
```
            CHARACTER*(4) W(100), SURP, DONE
            PARAMETER(DONE = 'DONE')
            DO 100 I=1, 100
                READ *, W(I)
                IF (W(I) .EQ. DONE) GO TO 110
100             CONTINUE
            PRINT *, 'SURPLUS WORDS'
101         READ *, SURP
            PRINT *, SURP
            IF (SURP .NE. DONE) GO TO 101
110         CONTINUE
```

9.7 ANSWERS TO EXERCISES

1. The processor would attempt to use either the memory cell COLA(8) or UNCOLA(8), but neither of these cells exist. The subscript is out of range. Error!
2. Put IF(AGE .GE. 12 .AND.AGE .LE.65) THEN just before the IF-THEN statement and ENDIF just after the ENDIF statement.
3. `INTEGER POPL(-1000:1980)`

9.8 ANSWERS TO EXERCISES

1. `INTEGER A(100,3), B(3,100),I`   Legal; declares two INTEGER arrays A and B.

   `REAL QRT(3,49)`   Legal; declares a REAL array QRT.

   `REAL P(10), Q(4,2)`   Legal; declares two REAL arrays P and Q.

   `REAL X(N,100)`   Illegal; length declarators must be constants.

2. `A(4,3) = 0`   Legal.
   `B(4,2) = 0`   Illegal; 4 is too large.
   `A(3,50) = 0`   Illegal; 50 is too large.
   `I = 10`   Legal.
   `P(8) = Q(3,2)` Legal.

3. The program prints a message indicating that the windchill factor for that temperature is off the chart.

4. A two-dimensional array arranged like a calendar with seven columns (one for each day, Sunday through Saturday) and five lines (one for each week, or partial week, in the month) works well. The entries in the array need to be set to the day of the month corresponding to their position (days not in the month should be set to some value that is not a day of the month, like zero).

MAY84

0	0	1	2	3	4	5
6	7	8	9	10	11	12
13	14	15	16	17	18	19
20	21	22	23	24	25	26
27	28	29	30	31	0	0

To find out what day of the month the second Wednesday falls on, look at MAY84(2,4). The "2" is for the "second week," which corresponds to the second line of the calendar; the "4" is for "Wednesday," the fourth day of the week.

In general, you need to check the first line of the array to see if the month has the day you're looking for in the first week to know which line to look on. For example, if we were looking for the "third Monday," we would see, by looking at the first line and seeing no Monday there, that the third Monday would be on the fourth line. Therefore, to find the Nth occurrence of the day "D", we need statements like this:

```
IF (MAY84(1,D) .NE. 0) THEN
   M = MAY84(N,D)
ENDIF
IF (MAY84(1,D) .EQ. 0) THEN
   M = MAY84(N+1,D)
ENDIF
```

9.10   ANSWERS TO EXERCISES

1.
```
READ *, A(1),A(2),A(3),A(4)
PRINT *, A(4),A(6),A(8),A(10),A(12)
PRINT *, A(2),A(6),A(10)
```

2.
```
PRINT *, (A(I), I=1,5)
PRINT *, (A(I), I=2,10,2)
```

3.
```
PRINT *, (A(J), J=1,N-1)      Is legal.
READ *, (J,A(J), J=1,N)       Implied do list parameters
                               may not be changed while
                               the list is being used.
                               This READ would change
                               J by giving it a value from
                               a data line.
PRINT *, (A(J), J=1,C(N))     Is legal.
```

4. Trouble. We should test for that case. Here's one way.

```
      DO 300 NUMB=0,NUMCAT-1
         THISB = BAR(NUMB + 1)
         DO 200 THISB = BAR(NUMB+1),1,-60
            PRINT *,'BAR',NUMB,':', (XCH,COUNT=1,THISB)
200         CONTINUE
300      CONTINUE
      END
```

5.
```
PRINT *, ( (I+J, J=0,3), I=0,2)
PRINT *, X(1), X(2), ( (Y(I,J), I=1,2), J=1,3)
PRINT *, ( (Y(I,J), J=1,3), I=1,2)
```

10.1   ANSWERS TO EXERCISES

1. We don't know about your system, but on ours, the printer can PRINT

```
:ABCDEFGHIJKLMNOPQRSTUVWXYZ0123456789Z+-*/()$= ,.>"'=' !?);'''(+|
:ABCDEFGHIJKLMNOPQRSTUVWXYZ0123456789Z+-*/()$= ,.>"'=' !?);'''(+|
:ABCDEFGHIJKLMNOPQRSTUVWXYZ0123456789Z+-*/()$= ,.>"'=' !?);'''(+|
```

2. No. Just remember to put a single quote (apostrophe) at the front of the first line, and at the end of the last line, and a READ statement will read the whole text as one string. You might have some trouble with extra blanks if you don't fill each line completely, but we'll see a way to write a program to remove them (in Section 10.3).

10.2   ANSWERS TO EXERCISES

1. It computes the number of characters in PHRASE, ignoring trailing blanks.
2. It is reversing the order of the first N characters in PHRASE.

3.
```
PRINT *, PHRASE(1:40)
PRINT *, PHRASE(41:80)
```

4.
```
PHRASE(40:41) = '++'
```

5. There are several ways to do it; here's one.
```
CHARACTER*(32) NAME
CHARACTER*(1) COMMA
INTEGER POS
COMMA = ','
READ *, NAME
DO 100 POS = 1, 32
   IF (NAME(POS:POS) .EQ. COMMA) GO TO 200
```

(Continued on following page)

```
100       CONTINUE
          PRINT *, NAME, ' IS IN FIRST MIDDLE LAST NAME FORM.'
          GO TO 300
200       PRINT *, NAME, ' IS IN LAST NAME, FIRST MIDDLE FORM.'
300    END
```

Notice that we've used the exact equivalent of an array search loop in this program.

10.3 ANSWERS TO EXERCISES

1. Before the assignments, during the assignments, and after the assignments, the *length* of each is 4. They were declared to the length 4 by the statement

```
CHARACTER*4 ONE, TWO, THREE, FOUR
```

and that's fixed.

After the assignments, they have these values:

Memory cell	Value
ONE	'+ '
TWO	'+ '
THRE	'+ '
FOUR	'+ '

Don't believe our answer? Look:

```
ONE  =  '+'
```

leaves ONE with the value '+   ', so ONE//ONE is the same as '+   ' //'+   ', which is this string (of length 8);

'+   +   '

So the assignment

```
TWO = ONE // ONE
```

is equivalent to

TWO = '+   +   '

Since TWO is a CHARACTER*4 memory cell, only the first four characters of '+   +   ' will fit, giving TWO the value '+.   '. Etc. Compare that with the effect of this program.

```
CHARACTER*1 ONE
CHARACTER*2 TWO
CHARACTER*3 THREE
CHARACTER*4 FOUR
ONE = '+'
TWO = ONE // ONE
THREE = ONE // TWO
FOUR = TWO // (ONE // ONE)
       .
       .
       .
```

Now, after the assignments, the cells have these values:

Memory cell	Value
ONE	'+'
TWO	'++'
THREE	'+++'
FOUR	'++++'

2. The first string will wind up like this:

'RUSSELL, LORD BERTRAND'

and the second will wind up with a leading blank, like this:

' RUSSELL, LORD BERTRAND'

Add a loop to the program that removes leading blanks similar to the part that removes trailing blanks.

3.
```
CHARACTER*(33) NAME
INTEGER POS
READ *, NAME
POS = INDEX(NAME, ',')
IF (POS .EQ. 0) THEN
  PRINT *, NAME, ' HAS NO COMMA--ERROR'
ELSE IF (INDEX(NAME(POS+1:), ',') .NE. 0) THEN
  PRINT *, NAME, ' HAS MORE THAN ONE COMMA--ERROR'
ELSE
  PRINT *, NAME, ' IS OK.'
ENDIF
END
```

Data   'LANGSFORD, RAYMOND G.'

Output   LANGSFORD, RAYMOND G.   IS OK.

Data   'AL SMITH'

Output   'AL SMITH   HAS NO COMMA-ERROR

(Of course, there are many other possible solutions.)

11.2 ANSWERS TO EXERCISES

1.
```
REAL FUNCTION VTPRIS(A,B,C,H)
REAL A,B,C,H
REAL ATRI
VTPRIS = H*ATRI(A,B,C)
END
```

2. It needs parentheses after the FUNCTION name:

```
REAL FUNCTION R( )
```

This is an unusual FUNCTION because it always produces the same value (namely, 2.0). Thus, C = R( ) would be equivalent to C = 2.0.

3. The function ATRI was written to accept three arguments, each of which is a single REAL number. Any invocation must pass along the arguments in exactly this manner. The invocation in this exercise provides only one argument, and even this argument has the wrong form (it is an array, not a single number).

4.
```
REAL FUNCTION ATRI(L)
REAL L(3)
REAL S, H
S = (L(1) + L(2) + L(3))/2
H = S*(S-L(1))*(S-L(2))*(S-L(3))
IF (H .LT. 0.0) THEN
   ATRI = H
ELSE
   ATRI = SQRT(H)
ENDIF
END
```

11.3 ANSWERS TO EXERCISES

1.
```
      REAL FUNCTION MAXVAL(X,N)
      INTEGER N
      REAL X(N)
      REAL VAL
      VAL = X(1)
      DO 100 I=2,N
        VAL = MAX(VAL, X(I))
100     CONTINUE
      MAXVAL = VAL
      END
```

2.
```
      REAL FUNCTION SUMLOG(X,N)
      INTEGER N
      REAL X(N)
      REAL S
      S = 0.0
      DO 100 I=1,N
        S = S + LOG10(X(I))
100     CONTINUE
      SUMLOG = S**2
      END
```

3. The array A is not a dummy parameter and cannot, therefore, be declared to have a variable length. Only dummy parameters may have variables in their dimension specifications, and those variables must be other parameters in the parameter list.

4. The invocation omits the second argument, which specifies the length of the array.

5.
```
      REAL MEAN, MAXVAL
      REAL A(12), D(12), MU
      READ *, (A(I), I=1, 12)
```

```
        MU = MEAN(A,12)
        DO 100 I=1,12
          D(I) = ABS(A(I) - MU)
100       CONTINUE
        PRINT *, 'MAXIMUM DEVIATION:', MAXVAL(D,12)
        END
```

11.4 ANSWERS TO EXERCISES

1. The first two are legal.
   The third is illegal. The name POMEGRANATE is too long.
   The fourth is illegal. A parameter must be listed by name only. If it is an array, the parameter declaration will say so. If it is only a memory cell, it doesn't need a subscript.
2. They are all legal.
3. It would print the line

   ```
   9       16        25
   ```

4. It would print

   ```
   A=DOG  NONE BAT
   ```

11.6 ANSWERS TO EXERCISES

1. ONE: legal.
   TWO: legal.
   THREE: illegal—LENGTH isn't in the parameter list of the SUBROUTINE THREE, so it can't be used as an array size declarator in the SUBROUTINE's parameter declaration section.
2. It is illegal to change the value of an array size declarator. Thus, the statement $N = N + 1$ is illegal in this context.
3. Change the FUNCTION LOCSML so that the second IF statement becomes

   ```
   IF (A(I) .GT. A(LOCSML)) THEN
   ```

   Also, change the name of the FUNCTION (and all references to it) to LOCBIG since it now LOCates the BIGgest element in the array.
4. After execution of the CALL statement, the cells ONE and TWO would both have whatever value TWO had before execution of the CALL statement.
5. The statement CALL BADSWT (1,2) lists two *constant* values as arguments, yet the SUBROUTINE BADSWT *changes* the values of the arguments given to it. It is immoral to change the value of a constant (according to the standards of ANSI).

11.7 ANSWER TO EXERCISE

1. Change the second argument in the CALL PLOT statement to X**2.
   label 100) to X**2.

12.2 ANSWERS TO EXERCISES

1.

2. After the first pass, we get
   123
   125
   121
   597
   642
   700
   After the third pass, we get
   700
   121
   642
   123
   125
   597
   What do you have? A mess.
3. After the first pass, we get
   700
   121
   642
   123
   125
   597
   After the last pass, we get
   121
   123
   125
   597
   642
   700
   What do you have? The list in increasing order.
4. a. Two changes would be made. The relation in the test for a new biggest value would be changed from .LT. to .LE., and the first Comment line would be changed to

   COMMENT: FIND THE (LAST OCCURRENCE OF) BIGGEST

   b. Entries in the list that have the same left parts would not be in proper order. Exercise 3 would come out like this:
   123

125
121
597
642
700

If you were sorting names, all the SMITH's would be messed up.

5. ZEROS: variable length—REAL A(N).
ONES: assumed length—REAL B(*).
THRESH: variable length—REAL A(M,N).
INIT: constant length—CHARACTER*(15) STATES(50).

12.3 ANSWERS TO EXERCISES

1. See Section 12.1; four steps.

2. Step 1 was the problem statement on the first page of this section.
Step 2 was the I/O description which followed.

Step 3 involved all of the analysis of the conversion process and the gradual refinement of the algorithm from the original form (conversion algorithm), through the digit conversion algorithm and the digit selection algorithm.

Step 4 was the last, coding the algorithm in Fortran and debugging it.

3.
```
GO TO (10,20,30), K
GO TO (200,200,100,100,200,200), I
```

4. Because we want to select the *first* option (statement 100) when D has the value 0, the *second* option when D has the value 1, and so on.

5.
```
        SUBROUTINE DIGIT(D, A,B,C, R,N)
        INTEGER D, N
        CHARACTER*(1) A,B,C, R(16)
        CHARACTER*(1) RDGT(3)
        INTEGER T(9,3), L(9), LNRDGT, I
        DATA L(1), T(1,1)                       /1, 1      /
        DATA L(2), T(2,1),T(2,2)                /2, 1,1    /
        DATA L(3), T(3,1),T(3,2),T(3,3)         /3, 1,1,1  /
        DATA L(4), T(4,1),T(4,2)                /2, 1,2    /
        DATA L(5), T(5,1)                       /1, 2      /
        DATA L(6), T(6,1),T(6,2)                /2, 2,1    /
        DATA L(7), T(7,1),T(7,2),T(7,3)         /3, 2,1,1  /
        DATA L(8), T(8,1),T(8,2),T(8,3),T(8,4)  /4, 2,1,1,1/
        DATA L(9), T(9,1),T(9,2)                /2, 1,3    /
        RDGT(1) = A
        RDGT(2) = B
        RDGT(3) = C
        IF (D .EQ. 0) RETURN
        LNRDGT = L(D)
        DO 100 I=1,LNRDGT
          N = N + 1
          R(N) = RDGT(T(D,I))
100       CONTINUE
        END
```

12.4   ANSWERS TO EXERCISES

1. a. **Hashing** seems like the choice. If people's names are the account names, there are far too many possible names to consider using direct access, and since there's lots of memory available, the odds are that access will be very fast if the hash function is chosen reasonably.

    b. **Sequential access** seems like the right choice. It's very efficient of memory space (both for data and programs), and the number of items will be so small that the time lost will be insignificant.

2. Suppose the first account name is $d_1d_2d_3d_4d_5d_6d_7d_8d_9$ and the second is $e_1e_2e_3e_4e_5e_6e_7e_8e_9$. They will have the same hash number if the set of digits d_1, d_5, d_8, and d_9 is the same as the set of digits e_1, e_5, e_8, and e_9. For example, no matter what digits are used to fill in the x's, all account numbers of the form 7xx x5 xx35 will have the same hash number as numbers like 3xx x7 xx55 and 5xx x3 xx75. Actually, the overlap problem is even more serious: the last number depends on a product that can have the same value even when the digit sets are different.

3. The add process becomes an infinite loop. It will endlessly cycle through the items, looking for an empty spot. One cure would be to keep track of the number of items currently being stored and to check this number against the array size each time another add is attempted.

4.
```
          SUBROUTINE FIND(NACCT,ACCT,ENTRY,LEN)
          INTEGER NACCT,LEN, ACCT(LEN),ENTRY(LEN)
          INTEGER HASH, POSN
C                   COMPUTE HASH NUMBER TO BEGIN SEARCH
          POSN = HASH(NACCT)
C                   SEARCH FOR NACCT
    100   IF (ACCT(POSN) .EQ. NACCT) GO TO 200
          IF (ACCT(POSN) .EQ. 0) GO TO 200
          POSN = POSN + 1
          IF (POSN .GT. LEN) THEN
            POSN = 1
          ENDIF
          GO TO 100
    200   IF (ACCT(POSN) .EQ. 0) THEN
C                   NOT HERE!
          PRINT *,
          PRINT *, ' NO ENTRY FOR ACCOUNT NUMBER ',NACCT
          ELSE
C                   FOUND IT!
          PRINT *,
          PRINT *, 'ACCOUNT:',NACCT,'   ENTRY=', ENTRY(POSN)
          ENDIF
          END
```

5. Are you convinced?

6. To delete an item in the direct-access case requires one step. In the sequential-access case, you need NITEMS/2 steps (on the average) to find the item you want to delete, then you need one more step to swap

the item that's currently at the very end of the array with the deleted position.

The form of hashing we presented makes it difficult to delete an item (other forms make it simpler). To delete by just marking the item deleted, you first have to find the item. That takes one step in the best case, and an average of NITEMS/2 in the worst case.

In the binary search method, to delete, first you have to find the item. That takes no more than log (NITEMS) steps. Then, to keep the items in order, you have to slide all items which occur after the deleted item up one position. On the average, that will require NITEMS/2 steps.

13.1   ANSWER TO EXERCISE

1. c.

13.2   ANSWERS TO EXERCISES

1. b.
2. a. (Assuming that FORMAT 1000 and memory cell NEXT are appropriate.)
3. c or d.

13.3   ANSWERS TO EXERCISES

1. None of the answers is correct. Answer c comes close, but is lacking the required RECL = *rn* specifier.
2. *****A***** should be

    ```
    READ(UNIT=1
    ```

    *****B***** should be

    ```
    READ(UNIT=1
    ```

    and *****C***** should be

    ```
    WRITE (UNIT=1, FMT=1000, REC=REC 2) CNAME, CPHONE
    ```

13.5   ANSWERS TO EXERCISES

1. b.
2. a.
3. You could add these statements (or the equivalent). In fact, you could replace the IF-THEN statement that removes dollar signs by these statements:

```
          .
          .
          .
      INTEGER CH
      CHARACTER*(1) T
          .
          .
          .
      DO 100 CH = 1, 80
          T = PAYCH(CH:CH)
          IF (T .NE. '.' .AND.
    +         (T .LT. '0' .OR. T .GT. '9')) THEN
              PAYCH(CH:CH) = ' '
          ENDIF
100       CONTINUE
          .
          .
          .
```

14.2 ANSWERS TO EXERCISES

1.

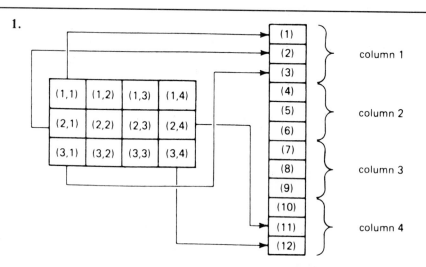

2. To refer to elements (in a two-dimensional array) "by columns," you must know *how long* the columns are. (It doesn't matter how long the rows are.) An *m*-by-*n* two-dimensional array has columns of length *m*. Therefore, you could set up the array as long as you knew *m* and an upper bound on the total amount of room you'd need for the array. Thus, knowing *m* exactly and that $n \leq 100$ is enough.

3. (I,J) corresponds to element $N*(I - 1) + J$. Note that N is the value you need to know precisely.

4.

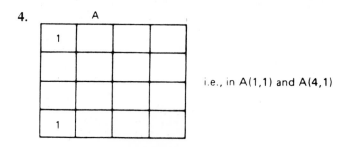

i.e., in A(1,1) and A(4,1)

5. The array declaration was REAL X(L:M,K:N). To compute the position of X(I,J) in the one-dimensional array which the Fortran compiler uses to represent the array X, use the formula below.

X(I,J) is element number s

where s is
$(M - L + 1) * -K - I - (L - 1)$

Note that s lies between 1 and $(M - L + 1)*(N - K + 1)$, inclusive.

14.3 ANSWERS TO EXERCISES

1. You would not want to store a triangular array by columns because then you would need to know how long the first column is in order to skip around it to reference the other columns.

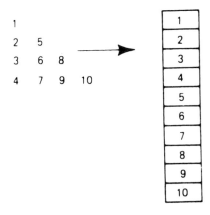

If the first column has four elements, then

$$(\text{row, col}) \rightarrow \frac{4*(4+1)}{2} - \frac{(5-\text{col})*(6-\text{col})}{2} + \text{row} - \text{col} + 1$$

2. Store it by columns. Then

$$(\text{row, col}) \rightarrow \frac{\text{col}*(\text{col}-1)}{2} + \text{row}$$

14.4 ANSWERS TO EXERCISES

1. The declaration of the array STACK would have to be changed to REAL. Also, the parameter VALUE in SUBROUTINEs ADD and RE-MOVE must be a REAL.

2.
```
       SUBROUTINE REMOVE(QUEUE, FRONT, BACK, VALUE, N)
       INTEGER N, QUEUE(N), FRONT, BACK, VALUE
C                 REMOVE FRONT ELEMENT
C                 (WRAP AROUND IF NECESSARY)
```

```
FRONT = MOD(FRONT,N) +1
VALUE = QUEUE(FRONT)
END
```

3. Add a test to see if FRONT equals BACK right after the wraparound statement.

14.5 ANSWERS TO EXERCISES

1. None. It does restrict the system to using no more than 1,000 list elements at any one time, but as time goes on, elements can be re-used time and time again.

2. One possibility is:

	SLIST	KLIST	FREE
	6	11	1

		QUANT	NEXT
1			4
2	SUGAR	1	5
3	PEACHES		0
4			10
5	FLOUR	5	0
6	EGGS		9
7	PEAS	3	12
8	WHEATIES		3
9	BUTTER		8
10			13
11	OLIVES	1	7
12	JELLO	6	2
13			14
14			15
15			0

3. There's a crude way to do it—just enter a phony BOUGHT command and then a phony USED command to make the system think we're now out of the item.

The right way to do it involves just two changes. First, add a new command ADD into FUNCTION COMMAND, associating it with the number 6. Second, add statement number 359 in the computed GO TO list between 350 and 360, and insert it after statement 350.

```
C                       'ADD ITEM TO SHOPPING LIST'
359      CALL ADD(ITEM,Q,FREE,SLIST,QUANT,NEXT,END,GROC)
         PRINT 3590, DBLSP, 'ADDED ',ITEM,
     +                ' TO THE SHOPPING LIST'
3590     FORMAT(A, A, TR1, A, TR1, A)
         GO TO 300
```

INDEX